AN HONEST LIFE

A novel

By

J F CONROY

For information contact: jfconroyinfo@gmail.com

Edited by Emma Walsh @ The Literary Professionals.

Cover design by Bespoke Book Covers.

ISBN: 978-1-83853-563-6

Dedication

This story is in memory of Jessica McCann and Stephen Fahy of Bishop Thomas Grant School, Streatham, South London. Jessica and I were in the same class in our first year of secondary school. I remember Jessica being bright and bubbly. Sadly, she was tragically killed in a road traffic accident before she arrived at school one morning.

Stephan Fahy and I grew up together in the same primary school before we attended secondary school. I remember him for his great sense of humour. When Stephen was a teenager, he unexpectedly died of meningitis during the summer holidays.

I have often thought about both of these friends and their families and the life they could have led.

CHAPTER 1

Holmewood Road was a street of single-fronted, terraced houses which backed onto row after row of similar homes. It was located north of Dublin, not too far from the main route linking to the airport. The houses were originally a sandstone colour, but following years of industrial pollution, they resembled a tired, smoky-grey colour. The windows and doors had a glazed, red-bricked surround which contrasted strangely with the wooden window frames and porch. It was a strange mix of styles that stood out more for its incongruity than for its consistency, odd in a street full of houses that were all the same.

Whenever it rained, the bricks gave off a rainbow marble glow bringing the old facias alive. In autumn, when the sun was low, the sky would turn an earthy copper colour, visible from one end of the street. The shimmering effect would be quite breathtaking, as if finishing its curtain call for the year before winters' early nights loomed in. Closeby was a factory that produced coffee, ideal for supplying the many café franchises at the airport. On a dry day, with a light wind, the aroma of fresh coffee beans wafted on the breeze.

Martin and Bridget Lynch lived at Number 22 with their two children: Shane, seventeen, and Sinead, thirteen. A council-owned property, it had been home to many tenants over its lifetime. As you entered the house, inside the porch above the door, children of the past had etched their names into the chalky brickwork. Amongst the array of Marys', 'Darrens' and 'Decco + Brenda forever' scrawls was an inappropriate limerick. The indentation had been coloured-in with a black felt tip pen to ensure longevity. It read: 'Jack and Jill went up the hill to fetch a pail of water, Jill the dill forgot the pill, and now they have a daughter'. Over the years, as representatives from the education board had visited the house to address young Shane's truancy, not a single person had ever overlooked the limerick, and yet it remained.

The large front window was a bay window with a worn seat covered in cushions. It was one of the most comfortable places in the house and had the best view of the goings-on of the street. It also had the permanent feature of a glass ashtray tucked in the corner, always full of cigarette butts and discarded chewing gum. Over the years, each of the panes at the top of the window had been smashed in turn. Once, a football had been kicked awry. Another time, Shane had lost his keys and broken in. A pigeon impact had once smashed the centre pane. The neighbours often joked about the pigeons becoming disorientated due to the pungent smell of coffee throughout the neighbourhood, causing them to nosedive into vulnerable houses. The Lynch's house hadn't been the only one to suffer such damage. Repairs, and the apparent need for repairs, were common throughout the street.

The property had needed upgrading for many years but had been left to decline by the county council. The Lynches had reported many complaints and requested repairs; each request was lost in the council department vacuous loop. Years of being ignored meant they eventually gave up trying, and the property was slowly falling apart.

Number 22 stood out from the street for all the wrong reasons. Neighbours were reluctant to park their cars outside for fear of damage by the drunken exploits of late-night drinkers or teenagers throwing their bikes down on the pavement and accidentally scoring the paintwork. Over recent years many residents had purchased their homes from the council. Extensions, double-glazing and porched doors added value to the properties and emphasised the lack of attention given to others.

As the street improved, a small neighbourhood watch scheme developed, designed to improve the street's reputation. The committee would discuss amongst themselves the best way to approach the Lynches. Bridget was often at work on different shifts, and the only response they got from Martin was, 'Will it cost us anything?' so it wasn't long before improvement of the area continued without the Lynches.

It was the kind of neighbourhood where everyone knew everyone else. Children would knock for each other to come out and play. Mothers would enter their neighbours' open doors to borrow anything from milk to shampoo. Despite the hardships and the varying degrees of decline, it was a good neighbourhood. Good people lived in these houses. Every family on the street had their own challenges, but for the most part, they looked out for each other and the kids. They did their best with what they had.

Across the road, at number 27, lived Mr and Mrs Mercer. They had lived on the street for decades and witnessed many changes. Retired now, their garden got all their attention. Thick foliage climbed the fences on either side of them and offered privacy from neighbours. Within the haven of peace, bedding plants and brightly-coloured flowers provided an Eden-esque feel for the relatively short summer period. The scent of lilies permeated the patio area, making eating outdoors a pleasant prospect during warmer months. However, on occasion, their tranquil setting was interrupted by the pitter-patter of canine paws cantering around the barren yard next door. Intermittently, the peaceful silence was sundered by the neighbour's dog, Nugget, as he leisurely strolled towards the perfect spot, circled, hesitated, then noisily emptied his bowels, leaving behind a putrid mess that demonstrated the lack of due care and attention given to his diet. Picture-perfect peace on the Mercer's patio could be ruined in the blink of an eye as following Nuggets' release, kamikaze flies divebombed the mess. Yet, despite this unpleasantness, the Mercers were one of the few neighbours who had good relations with the Lynches. Mrs Mercer looked out for Bridget and Sinead. With no children of her own, she doted on the girls across the road and treated Sinead like a much-loved granddaughter.

Holmewood Road led into Holmewood Gardens. The terraced houses formed a triangle shape with an open green in the middle. A willow tree dominated the centre of the green, its pendulous branches forming a canopy that shielded loitering teenagers from prying eyes. Empty rizla packets and cigarette butts littered the base of the tree. This was the place the teenagers hung out at late into the summer nights. The smell of cannabis giving away their presence until the midges became too much to bear, and they moved on, searching for the next safe, sacred space.

With its timber decking and modern equipment, the children's playground was the most popular spot for them then. Shielded on one side by a thicket of trees, once the younger kids were gone, it was the teenagers' territory. In Spring, the open green came alive with the blossoming of hundreds of incandescent bluebells. However, their fate was short-lived, but for a few weeks, they continued to litter the grass verges in rows bringing radiance to the neighbourhood.

In the autumn, when the leaves turned golden with rusty hues, the children took great delight in stamping and crunching on the banks of lost foliage as they passed through the park. These natural adornments made the area quite pretty, and at certain times of the year, the neighbours felt quite proud of where they lived, despite its lacking. On the bend of Holmewood Gardens, a convenience store partnered with a hardware store stood. It had a large car park that had the unfortunate capacity to draw in local chancers who either loitered outside or tried to cause trouble inside. However, once the chancers realised who the owner was and their swelling had gone down, due respect was usually given.

Across the road from the store had once stood the single source of employment for locals for decades, the local aggregate factory. After its closure, the building decayed quickly over the years as local kids found another space to congregate. Yet its demise had rejuvenated the air quality in the surrounding areas. Though no more smoke fumes emanated from its chimneys, the houses nearby continued to show the stains of its presence. A decision to demolish the site for health and safety reasons pleased the locals. The land was sold off, and a discount supermarket called Safeway and a modest primary school took its place to cater for the overpopulated area. Safeway provided the locals with alternative employment opportunities and the mothers with discount prices on the food shopping. All the services a community could need to thrive.

The supermarket received plaudits from the full time mothers for its low prices and convenient café that served as a time killer in the morning school runs. Individuals of the group showed their disproval of having to slot a euro into their trolleys for use. Due to a magnetic grid in the car park exit, it restricted them from moving the trolleys off the premises. This faced them with taking their shopping via mini cabs or the bus service. Pandemonium broke out when they discovered that a 22 cent levy charge was incurred on their shopping bill for each carrier bag required. This belittlement meant not only were they forced to carry their shopping home, but they were also charged for the privilege of it.

As the school became embedded in the fabric of the community, different factions of parents emerged. There were those from the local area whose kids often arrived late, without lunch and missing books. Some children walked to school by both mothers and fathers due to the chronic unemployment in the area, leaving both parents at home.

Then there were the children who came farther afield. They

were delivered in cars by their mothers, typically stay-at-home mothers with the luxury of working husbands dressed smartly in the uniform of the day; skinny jeans and UGG boots, and a 'no-makeup' look that denied the effort gone into presentation.

The local mothers smacked gum as they flicked through Facebook threads, laughing uproariously as they shared jokes and comments. Some of the out-of-town mothers took issue with the dress and behaviour of these mothers. Their too-tight leggings, visible G-strings, and regular pyjama bottoms many sizes too small offended their sensibilities and were brought to the Principle's attention them of suitable attire when escorting their children to school. Letters were sent out to all parents reminding them of suitable attire when escorting their children to school.

CHAPTER 2

The Telegraph, the area's local and much-frequented pub, stood proud, majestically flaunting its proximity within the neighbourhood with disdain. Despite its demise, a major overhaul was yet to take place. It was a large L-shaped pub, accessed by the main entrance on the street corner, with a large car park behind it.

The main entrance boasted hefty, solid-oak doors leading into the large main bar to the saloon's right. To the right of the entrance, in the hallway, was an unobtrusive doormarked 'private'. It led up a staircase to a function room. Admittance was by invitation only.

Inside, the function space was an unpretentious bar, backed by mirrored glass reflecting the recessed optic bottles, giving the illusion the bar was double in size. The room had a comfortable and traditional feel, with wooden beams that led the way to a stone fireplace at the far end of the room. Aged, leather chairs offered comfort to those lucky enough to gain admittance. Asides from the usual birthday parties and funeral gatherings, the private bar hosted various events, poker games, and meetings that took place off the record and out of sight.

Nicknamed The Graft, it and the hardware store were owned by Declan Hennessey, a Dubliner raised but not born. A businessman of sorts, he ran one of Dublin's most notorious organised criminal and money-lending outfits. It spanned the Northside of the city, from Drumcondra through to Ballymun and up to the airport. If punters in the neighbourhood had a request for a particular item, Declan had a team of personnel who could locate and secure that item at a reduced cost. It was an enterprise that had enormous appeal and variety and ran entirely on cash revenue.

Declan was a revered local rogue with a deserved reputation having a short fuse and a violent temper. He rarely had cause to use it though, as he surrounded himself with associates who were more than willing to do his bidding. The Telegraph served as a front for Declan's numerous business activities. The pub itself ran a profit that diverted suspicion away from his other activities.

One of his more sacred personal events was the Saturday night poker game that ran by invitation only. Guests would congregate in the main bar downstairs to loosen up before being escorted upstairs from around 9 pm. A discrete pat-down by the bouncers ensured the integrity of the night and the safety of the patrons. Declan's door staff ran a tight ship, and guests knew better than bringing a friend to the poker sessions.

Everyone knew the function room was off-limits on Saturdays, and it had been in practice for so long that it was never questioned why a 50th birthday party had to take place on a Friday or Sunday night. The locals knew the score, and if Declan, on the rare occasion, had to take care of any unruly behaviour, there was never any call for the Guards to pay a visit. A gentleman's agreement existed with the Staff Sergeant on duty to give Declan a heads-up if there were any complaints.

While the downstairs bar served legitimate spirits and liquors, the upstairs bar served illegal and contraband liquors that came in via Declan's connections in Dublin port. Declan had Eastern European associates in the UK who delivered into the Irish capital's docks discreetly. Though it had been risky at first, Declan had trialled the arrangement with trusted acquaintances to scope out the operation. Once satisfied it was safe to collect, he had the contraband delivered straight to his hardware store and stocked in its basement. The dry basement served as a perfect location to store stock.

Initially, it was just liquor and cigarettes. However, due to the influx of European criminals operating in and out of Ireland, new opportunities had opened up to stocking all kinds of fake branded clothing. Initially, Declan had been reluctant to branch out (booze and cigarettes would never go out of fashion), but it was his son Kieran who had opened his eyes to the demand for fake fashion amongst the youth on the streets.

Declan had met his wife Kathleen in his early thirties and was smitten with her from the off. Kathleen had been as attractive in her personality as she was in her looks, and many had pursued her. When she first met Declan, it hadn't exactly been love at first sight. Yet, despite Declan's shortcomings – he was a risk-taker and made rash decisions – his confidence and boldness won her over. Kathleen felt safe with him, in spite of the danger that surrounded him. As time went by and their son Kieran arrived, however, the novelty of his bad-boy image quickly wore off. Kathleen's parents had never approved of him, and as their relationship developed, their concerns became more vocal.

They thought she was throwing away a prosperous career in teaching and the chance to marry well. Instead, she took up with a risky man who dabbled in questionable business affairs. In the beginning, Kathleen's family had intervened and tried to persuade her to hold off on the marriage. However, it was easy for Kathleen to dismiss their concerns about Declan as prejudice, as Declan was a black Irish man living on the fringe of the criminal underworld in Dublin in the 80s. Never welcomed into her family, it was easier to assume it was his colour that was the problem, not his rogue lifestyle, and perhaps it was both reasons that were enough for her family to reject him. Yet despite it all, or maybe because of it, their relationship flourished.

At first, Kathleen rebelled against their disapproval. Kathleen felt loyal to Declan. They had their ups and downs, but unlike Declan's arguments with his punters, he never threatened or raised a finger to Kathleen. He adored her and always kept his cool around her. Their married life started in the flat above The Telegraph, but it wasn't long before living over a bar lost its appeal. Their flat soon became the headquarters for many of Declan's 'business' meetings, and to Kathleen's great dismay, her home became an open house.

After about a year of gentle hints about needing their privacy going unnoticed, things came to a head when Declan held a meeting in their front room with eight of his associates. To their delight and Declan's horror, they soon realised just how 'private' the space was when mid-conversation Kathleen, with a well-timed entrance, sashayed out of the bathroom with just a towel wrapped around her waist. She walked through the sitting room deliberately, slowly and unselfconsciously. Her slim figure and full breasts stopped time as, feigning nonchalance, she excused herself to Declan's associates who sat open-mouthed, afraid to look and yet afraid to miss a thing. She blinked in astonishment in front of the team of men and spoke innocently, 'Oh sorry, lads. I hadn't realised there was a meeting going on in here. Don't mind me, carry on as you were, pretend I'm not here.' Wiggling her hips as she swept past them, she dipped her head to hide a smirk. Declan was enraged, simmering with anger at her exhibitionism but knowing she had made a fair point.

Later, when he had cleared the men out and started to think seriously about a move, she apologised with sarcastic sympathy. 'I hope they were not offended by a half-naked woman walking into their meeting place,' she asked, mock innocently, 'Please God, they'll be able to look me in the eye the next time we meet.' Like a gentleman, Declan graciously gave in, and six weeks later, they moved into their new home.

The flat above the pub had a service entrance at the back that led to a hallway and staircase back down to the first floor. Divided into bedsits, one room was set up as a break room for bar staff. Previous employees had vanished mid-shift whilst on breaks, so this new space kept staff on-site and in sight. The staff room had a single bed often used as a dumping ground for clothes and knock-off gear in transit. A bland grey sofa slotted under the window facing a television and a mini kitchen kept tea and coffee supplies. Tenants were forbidden from entering the pub via the main entrance as it was deemed inappropriate. CCTV monitors were installed in the break room, and these covered all areas downstairs and recorded goings-on. With a business like Declan's, it paid to be vigilant.

The pub ran much like clockwork. Declan had a low turnover of core staff and left things very much in the capable hands of his manager, Dillon. Regular nights took place without fail, traditional music on Sunday evenings, bingo on Tuesdays, a DJ on Saturdays. There was no need to fix what wasn't broken. On the rare occasions that a booking was cancelled, disgruntled noises were made to Dillon about the missed event and the craftiest, and most persistent complainers got a free drink to quieten them down.

One regular customer, who knew the benefit of complaining at the right time in a busy pub, was Old Man Mick. An elderly gentleman who had frequented the pub for years, he took it upon himself to polish the tables and collect the empties for no reason and over the years became a sort of unofficial custodian. Nobody quite knew his age as his face was puce from years of heavy drinking. Age spots covered his arms as he cleared glasses with laboured breathing that revealed rotten teeth that would have been a good advert on cigarette boxes. Dillon granted Old Man Mick a free pint each evening, and he felt valuable and necessary. Even though he could be a nuisance from time to time, Declan welcomed free labour and a second set of – albeit rheumy – eyes on things.

Keeping things running smoothly was important for Declan. He had no desire to expand, take on new territory or conquer new shores. As the years went by he had fallen into contentment, lost his ambition and unfortunately, taken his eye somewhat off the ball. Little was he to know that a course of events was about to follow that would teach him a valuable lesson about the consequences of not paying attention.

CHAPTER 3

Declan was as Irish as they came, but his inauspicious start haunted him. His parents, Clara and Bernard, had travelled from Trinidad in 1960 with dreams and aspirations of a new life in the UK. The harsh reality of their arrival soon overrode their ambition. The unwelcoming stares and the unfamiliarity of one-word answers to basic questions dented their confidence. This was not the dream life they had envisaged. They found the country hostile, the people suspicious, and the opportunities limited. To complicate their life was the unplanned birth of Declan in their first year. Unmarried and broke, Bernard couldn't hold a job down for any length of time due to excessive drinking. He felt hard done by and fuelled by drink he would often say, 'We came from the warmth to live in this cold, unforgiving country.'

With work and money scarce, soon they had nowhere to live. Clara had turned from an optimistic and resourceful young woman into the broken and fearful wife of an alcoholic. Eventually, when things became unbearable, and with nowhere to live and nowhere to turn, she hopelessly left her three-month-old baby at an orphanage in South London. The plan was to return, but neither parent ever came back.

As the nuns inadvisably named the boy, Declan was one of three Black babies in the orphanage. These babies were harder to place with families back then, but by chance, a desperate Irish couple, Donal and Geraldine Walsh, who had been working in London, had registered with the charity. God had not blessed the couple with children. On their scheduled appointment, they were told about Declan whilst on a tour of the orphanage.

He was a young baby boy with a strong Irish name, and before they ever met him, they were keen. They immediately fell in love with this beautiful baby. His huge dark eyes locked on to Geraldine's like magnets the second she picked him up, and his fate was sealed. The adoption documentation was processed, and after passing the assessment criteria, they travelled back home to Dublin to start life with their new family.

Their welcome return was as joyful as it was surprising. Friends, family and their new congregation welcomed Declan into the fold. Declan was instantly accepted as part of the community despite a few comments and stares from small-mined people. When Declan was six years old, his adoptive father Donal passed away from a sudden heart attack. With no income, Geraldine was forced to move to a much cheaper and less salubrious neighbourhood. Their lives changed utterly. Geraldine found she had to harden up her son in the face of the vagaries of their new life. Her wisdom and common sense taught Declan to rise above the challenges of their new harsh position in the streets of inner-city Dublin.

1976

Galivanting around the streets with friends, Declan often drew attention from the Gardai. One evening a group of rowdy teenagers were up to mischief, messing and calling things out to women on their way home from work. Officers on patrol saw them, and Declan stood out immediately. Keeping an eye on them, the officers watched them from their patrol car across the street. Geraldine had warned Declan many times that he would always stand out, and as such, his behaviour had to be beyond reproach.

Declan mainly had kept to himself and did no more messing than would be expected of a young lad his age. He knew well to be courteous if ever stopped by the Guards. He was surprised and prepared when he noted the patrol car following him home after the group dispersed. It slowed to a crawl beside him for 20 metres before stopping ahead of him. Two Guards stepped out.

The older, more experienced one raised a hand to indicate Declan to stop. 'Good evening, young man.'

'Good evening, Guard, and a bitter cold one it is at that,' Declan replied cheerfully. The second Garda was clearly a recruit. He stood awkwardly, glancing at his senior colleague expectantly, as he referred to his pocket notebook to camouflage his shyness.

'Can I ask what you're doing around here, young man?' asked the senior Garda, 'this area isn't exactly a tourist attraction in the daytime, never mind during the evening.'

Declan stared sightlessly into the darkness as the hairs stirred on the back of his neck.

Looking back at the Guards, he replied gently, 'I live here, Guards, two streets away on New Park Road.'

Looking bemused, the officer removed his cap, reached for his notepad and pen on the dashboard inside the car and asked, 'What's your name, son?'

Declan remained silent. The officer stumbled and banged his head on the inside of the door frame.

Embarrassed now, his eyes narrowed and raising his voice, he said, 'Now listen here, young man. Across the way there, is Garda Clint

Eastwood and myself, well, my name is Garda John Wayne. We are freezing our balls off here when my young cadet and my good self should be back at the station sipping a cup of tea to keep warm. Believe it or not, we're concerned for your welfare. Look around you!' The officer twirled his head around to an invisible audience. 'Christ! I'd be worried in this uniform on my own around here.'

Pausing for a few seconds, he collected his composure and exhaled slowly in Declan's face. His breath misted up, and there was a faint whiff of mint.

'I'm just asking for your name, young man,' he sighed.

The tension eased. Declan spoke, 'Declan Hennessey, Sir.'

The officer's face softened. 'Ok – sit yourself in the car, young man. This cowboy is gonna take you home to your doorstep to meet your parents.'

The car was warm and oddly comforting. Sitting in the back, Declan couldn't quite figure out was he in trouble or getting a lift. He remained silent and didn't make eye contact in the rear-view mirror. He wasn't frightened, but he was concerned that his mother would be upset that Guards were escorting him home and knew she'd be worried about the neighbours watching a scene. As they pulled into New Park Road, Declan pointed out his home. Ratcheting the handbrake up caused the cadet to flinch.

The senior officer turned around to Declan and lazily said, 'Ok then, home sweet home. Step out of the car, young man and ask your mother or father to come out to the front door, please.'

Declan nodded and hopped out.

Turning to the cadet, the senior officer flashed an *I've-seen-it-all-before* look and remonstrated, 'Watch and learn from here on, son. This will be a learning curve for you tonight.' His last words trailed off to a grumble as he heaved himself out as the front door opened.

Geraldine appeared, and Declan spoke briefly with her. Stepping forward, she nudged Declan slightly behind her, whispering to him, 'Let me do the talking, a stór.'

Approaching the front door, the senior officer took a long deep breath through his nose and met Geraldine's gaze before he greeted her. 'Good evening, Mam,' he nodded. 'We were on patrol in town and spotted this young coloured man separating from a group of males. We stopped him and questioned his well-being, and he told us he lived here. Geraldine interrupted him. Raising her chin firmly, she locked eyes with him and, her voice steady, replied, 'I beg your pardon, officer; what is the term coloured?... Aren't we all some colour, officer?... Indeed, you look a bit blue in the cold tonight, and I have no doubt you turn red when you are embarrassed. So, with respect, coloured is an inaccurate way to distinguish my son from yourself. My son is a young BLACK man! Have you upset my son this evening, officer? I have brought him up with decency and manners, and I know he won't have been out causing trouble with his friends.'

A shocked and tense silence fell on the group. Geraldine's gaze hardened; anger crept into her voice. 'You're Mary Flannigan's husband, are you not?'

The officer's face reddened as she glared at him like a bold child.

'I'll be sure to mention to Mary in Church on Sunday that you have escorted my Declan home safely, and you'll be looking out for him from now on, Garda Flannigan.'

She tilted her head slightly and fixed her gaze over his shoulder, at the younger guard, now holding his lips tight to keep from laughing.

Garda Flannigan motioned his cadet to sit back in the car by nodding his head towards it in an attempt to regain composure. He walked back to the car and caught Geraldine's eyes before getting in. She nodded once. Then he caught sight of Declan, standing just behind her. A broad smile brimmed across the young lad's insolent face. With his hands on the steering wheel, he waited for Geraldine to return indoors.

As her door shut, his cadet piped up happily, 'I thought it was great the way you kept your composure. I take it that is what you call diplomacy on the job there, Sir.'

1985

As the years went on, Declan developed many great friends and the occasional ignorant enemy. Besides his colour, another factor stood out about Declan: his unusual strength and complete lack of fear. Declan never lost a street fight, and the more he won, the more he invited. By his early twenties, he was renowned throughout Dublin for brute strength and fearlessness, but every streak of good luck must end.

Declan became involved in an undesirable gang that ran most of the criminal activities in the northside of Dublin. They recruited him as a money collector as his reputation preceded him. His conscience told him to stay away from them, and he did for a while for his mother's sake. Until six months later, after persistent invitations and the allure of money and power, he joined the gang. A fortnight into his new job, Declan's life was nearly cut short for good. A routine money collection went wrong, and three against one, he was left to be slaughtered in wasteland near Dublin's docks. The only thing that ended up saving him from being killed was his streetwise guile.

It was a painful lesson for Declan and one he was not willing to take lying down. Knowing who was behind the attack, he visited his employer, Conor Casey, a lesser-known Dublin criminal. He knew he was in too deep, but his pride was wounded. That evening, whilst the shame and the bruises were still fresh, he walked into Conor's busy pub and confronted him, man-to-man.

Within seconds, five of Conor's sidekicks surrounded him. With no time to think, Declan lunged at Conor, pushing him to the floor. Five sidekicks piled on top. Stray punches, grunting noises and the yelps of regular bar-goers forced the fight outside, which suited Declan as he needed space to retaliate. With sheer strength of will, Declan began fending off the men with vicious blows to the head. Unknown to him, Conor had at this stage emerged out of the melee and raced back inside for his weapon.

Suddenly a gun fired, and everything stopped. Declan felt a red-hot poker drive through his shoulder and realised he had been shot. He dropped to the floor and rolled behind a pool table to shield himself.

Nobody in the pub indicated Declan's position to Conor. Searching wildly for Declan around the front bar, Conor felt a kick to his ankle from under the pool table and hit the floor. The gun fell, and Declan kicked it under the pool table out of reach. Declan shot up and grabbed Conor, shoving him against a nearby fruit machine. Lights flashed and blinkered, and a repetitive jingle jeered the men along until Declan smashed Connor's head repeatedly against the glass screen. The fruit machine applauded his win, with no pay-out.

The silence started to dissipate as a few locals stood up, chuckling and clapping. Blood soaked through Declan's shirt as he leaned back, took a breath and prepared to leave. Something changed forever for him that day. People knew he was not to be messed with, and there was no turning back; he had made enemies now. Enemies that would never forget. Sitting alone, watching the sun slowly sink beneath the backdrop of the city, Declan felt sure he had found his path in life. One day he was going to own the town.

Declan set about building a trusted team around him. Word spread across town about his plans, and meetings began with a renowned local criminal, Aiden O'Driscoll. One of the meetings took place in an isolated pub in the back of the beyond. It was at the behest of O'Driscoll; a meeting Declan couldn't turn down.

'Sit yourself down there, now. RELAX. I'm not here to put the heavies on you, my man. Aiden O'Driscoll, by the way. Do you want a drink?'

'No, thanks,' was Declan's short reply.

'Good for you – keep yourself focused. I'm here to gently persuade you about how things are going to run smoothly for us both. I have a line of business that runs through Darndale that is important to me. I bet you're thinking, "Why is this wiry old goat telling me this?" I bet you're thinking, "What's in it for me?" Well, absolutely FUCK ALL, young man.

'I tell yeh; there are a lotta folk around here who have given you the gentle nod for what you've done. That Connor Casey had it coming for years. He was reckless with a drink inside him, making threats he couldn't back up. He'd squeal to the Guards as they had him in their back pocket. That's why I never challenged him. I couldn't trust how deep the Guards were into his operations. I have a small piece of advice for you, Declan. Take it or leave it.'

'Get yourself a pub. Get yourself a few good men around you, men who you can trust. Get folk to respect you, and then everything will fall into place. Leave Casey to me. He is finished; you can start anew. Make new contacts and mind yourself with the Guards. They've lost their key man to what goes on in town; they won't like that. The North is yours, and the South is mine, plain and simple. I don't want anything to do with you and vice versa.'

Declan cautiously replied, 'I can live with that.'

O'Driscoll waved his men away before he continued, 'There is one condition mind you,' his eyes pinned Declan's.

'I haven't put myself through this shite to be conditioned by anyone,' Declan remonstrated.

'Relax! Let me explain. I have two lads who work for me; they're brothers. You'd think they'd be as thick as thieves… pardon the expression there, but they're always at each other's throats. I can't have the pairing anymore. I want you to take one of them on. He's trustworthy, one of the best; I'll give you my word on that,' O'Driscoll pointed his finger on the table, reaffirming his comment.

'These brothers will be our go-between. Keep the lines clear for us, you understand? You suck my dick; I'll suck yours, so to speak.'

'Sounds like you're not giving me much choice,' Declan replied diffidently.

'I'm giving you a hand of experience. I don't want you to fuck up before you've even got your feet off the ground. The Guards will be all over you, so an experienced hand in the team will be invaluable to you. Take it or leave it.' Offering his hand, O'Driscoll waited.

Declan countered, 'What's yer man's name?'

'His name is Brady. You're gonna get on fine with him. He's an ugly fucker but don't let that put you off warming to him,' O'Driscoll said affably.

'And what's in it for you?' Declan asked.

'As I say, I have business interests that yer man Casey knew fuck all about, and that will be of no concern to you either. A goodwill payment will come your way once a month to not ask questions. I don't want to associate with you at all. The last thing I want is the Guards sniffing around my businesses if you fuck up.' O'Driscoll's answer came out sharp. There was a pause before he spoke again.

'Look, lad, I'm just looking out for myself. Keeping our affairs separate will mean no conflict. I want you to ensure we don't step on each other's toes. You have a bright future ahead of you if you play by the rules. Make no assumptions about what you're getting yourself into here, though the Guards will be all over your backside; get a legit business, start from there, and take the advice given to you.' He offered his hand to Declan again; it was an invitation to stand up and end the meeting.

CHAPTER 4

At the beginning of the month – payday – locals in The Telegraph had money in their pockets. Declan enticed drinkers by showing live Premier League football, then prime-time boxing starting from around 9 pm. It was expensive to showcase events live on satellite, but it paid off. It encouraged punters to revel in the excitement and kept the pumps going all night long. Around 10 pm, buffet food was offered on the house, giving the drinkers a chance to slow down to drink more later. As the evening drew in, bouncers appeared discreetly inside the bar to keep an eye on things and move on any undesirables that may have overindulged.

On Saturdays, the upstairs function room buzzed with anticipation for the evening's gambling sessions. As punters arrived upstairs, mobiles were confiscated. Drinks were served on request – these were legitimate brands – and no money changed hands on these nights. As the night went on, the brands were swapped with contraband brands poured into the empty bottles. The staff used a metallic pen to score the base, marking out the contraband, so Declan was never served the cheap stuff. If some of the players noticed the difference in taste, it was never questioned.

Declan, despite his reputation, had an unerring, though not rational, sense of fairness. Even though he happily fleeced his punters at card games each week, he always felt that presenting a bar bill to the loser was a step too far. Perched like a hawk on the edge of a barstool, Declan sat back in the shadows where he could oversee the tables and punters throughout the night.

As he visually managed the floor, card dealers kept in constant eye contact with him. Requests were made and answered by a nod or a whisper in the ear if the sum was substantial. When a punter won big, he would motion the staff to applaud them and offer them a complimentary bottle of champagne (contraband). After all, he knew the probability would be on his side the following week for him to re-coop any losses.

Martin and Bridget's brother, David, were in good spirits from shifting boxes from a house clearance that had finished earlier than expected and headed into The Telegraph. In the early days, David accompanied Martin to keep an eye on him for Bridget's sake, steering him out of trouble. The pair soon became thick as thieves, and David rarely told Bridget any of Martin's antics. Declan often used David as a gofer to collect goods from the store and pub using a tatty van.

A relaxed doorman had turned a blind eye to two young men with a fake ID. After a couple of shandies, the gob on them caught his attention. After declining to leave and ranting the air full of expletives, the doorman apologised for falling on gobby number one, rendering him unconscious. His refusal to wake up meant that gobby number two had to carry him out and wait for him to come around.

As they entered the bar, the doorman, Billy, sauntered over to them, acknowledging them with a drop of the head. 'How's the form, fellas?' he inquired.

Martin replied, 'Bout ye.'

'That's a terrible problem to have as a trained door supervisor there, Billy,' David said sarcastically, 'all that falling over on folk.'

Surveying the crowd ahead of him, Billy answered. 'Well, I hope bucko forgives me when he comes to. When the great unwashed starts twisting hay after a couple of pints, you know they're going to be a pain in the backside for the rest of the night. Do you know what he called me? A WANKER. I nearly blushed. That's the problem with the youth of today. No fucking respect.'

'By the way, are you still after those dodgy fire sticks for the free TV service? Some have come about now with all the upgrades and all the channels. You just have to sync it now and then.'

Martin shrugged, 'I'm a bit short of cash at the mo…'

Billy interrupted, 'Don't fear, I can sort you both out for a sitting upstairs later if you're keen on some winnings.'

David offered a shake of the head before Martin piped up, 'Aye sure, why not.'

Billy obliged and focused on raised voices coming from the gents before he wrestled through the crowds.

Martin had been an avid gambler since a young man. He was very sharp when it came to card games and had an impressive history of winning at Declan's tables, something that no other punter held claim to. David was a casual player; he knew his limit and always lost the lot but never a penny more. He was competent enough to call it a day when he lost. Martin, however, was the complete opposite, and though he lost big, he won big too. Declan was waiting for the day to recoup his losses.

The evening session drew on late into the early hours. One table remained. Martin was once again on form and close to pulling off his most significant windfall to date. David had been one of the first to drop out and was, as usual, resigned to his losses. Adrenalin coursed through Martin's veins, making him feel giddy and brave.

'I can take them, David. If I pull this off, I can buy a batch of those chipped Amazon fire sticks and make more money. I'm nearly there, can you spot me any more euros?'

'Do you take me for a bigger fool than I am?' David growled. The air was tense now, and the dimmed spotlights cast pools of light among the beer bottles cluttering the table. As elbows juddered in conversation during intermissions, ripples of light moved across the felt cloth. Martin had played it cool, and his poker face had earned him a crucial position as one of the last two players left in the game. As luck had been on his side all night, he felt he had the hand of his life. David cringed when he heard Martin call the dealer over. He knew no good would have come of it.

'Take yourself the feck out this minute if not sooner,' David muttered under his breath.

Martin flicked his wrist dismissively and replied, 'Hold your whisht, man.'

Hearing the interruption, the dealer ushered David over to the bar. Declan rose from his stool and strolled over to him casually. David's palms started to sweat as Declan's piercing eyes pinned him to the bar. He mentally berated himself for showing fear. Declan preyed on terror, and David hated to feed it. Pinching two cigarettes from a packet, Declan gestured for David to join him on the balcony. The breeze picked up as he pulled open the adjoining doors. Declan had a worrying stillness about him. He stuck a cigarette in each of their mouths and lit them. Smoke funnelled out of his nose as he took a deep drag. He spoke in an unhurried tone.

'This is the only reason you need to part your lips. Take your drink, shut your mouth and stay seated for the remaining hand.'

Declan's stare sucked something out of David as he returned to his seat chastened, sitting back to watch the game silently. Martin was chatting animatedly with the supervisor before a nod from the card dealer caught Declan's attention. The room went quiet except for whispers of discussions at the bar as Martin appealed to Declan for a potential loan to cover his hand. David tried to intervene again. Declan winced and flashed him a look; David sat back.

Martin had tunnel vision and only saw one solution to getting his prize. He had recently finished paying off another loan with a revered family, the O'Driscolls. Part of the deal was that he worked for them. He didn't know what was involved, but his choices were limited once again, and he had agreed to it. Declan was unaware of this, as was Bridget. After a moment or two of further discussion, Declan called out the terms of the loan for Martin and the other players to hear. Typically, this was a departure from the usual informal way Declan and his colleagues conducted their business arrangements and was noted by the men.

'Right Lynch, you are borrowing €2,000; that's €170 each month over 24 months. Are you able to meet the loan payments each month on time with no exceptions; if not, there will be consequences.'

Martin heard the words but took little heed of their meaning. He was single-mindedly focused on his win. The alcohol had slowed his senses down; his eyes had become puffy, and his face clammy. He looked up, nodded, and shook hands to seal the deal. Speaking in a low undertone, Declan muttered, 'Just give me an excuse, any excuse, and I'll come knocking, Lynch.'

Snatching his hand back, Martin sat back at the table, his spirits somewhat dampened. Seeking one last chance to talk sense into him, David grabbed Martin by the forearm and pleaded, 'Please tell me you haven't chanced your arm?'

Martin shook him off dismissively and turned back to the table to receive his chips. An unsettled feeling coursed through him. After passing the chips over, Declan moved back towards the table, pulled out a chair, and positioned himself directly in Martin's eye line. Feeling a soft panic, Martin's stomach shifted as his eyes blinked rapidly. As the dealer spoke, he felt his breath catch as reality started to hit. Both Martin and Declan's heart rates quickened for differing reasons. As the tension grew, Martin's elbow slipped off the table, his senses dulled.

'Alright, I'm all in,' he confirmed. A note of impatience had crept into his voice. His heart fluttering, he pushed all his chips forward.The cards turned over. Martin tracked the turnover of cards and the players' subtle assessments of his hand and was satisfied his hand could win the game. It was not to be. When he revealed his hand, the players gasped in anguish for him. In the cruellest of twists, Martin, was beaten. He couldn't believe it.

He sat dumbfounded, staring at the cards. Heat climbed up his neck, and the surrounding air became uncomfortable as he struggled to breathe. His head fell into his hands. In shock, reality kicked in. He had just lost two grand. He started to sober up. The other players got up and embarrassedly patted Martin as they stumbled past him towards the exit. Others stayed and gathered by the bar, recollecting what could have been. Martin felt David's breath on the back of his neck and knew what was coming.

David glared at him, his jaw tightened, struggling to hold back profanities. Anger crept into his voice. 'Do you realise what you're putting my sister through this time?' he demanded, taking a step back. 'She will find out, and there will be ructions – Christ, Martin. She has enough to contend with. You never learn, man. How are you going to pay Declan two grand plus whatever interest AND pay the O'Driscolls at the same time?'

Turning his head, David gave Declan a fleeting stare to check he was listening before continuing. 'If either of them finds out you're involved with the other – they'll both kill you... and if Bridget finds out what you've done...' he paused and bit his top lip, upset now rather than angry. 'You're gonna send my sister to an early grave, Martin.' Shaking his head, he turned and left, disgust written all over his departing form.

Declan, still seated at the table, watched this exchange. He loathed Martin Lynch and had hated for years. The mere mention of his name gnawed away at him. The feelings ran far back and deep. Martin had little idea of why. It stemmed back to when they were just teenagers and Martin had courted Kathleen, way before Declan had ever met her.

Their relationship was short and tragic before they separated. Declan knew of their brief history together, but the thought of Martin's hands on his wife made his blood boil. The fact they shared a past that didn't involve him tore him up. Martin's presence in his life irritated him.

Every time he saw him or heard his name mentioned, he felt the anger churn inside his gut; it was a visceral reaction. The fact that there was still contact between Kathleen and Martin, through their wives' friendship, didn't help matters. He was always on the lookout for a chance to bring him down, and now he had him right where he wanted him.

Dragging himself up to the bar, Martin slumped against the counter dejectedly. The bartender waited for Declan's acknowledgement to serve him. Unease trickled down Martin's spine as he took his drink and trundled out onto the balcony. The cold night air was sharp. Declan walked unhurriedly over to him, lighting a cigarette then drawing the doors closed behind him. Leaning to one side next to Martin, he looked him up and down. Arching a brow, he took a long drag on his cigarette and deliberately exhaled in Martin's face. His face hardened. His mind had been racing. His head conjured up flashing images of Kathleen and Martin together. Their lips kissing, her laughter. Declan's anger brewed. Suddenly, his head cleared, and his eyes sharpened. 'Remember Lynch, FIRST of the month.'

Martin attempted to laugh, but a mirthless sigh was all he managed before downing his shot. Declan's gaze was unflinching as Martin stared ahead, failing to meet his eyes. Declan smirked and enjoyed watching Martin suffer. Martin was in a world of hurt now.

CHAPTER 5

The following morning Bridget had already opened the curtains and vented the room whilst Martin lay splayed across the bed. The sheet was wrinkled in knots, and saliva stained the pillowcase. He woke up with a continuous thirst. First, he remembered who he was before recalling where he was. Sunlight stabbed him as he squinted his eyes opened and zapped inside his head, causing it to pound. The potent aftertaste of garlic soured the back of his throat as a phlegmy film sealed his lips shut. The sight of the pint of water he should have drunk before sleeping induced more feelings of remorse. He stank. He farted. It stank. He needed the toilet but didn't have the energy to pull himself out of bed. Noises and laughter from the youngsters downstairs kept him from drifting back to sleep. Sitting up, he pulled Bridget's pillow over to rest it behind his neck. 'Bridget… Bridge!' he roared.

Peering her head around the door frame, Bridget watched as he unceremoniously scratched his balls under the duvet.

'There you are, love… a cuppa if you could be so good. Could you bring it up with breakfast? The full fry up if you so please… thanking you in advance.'

A middle finger salute appeared in the doorway as Bridget's head disappeared. Shane's friend Kieran who had already turned eighteen had arrived; they were the best of pals. Martin could hear him downstairs playing the fool with Sinead. The two of them were mimicking Shane's grooming procedures that he deemed necessary before he was able to pass himself fit to leave the house. Martin groaned to himself, wondering would he ever get a break. Kieran was the son of Declan and Kathleen. Even his own home wasn't safe from the Hennesseys.

Mind you, Kieran was a nice enough lad, he thought. He was shy with little confidence, which was odd considering who his father was in the neighbourhood. It was for that reason he hadn't many friends. Teenagers' parents had warned them to stay away from him, assuming he took after his father. His looks belied his temperament. Rising over 6ft in height, his muscle definition was like that of a middleweight boxer. His raw features and square jaw resembled his father's, but he had a natural smile like his mother.

Despite his physical appearance, Kieran lacked self-esteem and was reserved and nervous, probably, thought Martin, due to witnessing his father's brutal way of life growing up. He had been friends with Shane since they were babies, brought together by their mothers' closeness. His friendship with Sinead had bloomed not long after as he was always over at the Lynches' house. Sinead doted on him like another big brother. Despite the animosity between Declan and Martin, their wives, Bridget and Kathleen, had been friends since they were teenagers growing up in the same neighbourhood and had remained good friends throughout adult life.

Shane and Kieran were as thick as thieves since they were old enough to go and play on their own. They were always up to something, and spent most days exploring on their bikes, left to their own devices. They took excessive pride in their appearance in their late teens, but their bikes remained tatty old relics. Kieran had learnt the hard way that there was no point in having nice things around this neighbourhood. His first brand-new mountain bike was stolen after only a week.

No sooner had he chained it up than some toe-rag decided they needed the bike more than Kieran. From then on, Kieran rode a cheap second-hand bike the same as Shane's, a bike of no interest to anyone. However, Shane's was more than uncomfortable as it no longer had a saddle. Initially, it did, until one day when the bike was abandoned across the pavement outside his front door. Leaving it there overnight, one of the neighbours felt obliged to let their dog urinate over it, leaving the saddle smelling like a soiled nappy. Shane tried to clean it but to no avail. So, the seat had to go. He had gotten used to riding it standing up and only once or twice had forgotten and sat down, much to the hilarity of Kieran riding behind.

Kieran and Shane set off with no place to go as the sun warmed their backs with an energy drink as a substitute for breakfast. They rode their bikes blithely along and chatted without a care in the world. Their usual route took them past the college grounds by Dublin City University. Around lunchtime, the senior girl's hockey team practised for their forthcoming matches. The lads had front row seats and watched the girls through the slatted fencing performing their set play routines.

Shane spoke admiringly, 'Just look at them. I think it's a crying shame they have to wear that kit. It would be perfect if they had body paint on in the form of their kit. What a sight for sore eyes that would be. Can you imagine the influx in revenue within the sport? It would be a packed stadium week in, week out. Can you imagine if the sprinklers came on at the end of each match, that would be a riot!'

Kieran chuckled, 'You've really put a lot of thought into this, haven't you?'

Shane beamed. 'Which ones take your fancy? Come on; we'll split them into two teams.' Shane bounced to his feet and egged Kieran up to pick first.

'Right,' said Kieran, 'I'll pick long-tall Sally there… there look, with the stick to ball now.'

Shane nodded in respect and smiled, 'I knew you were going to pick the high school pin-up. You're so predictable.'

Kieran looked pleased with himself. 'I've picked the best now you can pick from the rest.'

Shane challenged him. 'Look at your lass. Her hair done up to the nines. Full makeup and nail varnish on, and her frightened to break her nails. Girls like her think their shite doesn't stink. They look down on lads like us. You'd never get a shag off her until you've taken her out and lavished dinners on her for months. Even then, she'd be posting it online and looking at her phone all night, checking her social media instead of chatting to you. Those girls don't put out, and when you do get a taste, you'll have to do all the work. What you want is an average girl. A five out of ten lass. First date, you'd be able to take her to the pictures and guaranteed you'd reach first base with her for a tenner well spent.'

Kieran looked horrified, 'What's wrong with talking to them on the first date to find out what they're all about, or if both of you even like each other?'

'Plenty of time for talking shite when she's on the rag each month,' Shane countered.

Shaking his head . Kieran sighed, 'I hope you have a completely different outlook on life when your Sinead starts dating lads.'

'Ah, look at you, Kieran,' Shane mocked, 'once your face clears up, the lasses will be flocking around you, don't worry. You're my bro, but you're so NEW at times, too fucking soft with the ladies. You should be shifting lasses by now, not trying to get to know them.'

Kieran stood his ground, 'Look, I'll do things my way and at my pace. If I think long tall Sally is for me, then I'll get to know her before you know… taking things further.'

'I think there will be quite a few long-tall Sally's ahead of you in life before you want to settle down with this one,' Shane jeered.

The pair laughed and joked about their misspent youth, reminiscing about how they used to wait for Kathleen's new clothing catalogue to arrive eagerly. How they excitedly huddled around it, checking out all the hot models in the lingerie section. Kathleen only became aware of their attention by accident when she had questioned Declan if he had ordered some items as a surprise for her after noting the folded back pages, and he laughed outrageously at her.

She started leaving post-it notes between the earmarked pages that read 'Respect our bodies', but she never questioned the boys to avoid embarrassing them. Shane ended the conversation about girls as his second most pressing need came to the fore; he was hungry again and said, 'We'd better slink off now for food before my stiffy gets stuck in this fence and I starve.'

After a lunch of takeaway chicken and chips, paid for by Kieran, they stopped outside The Swan public house. A pub and nightclub they had aspirations of gaining entrance to any day now. Both Kieran's and Shane's parents had spoken of its history. The lads joked about which lasses from the hockey team they would like to take there. As they loafed around outside, they saw a red sports car parked in a bay along the high street. They headed over to check it out.

'That's some flash car. Do you recognise it?' Shane questioned Kieran.

Shaking his head, Kieran replied, 'Nah, it doesn't belong to anyone I know.'

The lads were about to be introduced to the Finnerty brothers. Whilst unknown to the boys, they were well-known to the adults of the neighbourhood. Patrick, the elder of the two, was the more considered and by right of seniority, the natural leader of the duo. Then there was Thomas. Thomas was an individual who lacked charm in every way imaginable. Despite this, his confidence was unerring. He had no moral compass and imposed fear and pain without remorse. People who knew him stayed away from him and spoke of him having a split personality or mental health issues. He had an unhealthy glare in his eyes.

The brothers shared the same weaknesses, mainly easy women and potent weed. Patrick was tall and attractive; his hair was long and thick, and he had a Mediterranean look about him. He was easy on the eye and appealing to women and never short of their company. Thomas didn't have the same luck. He'd never had any real relationship due to his cruel nature and lack of charm. Not that he minded anyhow; to him, women existed for his sexual gratification. On one occasion, Patrick had had to rescue his younger sibling from madams who had held him hostage in brothels when he took out his cruelty on the women there. Despite his brother's failings, Patrick remained obstinately loyal to him.

The brothers were born and raised in Limerick and spent most of their youth in care. They had convictions from as far back as their early teens that escalated into their adult life. Developing a reputation in Limerick, their names soon made whispers in the netherworld. Both brothers worked for Aiden O'Driscoll and his associates. O'Driscoll had aspirations of flooding his south Dublin outfit with class A drugs, funnelling it into other major cities and towns, making him the country's number one supplier. The brothers fitted well into his hierarchy, spreading fear across the south of the city; one functional, the other terrifying. Aiden hadn't anticipated that the brothers had their own agenda that didn't fit into his plans. They planned to take over supplying the Dublin suburbs eventually, and this included Declan's district. The Finnerty brothers had an impossible task ahead of them.

Shane removed his top and tied it around the handlebars as he glanced in the driver's wing mirror. Wincing, he checked the progression of a pimple on his chin. They continued to chat as Shane leaned closer to the mirror to squeeze his zit. From the corner of his eye, Kieran saw two figures darting towards them. Before he could shout a warning to Shane, one of the figures swung his arm back and slammed Shane into the rear of the car parked in front. His body creased over his handlebars, hitting the headlights. The same assailant lunged at Kieran's shoulder and tried to swing him up against the car bonnet. In a simple reflexive motion, Kieran blocked the swing and ducked.

Huddled on the pavement now, the second assailant waded into Kieran, kicking him as he tried in vain to get to his feet. The first guy had now recovered his footing and joined in kicking Kieran. Blood streamed from Shane's mouth as he lay on the pavement coiled up in agony. A couple of people walked past them without batting an eyelid. Kieran instinctively shielded his chest and face and stayed in a foetal position. He yelped as he absorbed the blows, crying out guttural noises that made no sense. The taller attacker backed off almost as quickly as he had come at him. Behind him, he could hear Shane's moans as pain radiated across his face from where he'd hit the road. He coaxed his partner to back off and pulled Kieran into a standing position.

'What the fuck are you doing at my car, boy?' the man demanded, shaking Kieran roughly.

Kieran, gasping for air, mumbled, 'Nothing, I swear, we were just looking. I'm Kieran... Kieran Hennessey... my father... my father is Declan Hennessey.'

Looking at each other sharply, the goons' eyes opened wide. It was Patrick and Thomas Finnerty

Patrick winked at his brother. 'Well, what do you know. Is this a coincidence or what? This is our welcome greeting, boy. Tell your father he'll be seeing a lot more of us around his neck of the woods.'

Kieran felt cold travel through his body. He caught the overbearing scent of deodorant.

Patrick continued, 'You've heard of Mr O'Driscoll, haven't you, boy? We have a spot of business with him, and we plan to be making our acquaintance with your old man real soon. Your father has made a name for himself over the years, and I respect that; we both respect that.'

Kieran didn't attempt to move. Cowering, he looked up briefly before dropping his head back down. Patrick carried on menacingly. 'Unfortunately for him, a change is going to come soon. We plan on sticking around for some time here. Getting our feet under the table if you get my drift.'

Shane tentatively guarded his face as he huddled up against a wheel arch.

Thomas shouted, C'mere, what ya looking at? Wrenching him

away from the car by the scruff of the neck, he dragged him along the pavement towards the kerb and whispered gruffly, 'Your matey just saved your backside.'

Shane caught the aroma of stale weed clinging to his breath as he cowered.

'If you've smashed our window, we'll make sure you'll never be able to ride a bike again.'

Before Shane could explain himself, afraid of another attack. He knew to stay down. The footsteps treaded around the car, heels scuffing the tarmac as they faded. Kieran stared straight ahead, scared to make any sudden movement. Thomas discerned his fear. 'I bet your father is REAL proud of you. Some tough kid, the famous Declan Hennessey has raised!' he sneered.

He sniggered, seemingly inflicting enough punishment for the time being. From where he lay on the pavement, Shane heard the sound of phlegm being coughed up and hitting the road, a car door slam, then the rev of the engine as their tormentors departed. The car screeched off along the road, fishtailing, leaving a waft of burning rubber lingering in the air. Kieran and Shane choked on the fumes as they slowly came back to themselves. Speckles of blood blotted the pavement. Their first encounter with the Finnerty brothers had left its mark.

CHAPTER 6

Splotches of blood trailed behind the lads as they slumped on the steps of The Swan, consoling each other. Shane had already phoned Bridget to contact Kathleen to collect them. Kieran's phone shattered during the assault. Neither was up to riding their bikes back home. Declan was advised of what happened and sent his sidekick Billy to collect them and their bikes. On arrival, as the window of the car buzzed down, a broad cheesy grin spread across Billy's face, and he chuckled.

'Was it a couple of college girls that took offence to your advances, boys?' he smirked.

Too tired to object much, both lads weakly gave him the finger as they hobbled into the van. Billy loaded their bikes into the back. Declan's instructions were to take the lads home, dropping Shane off first. He hadn't entirely bought into Kieran's summary of what happened and wanted to question him.

While he waited, Declan mulled over who might be stupid enough to challenge his authority and take a cheap shot as his son. He lit a cigarette out the back and started pacing, the thoughts of it getting him more and more riled up. Without realising, he recited names off to himself as they swarmed around his head. None of his enemies sprang to mind as the obvious contender. Fidgeting, he popped a piece of chewing gum into his mouth, dropped his cigarette, and steeled himself for his son to return.

Billy chattered away obliviously in the car, giving Kieran time to collect his thoughts before his father interrogated him. On arrival, Declan came out and spoke with Billy as Kieran drifted, hobbling, inside.

'Did he say much on the way home?'

'No, Boss,' Billy replied, 'I didn't want to challenge his story. He looks pretty shaken up; it seems like the attack came out of nowhere'

'Ok, good man,' Declan countered, 'I want you to go back to The

Swan with Johnny. Have a scope around the bar, then ask the bar manager NICELY if you can view the CCTV footage.'

Spitting his gum out, he rubbed his stubble frustratedly. 'I want to know what the fuck these characters look like.' Pointing his finger aggressively at Billy, Declan raised his voice. 'See if you can catch the number plate on the car outside before I question O'Driscoll; he's the only one may know who would pull a stunt like this. This is something way out of character for him.'

'Right, Boss, anything else?'

'No.'

'Take it easy on the lad in there. Do yourself a favour and tread lightly with him; if you go in all guns blazing, you may miss something significant with him.' Billy's chest released a deep sigh.

'I know you mean well, Billy, but I think I know my son by now,' Declan replied, annoyed.

Closing the front door, Declan could hear the shower running. It gave him time to compose himself so he could gather his thoughts before questioning his son. Kieran appeared refreshed but still limping as he perched himself on a stool. Declan had made two teas. Kieran took a sip, pursing his lips against the heat; he grimaced and pulled away.

Declan's mouth opened before he realised his mistake,

'Christ, Son – don't tell me you flinched like that when you got hit.'

Kieran looked to the floor. Declan immediately regretted the remark.

'Kieran, sorry lad, from the start, think slowly and tell me exactly what happened.'

'It all just happened so quickly, Dad,' feeling vulnerable, Kieran squirmed.

'Son – nobody attacks you for no reason, even if they don't know who you are.'

'We stopped for a breather after the takeaway, then this swanky motor was parked outside The Swan. All Shane did was look at the motor…'

Declan interrupted. 'What do you mean? I need exact details, Son. Did he look at it or in it?'

Kieran had an evasive tone in his voice. 'Erm, into it, Dad.'

'Right Son, what next?' Declan's piercing eyes offered no comfort.

'Then, from nowhere, these two fellas came outside from the pub and smashed Shane across the car before kicking me to the ground. It all happened so fast; that's all I remember.'

'Did they talk to you at all? Did you hear any of their names? It's important, Son, any detail.'

'I wanted them to stop, so I told them you were my dad, and they stopped.'

'So, they knew who I was then?' The remark came out with anger.

'They laughed when I told them and said they had plans for the whole city. Dad, honest, that's all I can remember.'

'Did you fight back?' Declan urged.

'Dad, I was too scared; also, Shane was in a bad way,' Kieran's voice faltered.

'For Christ's sake, Son, you should have kicked, fucking bit them – anything. Don't tell me you lay there and took it? As soon as they sense fear in your eyes, they have already won. You've got to work on that; otherwise, people will never respect you. You can't follow in my footsteps and have everybody around you thinking you're a pussy, Son.'

'I'm sorry, Dad, it all happened so fast.' Kieran felt broken inside.

'Son, how many times do I have to tell you? You need to be alert and vigilant all the time. You are not like other young men in this city; you are the son of Declan Hennessey; things are going to be different for you.'

'I don't want your life, Dad. I want to go to college and do something different.'

'But you still have to know how to stand up for yourself, Son. I bet you begged those two fuckwits to stop kicking you instead of trying to get up. You always find trouble with that fucking Lynch boy by your side. He's just like his old man, a good-for-nothing lowlife who will never amount to anything.'

'That's not fair, Dad. He's a good mate.' Looking at his father, Kieran half-heartedly shrugged his shoulders.

Declan decided to back off a bit, realising he had gone too far. A car came to a stop outside. Kathleen had arrived home. Kieran averted his eyes from his father's. Declan knew he had to leave to avoid a confrontation with Kathleen over their son. Kieran stood up straight and flinched. The slightest of movements sent ripples of pain through his back and groin. Declan's eyes softened as he saw his boy's. pain, not with pity but with regret for how he had handled the conversation.

Without saying another word, Declan turned to go. Greeting Kathleen with a kiss, he nodded at her, confirming he had spoken to Kieran. Unable to resist one last remark, his pain turning to anger, he snidely aimed it at Kathleen. 'This is what you get when you mollycoddle the boy. Look at him in there; he still has his mother's milk over his face.'

The knuckles of Kathleen's hands turned white as she clenched the heavy shopping bags. Rage rose in her chest from the effort to remain silent. She knew she'd get her right to reply later, now was not the time. Declan left the house and got into his car. Slouching in the driver's seat and thumbing his forehead Declan also knew that Kathleen would make him pay for that remark.

CHAPTER 7

A surge of worry coursed through Martin's veins as he digested what he was seeing. A message from Bridget about the lads getting into a scrap earlier had put him on edge; now, a hard lump lodged in his throat as he saw his son's face. Blood, dried blood, and vulnerability written all over it.

Trying to diffuse the tension, he said, 'Hey there, boy wonder; I've only just finished paying for that bike on tick – at least it is still in one piece.'

Shane slumped onto a chair in the kitchen, leaning on its hind feet as he tried to take the weight off his back.

'That's right, Dad, check the bike over before me,' he half-heartedly joked. Pain surged as he attempted a smile.

Martin had already prepared a bowl of warm water with disinfectant. Sitting in front of Shane, he tenderly dabbed cotton wool over his marked face. Drips ran down his neck, staining his collar, as a searing pain shot through his face. Each dab of disinfectant stung; it brought back memories of scraping his knee as a young child. Martin let Shane open up the conversation with details of the attack. The warm cotton wool layered with blood created swirls of red in the bowl, like an artist's paintbrush, darkening on each visit.

'Do you wanna tell me what happened? Remember, this is not your mother sat in front of you, Shane.'

'For once, Dad, we didn't do or say anything to piss these guys off. Honest!' A squeal pierced the air as the disinfectant soaked into his bloodied nose. 'We've never seen these guys before. I was looking into the car's wing mirror, and this bastard walloped me from behind. I didn't stand a chance. Then they laid into Kieran.'

'Were they trying to pinch the bicycles off you? You didn't try and fight back, did you? Don't be embarrassed; sometimes doing nothing is the best response.'

'The bikes are worth shite, Da; I was in too much agony to care,' Shane sighed.

Martin gestured with a gentle nod. 'That's good; with an unprovoked attack like that, you don't know whether these guys were tooled up at all. How is Kieran bearing up? I'm assuming he took a beating as well. His old man will go berserk when he finds out.'

'They spoke to Kieran briefly, but I couldn't work out what they were saying.'

Martin probed gently, 'Did they rob you both?'

'No, Dad. They just gave us a pasting, jumped back into their flash car and took off like shite off a shovel.'

Martin gently wiped Shane's face clean, and cupping his son's cheeks, he studied his face. 'I can't imagine any harm coming to you and what it would do to me and your mam. Let's hope it was a one-off, and you'll never bump into those bastards again.'

'No fear, Da. I'll turn a corner if we see them again.'

'Good lad. You're in the safest company when you knock about with Kieran, your mother, and I trust him,' Martin countered.

'I think Kieran is more wound up about his dad grilling him than his bruised ribs. At least both our bikes are still rideable.'

Martin shook his head, 'That bicycle of yours is a death trap. I took a ride on it to the bookies a couple of weeks ago, fearing I'd miss a race. I went to sit on it, and it felt like a torpedo had gone straight up me arse. I took a long hot soak back home and used your mam's ginger body scrub shite with them grains in it. Next thing I know, my backside felt like it was the ring of fire. I told your mam, and she broke her heart laughing. That is until I told her I used her Revitalift face cream to numb the heat around my arsehole. I tell ye, she took the head clean off me. It worked a treat, mind you.'

Shane's face ached as laughter beamed burst out of him. 'Da, that's savage; you're killing me!'

The mood lifted, Martin stood up and started clearing away the mess. Shane glanced with a hint of pride at his newly acquired war wounds in his reflection in the oven door. 'Dad, I'm grand now honestly, I don't need you to mind me anymore,' he said, 'is it alright if I chill out for a bit?

I want to head back out later to meet Kieran.'

'No problem, boy wonder.' Martin smiled. 'Promise me you'll keep a lookout from now on, and if you see that car about, stay away from it. Promise me now, Son, that you're not going be a langer and play the tough guy, ok? Be wide now.' Despite his admonitions, Martin secretly admired Shane for his resilience. His ability to dust himself down and get on with it.

There was a knock at the door. Martin piped up, 'Are you feeling fit, Son? I need a hand unloading the van. David's here with some stuff for me. If the ribs are paining you, just hold the door open for me.'

David was anxious outside and called out, 'Fuck's sake, man, I haven't got all day. I need to get the van back before Declan scratches his head and asks questions.'

The two men heaved in the boxes and dumped them in the front room. Stretching his back out first, Martin dragged them across the threadbare carpet. Within ten minutes, a dozen heavy crates were stacked inside the sitting room. David left with not so much as a goodbye.

Martin was pleased with his hoard as he coolly rubbed his hands together and remarked in glee, 'Today I'm as happy as a pig in shite. Will you sit with me for a bit; I could do with your help sifting through these boxes.'

'What's in them?' Shane asked. Squinting his eyes, he peered into a crate and pulled out a book. Flicking through the pages, he dusted off the cover before disregarding it back in the box.

Martin scowled him and replied, 'Hey, careful with them there.'

Coaxing the hardbacks out from the box, Martin splayed them across the floor. Each stack must have had twenty-plus books. Picking one up, he gently rubbed its spine, caressing its cover. Looking at Shane, he spoke softly, 'I wasn't a reader as a youngster and never thought much about books until I met up with a man called Pat Ahern. Do you remember the fella, Shane?'

Shane's brain caught up as he answered, 'Who? Oh yeah. Was he yer man who Mam would never let into the house because he always had a fag in his gob and stank the place out?'

Martin shadow tapped Shane and replied, 'That's him. Unfortunately, it was those stinky fags that finished him off in the end. God bless his soul. I earned a good education from him, which helped me bring in a few euros after his passing. You see, Pat Ahern rarely worked throughout his life, yet he had a roof over his head for his family, and he always had money in his pocket for the betting shop. That's where I first met him and started my education with all these books.'

Rolling his eyes, Shane replied in jest, 'I think I'm going to need a brew before you carry on, Da.'

Martin interrupted, 'There's a couple of beers outside the garden there if you like?' Shane's eyes lit up; he didn't hesitate in getting and uncapping two bottles. They both settled cross-legged amidst the books on the floor.

Martin continued his story. 'Now, what old Pat did was trade old books. He bought them cheap and sold them on for a tidy profit. He had all that knowledge about books; he only passed on about 1% to me before he died. It was a crying shame. He knew he was slowly dying, so he introduced all his contacts to me: buyers, sellers and agents.'

Shane looked disinterested but was enjoying sharing a beer with his father.

Martin carried on, aware that Shane's attention had begun to drift.

'Pat was a very tricky man in business, and that's how he managed to make a living for himself. He struck up a friendship with contacts in estate agents in town. When elderly folk died and left their estate to their families, he was always the first point of contact when a property needed a house clearance. When the elderly die, their families usually come in and strip the house from top to bottom for hidden cash and heirlooms.

By the time all the vultures have had their pickings of any heirlooms, all that is left is old furniture and guess what else? That's right, sleepyhead, BOOKS! Pat would then get a call to view any books and slip the agents drink money if he cleared what he thought may be valuable. That was before the house clearance mob came in and cleared the lot out. So, now I get first pickings and delve through all these boxes to find myself a hidden gem.'

Shane blinked rapidly, went out and returned with two more beers. Martin had been preoccupied, wading through the books. Disregarding most of the contents of the first box, he held a book bound in leather aloft and spoke candidly. 'You see, Son, I look at books in a completely different way now. Take this one, for example,' the spine creaked as the pages fell open, 'look at the craftsmanship in its binding. It's timeworn but precious and I try to imagine the joy and anticipation folk had reading books years ago. You see, there was no telly or phones. Husband and wife either shagged, or they read books, or they did both. They sat in candlelight with no distractions from texting or calls. Children were read bedtime stories. A book was so much more respected back then as it was passed down through generations.'

Shane saw a completely different side to his father. Listening, he felt enchanted by his father's conversation. In this light, he saw a man who felt affection for something that didn't involve alcohol.

Martin continued as he swigged his beer. 'You'd be surprised, Son, how much certain books are worth these days in the right market.' Counting off his fingers, Martin continued, 'For instance, the series' first edition Harry Potter book is worth thousands of euros. In fact, many children's books are worth a lot of money. They must be first editions, though. The same if they have a dust jacket on them. They must be in mint condition to hold their value.'

Shane looked vacant. Martin snapped his fingers and explained, 'A dust jacket is the paper sleeve around the book.'

Shane nodded.

'Signed books need a provenance, that means you need to find out when and where it was signed. Books that were in short supply or demand fetch money too. If I could find one book that I can sell and make real money from; then I could put on the table, then I'd feel of worth, Son, and not be relying on your mother running herself into the ground to feed us all. You see, it does get to me, Son. I'm not worthy if I can't support my family.'

Feeling touched by Martin's honest take on life and regrets, Shane felt for his father.

Martin, conscious now he'd been getting emotional, tried to direct attention away from himself in a toast to Pat Ahern. Clinking bottles, they continued to sip, changing the subject to Shane's progresson to the next round in his football tournament.

Shane, still interested though, questioned, 'So, what's going to happen with all of these? Can't you take them down the car boot fair and flog them for a euro each?'

Martin replied, 'I find the car boot sales are a waste of time. Books are generally manhandled and get damaged easily, and you end up bringing them back home. There's an unwritten rule when it comes to books in this house: you never destroy them. Sinead will pick some for school and her pals, and your mam will take the rest into the nursing home. Everyone is a winner, Son.'

The trauma Shane suffered had taken its toll on him emotionally after the alcohol had slowed his senses down. With heavy eyes, he decided to sleep if off before meeting with Kieran later on. Martin appreciated the quiet time at home and picked his way through the boxes sniffing their history and marvelling in the promise of each one's potential value.

CHAPTER 8

In the Hennessey household, meanwhile, Kieran was having an entirely different debriefing with his mother. Sitting in silence, Kieran listened with his head bowed as Kathleen spoke in a no-nonsense voice.

'Right, my love, Bridget told me what happened briefly on the phone. Now in your own words, you can tell me the truth.'

Looking up, Kieran focused on Kathleen as she looked intently at him.

'Forget what you've told your father; just tell it to me as it happened, Kieran.'

Retelling the whole event again, Kieran explained how afraid he was for himself and Shane. 'I can't explain it, Mam; I got a strange vibe off one of those guys.'

'It sounds like they were off their heads on meth or something,' Kathleen commented.

When they'd finished talking, Kathleen, pleased neither of the boys had received any severe injuries, made Kieran take his top off so she could inspect the damage. Her cold fingertips tickled his ribs as she gently pressed each one. He flinched. 'Right, you were fortunate; no bones were broken. Now tell me, have you still got that pain downstairs?' she asked nonplussed.

Kieran blushed, stretching his top over his head, trying to ignore his mother's question.

'Come on now, love, I'm your mother, and I need to know that you're fit and healthy.'

Kieran had sustained a groin injury recently at a boxing gym his father had persuaded him to attend in a bid to boost his confidence and toughen him up. The boxing classes had done the complete opposite. Kieran lost his nerve, terrified at the sight of fists heading towards his head.

Instead, he snuck next door to use the gym area. Carrying out his own unsupervised weights routine, he had pulled a muscle in his groin, and the persistent pain hadn't subsided after a couple of weeks.

Kathleen persisted, 'You need to go to the doctors, and before you ask, NO, I haven't mentioned any of this to your father. I need to know that everything is in order downstairs for you to supply me with grandchildren in the future.' Kathleen managed a smirk.

'Jaysis, Mam,' Kieran groaned, 'you really are planning ahead. Look, I'll lay off the extra sessions until everything heals up. It's just a strain.'

'I tell ye what, if you won't go to the GP, then will you let my friend Dr Kavanagh examine you?' Bridget bargained with him. 'There is an Irish Countrywomen's Association charity ball that Bridget and myself have got tickets for that she's organising, I'm sure she'd help. Do you remember Dr Kavanagh?'

'No Mam, haven't got a clue.' Kieran dismissed her. 'Anyway, we're helping her with the planning for the ICA ball and she is picking us up from here for it on Friday, I'll ask her to give you the once over before.'

'Ah Mam, no,' protested Kieran.

'I don't want to hear any excuses, Kieran. You make sure you're here. Do I make myself clear?' she demanded resolutely.

'Can I go now? I'm meeting back up with Shane,' he asked.

'Come here and give me a hug,' Kathleen ordered.

'Mam, PLEASE.'

She grabbed him and held him close. 'No matter how old you get, my love, you will always be my little boy.'

Despite himself, Kieran accepted the hug, then disengaged quickly and, with red cheeks, snatched a freshly ironed hoodie and bounced out the door.

Fifteen minutes later, Kieran met up with Shane at the park at the top of Holmewood Road. Shane had been to the shops and had managed to get someone to buy him some discount beers. As they sat comfortably against the willow tree, a light wind rustled through the branches that startled the settling birds. The pair clinked their bottles and downed half the contents.

'I thought your father would have driven you all around the streets trying to pinpoint those two fuckers,' laughed Shane.

Kieran sniggered, 'Don't worry, I've learnt to tell my pops what he needs to know; my mam taught me that. How did yours take it?'

'My dad was grand. He was pleased that we both, more or less, got away with just a few bruises.'

'I sometimes wish my dad was more laid back like yours,' said Kieran, quieter now.

Shane's eyes twinkled. 'I'm also glad my dad ISN'T like yours. Feck sake, man, I'd always be grounded in your house – but I would have the benefits of snuggling up to your mam's bosom,' he guffawed, spitting beer droplets out of his mouth.

'Hey, cut that out. I mean it,' Kieran threw him a disgruntled look.

'You know I'm messing with you. Your mam does look grand for her age though,' Shane offered, mock contritely.

'Seriously!' Kieran pointed at Shane in warning as Shane guffawed.

Remaining subdued, Kieran threw him another bottle. Shane took a gulp and sucked his teeth as the fizz hit the back of his throat and came up his nose. 'This is the mutt's nuts,' he burped in appreciation.

Kieran carried on quietly as if unaware that the subject had somewhat ended. 'My dad is a good man. He means well even though he blathers on, and I love him to bits. I think he is the way he is because he never really knew his father. He had no experience of fatherhood to guide him, and I think that's why he is so overprotective of me and Mam.' He gulped his beer, letting his body relax.

'He does try to talk to me. I guess I know what he wants to say, but it comes out wrong at times, and then he loses his cool with himself but takes it out on anyone around him. He has spent much of his life looking over his shoulder and finds it hard to chill out around people.'

A football rolled in their direction. Looking around, Kieran jumped up and kicked it back in the direction it came from before sitting back on his heels against the tree.

'He never really trusts anyone – except his sidekicks, Billy and Johnny. At home though, he is the King of his castle, and Mam is his Queen. That's the only place he can truly switch off. I can tell him any bad news at that point, and he's cool; he says, "I'm glad you could tell me, Son." I know many people shy away from him, but he is a good man, deep down.' Kieran guzzled his beer, releasing a suction noise as he pulled the bottle from his lips.

'Outside the house, though, he's fucking scary. Mam has always told me to judge him for the man I see in front of me and not for the man people perceive him to be. He wants me to be this fearless figure like him. Mam says it's just not in my makeup.' Kieran sank back down into a sitting position.

Shane opened another bottle, then contemplated before speaking, 'I can honestly say I have never seen your old man chilled out. He always has this stern look on his face as if you've offended him, even though you haven't said a word. You don't know which way he will turn. He scares the absolute shit out of me, to be honest.'

A bottle cap flipped into the air as Kieran responded. 'He's not that bad really; he's just afraid that people will think of him as a soft touch if he acts nice.'

Shane gave a mirthless sigh. 'Well, I guess at least he cares. Mine has never given a fuck about anything. He takes one day at a time, nothing's planned, and everything is spent. I'll give him his due, as long as Mam is happy that there is enough money for the bills, he goes and does his own thing. That's generally in your dad's pub, by the way. My mam always looks like – she'll kill me for saying this – she always looks like she needs a bloody good rest. I don't mean a day off or things like that; I mean she needs to go away on her own.'

'You guys ever had a holiday?' Kieran asked.

Shane looked quizzical, 'Holiday... you've got to be kidding. We've never even been away for a weekend or even stayed a night in a hotel. What you never had, you never miss,' Shane shrugged unbothered.

Kieran nodded. 'Holidays are overrated anyway. Dad's always on the phone whenever we fly out, checking up on people and driving Mam mad. Last time we were away, Mam told him to leave the mobile at the villa when we went out. He refused, so she put his name down at one of these karaoke bars without telling him. We pissed ourselves when they escorted him up to sing. After that night, the phone always stayed in the villa.'

Laughter filled the branches above. Below, a collection of bottle tops formed a pattern spread out around them. Each one pressed into the earth, a reminder of past evenings spent telling stories and putting the world to rights. Both lads lingered on the last gulps of their bottle before uncharacteristically gathering them up to dispose of them in the park's bin. The sky was awash with a pink haze that bathed the skyline as sunset fell.

CHAPTER 9

Sinead was in remission after treatment from radiotherapy after having a biopsy that determined she had a primary brain tumour. The initial shock of her diagnosis had devastated the family. Bridget blamed Martin. She convinced herself it was for the wrongful way he led his life, jumping on the bandwagon of her sister's fervent religious beliefs. She believed it was God's punishment to teach them a lesson in life for Martin's misdemeanours. Martin also blamed himself and didn't need guilt from anyone else to confirm that.

The symptoms had started over months. Sinead complained of severe headaches in the mornings and fatigue before mood swings and signs of forgetfulness began. At first, Bridget and Martin had both dismissed them as growing pains. Bridget became concerned after they got worse over a few weeks. Initially, she had thought it was possibly an excuse for trying to get time off school. Sinead hadn't started the academic year well as she didn't particularly like her new teacher.

She began having mild seizures, and quickly, Bridget realised it was serious and had taken Sinead to their family doctor. After explaining the pattern, the doctor thought there might be something underlying her unsettling behaviour and referred her for an MRI. The results were damning and shook Bridget and Martin to their core. Sinead hadn't realised its significance at that time; she was relieved that a diagnosis for the pain she was going through was found.

After the biopsy, a course of radiotherapy treatment began. The intensity took its toll on Bridget. The hospital was on the other side of the city via a relentless journey through the rush hour commute on treatment days. Kathleen, as Bridget's close friend, offered to take them to the hospital. Martin's four-door estate car became unreliable. It played on Bridget and Martin's mind all the time. Bridget read up on the condition and the more information she collated in her head, the more daunting the prospect of battling the disease became. Her worst fear was that if the radiotherapy treatment failed, then chemotherapy would be required. It was a procedure that incurred more painful treatment.

The current treatment had severe side effects for Sinead. She endured challenging mood swings that triggered a nasty temper in her. Everyone at home had to take her spiteful tongue in these fits of rage, but Martin bore the brunt of most of them. He found it unduly upsetting in the heat of her temper when she referred to him as 'Martin' instead of Dad. He hated the unfamiliarity that made him feel distant from her.

Martin rarely reprimanded her when she was younger and didn't have the guts to now, fearing the spite of her tongue. They knew each other inside out, their likes and dislikes; despite Sinead's mood swings, their bond was as tight as ever. Shane and Sinead had witnessed many episodes of Martin's excessive drinking growing up. Sinead, in particular, had been more affected by what she had seen and vowed that alcohol was never going to run or ruin her life.

The smell of bleach overshadowed Sinead's earliest recollection of her mother. Bridget had supported the family with part-time cleaning jobs when Sinead was little. The rubber gloves irritated her hands, so she didn't wear any. The smell of bleach on her hands remained for days, every cuddle tarnished with the corrosive aroma. The nostalgia of days gone by was etched in her mind, not for the joy of family dinners together or outings to new places, but for the redness of her mother's hands and the smell of cleaning agents. Bridget tried to hide the discomfort of her work, but Sinead missed nothing and forgot nothing.

Though she loved her father and they had a bond nothing could break, she had a more mature view of his inadequacies than her age would indicate. She saw what her mother had endured to make up for her father's deficiencies. Memories of arguments between her parents upset her now and, despite her support for her mother, she felt sorry for her father. Sorry that he didn't have the guts to do something with his life. Sad that he lacked the self-awareness to make a change. She didn't yet understand the world of alcohol, how it could control and consume you, how it could destroy your self-esteem and belittle you around your family. Sinead was like her mother; she had her head screwed on and was practical and resourceful but not yet streetwise. She had her life planned out from day one. School first, then university, a job in architecture and design, marriage, babies, and happily ever after. She loved school and had many friends. She had a couple of very close friends who knew what she was going through. The pain and discomfortof her illness she could contend with but not control. The fatigue and nausea upset her. She was a fiery girl who never gave up, but this disease never gave her any warning. The radiotherapy sessions zapped her, and instead of being out on her bike with her pals, she had to contend herself with more sedate activities like reading and watching documentaries or quiz games. When her hair began to fall out in clumps, it distressed her that her illness was visible to the world. She couldn't hide it anymore and hated looking sick.

She stubbornly refused to wear a wig despite this and said she wasn't hiding away because she simply had no hair. She was a fighter. 'Cancer can go fuck itself' was a phrase she used to take back some control. It was the only time she was allowed to use bad language, and she glibly maximised the opportunity afforded her. It was a shock for the parish priest to hear it as he visited her to comfort the family through the early days of her diagnosis.

During the radiotherapy treatment, the frequency of seizures increased. When Sinead had an aura before an episode at home, both Sinead and Bridget were surprised Martin assumed the mantle. He would try to make the sitting room warm and comfortable before he started to help Sinead relax and control the strange negative feelings and racing thoughts. Bridget was astounded by his gentleness and capability in managing this task. It gave her a rare time to relax and take a break from the toll Sinead's illness took on her.

Sinead had recently taken up knitting and asked her neighbour, Mrs Mercer, to teach her. For years, Mrs Mercer had made soft toys for Sinead, who was always been impressed by them. Sinead started with small designs and moved on to larger, more complicated items. She had begun making a textured shawl and was pleased with her progress. Listening to music helped her switch off and submerge herself into a trance, and she often did both at the same time.

The term illness she contended with, the word Tumour she detested. It embarrassed her. The stigma attached to it had people smothering her with pity. She decided to give the illness a name, calling it *Trouble*. Trouble in her mind that could and would eventually go away.

It was a term that stuck with everyone close to her. Her illness really was trouble for the whole family. Some days, Martin and Bridget were like ships passing in the night. The night shifts took their toll on Bridget. Exhaustion plagued her regularly with the worry of keeping their heads above water each month and managing Sinead's hospital appointments. Trouble consumed her mind constantly.

Shane and Kieran fumbled through the front door. Martin shared small talk with the lads before entering the back room. The room, intended as a dining room ended up as a knick-knack room full of junk with a sofa and TV. It was the place everyone came to get away from things in the house. Sinead lay on the couch resting, listening to some music on her Walkman. Martin insisted she used it as a coping mechanism believing music helped control seizures even though the scientific proof of 'Mozart effect' was vague.

A free-standing wall unit from Sheila's home found solace in the corner of the room. It had stood there for years, and nobody ever ventured near it – except for Christmastime and New Year. The glass-panelled cabinet exhibited bottles of alcohol and was always in use during the festive period. The bottom section was like a time capsule of old family photo albums with negatives that ran in strips. LP records and religious ornaments used for dispensing holy water were stashed away out of sight.

Sinead was as pleased as punch that she had a Walkman; she had found it hidden deep within the wall unit and didn't care that it was out of date. It was the first edition of a Sony sports model gleaming in bright yellow. The original headphones were damaged, so she reclaimed a pair of orange foam ear cushions packed in another box with recorded TDK cassettes. Martin chuckled to himself as he caught the eye of Sinead, eyes closed, orange earphones tight on her head, happily listening to her dinosaur Walkman.

'Jaysis, that takes me back to my youth; didn't think I still kept hold of those,' he laughed.

Sinead grinned, undeterred. Clicking open the cover, she sniffed it and said, 'I love the smell of it. It reminds me of the big TV we used to have. When it used to get hot, it gave off the same smell from the back of it.'

Chortling to himself, Martin replied, 'You have such a take on things; it cracks me up.'

Martin's eyebrows knitted as he watched Sinead nodding her head in time to the music. 'Here, where did you get the batteries, Sinead? You told me you had none?'

Pulling the headphones off her head, she glanced up at him and, studying his puzzled face; she said, 'I took the batteries out of the mantelpiece clock, Dad.'

Cocking his head, Martin looked pleased with her answer. He admired that she was resourceful enough to work out what she needed and go and get it.

'So, time is standing still for us in here?' he asked. 'You should have asked me, darling. I would have taken them out of the smoke alarm instead. Nobody would have missed them. If this place ever caught fire, it would be the best thing to happen to it.'

Sinead's eyebrows furrowed, 'It's still home, Da… our home. We have to do the best with what we've got.'

Martin, feeling somewhat chastened, replied, 'You're right, darling… you're right. So, what else have you got there?' He nodded towards the photo albums in her lap.

'Are these pictures of you, Da?'

'Jeez, I often wondered where these photo albums ended up.'

'Oh my God! Da, was the full fringe the *in* haircut?! How old were you then?'

'Probably bout seven or eight. Before you start mocking me, your Nana Philomena was quite the inventive lady. We were the only family to take crockery to the beach to make sandcastles with, and that same mixing bowl was used as a template to cut our hair. Look at that straight line across the eyebrows...' he smirked. 'The skill wasn't in Nana's hands cutting it straight, but the calmness of us keeping still, so the bowl didn't slip across your face while she snipped. Quite a feat for a small child, I tell you.'

Sinead questioned him further, 'Did you used to get beat up as a kid then, Da?'

'I'll have you know; I was one of the cool kids back then. With my fringe tickling my eyebrows and me bouncing around wearing my ankle swingers singing along to Bucks Fizz, 'Making your mind up,' I tell yeh, I never had a care in the world back then.' He reached out for her and pulled her close. She rested her head on his shoulder.

Cuddling up together on the couch, Sinead elbowed him in jest and put her headphones back on. Martin closed his eyes contentedly, drifting off to the gentle thud from her earphones. Sinead's fascination with the Walkman was because she had never seen one in the flesh before. Most of her friends at school had smartphones for music, Sinead had to do with a portable CD player with headphones, but she was happy with it and loved to play her parents' old cassette tapes. She was a straightforward child, Martin thought fondly, not a bother on her.

A loud, repeated thud broke Martin's spell of snoozing. The lads were practising on a punching bag suspended in the hallway. Two years ago, Martin had given in to Shane's pestering and installed a second-hand one from the beam in the hallway. Erecting it wasn't a simple task in an old house like theirs. Martin needed David's help to suspend the fixings through the floor joists above them to take the weight of the punching bag. Bridget was less than impressed and insisted that the bag was removed after any practising session, leaving the hallway free of obstacles.

Shane and Kieran snarled and grunted as the bag absorbed their shots. Heavy panting followed after.

Martin yelled, 'Keep down out there lads, we're relaxing in here.'

Sinead had abandoned the Walkman now as the batteries had run down and reverted to a CD player. Shuffling inside the cabinet, she found a Robbie Williams' CD and checked for scratches before inserting it. Martin closed his eyes again as Sinead turned up the music. The next track was 'Angels.' The music started. Perking up on the sofa, Martin decided to sing along, trying to overpower the lads' laughter in the hallway. Sinead looked unimpressed. As the door opened slightly, the lads giggled away to themselves, each one egging the other on to enter the room. Shane pulled out his phone from his jeans and, setting the camera mode to record, edged the door open further.

Angling the phone through the gap to capture Martin, the lads recorded his performance. Martin knew the track word for word, but the sounds he emitted were nothing short of horrendous. As the track ended and Martin howled the last line, the lads fell over one another in fits of laughter as they burst through the door.

Catching his breath, Martin straightened himself up and proudly said, 'Well, lads, you can't beat the classics.'

Shane, recovering his equilibrium, chuckled before saying, 'You just crucified that one. This version is going straight onto YouTube, Dad.'

Looking disgruntled, Martin ushered the lads out of the room. Slapping. his backside, he shouted, 'Arhh, YouTube, my arse, beat it up your hole.

The lads composed themselves long enough to review the recording before uploading it to YouTube. Martin had no concept of social media sites. He didn't understand their relevance in society or the power and influence they had over their users. However, the lads did, and days later, Martin had become an unknown celebrity as Shane and Kieran's friends shared the video far and wide. It had been picked up and shared by influencers generating more likes. Tens of thousands of people commented on the video, and it soon caught the attention of the local newspaper. A reporter had watched the video, and it wasn't long before they contacted its source to arrange to interview Martin.

Once they met the family, the story's focus changed entirely after talking about Sinead's plight. A few days later, the paper established a charity appeal for the family to help them with the increasing costs of her illness. Despite everyone laughing at Martin, he didn't care a bit; from this short video, something significant had begun.

Meanwhile, during a day off on his world tour in London, Robbie Williams was interrupted during a heated football video game with his entourage. One of the sound engineers had viewed Shane's video on Facebook and showed Robbie. Feeling embarrassed for the singer, Robbie commented wryly, 'At least he's getting all the words right.'

Laughing in his face, the sound engineer replied, 'There is a resemblance to his pitching though, Rob, you can't deny that.'

Robbie laughed and countered, 'I don't sound that bad even when I try to sing first thing in the morning during a soundcheck.'

Reading the comments on the video, he saw many comments about Sinead and good wishes for her treatment and decided to find out more. After learning of her plight, he had his assistant organise front row seats for Sinead and her family for his upcoming Manchester show at the AO Arena. Return flights and a hotel suite at the exclusive Stock Exchange Hotel were on the list to make her visit as comfortable as possible with medical assistance available if needed. Little did Sinead know she was about to receive the offer of the trip of a lifetime, thanks to her dad's awful singing.

On revealing the news to the rest of the family, Shane instantly backed down from going as it interfered with his street credibility. The fact there was no grime artists as supporting acts confirmed his non-attendance. Bridget also had concerns about travelling as it meant losing two days' work in a row and leaving Shane to get up to no good with his friends. Bridget's decision was final.

CHAPTER 10

Bridget had booked two days off a couple of weeks ago. The care home where she worked appreciated her loyalty and dedication over the years and understood that she had found the last few months particularly hard managing fitting in work shifts and Sinead's hospital appointments. She felt terrible turning down shifts and feeling indebted to colleagues for covering her duty when she had to be in the hospital and was exhausted trying to juggle everything.

She had planned a day off doing something very rare, absolutely nothing, and couldn't wait to relax without worrying about fitting around everyone's needs or schedule. Martin had gone out early. He was vague about what he was up to, and Bridget hadn't pushed for more information; ignorance is bliss. Shane was waiting on Kieran; they were meeting up with friends to go goofing around town. As he left, he'd mentioned something about checking out new trainers that he wanted to buy. Considering he only had his lunch money in his pocket left by Martin, he would come home empty-handed. Bridget hadn't got involved; she didn't want anything to ruin her peace today.

The phone rang, Kathleen's name flashed up on the screen. 'Morning, B, I have the car loaded up with dresses for you to try on for the ball. Kieran is more of a hindrance than a help, but we'll be over in about an hour. I'll get some munchies along the way.'

'Oh Kath, it was lovely of you to offer,' she sighed, 'but I'm not in the mood for trying on dresses or gallivanting around town.'

'Christ, Bridget! You need to get out, and you need to have ME time; you deserve it. When was the last time you and I had a girl's night out? It won't cost you a thing because they've given me two tickets to the ICA ball in exchange for speaking at the event. It's all about empowering women and they're asking local women from the area to talk. I think they just asked me because my name is over the pub door with Declan's. I agreed to say something, though God knows what, I'll figure it out later. There's a three-course meal, complimentary wine and champagne, MORE free wine.' Her voice was good-humoured.

'I haven't any get-up-and-go in me at the moment, Kath,' Bridget sighed wearily but cheerfully.

'What's your favourite wine?' Kathleen asked.

'I'm long gone caring about what wine I drink. As long as it does the job for me and helps me unwind of an evening and eventually sleep, then that's my wine,' Bridget replied absently.

'Come on, your favourite wine?'

'I guess it's anything from the Marlborough region, a Sauvignon Blanc,' she giggled as she put on a French accent.

Kathleen replied with a buoyant tone to her voice, 'Right, I'll pick up a bottle before coming down to you. I'm not taking no for an answer.'

'Kath, are you trying to turn me into a lush or something? It's eleven o'clock in the morning; I don't drink early in the day.'

'You need to relax, Bridget, and you need someone to take care of you. That's my job today. After we're done at your house, I'll go home and get myself ready and come back and collect you this evening, and we can have a few drinks in my house before we head off. Dr Kavanagh is joining us. She has the tickets; she's head of the committee. I'll make sure to get your favourite wine in; it won't cost you a thing. Tell Sinead I'll do her makeover for her today as well when I get there.'

Bridget relented somewhat and started to consider that maybe a night out with the girls was just what she needed. 'Oh right; that's Dr Kavanagh from the surgery; she's lovely – always cheerful with Sinead. Ok, you've twisted my arm, see you in a bit,' she smiled and hung up, turning to see Sinead bouncing on the spot, listening intently, thrilled at the promise of a makeover.

Ladies' day at Number 22 started at lunchtime when Kathleen arrived over with an armful of dresses and a bottle of wine for later. Bridget felt a little embarrassed having Kathleen around, as they usually went to hers instead. The Lynches' house was unpleasant even when tidied up. There was an unearthly smell from the kitchen. Rising damp appeared on the inside of the retaining wall, with black mould filtering down from the corners. The mould freckled across the inside walls causing the wallpaper to peel.

Panicking about cleaning up, Bridget opened up new air fresheners, placing them in every downstairs room. Boxes were stacked around the hall and sitting room, cluttering up the house. Martin had acquired batches of goods to sell that he believed were highly profitable and stored them at home. Though he always ended up owing money somehow and tried to joke that, at the very least, the boxes helped to insulate the house.

Keeping a keen eye out, excited to be included in the proceedings, Sinead stood waiting, fingertips pressed white against the front window. She spotted Kathleen and Kieran arriving and yelped with delight, flinging the front door open. Kathleen entered with a large vanity case, issuing instructions to Kieran, who was trundling along brandishing an armful of evening dresses. They were restricting his view and, as he walked in, he stopped awkwardly in the hall. The dresses slid out of their plastic dry-cleaning membranes and spilt to the floor. After a brief commotion in the hallway, Shane and Kieran finally escaped and left.

The two women and Sinead entered the kitchen, and seeing it empty, Kathleen looked up at the ceiling and asked quizzically, 'Martin still in bed?'

As the kettle grumbled, Bridget replied, 'No, he was up and out this morning. Prattling on about dropping a car off for somebody. He was getting on my nerves, so I didn't push him on who it was for.'

Bridget brought over three steaming mugs of tea, and Kathleen whipped out a box of cream eclairs that looked delicious. They kicked back and relaxed and breathed a sigh of satisfaction.

The day was as fun and relaxing as Bridget had had in a long time. Kathleen gave Sinead dibs on getting her makeup done first. Moving from one room to another, unable to sit still, Bridget chatted idly to Kathleen and Sinead as she continued straightening up the place. Mild laughter warmed the atmosphere. At times, Bridget caught Kathleen and Sinead in animated conversation and stopped to peek; she observed Kathleen in deep concentration as she applied makeup on Sinead. Bridget smiled warmly and took a moment to savour the scene. She sighed with contentment and continued her tidying.

Kathleen had applied the makeup subtly, leaving Sinead's innocence to shine through. Sinead looked beautiful. A beaming smile creased her face and her eyes sparkled as she paraded around with a mirror catching the light at different angles. Delighted with her new look, Sinead retreated to her bedroom to find an outfit, swiping one of the éclairs on the way out. A minute later, music boomed from her room; both women looked at the source of the sound, then each other and smiled.

Finished now with her tidying, Bridget looked through some of the dresses, trying a few on, while Kathleen doodled on a piece of paper, working on her speech, writing out sentences, crossing out words and looking anxious. The music of Courtney Maria Andrews played in the background as Bridget hummed along, interrupting Kathleen's train of thought. The front door opened and slammed shut. Appearing sheepishly, Martin looked out of breath as he tried to hide his surprised look. He hadn't expected anybody to be at home.

'Good morning ladies, it's lovely to see you two, and you're looking ravishing as ever Bridge, that dress looks terrific on you, what's the special occasion?'

Peering up at him, Bridget rolled her eyes and shook her head in annoyance. 'It's for the ICA ball, Martin. I mentioned it to you weeks ago.'

'Oh, right you are. I was a million miles away then.'

Bridget had her back to Martin. 'I can't undo this blasted zip,' she muttered, summoning him over to help. As he worked on the zip behind her, she took the opportunity to question him lightly. 'So, I've noticed you've been out and about more recently. Is there something you're not telling me, Martin, and don't give me any of your guff?'

Looking evasive, Martin grinned and quickly changed the subject. 'Ah, stop your yakking woman. I don't know what you're on about. Can you wet the tea for me and be sure to make one for yourself as well. I left my frigging driving gloves out last night, and I'll be damned if I can remember where I put them.'

'You left them on the TV last night,' Bridget pointed out, annoyed at the quick topic change.

Martin's eyes brightened as he glanced over at the plate of eclairs.

Catching his look, Bridget warned, 'Keep your clammy fingers away from that plate. Those eclairs have Sinead's and my name down for them.'

Taking a deep sigh, Martin rested his hands on his hips and tutted. 'If I've told you once I've told you a thousand times, Bridge. If you continue to eat these kinds of foods, you'll keep getting fatter.'

An annoyed look rippled across Bridget's face as she muttered something deliberately under her breath.

Kathleen made a mock attempt at lashing out with her notebook at Martin in defence of Bridget. 'Martin Lynch, the tongue on you. I tell you; you wouldn't be getting away lightly with a jibe like that in my house.'

Pretending to shield himself from heavy blows, Martin went to grab at the notebook.

'What have you got here then? Let's have a gander?'

Kathleen pulled it closer to her, tapping a finger on her lips in mock secrecy.

'I'm giving a speech at the ICA ball. They hold this event every year and have asked me to speak at it as a local business owner this year. I've gone completely blank on how to finish it. I need to end it with something poetic or meaningful. Any ideas?'

Martin smiled delightedly at the implicit compliment. 'Kathleen, you've always been a woman with plenty of cells bouncing around in that head of yours… but if you want my input…'

He pulled his shoulders back, and in a faux-posh accent, said, 'I've always considered myself to be a bit of a poet. I've often written a few pieces when enlightenment strikes me. Let me offer you some words of wisdom…'

Covering her mouth, Kathleen chuckled as Bridget interjected, 'Fuck off, Martin, this is serious.'

Ignoring her, he looked up to the heavens, pointed his index finger to the side of his head, closed his eyes and began to recite his words of wisdom to himself. The women's eyes met, and both, laughter now subdued, quietened to listen. Opening his eyes for a brief moment, he remarked comedically, 'You may want to set your phone to record this.'

Trying to hold a straight face, both women grinned and took out their phones.

Taking a deep breath, Martin closed his eyes again and began:

'What makes life valuable is that it doesn't last forever; what makes it precious is that it ends. I know that more than ever. Time is life, so don't waste it living someone else's life; make yours count for something. Fight for what matters to you, no matter what. Because even if we fall short – what better way is there to live.'

Exhaling slowly, Martin opened his eyes to his audience. Stifling a laugh, Bridget, gazed at Kathleen who, open-mouthed now, said, 'Well, aren't you the cat's pyjamas, Martin. That was beautiful. Did you make that up yourself, or was it something you memorised from one of your books? Would you mind if I included it in my speech?'

Before Martin could revel in glee, Bridget spoke up with a ghost of a frown, 'I'm not buying this blarney. Something smells fishy here to me. I know you, Martin Lynch, better than you know yourself. Poet my arse!'

Martin contorted himself into a dramatic pose, 'The world is full of non-believers and philistines. I bid you ladies farewell for today and leave you to reflect over my words.' Walking backwards, Martin bowed in front of them as he moved to the front door.

Intrigued now, Kathleen interrupted his departure. 'But Martin, you haven't had your cup of tea yet; I'd like to hear some more; sit yourself down here.'

Martin, clearly delighted to be in demand, paused and offered, 'I can recite one of my more favourable poems if I may?'

Kathleen pretended to clap her hands, and Martin began. 'There once was a young woman called Hannie, who teased all the boys with her –'

Bridget interjected quickly, 'We can see where this one is going. We'll leave it there, for now, Martin.' Both women were laughing.

'Come on, Martin, you must have picked up some useful phrases in the books you sell?' said Kathleen.

'Alas, my sweet beauty, I must leave and venture out into the wilderness… Oh, Bridge! My Gloves?'

Bridget answered sharply, 'TV, Martin, you Jackeen.'

'Right you are,' Martin added. With another bow and a flourish, Martin exited the room, chortling away to himself.

CHAPTER 11

Shuffling herself in a dress, Bridget glanced down at herself, feeling confident. Kathleen studied her in it and remarked, 'Hmm, that one isn't right.' Her chin rested in between her index and middle finger knuckles as she thought aloud. 'You have a great figure for an aul gal. Your arse is still in great shape, but your tits have sagged somewhat, mind you. You need something that is gonna give you more support and lift your bosom. That frock does nothing for you.'

Bridget slumped back in her chair. 'Well, I suppose there was a compliment in there somewhere,' she chuckled, taking off the dress and moved on to the next one. Dropping each dress to the floor as she tried them on, she casually paraded in knickers and a bra that didn't match. An hour later, following intense deliberations, both women had selected the perfect dress. The remaining dresses lay draped over the sofa. Bridget was happy, and Kathleen was exhausted but pleased. Feeling relaxed, she signalled for the wine. Bridget obliged, pouring generously as the bottle clinked against Kathleen's glass. Bridget stuck to a mug of tea. They gossiped freely, knowing Sinead was out of sight.

An hour later, after all the usual topics of conversation were exhausted, Bridget tentatively turned to Kathleen and, looking down, said, 'Can I ask you something? It's been bothering me for some time, years actually, but if it offends you, please just shut me down.' Clasping her hands together, she rubbed her index fingers against her front teeth.

'Christ, B, how many years have we known each other? There is nothing you can't ask me. Fire away, woman,' Kathleen rolled her eyes.

Looking flustered, Bridget tried to find her words. 'Ok, fuck it. I've always wondered, did you ever think that you and Martin would have made it together even if you hadn't lost the baby?'

The question hung silently in the air as Kathleen, surprised, inspected the stem of her glass and gathered her thoughts. She raised her eyebrows, then smiling ruefully, said, 'Right!... One of those questions.' Kathleen took a large swig of wine with a small smile, then looking into the glass was surprised to see it empty. 'I wish I had left the car at home now so I could finish off the rest of the bottle.'

Bridget tried to backtrack, 'I'm sorry, I pushed you. I should've let it lie.'

'For God's sake, B, what are friends for if we can't speak our minds?' Kathleen retorted. Leaning forward, clasping her legs, she searched for words to begin.

'Ok. Well, firstly, it wasn't a miscarriage. I carried my baby full-term. She was born asleep. People didn't realise back then that the loss of a child stillborn was still as traumatic as losing a child that had lived.' A three-second beat passed as she stared into thin air. 'The difference is when a child dies, a mother still has the memories of the child. I had none.' She paused, rubbing her finger around the rim of her glass until it dried out with an annoying squeak.

'I never got to buy her pretty dresses or do a simple thing like change her nappy for the first time,' pale and saddened, Kathleen's face changed. 'As each month and each year went by, I pictured how her face would have changed as she grew up. Nobody understood my grief.'

Tapping her wine glass, she nibbled her bottom lip. 'My mother never thought much of Martin and thought even less of him after that. You have to remember I was only twenty-two then. I think at the time, I had post-natal depression, but of course, there was little advice given to women at the time. Nowadays, there are support groups and blogs to help women. I had nobody really who I could talk to.'

Taking a deep breath and slowly exhaling, Kathleen tried not to let it consume her after all those years. 'So, with that and Martin's partying, we were doomed from the start. It's completely different for fellas; they carry nothing, so feel nothing. I didn't hold it against Martin. Everything was in God's control and not ours.'

As the room remained silent, Bridget felt embarrassed that she'd broached the subject, so she busied herself leaving to make tea. It gave Kathleen time to compose herself. Bridget peeped in on Sinead before she returned.

Feeling guilty but resolute, she still pursued her question, 'You still haven't answered my question, Kath? I know he's my husband, and it was a long time ago, but I need to know if there was ever a chance that you and he were supposed to end up together.'

Kathleen was reluctant to answer, concerned not to offend her friend. Gazing across with a soft smile, she continued, 'It was no fairy story, Bridget.'

'In the beginning, we flirted with one another. Mind you, Martin did with all the girls. You remember the saying, "If sin had a twin brother, his name would be Martin Lynch?" We finally spoke to each other at that party Noreen Ryan threw at her parents' home. Do you remember? The big house with the railings on Josephine Avenue. Martin came up behind me and made a joke about it, "If we had kids, we'd lose them in this house." That was probably the first and only time the real Martin was talking with me with no drink about him.'

Bridget was now regretting her question. She felt vulnerable and worried about what was to come.

Kathleen continued talking without noticing. 'We bumped into each other again a week later in some pub in town. I purposely found out that he'd be there. We got talking, and he asked me out. I was on cloud 9. I felt like a beauty queen at a pageant, all beautiful and special. Martin knocked for me on our first date, and my mother smelt the drink on him and put her back up straight away. Once that woman formed an opinion, she never changed it.'

Suppressing a smile and nodding sagely, Bridget added, 'God love her.'

Kathleen found her rhythm again. 'I didn't have Martin back at the house again; it wasn't worth the argument. My father kept saying to my mother, "It's just a phase; don't interfere, and it will fizzle out." I was determined to prove her wrong. The dates with Martin were lovely at first. We'd watch the latest films then head out for something to eat before he'd take me home to my gate. I made excuses for my mother, but I think Martin worked it out. Different classes and that. I was just fooling myself.'

Kathleen looked across at Bridget with a timid smile, breaking her train of thought. Bridget averted eye contact.

'The dates turned into trips to the pub and parties. Good times at first, but when the drugs kicked in, I saw a different side to Martin. You could see the chemicals rushing through his bloodstream behind his eyes.

Full of himself and doing everything to excess. I couldn't believe it when I fell pregnant after three months. Telling my mother was, and still is, the most challenging thing I have ever had to do. There was no coming back for Martin in her books.'

A creak of a door and the sudden patter of shoeless feet caught Bridget's attention. 'Sinead Lynch, if I so much as catch you within earshot of this conversation, I will swing for you, child.'

A shudder of Martin's boxes in the hall gave Bridget all the indication she needed that Sinead was nearby as she flew back upstairs, and they heard her bedroom door ease shut.

Kathleen found her thread back into the conversation. 'Mother badgered me for weeks, wanting to take me over to the UK for a private abortion, you know. I never told Martin that. I dressed everything up for everyone, pretending my family supported us, and we were happy to be expecting. The pubs and the late nights were off. Everything changed so quickly. I ended up walking *him* home, and on one occasion myself and his mother put him to bed.

'The pregnancy took its toll on me, and I couldn't take the smoky pubs, so every time I saw Martin, he was hungover. I still thought Martin would change when the baby was born, but the mere mention of the baby frightened him. I think I knew we were doomed from early on. Martin's charm had worn off on me halfway through the pregnancy, and by the time my pregnancy came to an end, there was nothing left of us.

'Even if we had stayed together for the baby – if she had lived – I couldn't handle his shenanigans. I knew he was copping off with other girls before the baby was born. So, it came as no shock when we finished after the birth. I probably would have raised her on my own and gone back to teaching as she grew up.'

Kathleen leaned forward, exhaling gently. She was relieved to get this off her chest. 'We were never meant to be together, Bridget. Lucky for you, he'd got that out of his system by the time you two got together. The one thing that has stayed with me above anything else is that I'll never forget my mother's eyes when she was told the baby had died. It was like all her wishes had come true without having to say a word. I never forgave her for it, and I couldn't even listen to what she said when it came to marrying Declan. I never trusted her again.'

There was a stillness in the air before Kathleen broke the silence,

'Is everything ok between you and Martin, Bridget?'

The question was a stake to the heart. Bridget accepted it and bled. She sighed wistfully, 'Good days and bad days, Kath. I still hear those three magic words from him regularly, but they have changed now. It's usually "Where's my dinner?" or "How much longer?"' A look of regret pained her features.

'I'm up to ninety juggling around schedules and appointments. I don't have time to think. I'm worn out all the time. With Martin at home all the time, it feels like I'm the only adult with three children to look after.' As Bridget gripped the hot tea, its warmth soothing her, she thought about her marriage.

'Do you still love him?' Kathleen twisted the stake, scanning Bridget's eyes for signs she was pushing too hard. 'Let me rephrase that… Are you still getting busy under the bedsheets?' she tried to lighten the mood.

Bridget winced at the intrusion. 'Crying out loud, have you got no tact?' she queried, half-annoyed, half-amused. 'Aren't you supposed to dance around the question a bit before going in for the killer sting? Now that's *really* going to put me in the mood to open up to you.'

A small smile broke at the corners of Bridget's mouth, relaxing Kathleen somewhat, who tried to lighten the subject with sarcasm. 'Flattery will get you nowhere, my dear. I just want to know that you are ok. You're pushing yourself all the time. If you love him, you need to make some quality time together. Talk things through. I can have Sinead at mine anytime to give you a night out or a weekend away,' Kathleen offered.

Bridget, now exhausted, answered, 'It's not just that, it's everything. Life is just very hard these days. Even when we have all the family together, I can't relax. If it's not Martin and my sister Sheila staring each other out, then I'm watching over my shoulder to see if Shane's necking back people's pints. I worry that he may start drinking at a young age and end up like his father. All I would like to do is relax in company without having to worry about anything. Just for one day to start with. It's not too much to ask for, is it?' Rubbing her forehead with the back of her hand, Bridget slumped back into her chair. She felt untethered.

'Well, as we are both opening up to each other, there's something I need to get off my tits.' Making herself comfortable, Kathleen crossed her legs leaned in and spoke. 'B, you are the bravest, most reliable person

I know. You take what shite life throws at you. You plough on through it while others are holding you back as you're trying to keep your head above water.'

Bridget mustered a smile.

'Your sister Sheila is one of those people who hold you back. My God, you are so blind you can't see what's in front of you. Your *sister* Sheila has always fancied Martin. It put her nose out of joint when he fell for you and not her. Everyone could see it except for you, B. She's always been jealous of you. Ok, she's done well for herself finding a loaded man who can support her lifestyle. I see there are no children there, though. Funny that? I'm not taking anything away from her – she's a fabulous auntie. Sinead loves her to bits.' Kathleen's nose wrinkled, and she continued, 'But she is so pretentious, she's so *Holier-than-thou.*'

Bridget didn't respond to Kathleen's candidness. Instead, she lost enthusiasm. A chink developed in the conversation between them, like a carriage released from a travelling train.

Unnoticing, Kathleen continued, matter-of-factly, 'Who in this day and age has the best room for guests with sofas covered in plastic sheeting, for God's sake? She wears expensive clothing, mind you a size too small in my view, but she overdresses as if she's presenting the news or something, even if she's going to the post office. And that accent! Talking all la-di-dah. She's the kind of woman who checks herself in the mirror before answering the house phone. She looks down on you; she looks down on all of us, especially Martin. Your sister is dragging *you* down. I mean the gall of the woman. She's a snooty bitch. I've never taken to her.'

Kathleen exhaled and sat back, spent. She glanced at Bridget and then away. Instantly she regretted her words. Bridget smiled hesitatingly to attempt to minimise the effect of her pain, but it was no good. The words wounded her as they pinched her features, and it was written all over her face. She stood up and busied herself collecting the mug and wine glass. The electricity suddenly cut off, the lights went out, and the music stopped. The credit had run out on the meter. The boiler chugged before it was silenced. The house was cold and full of hostility. Silence thickened between them. Kathleen couldn't meet her gaze.

Bridget smiled; she swallowed hard and resentfully said, 'Well! On a scale of 1 to 10, I think you've gained full marks in humiliating me today with both my sister and husband.' She took a short breath. 'I think we are done for today. I'll tell Sinead you said goodbye. Please see yourself out.'

Flustered now, unable to hold back the engulfing emotion, Bridget hugged her arms, squeezing onto her elbows. Her face spread crimson down her neck. Her eyes blinked against tears she wouldn't let fall, and she turned away.

Kathleen knew she had gone too far. She pushed herself to her feet, sighing with regret. Standing behind Bridget, she lifted her friend's hair behind her ear unselfconsciously. Touching her shoulder, she squeezed it before saying, 'B, I only want to see you happy.'

Bridget's head hung low as her chin trembled. She sucked in her breath as though to add something, but no words emerged. Kathleen collected her bag and left. The front door closed. Kathleen got into her car and idled the engine. She sat and waited. Walking over to the front door, Bridget leant her back against it, raising an arm to her throat to steady herself. Her eyes watered, and tears spilt down her cheeks. Using the heels of her hands, she wiped away the tears. As she pursed her lips in thought, she let out a weary sigh wondering how such a lovely day could have ended like this. Both women listened out for each other; neither was prepared to make a move towards each other. Kathleen's engine revved, and she drove off down the road. Suddenly, hitting the steering wheel in frustration, she slammed on the brakes and shouted, 'SHIT, FUCK, SHIT and FUCK THIS SHITE! ... FUCK IT!'

Biting her lower lip, she bowed her head, shaking it as if to dislodge what had just taken place. 'FUCK THIS!' she roared again and spun the car around with haste, hazards flashing as she executed an illegal U-turn. Pulling back up outside the house, Kathleen sat thinking in the car as the engine hummed. Bridget hadn't moved from the front door. She heard Kathleen return. Kathleen got out of the vehicle and knocked, panting. The door opened, and their eyes met; the tension was palpable.

With a weak smile, Kathleen asked, 'Are you still coming with me to the ball tomorrow tonight? It would be a crying shame not to show off your lovely figure in that dress.' Kathleen held her gaze, determined not to break eye contact.

'Well, of course, I am,' Bridget answered, unnerved but delighted.

'Good, that's settled then.' Kathleen's eyes lit up; she let out her withheld breath, nodded and got back in the car.

'Are you still coming to collect me tomorrow evening?'

Bridget countered.

'Well, of course, I am,' Kathleen emphasised it with a defiant nod.

'Good, that's settled then,' Bridget mused.

As Kathleen jumped back in to drive off, she missed a few final words spoken by Bridget. Her window lowered as Charles Bradley played on the car stereo. 'What was that?' she asked.

'I said, remember, I want to drink a bottle of that Sauvignon Blanc when we reach your house,' smiled Bridget.

'Don't worry; I'll get two.' Kathleen beamed and blew a kiss as she drove off. Bridget closed the door and slumped back against it, raising her eyes to the ceiling. She chuckled to herself as the tension eased between her shoulder blades, tears brimmed.

Sinead appeared and cuddled into Bridget, nestling her smooth head into her mother's chest. Sinead looked up at her; she had a twist of a smile jutting out on one side of her face, and in a bright voice, said,

'Mam, sometimes you are all wrong, and other times you are all right. By the way, Auntie Sheila *can* sometimes be a bitch.' Her eyes twinkled.

Bridget held her at arm's length, looking her in the eyes, and said, 'Sinead Lynch, how many times have you to be told not to eavesdrop on adult conversations. Go on, child, away with you.' Bridget waved her off like a wasp.

Sinead giggled as she skipped away. Standing with her hands on her hips, Bridget chuckled to herself, gently shaking her head as her mouth spread into a grin. As she inserted the spare key into the electric meter, the boiler chugged, reigniting life back into the home as warmth and love filled the house again.

CHAPTER 12

The first of the month had arrived. Screeching bike brakes disturbed the calmness of the sleepy streets on a Sunday morning. Letterboxes shuddered as the newspaper boy disrupted people's beauty sleep and antagonised snoring dogs. Early risers pottered around their homes, marked out by the steam generated from their boiler flues at the back of their houses. Martin was one of those people whose spirit always lifted when the early morning sunshine greeted him. Sunday was his day of rest. His favourite day. He wanted nothing to spoil it.

The morning mist gradually dispersed as the sun warmed through the frosted pavement. Shortly before 9 am, a small white van cruised along Holmewood Road before parking two doors away from Number 22. The driver retrieved a hardback ledger from a satchel in the footwell and shut the car door. His trained eyes scanned up and down the street as he dusted off imaginary hairs stuck to him.

Dressed in dark trousers and a tight-fitting penny collar shirt, his top button restricted his neck movements somewhat as he made a quick scan of the scene. Over that, he wore a dark pea coat. A thatch of dark hair, cleanly parted to one side, was gelled back. He was an ex-army officer who still carried the strict code of conduct of the armed forces into civilian life.

He rapped his knuckles forcefully on the door of Number 22. There was no answer. He watched the windows for any ghost-like movements behind the nets. Knocking louder provoked movement, noises and, eventually, muttering from inside. The debt collector stood back against the kerb and waited. The slap of bare footsteps on lino making their way towards the front door slowly grew louder. Lock after lock disengaged before finally the door opened. The collector scuffed his feet as Martin acknowledged him, judging him by his dishevelled look.

He greeted Martin formally. 'Morning, Sir. Today is payment day; you can sign the receipt book just here, once I have collected monies owed.'

There was a pause as Martin processed the information. Swiping his hand across his face and palming back his wiry hair, he tried to gain composure before he answered. Attempting eye contact, the collector glared at him.

Martin spoke hoarsely. 'Erhh…' He sniffed the air. The collector's cologne overpowered Martin's morning breath. 'The missus doesn't get paid until the money goes into the bank on Monday.' Snorting back bile, he cleared his throat before swallowing. 'I can't pay ye until later. Can ye come back tomorrow?'

The reply was met with steely eyes from the collector. 'Did you not fully understand the terms for this agreement Mr Lynch?' The man's manner was austere. 'Mr Hennessey assured me all clients are made fully aware of consequences of failing to make agreed on payments.'

Martin responded with contempt, looking annoyed, 'Well, I have to get back to my bed now. I'll be seeing you back here tomorrow, my good man.'

Standing motionless, the collector ended the conversation with a curt, 'Duly noted, Sir.'

Turning around, Martin scratched his backside before slamming the door behind him. The collector glowered and retreated to his van. He made a call that lasted no more than a minute. By then, Martin had already bolted the front door and darted back to bed, where he hibernated for the rest of the morning. Declan advised the collector to take no further action. Declan himself was going to collect payment instead next time.

CHAPTER 13

The following morning Declan collected Billy and Johnny, and they headed out to a 24-hour café up by the docks on an industrial estate. The conversation remained quiet as awing seagulls circled them as they entered the café, giving Declan concerns for his paintwork. It wasn't the only thing on his mind.

The lads knew the number of their preferred meals and ordered quickly. Treating them to a hearty fry-up, Declan settled for a black coffee. As Billy and Johnny lined their stomachs, Declan glanced around anxiously. He wanted to talk frankly with them.

Johnny finished first and, noticing Declan's subdued mood, remarked, 'You alright, Boss? It's unlike you to turn down a square meal. Everything ok at home?'

Billy looked up as he chewed bacon rind. 'Something you wanna get off your chest, perhaps?'

'Something serious is troubling me; well us, if the truth be told.' The pair froze, making eye contact with one another.

'Go on. If it's about that Lynch fella,' Johnny pointed his finger defiantly, 'no problem, he'll get the message once we've introduced ourselves as collectors.'

'No, that's not it. I'll be marking his card this morning, don't you two worry about it,' Declan tapped the table with his fist. 'Something is going on with the shipments that is not right.' He eyed both of them speculatively. 'The last cargo drop that was organised via Jim's intel was set upon before our team arrived. Jim swears his man at the port is good, so I trust his judgement there. But this is the fourth drop in a row where we have been duped; someone is getting there first. Now, that's no coincidence.'

Both men looked quizzically back at Declan, avoiding looking offended.

Declan continued, Jim's intel is tight; I trust him, so the weak link must be closer to home. Do you two trust everyone else down the chain? Either we have a snitch inside, or someone is talking loosely about our operations.' Declan's phone rang, he ignored it.

'Our mark is being robbed before we get there to claim it ourselves. The trailers have been ransacked before we turn up. The driver then rings in the Guards, who turn up just as our lookout makes his getaway. So far, we have lost thousands of euros of potential street revenue from these missing cargos. This last hit was the high-end sportswear line that we had just gotten into. We can't sustain much more of this. Someone is threatening to shut us down, and I have an idea who it might be.'

Billy stiffened in his seat as he followed the line of Declan's thought. Declan admired that about him. 'Do you think the O'Driscoll's have grand ideas?' asked Billy.

'No. It's not him. Aiden may be a sleeveen, but we have the gipsy brothers who look after trading patterns between O'Driscoll and our territory. Our Brady was the only one I had doubts about.' Declan gestured with his hands for them to come closer. 'I mean that in the way that he may have been slack in his talk with his brother, Pádraig, who works for O'Driscoll. It's surprising what even trustworthy people can reveal with a drink inside them.'

'What are you talking about, Boss?' probed Billy.

'See, lads, I had no choice,' Declan went on,' I had to check that Brady was loyal.

The men squinted at each other in confusion.

'I deliberately fed him false information to test him. It seems our Brady is tight.'

Billy looked uncomfortable, 'So, is Brady the only one you've tested?'

Declan narrowed his eyes, a deep crease formed between his brows. He answered without making eye contact. 'Did you really have to ask that question?'

'Yes, I did, Boss. If you have misgivings about Brady, he comes from the same stock as us,' Billy's folded his arms in protest.

'I had to be sure it wasn't him before telling you guys because I know all three of you go way back.' The plastic back on the chair strained as Declan stretched his back, pulling himself upright. Spreading his arms out conciliatorily across the table, he said, 'The answer is NO! I haven't doubted either of you. We all started together. That's a bond you can't break. I feel bad enough questioning Brady's loyalty without you reminding me.'

Johnny punched Billy's shoulder in an effort to get him to lighten up.

Purposely making eye contact this time, Declan asked, 'Are we cool, guys? I need to know we have each other's backs?'

Johnny winked in acknowledgement. Billy, still aggrieved that neither of them had been informed of Brady's trust being in dispute, simply nodded to end the argument.

Declan went to appease him, 'I've always trusted you two hundred per cent lads – no questions asked. Don't ever doubt me again.There's no fireside like your own fireside.'

They all stood up as Declan insisted on an embrace, placated now they returned to their light-hearted banter. The mood lifted. Just in time for their next port of call – Martin Lynch's address.

The three men arrived at 8.30 am into Holmewood Road in an old estate car, chosen purely to be unrecognisable to the residents or clients. No warning ever helped matters in this line of work. Declan parked on the opposite side of the street, tucking back a few houses down, just out of view of Number 22. The steady pitter-patter of raindrops obscured their view.

Once the engine was off, the windscreen quickly misted up. Rubbing his sparse stubble, Declan sighed. His muscles felt tense. Anger brewed inside him over Martin's blatant disrespect. Not having money ready on time was one of Declan's biggest irritants. Considering this was the first payment of the new loan agreement, Declan took this as a significant insult. Seething with anger, his mind went into overdrive.

The Finnerty brothers were making a name for themselves on his streets, and he wasn't one bit happy about it. Was Martin Lynch trying to set him up? No one he had ever loaned money to had treated him so disrespectfully before. Was this a set-up? Was Martin involved with the Finnerty Brothers and trying to test his resolve? His fury grew as his thoughts continued to run away from him. He was going to make an example of Martin and everyone would know about it. Nobody fucks with Declan Hennessey.

He turned around to address Billy and Johnny in the backseat. His face like thunder, he hoarsely instructed, 'Gents sit here for a minute; this shouldn't take long.' Stepping out of the car, he shrugged his shoulders to unruffle his coat. Tucking his shirt in, he crossed the road. Taking a breath, he collected his thoughts and appeared calm as he approached the front door. The wintry mist caused his nose to run. He sniffed loudly. Rapping his knuckles on the door, he waited for 20 seconds. There was no answer and no movement from inside. As he exhaled, the vapour disappeared against his face.

Stepping back, he studied the windows, then moved to the front bay window and peered through. Angrily, he knocked again – harder – before he walked back to the car and got in. Squinting into the rear-view mirror, he issued instructions. 'Johnny, take a walk around the far way down the alley. Check for any lights or movement at the house. Billy, cross over and slowly walk past the front of the house to the end of the street. Do the same on your way back and listen out for anything.'

The pair jumped out, walking in different directions. A couple of minutes later, they arrived back and settled themselves back in their seats. Rubbing their hands together to get their blood circulating, they reported back that there was no activity.

'Right so, we wait,' directed Declan.

Billy rustled a newspaper, opening it to the crossword that had perplexed him earlier. Slipping a box of cigarettes out of his pocket, Johnny offered them to Declan. Declan twisted his shoulders around and took one from the pack with one eye on the door. He lit it, taking a deep drag. Unwinding the window slightly, Johnny lit his own before sliding the box back into his coat.

Billy revealed his face from behind the newspaper and glanced across to Johnny, 'Where the fuck's mine?'

Johnny stared straight ahead of him. 'Don't fecking start.'

Declan turned his head around with a cursory glance; he appeared to wink as smoke caught his eye. He quizzed Johnny, 'Why won't you give him a fag?'

Johnny looked to Billy, scowled, then looked back to Declan and said, 'He has a bad habit of lighting a fag, taking one drag from it and letting the rest of it burn away.' He turned his head to Billy looking remorseful and said,' It's torture watching you light a fag knowing that it's going to waste. It breaks my heart when I'm gasping for a fag and realise I've run out; then I recall you wasting one of mine.'

'Just give him the blasted fag,' Declan ended the dispute. He took a deep drag and let the smoke funnel out of his nose. 'I'll throw a box your way back at the pub.'

Johnny begrudgingly gave Billy the cigarette, lighting it and taking a long drag before handing it over. True to form, Billy took just one drag from the cigarette, and Johnny watched in dismay as the rest of it burnt away.

Shaking his head, Johnny muttered, 'That's sacrilege to waste that fag.'

Billy snapped back, 'Arhh!... away with you... I only smoke when I'm bored or stressed; for God's sake, man, it's only one fag.'

Creasing the newspaper, he tapped it with a pen, 'Ok brains of Ireland, erhh – 10 across – Obese?'

Squinting as he concentrated, Johnny reached across to grab at the newspaper. 'Is that the only clue? Let's have a dekko.'

Shielding the newspaper, Billy defensively replied,' By the living jaysis, I'll swing for you,' he snatched the newspaper back admonishing, 'and don't be making any fucking words up again. I could only come up with *Chubbiness.* The e.s.s seems to fit, but I'm stumped.'

Silence descended momentarily before Johnny's eyes lit up with inspiration, 'I know – GOT IT... wha-cha-ma-call-it... *Fat Bastard,*' he declared triumphantly.

'For fuck's sake, man, can't you think before you blurt things out? Your mouth is the size of a skip and full of useless shite too.'

'You said 10 across! That's 10 letters. What?' Billy demanded, insulted.

'Arhh, leave it out. You're about as much use as a back pocket in a shirt, you eejit.'

Declan, fed up listening to the two bickering like an old married couple, started the ignition to turn on the radio. A couple of tracks played between adverts and the overbearing DJ's small talk before, 'Forget You' aired. The lads knew the song. All three mumbled in unison every time the chorus played the lyrics to 'Fuck You.' Sixteen times a rendition of those two words echoed in the car; 'Fuck You–Hoo–Hoo.' The track faded, and the DJ prattle returned when there was activity by the front door.

Declan turned the ignition off; all three sat still in silence. Shane appeared to be leaving the house. As soon as his feet touched the ground outside, the front door slammed shut behind him, followed by the sound of three locks clicking shut. Glancing in both directions, Shane proceeded to walk off in the direction to the shops. Suddenly, he froze for a few seconds, patting his trouser pockets. Turning back, he knocked on his door in an agreed pattern to draw Declan's attention.

'You see. lads?' Elated, Declan swung his arm back, clicking his fingers inches from their faces. The three men watched as the door reopened and Shane disappeared back inside. No sooner had he gone in than he left again, this time dropping loose change into his pocket. Continuing to the end of the street, he turned left and disappeared.

Declan turned his head around once more to the fellas and said, 'Back to business, lads.'

Levering himself out of the car, Declan dusted off some fag ash from his trousers. Then, clearing his throat, he popped a tic-tac into his mouth and strolled casually up to the Lynches door. He raised his hand to the door and knocked, two short raps in quick succession, then three spaced out raps. He waited. Footsteps tramped down the stairs before a mumbled voice raised behind the door. Palms shunted bolts across, and the door fully opened. A cold rush of air entered and spiked Martin's skin. He stood there, speechless. Then, furious with himself, he cursed under his breath.

Tilting his head, his hands clasped behind him, Declan waited for Martin to say something. Martin bristled in panic, 'I was just putting the money in an envelope for collection.' He mimicked the movements. His voice wavered as he continued, 'Bridget left it on the side this morning when she came back in from her nightshift… hold on, I'll be back in a tick.'

Running his hands through his hair, he held onto the back of his head, agitated, as he vanished into the back room. He reappeared with an envelope in his hand, his bottom lip quivering. Declan took the envelope. Purposefully, he counted the money out slowly in front of Martin. When satisfied, he put the envelope in his inner coat pocket.

Relieved and letting his guard down, Martin was trying to make small talk about the weather. From nowhere, Declan swung his arm back and landed a swift punch to Martin's gut. Winded from the blow, Martin lost his footing and dropped to his knees. Declan dwarfed over him as he laid crippled in shock. Martin's face turned red, then purple, as the veins in his neck protruded as he doubled over in agony. Letting out a moan, shoestrings of saliva dripped from his lower lip.

After ten seconds, the first breath he drew in contained the smell of Declan's stale cigarette smoke. Declan knelt, peering over him, and spoke in a quietly menacing voice, 'Didn't you think I was serious about the agreement? I *told* you there would be consequences.' Spittle dripped further onto the doormat in the hallway. '*These* are consequences.'

Taking two steps back, Declan glared at Martin, who was trying to regain the rhythm of his breathing. The punch had held real malice. The non-payment scenario was just a cover story for his real feelings. It was having control over Martin that he thrived on. It wasn't the fact that somebody else had once made Kathleen happy before she met Declan. It was the fact that it was Martin Lynch who had. As far as Declan was concerned, Martin was a lowlife who ruined everything he touched.

Rage for Martin had been eating away at Declan for years. Now, he had him right in his pocket, just where he wanted him, so he could make his life miserable. A wry smirk of satisfaction stretched across Declan's face as he walked calmly back to his car. He turned back to Martin, his voice raged with spite, 'We'll be around on the first of next month.'

The engine started; Billy chuckled to himself as the car pulled away. As it crawled past Number 22, Martin remained slumped in the doorway. Winding the window down, Johnny shouted out at him, 'Put some clothes on there, buddy! It's freezing out here.'

Declan's morning's work gave him complete satisfaction. Martin wouldn't dare pull another stunt like that again. The car sped up as the men squabbled over packets of owed cigarettes. Declan revelled in his power. He glanced one eye into the rear-view mirror at Billy and Johnny before he slammed on the brakes. Turning around, he curtly said,

'Portliness, ten letters. Obese.' Then, smiling, he winked once, glanced back at the road and drove on.

CHAPTER 14

After Sinead had been diagnosed with a primary brain tumour, radiotherapy treatment had successfully advanced her recovery, but she remained unable to attend school. The head of the year at her school liaised with Bridget about home-schooling for her. The Department of Education had arranged for a teacher to visit her and support Sinead's schooling. Mrs Callaghan was the teacher assigned to her.

It was a Monday morning, and Sinead was in good spirits. She was watching TV whilst waiting for home-school to start. Bridget was fast asleep from her night shift, and Martin had been tasked with a list of chores to carry out before Mrs Callaghan arrived promptly at 11 am. Martin directed her into the sitting room where Sinead was concentrating on her knitting; her shawl was coming along beautifully. On seeing her teacher, Sinead jumped up and hugged her, delighted. While still that of student-teacher, their relationship had an extra intimacy from the close bond built throughout Sinead's illness.

Mrs Callaghan was a short, plump woman who struggled to walk correctly because of a hip disorder. She dressed like an old-fashioned librarian; formal skirts and high-necked cardigans, with a pair of glasses hanging around her neck that remained a permanent fixture. The teacher never wore any makeup but swore by the use of *Oil of Olay.* She had lived her whole life with her elderly mother, who on becoming housebound, refused to go into sheltered housing until she sadly died. After all, she died alone in the end, something Mrs Callaghan carried guilt over that she couldn't shake off. It took a year for her to get through her initial grief and return to teaching. Even though pupils always called her Mrs Callaghan, she had never married, and she never corrected them as it only led to more awkward questions.

Sinead's composure and fortitude in dealing with her illness inspired Mrs Callaghan, and she was very fond of her. She was scheduled to tutor for a couple of hours each morning, five days a week, but she often stayed most of the afternoon. She was lonely and enjoyed the company, and Bridget and Martin didn't mind. Sinead was very bright and sharp-witted. She had the potential to excel at whatever she put her mind to but needed some gentle pushing to do so. Mrs Callaghan was just the person to do that.

Absorbed in the programme she was watching, Sinead gestured to Mrs Callaghan to sit with her. As she plunged into the sofa, making herself comfortable, she recognised the programme with a nod. 'Ah, I love University Challenge,' she sighed, settling down to watch.

'So, my dear, is this an educational programme for you or a form of entertainment?'

Glued to the television screen, Sinead's eyes glazed over from not blinking; she broke her concentration to shrug, 'I don't know?... I just like the sound of their funny voices. I don't understand what they're all talking about. The way they answer questions makes me smile.'

Mrs Callaghan replied, making a point, 'The contestants generally have worked hard to get top grades to get into the best universities.'

'Dad says it's because they're all English twats who've never had a girlfriend,' Sinead replied guilelessly. 'The best bit is at the beginning when they read out their names. At first, I thought they were made-up names, but then as each show went on, I realised that's what they're actually called,' she laughed without taking her eyes from the screen.

Stifling a laugh, Mrs Callaghan smiled indulgently at Sinead's endearing way of viewing the world. As the two watched the show, Martin hovered around, poking his head into the front room to check in on them. Martin studied the TV and lounged in the doorway, with his arms crossed and his chin on his chest,

'For the love of God... I can't see what she sees in this shite –'he addressed his remark to Mrs Callaghan.

Mrs Callaghan, straightening her posture, and spoke defiantly. 'Mr Lynch, you forget yourself with your tongue.'

'I'm sorry, Mrs Callaghan, my potty mouth lets me down,' he replied, faux contritely in response to Sinead's disproving head shake. With that, he left the room to continue his pottering. A waft of *Sunflowers* perfume caught Sinead's senses as Mrs Callaghan undid her cardigan, it was comforting. Sinead invited her to slip her shoes off as, lessons forgotten, they began to immerse themselves in the questions fired at the students.

QUESTION: *What five-letter term describes a curve on the surface of a right circular cylinder that cuts the generators of the cylinder at a constant angle*?

Giggling to herself, Sinead whispered to Mrs Callaghan as her fingertips touched her knee, 'It makes me laugh the way they all take it so seriously. If it were me, I'd just say, dunno?'

Mrs Callaghan reminded her, 'If you knuckle down and pay attention to your studies, you too could be on that show one day, my dear.'

From the hallway, Martin poked his head around the door like an inquisitive meerkat, afraid of missing out on something. Agitated, he sarcastically asked, 'Can you tell me something, Mrs Callaghan? In what walk of life, profession, or industry would you ever need to know the answer to that question?'

All three turned their heads back to the TV, awaiting the answer as the team delivered the incorrect answer and the quiz master corrected them.

ANSWER: *Helix*

Letting out a heavy sigh, Mrs Callaghan looked annoyed with Martin's question.

'That question would be part of a syllabus to a subject either to do with mathematics or sciences.' She studied Martin. 'It's not a matter of whether Sinead would need to know it, but if she could recall it after learning it, Mr Lynch.'

Feeling outsmarted, Martin knew he couldn't win the discussion. Conceedingly, he asked her, 'Can I get you a cup of tea, Mrs Callaghan, while you enjoy the show?'

She nodded, 'No sugar, thank you.'

QUESTION: *Which old measure was used for various liquids, but chiefly for ale when it was originally the equivalent of a quarter of abarrel of nine gallons*?

Martin, about to leave, turned and stood firmly like a headmaster with a glint in his eye. Arms folded in front of him, he spoke matter-of-factly, 'Arhh! Firkin Ale.'

'Mr Lynch, PLEASE! Not in my company and certainly not in your daughter's either. Save that kind of language for when you frequent the public house,' she scolded Martin.

'No! Mrs Callaghan, that's the answer… FIRKIN... Look! Arhh, would you look at that? The answer has already flashed up on the screen.' He dropped his hands in defeat.

'I can never tell, Mr Lynch, when you are serious.'

'For the love of God, woman, I'm telling you FIRKIN is the answer.'

'Dad... Mrs C… shhh,' Sinead signalled with her finger to her lips whilst she awaited the next question.

QUESTION: *What word for a quarrelsome and scolding woman derives from that of an imaginary Muslim deity, a stock character in medieval mystery plays*?

Martin became petulant. 'That would be your Auntie Sheila, Sinead,' Martin guffawed.

'You see, Mr Lynch; you've just proved my point.'

'Dad, really?' Shaking her head, Sinead joined in the castigation. Rolling his eyes, Martin rubbed his hands together and said to Mrs Callaghan, 'I'll dig out some biscuits for you, Mrs Callaghan, to go with that cup of tea of yours. Be right back now.' He left the room.

'Dad's quick with knowledge questions, Miss.'

With a bemused look, Mrs Callaghan smothered a smile and spoke gently, 'You're not the only person in this house who needs to finish off their education.'

Sinead, her mind moving on ahead already, missed the reprimand.

'Miss, is 'Snatch' a swear word also?' The question came out of the blue. Inquisitively put but not confrontationally so.

'I beg your pardon, Sinead.'

'I heard one of the lads talking when I was stood outside the front room door the other night. They said that a woman went into the men's toilets and said something about a snatch. Is it a rude word, Miss? Also, why would a woman go into the men's toilets with him? Surely, he would say to her she has made a mistake?'

'Young lady, do you know it is rude to eavesdrop on other people's conversations? You shouldn't take heed of what your brother and his friends are up to.'

'No, it wasn't Shane, Miss. It was when Dad's friends came around to pick him up last week. Erhm, what's the other one they said? Oh yeah, what does 'put out' mean?'

Mrs Callaghan's face reddened.

'Right, let's cut this conversation now. Any more ambiguous questions, then you should ask your mother. I'm sure she'll know how to deal with them and your father for that matter too. Right, we'll watch a few more minutes then get stuck into our schoolwork, love.'

Curling her legs up, Sinead nestled into the warmth of her teacher. They focused on the screen with frowns as they concentrated on the next question.

QUESTION: *A French word meaning 'DEATH PLEDGE' is the origin of which English financial term*?

One of the contestants hit their buzzer and blurted out '*Mortgage*'. The answer was correct, and he received a round of applause. Meanwhile, Martin's chores had been abandoned in favour of sitting in the kitchen listening to the TV programme in the background through the hall.

The dilapidated kitchen was the worst room in the house. Aged windows were smudged and grimy. The worktop counter was cluttered all the way along, blocking out any visible sockets. Small appliances were stuck to the surfaces, sealed down from sticky spills. A Belfast sink had a constant dripping tap and lay full of yesterday's dirty dishes. A sponge acted as a makeshift plug inside it. Random damp musty cloths lingered around the kitchen – nobody knew their age – and two marigold gloves trailed over the sink: one yellow, the other one pink.

After making tea, Martin came across a packet of biscuits that were out of date. Opening the pack, he ate one. Nodding to himself in approval, he filled a plate with them. Martin returned to the front room. With the tea tray and a juice for Sinead. Mrs Callaghan stared at him unnervingly, no doubt waiting for him to redeem himself from his previous blunder. Her narrowing eyes followed him as he laid the tray on the table. She glanced towards Sinead and wondered what hope she had of getting ahead in her education with Martin as her role model.

Instead of leaving, Martin braced himself in the doorway. In an attempt to defrost the situation, Mrs Callaghan directed a question his way. 'So, how's the whole book thing going, Mr Lynch? Sinead says you're interested in old books.'

Martin responded blandly, 'I buy them. I sell them. I have no interest in the story they behold.'

'That's a sad state of affairs, Mr Lynch.'

'I didn't mean to sound blunt; Mrs C. I appreciate their value and the way a book is constructed. The time and skill involved in producing them. I just don't have time to read them regularly. Bridget is the one who does all the reading in this house. God forbid if you interrupt her when she's into a good book.'

Sinead laughed and added, 'Da is right, Miss. Mam says that if she's left alone with a good book that's a page-turner, it's like being swept up in a world where characters come alive.'

Mrs Callaghan agreed. 'It's like being invited into another world; it's totally encompassing. Nothing else matters around you; when you are interrupted in the middle of a great book, it's like being returned with a bump to reality.'

Martin countered, 'Don't I know it. She has a face like I've wounded her somehow if I interrupt her! I mean, it's just a book.'

Mrs Callaghan replied, 'Mr Lynch, when you become consumed in a story, you want to finish it through to the end. It's not like flicking through your phone messages, and someone asks you something distracting you. A book is a more personal experience that doesn't need bear interruptions. You have to feel your way back into the story each time. Tell me, Mr Lynch, what was the last book you read?'

'Erhh, I read that sex book everyone was talking about. *A Whiter Shade of Pale* or something like that. Kathleen passed it onto Bridget. The one they made into a film. I forget it now. Anyway, it was a load of bollixs.'

'Well, thank you, Mr Lynch, for your critical analysis. Somehow, I don't think you'll ever be required to submit a book review to the paper.'

The conversation ended, and Mrs Callaghan dismissed Martin with a look. Sinead turned back to the screen as the next question came up. Martin whistled to himself as he collected the tray. In the kitchen, the laughter of Sinead overwhelmed the noise of the television. It was a blessing for Martin to hear her enjoying life despite her illness. It gave him confidence that her body was getting stronger and recovering well from the treatment.

Whilst Bridget thought Sinead's illness didn't affect him much, in reality, it was all he could think about. Many a night, Martin would stumble in from the pub after a few drinks, trying not to make any noise, and sit up late into the night listening out for Sinead's breathing. Sinead had suffered terrible episodes in the nights before being diagnosed. The pain in her skull, the erratic sleeping patterns and crying out from headaches stirred her. Even now, if Martin went to bed and heard a murmur from Sinead's room, it was enough to bring back all the bad memories and keep him awake all night lying there. No amount of alcohol could send him to sleep. He would lie there staring into oblivion until she finally settled.

Mrs Callaghan had prepared some reading exercises for Sinead. Reading wasn't her strongest subject, and it was never encouraged at home by Martin, though Bridget was an avid reader. Shane suffered from poor literacy skills, and the guilt from that played on Bridget's mind. She berated herself too for not following through with her own education as a positive example for her kids. Having Martin at home didn't help things either. He exerted little positive influence when it came to educating the children. Bridget was determined not to fail Sinead, and neither was Mrs Callaghan.

Sinead started reading out one of the stories set for the day. She stuttered through the words with broken sentences. Mrs Callaghan wasn't too concerned. The child had been through so much and missed so much school already. She was confident that with plenty of practice and encouragement, this setback would right itself. Stumbling on a word, Sinead scrunched her nose up before sounding it out slowly. Peering over her glasses, Mrs Callaghan encouraged her, 'Yes, that's right, PHEN–OM–EN–ON, Phenomenon. It means an occurrence that is witnessed and is… shall we say, impressive or extraordinary.'

Sinead carried on with a couple more pages as Mrs Callaghan marked work she had completed previously. Tilting her glasses down, she caught sight of Sinead looking puzzled. She glanced over and remarked, 'Everything ok, dear?' Looking closer at the page, it became clear what Sinead was struggling with. 'Ah, yes. Well, that word there is what is called a homonym. They are words with more than one meaning. For example: Hail, which means frozen rain and also to welcome or salute someone. Do you know any words that have two different meanings?' she asked Sinead encouragingly.

'Like, 'loose' Miss?'

Pretending to be engaged with her marking, Mrs Callaghan replied, 'Sinead Lynch, you really should stop listening to your father's friends' conversations.'

Sinead smiled happily and carried on with her reading. Pausing for a short break, she flicked through her well-thumbed dictionary. Hearing the room go silent, Martin popped his head back around the door then asked, 'Everything ok for you, ladies?'

Sinead was content, 'All good, Dad.'

Martin sat back in the kitchen and studied the racing post. The afternoon flew by as he listened to the gentle conversation in the other room that soothed his soul.

CHAPTER 15

Kieran had rested a little over the last couple of days. He'd hoped his groin injury would subside before his doctor's appointment. It hadn't, and it didn't matter anyway. Kathleen insisted on dropping him off at the surgery and waiting. Kieran accepted the lift, but only on the condition that she left him there alone and let him make his way home. He was a grown man now and didn't need his hand held by his mother. They arrived ten minutes early, and he tried to rebuff a kiss from Kathleen on getting out of the car. Heading into reception, Kieran didn't realise that a red smear highlighted his cheek as if a drunken floozy had left her mark.

An attractive young female receptionist guided him in the direction of the waiting room. The smell of perfume lingered in the air after her. Sitting awkwardly, Kieran forgot to remove his mobile phone from his back pocket and jumped up when it stuck into him. Embarrassed, he surreptitiously checked for screen damage, trying not to draw attention to himself. Kieran sat back down timidly and had a quick look around. Staring into oblivion, he accidentally caught a patient's eye but looked away seconds too late, leaving him even more uncomfortable. Coughs and spluttering emanated from patients on either side of him. Ten minutes dragged on forever. Yawning expansively, his eyes began to water. Again, he got caught staring at the same patient. A slight shake of their head dented his confidence for no reason. Then, with perfect timing, 'Kieran Hennessey–Room 5' flashed up on the appointment monitor.

He went to rise up, but at that exact moment, an older man did too and beat him to the exit, shuffling on his feet as if sliding on ice. The older man had a funny smell; Kieran didn't like to presume its origin. They both followed on down the corridor heading for the same room, at the same time, the awkwardness increasing with every step.

A voice called out behind them both, 'Mr Hennessey! Your

walking stick, Sir, I'll leave it at reception, so you can collect it on leaving.'

'Right you are, my dear,' the elderly man replied.

Kieran looked at the elderly gentleman puzzled and asked, 'Excuse me, is your name Kieran Hennessey?'

Peering up, the gentleman struggled to move his neck enough to look up to Kieran.

'Yes, young man, are you my doctor?' he enquired disbelievingly.

Kieran's brow knitted in frustration. 'No, I mean, my name is Kieran Hennessey as well.'

'Well, what are the chances, young man!' The gentleman forced a light chuckle.

Kieran smiled. 'Hold on, save yourself from walking, and I'll find out which one of us this appointment is for.'

Light on his feet, Kieran strode back up the corridor. Meeting the same young receptionist who greeted him earlier, he briefly explained the confusion with a bashful smile. Her eyes locked onto his and his cheeks reddened. She went to look up the computer, and Kieran, taken aback by her, tried to look away by looking down. Instead, he ended up glaring at the form of her breasts through her white tunic. A warm feeling spread through his groin. Mentally swiping wild thoughts from his mind, he slowed his breathing, willing away the further embarrassment. Turning around abruptly, he headed back to room five and his namesake.

A minute later, the receptionist emerged into the corridor. Whispering pleasantries, her sleek figure passed them both as she headed to consult with the doctor in question.

Reappearing with eagerness, she approached Kieran.

'It's Kieran Hennessey with the urinary retention... Oh my God, I'm sorry,' She blustered, mortified as she realised her error in front of the gentleman, and her cheeks blossomed red as she tried to apologise.

Kieran, further humiliated, irritably remarked, 'What made you think it could have been me?' Kieran felt belittled by the pretty staff member and couldn't get his confidence back.

The elderly gentleman glanced sideways, then up at Kieran and then back at the young girl and answered, 'Young lady, that's me then.' Attempting a half-hearted chuckle, it turned into a full-blown coughing fit that made his eyes water and weakened him. Kieran helped him into the treatment room and got him a handful of tissue from the doctor's desk.

Making his way back into the reception area the exit doors buzzed opened, a light gust blew in. Anxiousness washed over Kieran as his chest restricted; in a split second, he made a decision that was the release of tension built up inside him. As the automatic doors shunted to close, he strolled out between them and blew out a slow puff of air. Breaking into a stride, his heart rate quickened. How he was going to tell his mother he'd bottled it.

The rustle of keys in the lock caught Kathleen's attention. Kieran headed into the kitchen, lightly panting from the exertion of running home. He wiped away the sweat from his brow before removing his tracksuit top.

Shaking her head, Kathleen muttered, 'You turned down a free lift to run back home?'

'Mam, don't start. I needed the run to clear my head.'

'Right, let's have it?' Kathleen demanded gently.

'What?' Kieran pretended he didn't know what his mother was asking.

'What did the doctor say?' Kathleen nodded her head purposefully with a sharp stare.

'Leave off, Mam, I've just walked in. Let me have a quick shower first. I'll be down in fifteen.' Kieran went to leave.

'Hold your horses there. Before you go upstairs, I've got some bad news for you, and it's going to upset you. Are you ready?' Her pursed lips smothered a grin.

'Go on, Mam.' His face changed as worry set in.

She held her hands up in mock surrender and paused for effect, then spoke dramatically. 'So, here it is…' Her eyes glinted. 'While we were out, an intruder got into the house and headed straight to your room…' Her hand movements exaggerated the story. 'They turned it upside down and threw all your clothes onto the floor, stashing some under your bed. They really went to town up there. The rest of the house was untouched, though.' She held her hands out; palms turned up.

'Argh crap; did they take my Superdry jacket?'

Kathleen's voice changed to deadpan. 'They didn't take a frigging thing,' her eyes squinted fiendishly. 'I have a feeling it was an inside job, Kieran,' She burst out laughing at her wit.

Kieran replied with a hint of sarcasm in his voice, 'I don't suppose they did any ironing before they left, Mam?'

Rolling her eyes, Kathleen remonstrated, 'Now, how many times do I have to tell you? I am not walking into your room in that state. You have a wardrobe. Use it. We have a laundry basket; use it.'

'It's supposed to be in that order, Mam. I like to call it *Feng Shui*.'

'Well, I call it *Feng Shite* Kieran,' she riposted, annoyed now.

Kieran tried to diffuse things, 'If I tidy it up, can I bring a lass back up here?'

'Not on your nelly, Kieran. I'm not having some strumpet I don't know swanning around in her knickers first thing in the morning. As soon as I've gathered enough info on her from Facebook, I'll decide then.' His questioning had backfired.

'You're not joking either, Mam! It's a good thing I don't have a sister. Can you imagine Dad with any of her boyfriends?'

Kathleen choked on a chuckle, 'That doesn't even bear thinking about; the poor lass would never be able to date any lad around here. They'd all be too scared.'

Finding common ground, they both relaxed. Kathleen couldn't resist tormenting Kieran, 'That was a pretty young thing in the doctor's reception there.'

'Fuck sake, Mam, you promised,' Kieran protested.

'Did she admire the lipstick mark on your face?' Kathleen muffled a laugh.

'What?' Jumping up and examining himself in the chrome kettle, Kieran's reflection showed him the lipstick mark smeared on his cheek.

'Thanks very much for that, Mam. There's me thinking that she was boss-eyed looking over my shoulder. All the time, I'm looking like a harlot's plaything.' Clutching his hoodie and feeling hard done by, Kieran stomped upstairs for a shower.

From below, as he went up the stairs, he heard, 'Clothing for the basket, remember! And the only thing to grace the carpet in your room is the hoover.'

Half an hour later, Kieran emerged refreshed and invigorated, dressed in a bathrobe and boxer shorts. The smell of deodorant hung thickly in the air.

As he flounced into the kitchen, Kathleen chided, 'So, I take it you're going to sit on your backside all day now, is that correct?'

'Mam, I've got no evening shifts at the pub tonight.' His shoulders dropped in relaxation, 'I'm a man of leisure for the rest of the day.'

'Well, a man of leisure, keep your backside in this kitchen. I want you to tell me what the doctor said.'

'Oh, Mam!'

Kathleen looked at Kieran searchingly and snapped,

'Kieran, NOW.'

'Mam, the thing is, when I got there, I couldn't go through with it.'

'I knew it,' she said, slapping her hand on the countertop; she rolled her eyes. 'I knew I should have waited for you outside. Christ, Kieran, I trusted you to go on your own to be seen. What's the excuse this time? In fact, I don't wanna know... right, drop your pants.'

'What! You've got to be kidding me, Mam.'

'Look, I gave you every opportunity to have your problem assessed. I booked the appointment; I drove you up there. Christ, Kieran, do I really need to hold your hand – now drop them.'

'Mam, everything has changed downstairs since the last time you saw me.'

'Son, you are the most precious thing to me in this life. I will do everything possible to ensure your safety and health, no matter what your age is,' she pointed her finger at him, 'I want to be sure that there isn't a problem later on down the line that is stopping you from providing me with grandchildren. Now, for once in your life, do as your father does, because believe you, me, I never have to ask your father a second time to do this. Drop your pants!'

Kieran held his hands up in protest, 'No way, Mam, I'm not doing it!'

'Ok then, well, at least answer me this,' Bridget asked, 'Is everything in working order down there? Are you able to relieve yourself without any discomfort?'

'Mam! I've said all along, I've been able to go to the toilet properly.'

'I meant, are you able to... *relieve* yourself? You know, in your own quality time?' she raised an eyebrow.

'This conversation is so wrong, Mam.'

Kathleen sighed, 'Right, there is only one thing for it – to put my mind at rest...'

‘Don’t worry, Mam, I’ll promise I’ll make another appointment; you can sit outside if you want.’

‘No sirree, It’s too late for that. I gave you the opportunity to see your GP, and you couldn’t be bothered. So, to put my mind at ease, my little darling, I’m seeking my own medical opinion and, believe you, me, those boxer shorts will be coming down later one way or another. Dr Kavanagh has given us tickets for this event tonight, so I’ll text her for a proper diagnosis by going private. She may be able to fit you in for consultation later today as a favour to me. We’ll pick Bridget up along the route and drop you off for the consultation. Dr Kavanagh will assess you and put my mind at rest. Are we clear… look at me,’ her face was righteous.

Kieran huffed and puffed and searched for excuses. None were found.

Kathleen remarked, ‘Just remember, it’s me who you want to sweet talk your father about those new trainers that are out.’

‘Ok, Mam…’ Kieran relented. Rolling his eyes, he sloped off into the front room, sinking into the sofa with a can of pringles in one hand and a glass of coke in the other; a manoeuvre he had practised many times before without spilling a drop of his drink. Minutes later, Kathleen peeped in on him. All she could hear was the munching of crisps and the ricochet of bullets from the television.

CHAPTER 16

The rich smell of tomato and basil sauce filled the kitchen. Its residue clung to the saucepan discarded in the sink. Kathleen's efforts to make a nice dinner for her family put her mind at ease as she prepared herself to go out. A lemon drizzle cake tempted her on the side, but she resisted, saving her appetite for the evening ahead.

Gathering her thoughts, she spoke aloud to herself. 'Ok, dinner ready – Check. Dishwasher loaded – Check. Cab ordered – Check. Something, something, something. Shite, what is it? Think, think, think. Shite!... Bridget's wine!'

Dressed and manicured, she stood in front of the mirror, her hair fluffy and bouncy as she flicked her hand through it. Pouting, then smacking her lips to ensure lipstick was evenly applied, she checked herself one last time before shouting for Kieran. 'Downstairs NOW and don't be fobbing me off with excuses… I said NOW, Kieran. We need to make a move.'

Footsteps stomped down the stairs. Kieran looked guilty.

'God Kieran,' she said, 'did you have to overdose with the deodorant.' Waving away the unwanted scent, she scolded him. 'I've told you before; you don't need to use half a can each time. Now, did you open the window when you sprayed it on? You know, I've read stories about young lads overdosing with fumes from those things… Christ.'

Kieran didn't comment. Bundling him and herself into the car, Kathleen drove carefully and hesitantly to Bridget's to collect her. On their way back to Kathleen's, the trio stopped at Dr Kavanagh's clinic. Bridget remained in the car, happily re-applying her eyeliner. Dr Kavanagh greeted them on arrival. The women embraced with attempted air kisses that made their cheekbones clash. They exchanged pleasantries as Kieran tried to make himself invisible.

'Kieran, this is Dr Kavanagh. Dr Kavanagh, this is your patient who absconded from his appointment at his surgery today.'

'You're a woman!' blurted out Kieran.

'Indeed!' The doctor raised her eyebrows.

'Sorry, I should have realised when mam mentioned the ICA ball, the that came across rude… Mam, you never said?'

'Why would it matter?'

'It's just, my doctor is a fella,' he stuttered.

'Let me put your mind at rest, Kieran,' spoke Dr Kavanagh kindly. 'I have been a qualified doctor for over twenty years. I have seen all shapes and sizes of men's willies, and there are stories I could tell you that would make you shudder.'

Kieran conceded, 'Sorry, that was rude of me again.'

'Right young man, your mother has asked me to put her mind at rest. Don't worry; I won't be touching or prodding – well, not much.' She led Kieran into the practice room. Standing guard with her back to the door frame, Kathleen kept her head turned away.

Kieran protested, 'Outside, Mam, now please.'

Kathleen promptly left, leaving the door ajar as Kieran prepared himself behind a screen. The doctor knelt and began her examination.

'My, what a specimen we have here!' she tried to put him at ease.

'I hope Dr Kavanagh, you mean that in a medical capacity,' Kathleen chortled.

As colour flushed across Kieran's cheeks, he remained still and silent, staring at the ceiling. The examination was soon over but not soon enough for Kieran as he stayed behind the screen.

'Right young man – in medical terms, you have what is called a varicocele. You have abnormalities of the veins inside your testicle, leading to a backup of blood that cannot flow. That is why your testicle feels like a bag of worms.'

Kieran looked concerned.

'Your GP will refer you to a specialist once you go back to see him. This time you WILL go back to see him. You may require a medical procedure, but it's nothing that can't be put right for a young, healthy man like yourself.' The doctor disposed of her gloves and sanitised her hands.

Kathleen re-entered the room with a face like thunder. 'Is it likely to be from pushing himself too hard in the gym?'

Rubbing her hands briskly, the doctor shook her head. 'Kathleen, it can be caused by a variety of different things, stretched muscles or ligaments exerted beyond their natural tensile strength, leading to these symptoms. To be honest, we don't know why it happens most of the time.' Absently, the doctor added to Kieran, 'Young man, you can pull your boxers up now.'

'Wait, Kieran,' Kathleen held up a hand to stop him, then shouted out, 'Bridget! Will you come in here and take a look at this?'

Kieran's reaction was instantaneous. 'JAYSIS, Mam, that's not even funny. Has Shane's mam come in here, you never said?'

Kathleen brayed with laughter unapologetically. Kieran redressed himself and thanked the doctor, ignoring his mother as he stomped out angrily past her. As they arrived back home at Kathleen's, Kieran darted inside, avoiding clearing up his mess from earlier. Broken crisps mashed into the carpet greeted them in the front room. Blood vessels pulsed at Kathleen's temples as rage erupted inside her. As she attempted to scream up the staircase, Bridget restrained her by gently holding her arm out across Kathleen's waist like a forcefield.

'Leave the lad alone, Kath; open one of these bottles and slow down. You've been on your feet all day.'

'That boy has plagued my mind all day,' dropping her head, Kathleen surrendered to the alcohol and sighed. Clinking glasses overzealously, the pair slugged back a second glass before embracing in fits of giggles as wine dripped from their chins.

Kathleen lifted a strand of hair from Bridget's face with a light finger and studied her gently before she spoke, 'Look,' she started to say, 'what I said about Sheila and Martin, I was way out of…'

'I won't hear another word about it,' Bridget interrupted her. 'As Sinead said to me… sometimes we are all right, and sometimes we are all wrong. Me and you are strong.'

The women hugged and then pulled back and laughed. Conversation and cackling filled the air as they complimented each other on their evening dresses. They enjoyed the second bottle of wine before their cab arrived. The excitement of the evening brought back memories of their youth when they prepared to go out for an evening dancing and slept over at one another's houses. For one night only, they could make believe they were in their early twenties again, revelling in all its freedom.

The event was taking place at a private members' golf club. Glistening asphalt leading up to the entrance was fenced off by stone pillars with wrought iron gates defending the green fairways beyond. Rows of expensive cars lined up and gleamed under lighting from the stone façade.

On arrival, Dr Kavanagh greeted them as a pleasant breeze rustled in the foliage surrounding the main doors. Handing over their tickets, they were greeted with flutes of champagne. Fresh cut flowers adorned the reception desk, their aroma overpowering. Pleasantries and introductions were exchanged before staff escorted them to their table. Bridget and Kathleen held each other's fingertips as they proceeded in a line to their places. The scraping of chairs sounded as seated diners were forced to squeeze into their tables as the friends negotiated the narrow aisles between tables and chairs.

An orchestral melody drifted through the venue. They felt relaxed as they sat down at their corner table. Long, embroidered curtains with tasselled tiebacks revealed the glass doors that backed onto the view of the fairways, now overshadowed by the velvet dark.

'I hope we don't require the ladies too often tonight,' Bridget remarked, 'as I don't fancy squeezing through this cattle market for the sake of a wee.'

Starched tablecloths layered the tables, pinned down with corked red wine bottles from a region that nobody had heard of. Drowned lemon segments floated in jugs of water, partnered with ice buckets dunked with chilled white wine bottles. Chatter buzzed around the room as people raised their voices to be heard amidst the noise.

Bridget relaxed as the mix of wine and champagne loosened her up enough to drop her guard. Kathleen watched her best friend come to life; the shackles of domestic responsibility relinquished for the evening. She studied Bridget's face as she talked to another guest. Kathleen noted the shimmer of glitter that dazzled from her neckline in the candlelight. It dawned on her how beautiful she looked, and she thought to herself that her friend deserved more. A stray hand in front of her broke through her train of thought. The menu was laid neatly at her place setting.

Studying the layout of cutlery, Bridget lifted a knife and was surprised by its weight. She whispered to Kathleen, 'Now, this is luxury. I could never go to a restaurant with Martin with trimmings like this. I'd have to keep checking he hadn't stashed any of this good stuff away,' she chuckled.

Kathleen finished her wine and sucked her lips inward at the sharpness of it. Glancing at the wine label, she prayed to God that Declan hadn't had a hand in supplying the club with the robust flavour. As the evening progressed, the conversation at each table became louder as Prosecco fuelled the laughter. Feeling giddy after a couple of glasses on an empty stomach, Kathleen locked eyes with Bridget.

As light spooled across the table, the crystal glasses shimmered and, suddenly and without preamble, she asked, 'Why don't you leave him, Bridget? Not for his sake or the kids but for yours?'

Bridget's gaze strayed, causing her to blink rapidly. Kathleen placed her hand over Bridget's, apologetically but also reassuringly.

Sipping wine, Bridget curled her tongue, waiting for the bitter sensation to kick in before swallowing. Hesitatingly she replied, 'I know you mean well, Kath,' she sighed. 'The truth is I'm afraid to be lonely. I'd gladly suffer the ills of life and keep my family the way we are. Look, I know we don't have money, and have our own issues, but as strange as this may sound, I feel secure having Martin with me. I wouldn't have it any other way.'

Leaning forward, Kathleen pressed her lips against Bridget's forehead, 'I had to ask.'

The conversation ended as the serving staff filled the wine glasses. As the plates were cleared away, the front section of the room came to life as spotlights lit up the podium. Coffees were served as the speeches were about to start.

The compere introduced Kathleen to make her speech. Her voice boomed out of the microphone, a little overzealous as she pitched her way through her lines. Within minutes it was over, ending in applause and well-received (thanks to Martin's input) laughter. The evening was a huge success.

Once the tables were cleared away, Dr Kavanagh found her friends on the dance floor, and together the three women danced the night away. Shoes were flicked off at the end of the evening, rejuvenating the weary soles of their feet and showcasing their bunions as they rested them on adjoining chairs. Relaxed and happy, the women gazed around the venue, gossiping and wondering just how many people were planning on driving home given the number of cars parked outside. Everyone looked like they had overindulged during the evening's proceedings. Waiting for the cab to arrive to take them home, the two friends tottered on the pavement, linking arms and laughing like they were young again. The following morning, youthful feelings departed as the hangover curse kicked in, reminding their bodies of their exact age.

CHAPTER 17

The morning sky woke matt grey a week later and combed through with dark clouds threatening to rain. It was mid-morning before Martin fell out of bed at the sound of the post hitting the doormat. He sat up and looked at his bedside table. Heavy eyes and a lolling head focused on the list of chores that Bridget had scribbled out on the back of a church newsletter. Sinead had been up for hours, and her room was already tidy.

They sat down together in the kitchen for breakfast. Bridget had finished her night shift and had no time for any sleep. Her sister Sheila planned to come over later for lunch. Once the dishes were done, she took her cup of tea and retreated upstairs to get washed and dressed.

Meanwhile, Martin kept a watchful eye over Sinead as she was showing early signs of a seizure. Glancing into the back room, the aroma of scented candles hit him straight away. The room had a warm glow with the curtains drawn and the lights low. Sinead was lying down on her stomach with her legs waving in the air. She was wearing a cosy onesie with a leopard print design. It was one size too big, which suited her as Sinead often wore layers underneath to keep warm. Originally it was bought as a joke, but it had become a Christmas tradition now, and Martin loved seeing her face each Christmas morning as she opened her latest onesie. She ran with the joke and continued to wear them at home. Bridget also received one. She made her feelings clear to Martin about wearing it.

Sinead was listening to music on Martin's old Walkman and clicking her ankles together to the beat of the music. She glanced up with a broad smile.

Martin greeted her, 'How's 'Trouble' today? Is it causing you any discomfort?' His voice was tender.

Sinead pulled the headphones down around her neck and looked up at him. 'I'm ok Dad, I've gotten used to it now.'

'Right love, well jump up here, let me look at you; I want to see if your pupils are dilated.'

Sinead removed the headphones but left the Walkman running with the music reverberating around the room. Her back rested against the armrest as she sat up, she asked,

'Dad, can you push the box of tapes over to me. Oh, and when you come back in, can you bring me that box of liquorice Mam brought home this morning? Please?' she smiled winningly at him,

'Please? PLEASE!'

As Martin reached the door, he turned around, 'Oh, by the way, love,' he smiled. 'I wanted to you see this,' he slid a brown package over to her with his foot. 'See this DVD here, stick it on. It's from Robbie Williams, himself no less.'

Sinead's eyes opened wide. 'What's this Da, some kind of Catfish setup? I know you too well!'

'I'm not messing; it really is from Robbie Williams! He heard about your plight – well, actually, his team heard me singing first and then heard about your tumour and sent you this.'

Sinead's mouth dropped open.

'I'm not messing. There is a letter in here from him explaining how his team found out all about you; it's for real, cross my heart.'

Martin returned with the liquorice, which he had already started eating. It was an unwanted gift by one of the residents where Bridget worked. Sinead wasn't impressed but sifted through the box to find the ones she would eat.

Martin teased her. 'Oh damm, I've mixed up the DVDs now. Was it this one or… ah, got it right here with your name on it.'

'Da, stop messing.'

Martin sniggered as he fell back onto the sofa; Sinead nestled into his shoulder as the DVD played. A special message from Robbie Williams just for her. Robbie told her that he had seen Martin's version of his song, heard about her story, and wanted to wish her well in the video. Tears sprang to Sinead's eyes as he went on to sing the song that propelled himself, and Martin Lynch, into the limelight. Making the music personal, he changed the lyrics from 'Angels' to 'Sinead.'

Overcome with excitement, once the video ended, Sinead laid back down on her Dad's lap. Martin tilted his head back and prepared to relax and take a short nap. The flickering shadows of the candles bounced off the ceiling as Martin closed his eyes. All he could hear was the beat of the music from Sinead's headphones. Something caught his attention as he started to doze off. Stirring, he tapped Sinead on her forehead and gestured for her to remove her headphones.

Scowling at the interruption, she pulled one earphone back to listen.

'Is that, 'Long as I Can See the Light', you're listening to, darling?' Martin questioned her.

Sinead nodded.

Much to her annoyance, he continued, 'Do you like a bit of Creedence Clearwater Revival then, Sinead?'

She tutted, exasperated, and replied, 'Well, yer man has a funny voice, but the music is nice… and he talks about candles.' Pulling the headphones back over her ear, she snuggled back into a comfortable position.

Martin chuckled to himself and muttered under his breath, 'You have a touch of class with your taste in music, poppet.'

CHAPTER 18

Before he could nod off again, Martin heard the noise of female voices echoing from the kitchen. The door was closed, but laughter and loud voices carried through to the back room. That meant only one thing; Bridget's sister Sheila had arrived and was, it sounded, in good spirits. David had also made an unscheduled appearance and was catching up with both his sisters.

He teasingly asked, 'Where's Martin, is he even up yet?'

Bridget pointed beyond the kitchen, 'He's been up for ages; he's in the back room there with Sinead.'

David walked away to find him, miming a kettle at Bridget as he left.

The door to the back room was ajar. Martin could hear Sinead chattering away. Peeking his head in, David thought twice about breaking up the bonding session and instead returned to the kitchen. After a brief cup of tea, all three were ready to leave. Sheila wanted to say a quick hello to Sinead before going. Sheila led the way to the backroom, with David following behind her.

She tapped gently on the door, walked in, looked around and said, 'My, it's warm in here. How's my sweetheart today?'

Martin and Sinead both looked up; Martin responded first, 'I'm grand, thanks for asking, Sheila,' he grinned.

Sheila scowled. Sinead elbowed him to behave as she got up. She embraced her auntie. Sheila then turned back to Martin with a forced smile on her face.

Sensing her annoyance, he grinned back, 'So, what's the craic then, Sheila?'

Slightly mollified, Sheila launched into an update. 'I was just telling Bridget that we have a new parish priest who wants to make a name for himself in the diocese. He's young and keen, but we don't feel he understands the concerns of the parish.'

Martin bored already, interjected, 'You mean, you and your cronies can't get your way now.'

Sheila ignored the remark and carried on. 'Father O'Hara had set up a food bank that was attached to the church building. It had proved successful until some tearaways set fire to it, and it burnt to the ground. Not to be outdone by its demise, Father O'Hara then hired a shipping container racked out for shelving all the donations. Since then, loiterers have urinated behind the container which is still on church ground, and random homeless people have set up camp, hanging washing out; until they were asked to move on. It's an absolute disgrace,' she added, shaking her head with disgust.

Martin pursed his lips and winked at Sinead before asking, 'So, what was the outcome of it?'

Sheila perked up, 'We think that Father is too lenient with these people and their smells. Also, the reputation of the parish is undermined. We have set up a meeting with Father O'Hara, and the Canon is to attend as well to address the situation.'

Martin sneered and shook his head as he spoke, 'You know, Sheila; you need to start shedding that thick skin of yours and show some tolerance with the new fella. Yer man is reaching out to poor folk who have absolute fuck all –'

Sinead interrupted Martin with a slap on the leg for cursing.

Sheila took over, 'We agree with the Father's charitable work; we just question his approach to it. The container is an eyesore, and juveniles have sprayed a picture of male anatomy on its front, facing the street. It does not fit for the church or the area.'

Martin snorted. 'Listen to yourself, woman; you're nothing but a snob. That Bible of yours – THE GOOD BOOK – is just an ancient relic. It was devised thousands of years ago to give people some kind of guidance on living their lives. To help them to keep order within the communities they lived in. It was to make people sit back and think about the consequences of their actions… like: "Thou shall not steal", or "Thou shall not shag thy brother's wife," or you will face the wrath of God when you die. The ages, revolutions and democracies we live in, in today's society, allow people to express themselves. What is wrong with a drawing of a willy on a wall?'

Sheila snapped back at Martin's garish remark, 'You take that back, Martin Lynch. It's not just a willy. It had the other two bits attached to it as well. It was detailed. It was offensive. Also, for your information, it isn't on a wall; it's on a shipping container. We want the parish to help set up a refuge house for the homeless and not have someone's shite all over our church grounds.'

'I apologise, Sinead, for the S-word: she broke off, looking at Sinead, then returned her focus to Martin. 'Just because someone is homeless, it doesn't give them the right to desecrate church soil when the church is out to help them in the first place.'

Martin, still smiling and loving the conflict, winked at Sinead.

'Isn't it the bible that states, 'Necessity knows no laws?'

Scrunching her face in despair, Sheila countered, 'No, it doesn't, that's a proverb.'

The tension remained palpable as David's eyes batted to and fro through the exchanges; after remaining silent, he finally butted in. 'I think you'll find it was from one of those Dirty Harry movies.'

'So, in the space of a sentence, the good man has jumped from folklore to an outlaw.'

Sheila tried to stop Martin from controlling the conversation, but she'd fallen into his trap. Martin saw the irritation and seized it.

'You talk of privilege like it's a virtue,' he accused. 'Your whole life has been privileged, Sheila; you know nothing of hard times. These poor bastards, who have so-called *desecrated* your land, have fuck all. They didn't choose that life. They have lost everything and everyone in their lives. I'd like to see you do a charity event where you sleep rough for one night with your committee pals and last throughout the night. I'd certainly sponsor you for that.'

Sheila stood resolute as her face turned beetroot red. Martin had touched a nerve. '*Blah, blah, blah,* Martin, tell me now, how would you ever afford to sponsor me for anything?' she accused, angrily, 'would you take all of your empty bottles back?'

The remark ruffled Martin. Sinead's headphones were on, but she was still well aware of the discord and tried to tune out the words of destruction between people she loved.

Martin fired back, 'I'll tell you what privilege would be like for those homeless people seeking sanctuary on your church grounds. If the likes of you offered them the time of day with a cup of tea or the use of the church hall toilets, that would give them 1% of self-worth; the notion that they matter instead of you turning your nose up at them.

'I bet you have… you don't even need to answer that. I can see it in your face. It's evident in the way you look at people. You think that your own shite doesn't stink – Sinead, I apologise for that blasphemy. Your church has been privileged for its entire existence by not paying taxes. You tell me another organisation that doesn't have to pay jack-shite. Now you have to agree with me on that.'

Taking a deep breath, Sheila peered at Sinead and, dismissing Martin's comment, changed the subject entirely and asked Sinead, 'So, pet, what are your plans over the Easter holidays?'

Shrugging his shoulders, Martin raised then dropped his arms to his sides in surrender. 'The same as Jesus…' he quipped, 'disappear on Friday and turn back up on Monday.'

Sheila glared at Martin again in disapproval. David resisted laughing, knowing Sheila never thought Martin was ever good enough for their sister, so, he stayed out of it.

Martin continued, 'So, tell me, Sheila, what are your plans over the festive weekend, my sweet?'

Tempted to reply and continue the battle, she instead glowered at Martin. Bridget linked her arm to move her out of the room, but Sheila paused, resisting, and replied sternly, 'I'll be celebrating the good Lord's awakening in two weeks.'

Ignoring her, Martin focused on the framed photograph of Jesus Christ hung proudly on the wall. Initially, it had lit up when plugged in, but Martin had needed its plug for something else. He remained unbothered. 'Indeed, he was a great man who suffered for us all. But he must be looking down at us all now and thinking, "What the fuck was it all for... they've still learnt nothing. Wars and killings all over the world.' Biting her tongue and grinding her teeth, Sheila's voice quivered at Martin's blasphemy, 'You take that back now, Martin.'

Knowing he had riled her, Martin still pretended not to hear whilst gazing at the picture. He persisted in goading to get a reaction out of her. 'The thing is?… studying this picture makes me think that Jezzer was actually Irish,' Martin pinched his chin in deep thought. 'You don't get many other nationalities pastier in colour than an Irishman... and you could well believe that it makes sense judging by his lifestyle.'

Counting on his fingers, Martin carried on, 'One – he trained as a carpenter to work on the buildings and was often unemployed. Two –he went out drinking with the lads the night before he died. Three – he thought his mother was a virgin and bless her; she thought he was fecking God.'

David burst out laughing then immediately tried to stifle it as both his sisters glared at him.

'But me personally,' Martin added, 'I think the great man was actually a black man.' Bowing his head and holding his arms aloft, Martin pretended to calm the room.

'Now hear me out now and don't bite my head off. If yer man was born and raised in Jerusalem – I'm taking it that it is Egypt way – then. Them people have a touch of the sun and don't look like this,' Martin raised his trouser leg to show his pale complexion. He continued, 'So, I'm pretty sure that the fella was a black man actually.'

Sheila unwisely engaged with him, 'Well, thank you for your rational insight. Now again, in three points, explain why?' Looking pleased with herself, she leaned back, triumphant. It backfired on her immediately.

Martin paused for a moment and counted off his fingers again while answering. 'Well – erhh – one – yer man loved gospel; you can'tget away from that fact. Two – he walked around the townships calling everyone brother. Three – he couldn't get a fair trial. He should've signed up OJ's lawyer.'

Martin watched as his words had their desired effect on Sheila. The tightness in her jawline, the holding of her breath, her clenched hands. He could smell the heat rising from her… but nothing. She remained quiet, finally.

A few seconds elapsed, and she attempted a smile, and with a note of victory added, 'Well, as they say, Martin, mockery is the sincerest form of flattery, and I think deep down, you truly are a believer.' Remaining stoic until she thought she was out of hearing distance, Sheila shouted expletives at the front door.

David suppressed a smile behind her, brandishing his index finger aimed at Martin, while a broad grin etched across his face. Bridget trundled off after her sister and tried to calm her down. Loud voices echoed in the hallway amidst the cursing. Martin and Sinead remained silent.

The silence continued after the front door slammed shut. David left quickly, tired of listening to his sisters argue and squabble over Martin again. Realising her purse was left behind, Bridget offered to get it for Sheila to save any further discord. Hearing the door creak open, Sinead made a bolt off the sofa and ran outside to placate her auntie. Sheila, sitting in her car, started the engine whilst looking angry and tired. Sinead tapped on the window, startling her. As the window buzzed down, Sinead noticed a sheen of sweat above her auntie's perfectly shaped eyebrows.

'Aunty Sheila,' she asked, 'can you not argue with my Da when you come around again? It would mean so much to me if you could both get along.'

Abashed by the comment, Sheila felt flustered and dabbed her hairline with a tissue before she answered. 'Your father can be a difficult man to hold a conversation with, my sweet, but I will do my best for you next time. I'm sorry you were caught up with grown-ups' arguing.'

'I'm used to it, Auntie Sheila. I'm ok. It's not for me; I want you to do this for Mam.'

She was taken by surprise and feeling even more ashamed, an embarrassed heat suffused her, moving up her chest and blossoming into her cheeks. Sheila nodded, feeling the weight of Sinead's request rest heavily on her.

Sinead beamed and planted a kiss on her auntie's cheek before she quipped, 'I like your eyebrows, by the way.' In a dart, she retreated inside.

Sheila slumped in her seat.

A second later, Bridget dropped the purse onto her sister's lap and asked, 'And what was that all about?'

'Nothing, Sinead just asked me to look after you today.'

'She's a good girl, our Sinead,' Bridget smiled.

'I'm sorry for riling it up in there, Bridget. I didn't mean to start the day off with a bad taste in everyone's mouth.'

'I'm used to it by now Sheila, don't fuss yourself,' Bridget responded.

Sheila fumbled with her purse as an excuse without replying.

Back inside, Martin and Sinead carried on with their analysis of Martin's taste in music. Martin, nonplussed by the furore, started trying to educate her in the history of 1970s music when Sinead firmly interrupted

.

'Dad, it upsets Mam when you and Auntie Sheila argue. You argue every time you both meet; why do you do it?'

Martin sighed, 'The thing with your Auntie Sheila is that she always has good intentions when she's invited around, but our personalities clash on most topics of conversations. I try to be good, but to be honest, I can't help myself. By the time I'm finished with her, she has a head on her like a burst trout.'

Martin sniggered as Sinead pinched his nose in mock annoyance. Sitting back and looking puzzled, she asked, 'Why does Auntie Sheila talk so differently to us? You know, how can I put it? A bit posh-like?'

Martin replied in jest, while lowering his voice, 'I think it might be that stick she has up her –.'

'Daaad,' scolded Sinead.

'I'm only messing. Aunty Shelia has done well at school and furthered her education. It opened doors for her, unlike myself.'

'Dad, what makes you happy?'

Martin looked quizzically at the unexpected question. Reaching out, he tenderly stroked the side of her cheek before slowly answering. 'Let me see, now. Well there's a lot to love about life if you ask me. First off, there's my family, who I love madly,' he smiled at her.

'I love nature, the beauty of the world, the stars and the moon and the sun and the seasons; I love being on my own, looking at the sunset; let's say, any day in November. The way the sun sets in an orange amber-glow. As for what satisfaction I get from life. Well... I've tried every form of alcohol and the paraphernalia that goes with it,' he shrugged, 'if I'm true to myself, I'd have to say it's doing an honest day's work.

'Coming home and putting money on the table. Having my dinner then looking at that money and feeling tired, exhausted, but I've achieved something. That's the best feeling, working hard with something to show for it. But I haven't been able to feel like that in a long, long time. As a famous Irish man called George Best once said, "I spent a lot of money on booze, women and fast cars. The rest I just squandered."'

He laughed a little less confidently.

'You can still go back to a normal job, Dad. It would probably make Mam happier as well.'

Martin chuckled to himself, then sighed, 'This is what happens to me with every job I've ever had. The boss man calls me into the office for negotiations on my future employment within the company. After discussions, we conclude that I should leave the company, and we both agree on it.'

Sinead smartly replied, 'You mean they sack you, Dad, don't you?' Her eyes assessed him warily.

Martin burst into laughter and said, 'There's no pulling the wool over your eyes, darling.'

A sense of relief overcame Martin. He surprised himself. Telling Sinead some of his deepest feelings, admitting to his faults, felt strangely liberating in its honesty. She hadn't judged him for it either.

Sinead leaned back into the couch and closed her eyes. Martin continued talking.

'The biggest failure of our family is me,' he confessed. 'I can't keep my mouth shut. I've always dived in headfirst without thinking of any consequences, and it has got me nowhere in life. I've lived by the motto 'It's easier to ask for forgiveness than to ask for permission first, and it hasn't served me well.'

Sinead blinked, smirking, then astutely replied, 'You're feeling sorry for yourself, Da, aren't you?'

Martin, cornered, tried to deflect Sinead's painfully astute observation. 'Look, Sinead, you're a smart lass, so I'm not gonna string you a line. Things have been tough for us, but I have your mam, Shane and you as my lucky charms. I couldn't have wished for anything more.'

'I'm not a child anymore, Da, so stop talking to me as if I am. I know things are shit sometimes; you don't have to pretend life is all rosy. This damn tumour makes people take pity on me. I don't know what I hate more, the disease or the pity? Everyone always trying to shield me from reality.'

Martin fixed his gaze on her, 'Sinead Lynch, listen to me, I'm not shielding you from anything. I've set a precedent in this family for mishaps in life, so unfortunately, the bar has to be lower. Yes, things aren't and weren't always easy. Your nanny Philomena brought three of us up on her own. The old man was no good, and your nana did the best she could raising us. We were poor, and things were tough.

'Did I ever tell you that we were so poor, the first brother that got up always picked the best socks that didn't need darning and, because my sister's arse was so big, if we older kids ran out of underwear, we'd end up wearing her knickers –'

Sinead interrupted, laughing scornfully, 'Let me see how this goes now, Da – right… and at Christmas, if you were lucky enough, you'd get a satsuma in your stocking, and you were thankful.'

'Hey smarty pants,' Martin chided, 'this house only has one spot for a comedian, and I'm here as the top bill every week. Anyways, before I was rudely interrupted, spilling my heart out to you… When I a child, I was about to tell you that when I failed maths so many times, I can't even count on one hand,' he roared laughing at his own joke.

'But, despite all this, I have my talents. I can calculate odds and the horses form with the click of my fingers, and I know everything about books, but I have no time to read them. My life has taken twists and turns. I could have gone down a different path in life. My point to you is not to dwell on the past or think about all that has already gone before. Seize every opportunity life throws at you… oh yeah,' he remembered, 'and stay off the drink for a bit.'

Smiling at his advice and slipping on her headphones, Sinead closed her eyes once more and began to drift off under the spell of music. Martin settled down into the couch, the waft of the scented candles and the rhythm of the music through Sinead's headphones pleasingly soporific. The shadows of the candle flames swirled around on the ceiling and hypnotised him. Sinead lay drowsing as Martin gently stroked her scalp. Her breathing became deep and regular. The beat of the music acted as a lullaby as they both drifted off to sleep.

CHAPTER 19

It was the evening before one of Martin's scheduled driving jobs. Recently, he'd been regularly called upon to carry out some 'driving' duties for the O'Driscoll family. He couldn't refuse work as he had a debt to clear with them after agreeing to borrow money that he spent at Declan's gambling tables. He lost the lot. They owned him.

His task had been to deliver stolen cars ready to be shipped abroad to random locations in the heart of Dublin, hiding them in private lots by the river. Martin knew the cars weren't rental cars awaiting repairs, as the O'Driscoll's had insinuated. Martin played along with it, although they all knew legitimate work was not for the O'Driscolls. The cars were always high-end models, and the destination was only ever a one-way journey. Payment for each drop-off was left in an envelope stored in the boot compartment.

Anxiety plagued Martin during these errands, causing knots of fear to twist in his stomach. The consequences of something going wrong or getting caught would have a terrible effect on his family, and he was not naive. His appetite diminished, and the worry prevented him from sleeping the night before each job. As he tossed and turned in bed, his restlessness kept Bridget awake, and both of them emerged the next morning in a foul mood. Bridget often questioned Martin about what was bothering him, but obviously, he could not tell her. He sometimes said that he had had a bad run of horses beaten at the post. The less Bridget knew, the less stress was on her shoulders.

Soon after getting up, anxiety plagued him. Sweat patches bloomed under Martin's arms. He hadn't sprayed any deodorant on that morning. He'd been agitated, biting his nails as he prowled around the house, snapping at everyone. As he watched TV, Martin continuously flicked through the channels, unable to settle on one.

Drinking a sneaky shot of neat Vodka first thing calmed his nerves. In turn, it stopped him from shaking. It was the only spirit that couldn't be smelt on his breath. A small liquor flask was hidden inside his jacket pocket to get him through the day. Once the job was completed, it was only then that he would be able to relax.

Pacing up and down the hallway, Martin waited for his pick-up point confirmation to arrive at his phone. At the sound of the beep of an incoming message, he scrolled down through the information and repeated it back silently to himself. The details were sparse – just the pick-up point. The ignition key or card was always placed inside a magnetic box and stuck to the vehicle's underside. If it had rained the evening before or on the day, he knew he'd get wet and dirty lying down on the kerb to retrieve the key. Thankfully the day was due to be dry.

Martin wore a smart black suit with a clean, crisp white shirt and matching tie, but with a pair of white trainers. He found them comfortable to drive in. He deliberately wore the suit to blend in with other office workers on their daily commute. Staring into the wardrobe mirror, Martin repeated the address back to himself. It was too early to leave, but he wanted to get out of the house to get some fresh air. With time on his hands, his mind went into overdrive, thinking about what could happen if things went wrong – a decade in prison, he assumed. Not being able to see his family or talk to them frightened him. He wanted to make a change for himself and his family's future but, instead, he was drawn deeper into criminal activity. The worry and constant looking over his shoulder had caused him to lose weight, and his suit was roomy.

Martin left the house and strolled to the local cab office. The day was bright, and thankfully it hadn't rained in the last 24 hours. Walking past The Telegraph, he heard lively music. Checking his watch, he looked into the main bar. Staff were idly scanning the newspapers as only a few patrons loitered about. The music echoed down from the upstairs function room. As he reached the top of the staircase, he stopped to watch what was going on. Today was ballroom dancing day.

This was a club held twice a month and organised by Kathleen but run by a local couple, Eddie and Mary Cassidy. Mary arranged the dance routines and collected the monthly fees. Eddie set up the loudspeaker system and supplied and managed the music. Martin watched in awe as Kathleen glided elegantly across the floor. Martin caught Eddie's attention and walked over to him.

With confidence, he asked, 'My wife and I were thinking of joining this group. So, I thought I'd pop in to see how advanced the dancers were.'

Eddie looked pleased with Martin's interest and replied, 'It's not a competition here, lad; people come here to rekindle their misspent youth. Nobody here is looking for brownie points; it's just a getaway from what's out there.' Pointing outside the window, Eddie sat back on his stool. They both chuckled.

Martin nodded for approval to look through Eddie's catalogue of CDs.

Eddie said graciously, 'Ah go-ahead, lad.' His hands rested on his stomach.

Martin began to search through the rows of CDs. His fingers tracked along the titles until he found an artist that appealed to him. The contemporary dance was coming to an end when Martin whispered into Eddie's ear, 'When the next dance starts, could you slip this track on?' His eyes fixed on Eddie's, 'I want to surprise someone here.'

'Sure,' Eddie agreed.

Martin patted him on the shoulder in thanks. The participants parted to take a breather before the following dance routine began. Cruising in between the dancers, Martin approached Kathleen from behind. Loosening his tie, he released his shirt collar button and greeted Kathleen with a gentle tap on the shoulder. As she turned around, a surprised cheerful look on her face greeted him.

'Well, hello there, Martin,' Kathleen said in surprise. Tilting her head, she smiled at him.

A cheeky grin stretched across his face. It was a look that had got him everywhere with the ladies in his youth. Taking two steps back, he slowly bowed in front of her. While still maintaining eye contact, he held his hand out to her and, in an exaggerated voice, said, 'May I have this next dance, my lady?'

Though he was drawing attention from onlookers, Kathleen nevertheless admired the gesture. She looked bemused but entertained him. 'You certainly can, Mr Darcy.'

Pretending to pinch an imaginary ball gown on either side of her, she curtseyed in front of him. Martin nodded over to Eddie. Mary had buzzed around swapping dance partners and had the class ready for the next number.

'Valentine Moon' started to play over the speaker. Martin held Kathleen around her waist with his two index fingers pressed gently against the small of her back. Her body felt the same as it had twenty years ago. They both gazed into each other's eyes, unashamed of the fond memories of their youth returning.

For all of Martin's misdemeanours, he was held in high regard as an exceptional dancer in his youth. Back then, dancing was deemed in the same light as riding a bike – once you learnt it, you never forgot it. The slow pace sped up as the orchestral pitch breathed life into the routine. Kathleen's eyes kept on Martin's as he coaxed her confidently around the dance floor. She watched him as he concentrated on his manoeuvres. His trainers squeaked as he spun her around, bringing a wry smile to her face.

'Good choice of music. I know what you're trying to do. Just for this dance, I'll allow it, Martin.'

She studied his face for a moment as Martin's eyes were averted. Martin's posture and the music took Kathleen back to her youth. She recalled the freedom of life back in her twenties, the happiness, the carefree nature of her days. The way Martin used to look at her as a young man brought butterflies to her stomach. The way he looked at her now, she felt twenty-two years old all over again.

The music was infectious. Kathleen's hair clung to one side of her face with the momentum of the dance. Martin inhaled the perfumed breeze around them. Reaching the French verse, the moment took over. The passion in the vocals and the raucousness of the symphonies bellowed out across the function room, and it felt like they were the only two people there. Then, suddenly, it was over. The music came to silence. Standing apart, they held each other's fingertips lightly, reluctant to release them.

Kathleen's breathing slowed down, and her neck flushed. Her eyes were alight with nostalgia. In the blink of an eye, Martin saw all the heartache of her past flash before her eyes. It brought her back to reality. A tinge of sadness shaded her face. Martin was out of breath and covered in sweat. Their fingertips separated as the hairs on their arms bristled.

Tilting her head to one side, Kathleen took a few steps backwards and said lightly, 'Thanks, Martin.'

'Thank you, Miss Kelly,' he replied.

Kathleen's smile disappeared. As her face turned sullen, she said,

'You need to let go of that girl, Martin. She disappeared a long time ago. I'm Mrs Hennessey now and always will be.' Turning around, Kathleen walked away to mingle with the other dancers.

Martin, all of a sudden, felt the surge of youth leave him. He slowly walked away from the dance floor towards the staircase, passing Eddie on his way. He raised his hand and nodded to Eddie, who was sipping tea and eating a biscuit. Eddie acknowledged him with a return nod. Then, Martin froze as he heard his name being called out; he turned back around.

'Oh Martin!... MARTIN.'

His ears pricked up. It was Kathleen who emerged at the edge of the dance floor. Gawking at her, his eyes filled with excitement. He summoned bravado, trying to shed the lost puppy look from his face.

Their eyes fixed on each other for the final time when Kathleen shouted across the room at him, 'Oh Martin – you need to have a bath.' She gave him a wink before disappearing back amongst her fellow companions.

Martin looked down at himself, deflated. He saw that his clothes were rumpled and damp. Turning back around he glanced at Eddie, who had heard the comment and was choking on his biscuit in a fit of laughter. Lifting the lapels of his jacket, Martin sniffed the inside of his shirt. A sweet and ripe odour stung his senses. Wincing, he continued to walk downstairs and out into the fresh air.

CHAPTER 20

Declan arrived at the pub at noon and headed straight inside. He had called his associates earlier to come in for a meeting. It was an important meeting, and he made it clear that everyone should attend no matter what they had planned. They were all told the meeting was to discuss an issue that could jeopardise their incomes. Dillon had finished refilling the snacks and needed to replenish the upstairs bar. Kieran was also on shift behind the bar. It suited Declan that Dillon wasn't going to be around. He trusted him, but there was probably going to be some unsavoury comments made about specific individuals. Declan wasn't prepared to have his territory undermined.

Declan wanted Kieran around the group of men to familiarise himself with their faces before being brought into the fold. He glanced around at the bar. Rays of sun slanted in through the metal-framed windows and streaked across the tables. It felt soothing. Dust motes came to life, and dead flies basked in the morning glow inside the bay windows as a felting of dust lined the surface. He thought there was something pleasurable about the smell of stale lager and old cigarettes embedded in the carpet. First thing in the morning, years' worth of spillages created the perfect aroma of nostalgia.

The entrance doors swung open; the spring hinges cluttered shut. Billy and Johnny arrived and immediately argued about what pint they were going to sample first.

Declan squinted at them in the searing light and cut them off. 'You're fecking late – follow me.' Leading the way, Declan paced to the back of the pub. It was a secluded area that had a large round table which would host the meeting. Two patrons were tucked away at the table in conversation. With an intimidating look, Declan brashly said,

'You two – fuck off to another table. My young fella at the bar will see you right for a drink on the house.'

One of the men, a bear of a man, rose in indignation and stared Declan down, then thought better of it and trudged off. Settling down at the table, Declan was pleasantly surprised as he slotted into the groove of the big man's mould, where it was warm and snug. 'This is grand – feels like a fecking bear has been nestling here.'

Shuffling his backside, he made himself comfortable as he hollered out to the bar, 'Kieran – bring out the coffee and teas, son.'

Billy and Johnny didn't look impressed. They were hoping the meeting would turn into a piss-up. Declan sighed as all nine men turned up about the same time. Naturally, they were all concerned and so had arrived on time, intrigued and somewhat worried. All of them were seasoned criminals in their field. They sat down and, agenda aside, focussed on preparing their teas and coffees.

Brady, known as the bruiser, was one of the longest-established associates who worked for Declan. He was a man of few words. Brady asked once; then bruises appeared until Brady got the correct answer. He was tall, broad and as bald as a coot. His head showed a deep scar from a bottle attack. A knife scar ran from his temple down to his chin, giving him an even more frightening look. His brother worked for the O'Driscolls; it was he who Brady liaised with on transactions that were to take place in Declan's territory. Like Billy and Johnny, Declan trusted him.

Next to him was his close ally Emmet Byrne. An astute man, Emmet was also an ex-Guard. When he was a young man, he had joined the force, but an altercation out of uniform deemed him unfit to serve.He served time after he hospitalised an innocent man in a dispute over ayoung lady. He had contacts in the Gardai and knew the law inside out.

Alongside him was Jim Kennedy. He was an ex-docker who knew the port operational practices in detail. Jim had first-hand knowledge of the consignment routes and destinations. He had joined ranks with Declan after bitterly getting laid off from a shipping company following thirty years of loyal service. Jim still had reliable contacts within the port which he paid for intel on incoming shipments.

Across the table from him sat Ryan Quinn. Ryan was an ex-military man who was meticulous in everything he did. He was head debt-collector, and his attention to detail was exceptional. Everything was collected and managed via an old-fashioned accounts book. Nothing was processed on computers, online, or backed up. Ryan was of a breed who didn't like change. He stuck to traditional bookkeeping methods and told Declan that if modern methods of computer formats took over, he would tender his resignation. Declan respected him, his old-school methods worked, and he let him control the financial side of his operations in his own way.

The rest of the associates were second-level personnel. They followed instructions from the others and acted as stalwart figures for collecting monies and distributing stock to street traders in the suburbs and city. A rap of Declan's signet ring against the table silenced conversation. He had their full attention. Settling back in their chairs, jackets and shoes were slipped off. An unpleasant odour emerged from under the table; nobody laid claim to distributing it – it stank.

Waving away an imaginary fly, Declan breathed in his coffee before he spoke.

'As some of you are aware, recent planned activities for us to acquire certain goods have been breached. Our efforts have been undermined, meaning we either have a snitch in our organisation, or someone unknowingly is talking to parties outside our circle of trust,' Declan cast his eyes around at each man, before he continued.

'Every time we have targeted a trailer recently, another group have been informed and beaten us to the merchandise. Our latest target was a trailer filled with branded sports clothing that had left the docks and parked up outside town for the night. Once filtered through our merchants who supply to the streets, this could have provided us all with a handsome profit. All of you here are trusted men. Well, I thought you were trusted… until now.'

Shifting in their seats, startled faces scanned one anothers', searching for clues with daggered eyes. Declan's arms locked straight against the table as he stretched his back out. Others sat upright, mirroring his moves as if this would eliminate them from suspicion.

He carried on. 'I have trusted all of you men for years. Now information is being relayed to another source which is now tearing our livelihoods apart. Our chain of supply and demand is in jeopardy. If we can't supply, and there is a whisper that someone else can trade in place of us, all our contacts will desert us.'

Doubt spread across tense faces as each man looked to the man next to him. They sincerely trusted each other, and the thought that one of them was a snitch offended them all. The old-fashioned motto of Honour amongst Thieves was held in high regard within this band of brothers. Watching the mannerisms of the men around him suspiciously, Declan did have misgivings about two of his menial employees.

A week ago, he had set up a scenario to test them. He made a call in their presence that contained false information about a hit on a potential cargo trailer coming in from Europe. The run took place as planned, and nothing untoward had happened. He was sure these two men had heard the location, but nobody had beaten them to it as on previously planned hits. This, he felt, proved that there was no leak in his cluster of associates and confused him even further.

Kieran had finished serving teas and coffees when Shane sauntered in and perched himself at the bar. A packet of peanuts glided through the air into Shane's grasp. Kieran and Shane joked and giggled between them, one on either side of the bar as they laughed at video clips on their mobile phones. Declan gestured to Kieran to clear the table, and Kieran put down the phone and nodded to Shane to wait.

Bickering had erupted amongst the men at the table regarding who had the greatest length of service working with Declan. Twisting his neck, trying to stretch out the knots in his shoulders, Declan interrupted the chatter. 'Look, gents – we need some answers here today otherwise we'll all be finished before the year is out. I need you to put your ears to the streets to get me some answers. Someone is making us out to be fools; I won't settle for that.'

Back at the bar now, Kieran and Shane listened with rapt interest, facing away from the table so as not to be noticed. Shane was trying to make Kieran laugh with a series of exaggerated facial expressions. Kieran motioned for him to stop and tried to get his dad's attention.

Noticing Kieran staring at him, Declan said, 'Jaysis, son, speak up.'

Kieran felt a rumble of anger inside him. He hated when his father belittled him like this in front of his associates. He looked down sheepishly and with shaky breaths and said, 'Dad, I think the leak is coming from that side of the bar.' He pointed at the jukebox on the customer side of the bar. Declan looked puzzled.

One of the associates dismissed his comment by waving his hand away and saying, 'Arhh – away on with that, lad.'

Lowering his eyes, Kieran tried not to blush. Feeling the heat rise up his neck, he let it go and carried on filling the dishwasher when Shane, annoyed, spoke up and said to Declan, 'For crying out loud, listen to him. He misses nothing from behind this bar.'

Declan cocked his head at the sight of his son's friend sitting at his bar, munching *his* peanuts, telling him how to manage *his* business. Glancing at Kieran, he waved a dismissive hand at Shane. 'What the fuck are you even doing here, Shane Lynch? You're like a fly around a cow's arsehole; you're always fucking there.'

Standing his ground, Shane shouted back, 'Fuck's sake, listen to him, will you.'

Declan glared at Shane and bit on his lower lip. He could see the same defiance in him as he saw in his no-good excuse for a father, Martin. Declan stared at him menacingly. Shane held his gaze, refusing to withdraw.

Finally, Declan stood up, drew a deep breath, and the sharpness in his features softened as he nodded at Kieran before saying,

'Son, what's going on? Speak freely now.'

His gaze flitted around the table, daring anyone to challenge him. The group's attention turned to Kieran. It took him a few seconds to find his voice.

'I think there are what I call watchmen in here day and night. The first one arrives around lunchtime every day.' His voice wavered. 'They mingle with the punters and always join in with other people's conversations.' Kieran had their full attention. 'I think there's two of them. They look shifty and always drink a lager, then follow it up with a shandy. They swap shifts around teatime; then the second one always follows a pattern of making a call from about 5 pm and every two hours after that. It's always a short call, Dad.'

Rubbing a knuckle back and forth across the solidness of his chin, Declan, consumed with the possibilities running through his head, replied, 'They could be anyone, son. What makes you think they're reporting back to someone?'

Shane nodded encouragingly at Kieran to continue.

Kieran spoke up again, 'I've watched them. They never dial a number. They just press redial each time and during the changeover they exchange the phone over between them.'

A croaky voice from one of the associates spoke up and said, 'Jesus Christ, you mean to say the Guards are crawling over this place every day and –'

Declan cut him short, 'Believe, you, me, if that were happening, I'd know about that from my man on the inside.'

Kieran continued more confidently, 'I know they're not Guards. One of them cops off with *laid back Leanne* on a Friday night most weeks. He gives her one in the jacks at the rear of the bar before the crowds pick up. One night he dropped his driving licence in the cubicle, and I found it when I had to sign off the toilet checks.'

The table erupted in laughter in appreciation of Kieran's lack of discretion.

Brady scathingly commented, 'That sperm receptacle – I thought everyone had cottoned on to her.'

The table quietened down, and one of Kieran's new-found fans joked, 'You'll be chief of the Gardai in years to come, my boy.' He chuckled at his joke before catching Declan's eyes pinned to him.The table fell to silence, and heads swivelled between Declan and the joker as everyone turned to watch. Pinching the bridge of his nose, Declan tried to stay calm.

'Really, son, that's great awareness, well done, boy,' he reassured Kieran.

As the meeting drew to a close, Declan thanked the men individually with a squeeze on their shoulders. Giddy at the bar from the respect, Shane and Kieran watched as Declan sauntered over to them. He attempted small talk with the lads that soon became uncomfortable for all three of them. Kieran, knowing his father wanted to ask him more about the driving licence but didn't want to show a lack of authority. The driving licence was handed over to Declan without a word.

Declan smiled and said, 'I need you to be more upfront with me in future, son. That was great info today, well done.'

Taken aback by his father's praise, Kieran smiled nervously at his hands. Unsure, Declan reached over, and a quick embrace took place before both pulled away as if caught in the act of something. It was an unfamiliarity that neither party knew how to deal with. Leaving the bar with his back to the lads, Declan clenched his fist in joy; his son had made him proud. As he bounced through the doors, the sunshine strained his eyes; he hoped it would continue to be a good day until his mobile rang. Recognising the number, he unnervingly answered it. The person on the other line spoke without giving Declan room for reply. It was an informative call and not a conversation before the line went dead. His contact at the port had just delivered more bad news. Rolling his eyes to the heavens, Declan let out a heavy sigh.

CHAPTER 21

Declan toyed with his phone before he made a call. He greeted the caller, a beaming smile etched across his face, as he dangled the licence in front of him.

'Good afternoon, detective – we need to talk. I need you to run a background check on a Daniel Conway. You'd better pray he's not one of yours.'

'Don't ever ring me on this line again and be so blatant in your requests,' chastised Detective Muldoon. There was nothing playful in his tone. 'I have, just this morning, walked out of an intelligence meeting with other agencies from UK divisions and Interpol regarding European drug gangs aiming to distribute via Ireland. When, out of the blue, details regarding ownership of a vehicle registered to your good self cropped up. In answer to your request. YES… we need to talk, and you had better be open with me about everything you're involved in.'

The conversation continued briefly; there was only so much either could give away over the phone. They agreed to meet up before the end of the day. Declan hung up. He stood in the warm air, reflecting on everything he had built up. The sun's rays cast heat across his face. Why does the world seem a better place when the sun shines, he thought. That moment of brief respite left him as, feeling disheartened, he contemplated the business losses he was facing.

The meeting took place in a local coffee shop on the high street in town. Both parties deemed it safe by dint of its busyness with shoppers constantly hustling in and out of the branch. They had agreed to meet at 5 pm. By 5:05 pm, Declan had arrived and was looking around him. Faceless shoppers and business people darted in and out of the shop, mainly for takeaways.

Satisfied Muldoon hadn't arrived yet; Declan joined the queue and gazed at the selection of available coffee concoctions. Some of them Declan couldn't pronounce, and most of them he had never heard of. He smiled at the young girl who greeted him at the counter, his eyes focused on the menu when he caught the reflection behind her of the detective approaching the counter.

'Just give me two coffees I can drink instead of playing with,' he was curt. The coffees were left on the end of the counter and the pair took them, nodding their thanks, and made themselves comfortable at a table at the back.

Declan started the conversation. 'Apologies if I put you in a tight spot earlier,' he said diffidently, 'I was a bit too keen.'

Muldoon batted away the apology with a dismissive shake of his head as he stirred his coffee and replied, 'No harm done. This morning's briefing was a bit too close for comfort.'

The gaggle of low key conversation surrounded them, acted as background noise. Declan peered over at the next table where an elderly couple sat. Satisfied that their conversation wasn't going to be overheard by eavesdroppers, he settled more comfortably into his seat.

Peeling his coat off, the detective revealed a dark grey suit. Stress and fatigue plagued his face. A deep sigh followed as he palmed his tie against his shirt. He lifted a messenger bag onto the table and produced a manilla folder from it.

Leaning back in his seat, Declan eyed the folder like the finding of a bad smell. Cream foam skimmed his lips as he sipped his coffee. Glancing down at the folder, he raised his eyebrows at Muldoon before saying, 'Looks important. Is this what I'm getting for my money?'

Smothering a yawn with the wave of his hand, Muldoon placed his hand down on the folder before he began to speak. 'This city, and other connecting ones, have come to our attention as being locations of high-density drug smuggling. Interpol has informed us there is a European network connected with some new blood on the scene. They are planning on overrunning this city.' His voice had an edge to it, 'Bigger fish are outfrying you, my friend.'

The skin stretched over Declan's knuckles as he clenched his fists tightly. The gentle thump of the background music caused ripples in his coffee. Remembering his surroundings, he clenched his jaw harder to remain calm, and muttered, 'The fucking O'Driscolls.' The name slipped out before he realised he'd said anything.

The detective smirked as he relinquished his slight touch on the folder. He looked satisfied and said, 'That name check you asked me so politely to chase? That Daniel Conway turns out to be nothing but a pussy. A few driving convictions and another one for affray, that's all. He's certainly not one of ours, or ever was.' Muldoon fixed his gaze on Declan pointedly, 'So, I'll accept your apology for that.'

Declan didn't respond, uncomfortable with the direction of the conversation as it moved out of his control. The heat had started to funnel its way up his chest. Knowing that Muldoon had the upper hand over something, Declan didn't want to push his luck until more information was revealed.

'Officers from the Limerick division were included in today's proceedings which provided intel on two prolific criminal brothers. They have grand ambitions of running their organisation, exporting stolen luxury cars. The proceeds of which are then used to fund the importation of class A drugs on a scale that would devastate any major city in Ireland. Do the names Patrick and Thomas Finnerty ring a bell for you? They're already making a name for themselves working alongside the O'Driscolls' outfit.'

'All this is starting to make sense now,' Declan answered. 'A few of my clients have had visits from these chancers taking liberties.' The cogs clicked into place inside his head as he started piecing together recent events.

Muldoon continued, 'If the O'Driscolls' are mixed up with these two characters, Mr O'Driscoll had better know what he's letting himself in for.' His tone was curt. 'From what we've learnt about these two, I'd say Mr O'Driscoll is getting in way over his head.' Taking a sip of coffee, Muldoon licked the foam from his upper lip before revealing more information.

'These boys are a nasty pair of fuckers. They grew up and worked alongside a large family in Limerick called the Dooleys. Word has it, they started acting the bollix and arranging deals way above their paygrade. The head honcho of this outfit, who is referred to only as Dooley, naturally took offence to this and cut them loose.

'The pair were each given a golden handshake to start again in a new city, under the condition they never set foot back in Limerick. Dooley thought that was the end of them until the sneaky bastards came back and slaughtered his dog. Apparently, this Dooley character loved that dog and put a bounty on the pair to be brought back to Limerick to be taken care of and, with that, here we are today.'

Easing the folder towards Declan, he motioned for him to take a look. Casually opening it, Declan glanced through the pages. A selection of surveillance images drew his attention. The glossy images showed stills of individuals captured on surveillance footage stealing cars. Declan passed his hand over his mouth and pinched his chin. He indicated he didn't recognise any of them with a shake of the head and a rueful grimace.

Leaning forward and crossing his arms, Muldoon paused for a few seconds before he spoke softly, 'You wouldn't be holding back on anything back from me, Declan, would you now? This understanding we have works both ways.'

Declan, subdued, shrugged his shoulders. Waiting for a response, Muldoon looked tired and burdened. He dragged his fingers down his face before glaring at Declan. 'I'm sorry to say I believe you.'A small laugh rumbled from his belly before he tutted, 'You're being played then, my friend.'

Declan ignored the remark. Affronted, he braced himself and sighed before saying, 'Go on, you have my full attention.'

Another folder emerged from under the table; Muldoon opened it and pointed to the first photo. 'The surveillance team captured this guy driving one of these vehicles. It was reported stolen and dropped off at a designated spot they were watching,' the detective's hand guided Declan through each photograph, enhancing the story.

'Another guy arrived about thirty minutes later and retrieved the key from underneath the car, then drove it back to the docks where we later found out it was being shipped abroad. Anyway, this drop-off guy is then caught in the surrounding area on CCTV footage being picked up by another fella in a van registered to… wait for it – to you and your hardware store.'

A frown line appeared across Declan's forehead, and a pulse developed in his temple as he flicked through the rest of the photographs one-by-one. Muldoon chided him, keeping the tone light, 'Sorry, buddy.' The anger on Declan's face was enough to show the detective that he recognised the driver.

Sliding his overcoat back on, the detective quietly spoke. 'I'll leave these with you. The original set is with the investigating team. I don't think you appreciate the predicament our arrangement puts me in. I'm not running the fucking *Sweeney* over here. I can't just duplicate files and trace known cons at your disposal. Every file and access login is recorded on our systems. An officer's signature can be traced to everything accessed. I've had to download these files onto a USB to print them off. If word got out of any association between your good self and I, I'd be finished –'

Declan interjected, 'I think you forget how our little arrangement started way, way back when. It was *your* good self that came to me if my memory serves me well.'

Both men stared at each other reproachfully. Dropping his head remorsefully, the detective was silent. 'I haven't forgotten the lengths you went to finding and saving my daughter. I also haven't forgotten how much money it cost me either. The rank I held and the resources I had to hand did me no good; I had to go elsewhere to find her. She's been clean now for years and has started a new life. My wife would never have forgiven me if she was found dead with a needle stuck in her arm, living with that toe rag. I'm grateful for what you did, Declan, but I'm getting older and have a lucrative pension pot for retiring. I don't want to jeopardise this. I've returned the favour. You have one more lifeline, and then we are done for good.'

There was a pleading note in Muldoon's gaze. Declan's brows furrowed as he mulled over the photos. Glancing up, he noted the detective was buttoning up his coat.

Anxiously, the detective prompted, 'There's just one more thing?'

Pretending not to hear, Declan reached inside his coat, pulled out an envelope and placed it on the table. Disgusted by the blatant display and seething, Muldoon whipped it up and shoved it into his bag. Silence thickened as the detective, leaving his coffee unfinished, shimmied past the backs of chairs on his way to the exit.

Declan gathered the photographs up. His eyes absorbed the figure captured on the surveillance footage. As his tongue smoothed across his bottom lip, the features of Martin Lynch came to life. Declan began to think back through who might have used the van to collect him. Even though covered under any named driver, only a handful of people were intrusted in using it. Declan recalled how last week he was short-staffed and asked David to help out for a couple of days in the hardware store. In desperation to get him to cover the shop, he allowed David to take the van home. David was a skilled tradesman and was regularly called upon for odd jobs in the pub and installing security measures for Declan's various businesses. This allowed him to use the van without raising suspicion of its use.

Martin being brought into the equation riled him. Endless questions plagued his mind. What was he doing with the O'Driscolls? Was David or Martin the link to whoever took over Declan's haul at the port? Had Martin struck a deal with O'Driscoll or the Finnerty brothers? He trusted David, he thought, but this had now undermined everything he knew. Letting his guard down had come back to bite him on the backside. Someone was going to feel Declan's wrath. He had already decided who.

CHAPTER 22

Martin paid his cab fare with cash when he reached the pick-up point. The residential street he had arrived at was a private road. Detached houses and long driveways linked to detached garages sat back from the street in mature gardens. His mind went blank, and he examined his phone for the collection details. Nervousness was starting to set in again. Martin took a deep breath to compose himself and began to recite the details in his head again, noting each vehicle he passed. It wasn't until he got to the end of the road that he saw the matching registration in sight. Sighing with relief, Martin briefly scanned around before he laid down on the road beside the car to retrieve the key-box from the undercarriage. He found it easily and pressed the button to unlock the vehicle.

The alarm beeped once before he dusted himself down and sat inside. It was the most luxurious car Martin had ever picked up. A top of the range SUV in metallic silver. It was something he only saw in adverts on billboards on the drive up to the airport. He patted the inside of his suit jacket to make sure his leather gloves were there. After making the sat nav hard work, he left the side roads and joined the main motorway. Fussing about with the radio frustrated him as he couldn't find a broadcast with live horse racing.

His short fuse ignited as he yelled out, 'Bollixs, ye!' He found a station offering hits from the eighties and nineties and stopped fiddling.

The radio DJ announced, 'The next track after the break is '*Robbie Williams* with *Angels*'... see you soon.'

Martin rejoiced, 'Get in there... ha! Christ! I wish I had written that song. I'd be a fecking millionaire by now.'

The journey was a smooth ride as Martin cruised under the speed limit. Holding his grip on the steering wheel low to his thighs, he kept his leather gloves out of sight. As he neared the Moore Street Mall in town traffic slowed to a stop-start sequence as cabs pulled into laybys collecting shoppers. Slumping back and releasing the window for air, Martin's face beamed as the song's interlude played over the thrum of the idling engine. Feeling cocky, he belted out his own tuneless rendition of a classic. Shoppers gave Martin a second look as he warbled his way through each verse. The song faded out as the DJ broke into a spiel about a competition to win concert tickets.

Slowing down at a set of traffic lights, a loud siren echoed through the inside of his cavern of comfort and startled him. As the shrill noise stopped, Martin glimpsed into his rear mirror and saw a Garda patrol car following with its sirens flashing. An arm appeared out of the driver's side and gestured for Martin to pull over. His body tensed up, and the back of his shirt started to saturate with sweat. Tension coiled in his stomach as he fumbled for chewing gum; a sharp surge of mint woke his senses as he chewed exaggeratedly.

Finding a safe place to pull over, he turned off the engine and waited nervously. An officer heaved himself out of his vehicle and approached the driver's side. Quickly removing the gloves, Martin's knuckles pressed white as he clung tightly onto the steering wheel. The officer looked close to retirement age. Stopping, he stretched his back before eventually reaching Martin. Sweat droplets slowly ran from Martin's armpit down along his rib cage, settling into the waistband of his trousers. He turned to meet the officer's gaze. Martin gave a quizzical but innocent smile, hiding his anxiety. The officer nodded as his eyes scoped around for anything suspicious. The cold air spiked Martin's skin as the officer spoke.

'Do ye have any idea why we stopped you, young man?'
Martin looked perplexed at his question.

The officer continued, 'We noticed your passenger brake light was out. We're finishing our shift and were going to let you pass on by but we heard this racket coming from the inside of your car while you were waiting for the lights.' He rubbed his nose. 'So, we were curious young man... it sounded like a cat being strangled.'

Looking embarrassed, Martin couldn't help himself and remarked, 'Can I sing you an encore, officer.'

The officer smirked whilst still scoping out the inside of the car. The officer's back was now troubling him, he stretched again and remarked, 'Good evening now, young man... be on your way and be sure to get that bulb sorted soon... you know we are due a fall of snow any time now. The last thing you'll want is another driver ploughing into the back of you. Oh, and if I were you, young man, I'd stick to the day job and forget the singing. Where are you going?'

Looking meek, Martin replied, 'Home officer... just home.'

Sniffing the air in Martin's circumference, the officer ended the conversation, saying, 'Be sure to enjoy a hot bath when you get there...that cat you were strangling smells like it's pissed itself in here... bye now.' Limping back to his patrol car, the officer clutched his lower back.

With eyes focused on his rear mirror, Martin could see the officer's partner on his radio looking straight back at him. He waited while the officers buckled up and disappeared into the flow of traffic. Dropping his head on the steering wheel, Martin's stomach churned. He reached for his flask stored inside his jacket and emptied its contents. His phoned beeped; looking around him, he realised he had dropped it in the footwell. The message read: *Hurry up, bastard.*

On arriving with the car near the river, Martin was blinded by flashing headlights as he wiped down the dashboard and steering wheel. David was waiting to collect Martin at the drop off point. A flurry of sleet had obscured David's windscreen as the wipers powered to clear the sludge. The van was at least a decade old, and it was initially white before it had been eaten away by rust.

Martin jumped in. 'I arrive in luxury and get picked up in this shit heap.'

Leaning across Martin, David flipped the door open and held his hand aloft, saying, 'Well, if you'd rather walk – then...'

Wheezing with laughter, Martin replied, 'You wouldn't believe what I've been through on the journey coming off from the norrier. I got pulled over from the shades. For fuck's sake, I thought my time was up – do you have any drink in the cab, man? I've an awful throat on me.'

A dented lager can emerged from behind David's seat. He handed it to Martin while concentrating on the road ahead of him. Martin continued to fill David in on his exploits with the Guards. As sleet fell, causing havoc with the swishing windscreen wipers, David remarked, 'Arhh, shit wan… you're some jammy client, Martin.'

A brief altercation between the men started as David, trying to dispel the misted windscreen, opened the windows. Martin, freezing, kept trying to close them. Taking the same route as Martin took earlier, he could now see the funny side of his meeting with the Guards. Every gear change cranked as the clutch released too soon, causing Martin to shudder. The sleety coat of ice blurred the windscreen as David bobbed his head from side to side, searching for a clear patch of vision ahead. Draining his can, Martin exhaled deeply before he spoke. 'Can I talk seriously for a bit?'

David chastised him, 'When do you ever take life seriously, Martin?'

'Fuck off then.'

'Go on; I'm listening… shoot!' David countered.

'I'm tired of this shite. This tug today has put things into perspective for me. The thought of getting caught and doing time scares me, man. I can't be away from Bridge or the kids. It would finish me off. I know I've got some cash in the back pocket for this job, but it's just not worth it. How do I get out of all this mess I'm in?'

David contemplated his answer before speaking. 'Firstly, Martin, you need to keep your gob shut. I'm serious. I tried to save you in the card game but… no, no, you knew better – Martin with the drink inside him doesn't listen to anyone. If you came off the drink, Martin, your whole outlook on life would look completely different. There… I said it, is that what you wanted to hear?'

'Jaysis, there was no need to insult me,' Martin, ashamed, covered it with a joke.

'There you go again, Martin the jester, always putting on an act. We're all tired of it, Martin. Your wife, my sister, is deadbeat all the time. Fuck sake, man, if she knew what I know, she'd have walked away years ago. There you have it now, loud and clear. The question is, what are you gonna do about it yourself?'

Staring ahead, Martin acknowledged the truth silently but decided not to comment. They soon came to the end of the high street to head on back home when Martin recognised a figure at a bus stop. Looking closely, he made out it was their neighbour Mrs Mercer, waiting for the bus across the road. As the wind picked up along with the horizontal sleet falling, Martin nudged David to pull over and offer her a lift. Shaking his head but consenting, David ploughed across the two lanes slamming on the brakes and said, 'Sweet Mother Theresa, Martin, you do have a soft spot for all the aul ones.'

Cars beeped as their van blocked the lane. Martin jumped out to chaperone Mrs Mercer into the van. A cyclist braked and skidded behind the vehicle. When safe to do so, he rode past the driver's side. Enraged at the obstruction, the rider remonstrated with his arms as he passed.

'Fuck off, WANKER!' David shouted after him through the open window.

Mrs Mercer took her time getting in, launching into small talk as she sorted out her bags. Unaware of David's eagerness to move on, she flinched when David shouted out, 'Will you get a move on there, this traffic is fierce, and it's tipping down.'

The torrential sleet moved up a gear, blinding the windscreen even with the wipers on full tilt. In these conditions, nobody would have turned down a free lift home. For all of Martin's jesting with Mr and Mrs Mercer, he did respect everything they did for Sinead and Bridget. Mrs Mercer was in good form as she had won ten euros for her afternoon's activities in the bingo hall. Winnings Martin would typically dismiss as something insignificant to him, but he relished in her delight, for once.

Martin could see how frail and cold Mrs Mercer looked; he waited for a beat and asked her, 'Isn't there anyone you can travel to bingo with on cold days like this? I take it Mr Mercer isn't one for sitting around with a room full of ladies.'

Mrs Mercer shuffled in her seat uncomfortably; she replied, 'I don't have many close friends nowadays. I used to be close to my sister, but unfortunately, I lost her to the C-word many years ago.'

Martin paused before answering, 'I'm sorry, I hope she didn't suffer for long.'

Nodding, Mrs Mercer replied, 'I think she did, and what's more, I hope she still is to this day.'

David released a sudden burst of laughter. Martin, shocked and awed in equal measure, remonstrated, 'Steady on now, Mrs M, that's going at it a bit strong.'

'Well, I mean, she deserved it. After burying our mother and father, we moved from Enniskillen to Dublin. The stupid fool, me, let her handle the will. She shortchanged me after meeting this man – a CATHOLIC. I tell you! I tried to warn her about him, but no, she knew better. He squandered the money before he got a promise of work over there on the building sites, in London and she followed him like a lost lamb. She fell pregnant again and again and had three children, and no money to look after them, and yer man down in the pub every night. Some life she had, and I hope she regretted it ever since.'

Martin and David sniggered at each other before Martin answered, 'Well, I think we'll leave it there, Mrs M.'

The journey home was short as the sleet turned into sparse rain, although the forecast predicted far worse to come. Mrs Mercer appreciated the lift and told them so. Not because of the weather conditions but for the fact Martin could have driven straight past her, and she would have been none the wiser. For once, she had seen a different side to Martin. The van pulled into Holmewood Road and double-parked. Easing herself out, Mrs Mercer thanked the men again and said, 'Now, hang on here for a moment, I'll be right back.'

She left her bag on the passenger seat. Martin knew what was coming. He turned to David as the van idled and explained, 'Oh shite… she gives us a bottle of prosecco every month. Bridget won't touch the stuff because it's only 4%. It's like drinking fizzy water; you can't get pissed on it.' Martin tapped on the dashboard, 'Neither of us has the heart to tell her.' Breaking his heart laughing, David slapped the steering wheel.

Mrs Mercer approached the van out of breath, 'Now, I know you're not a wine drinker, Martin, but if you could see this gets to Bridget. It'll help her unwind on her night off. There will be another one for her next month. Now, I won't hear another word about it – take it,' she insisted.

Smiling graciously, Martin accepted the bottle and thanked her for the gesture. Mrs Mercer hobbled back indoors; David remarked, 'She's away with the fairies that one.'

Martin protested, 'Hold on now. She's a goodun'. A heart of gold for our Sinead and a grand neighbour to myself and Bridge.'

David shook his head in dismay at Martin's mawkishness as he shunted along the kerb outside Martin's house. Jumping out, Martin shouted back, 'Are ye coming in for a brew?'

David unwound his window and yelled back, 'Nah, I have to drop the van off before Declan realises I've been using it outside of hours. I'm going home for a shite, shower and, and then I'll be back to meet you in the pub later. What time are we meeting for Gerry's piss up tonight?'

'Come back in about an hour, and we'll head on up there together,'

Martin replied.

David nodded, then, looking up to the heavens, shouted back, 'This rain will cut the bollix off ye, I'll meet ye in there.'

The engine revved as he drove off. Winding down, Martin looked forward to a good night in The Telegraph. The aroma of sizzling sausages greeted him when he walked into the hall. With Bridget in his sights, he crept up behind her and surprised her by clutching her waist and kissing her neck as he brandished the bottle of prosecco aloft in one hand. She yelped and screamed out, 'Martin; you scared the bejesus outta me… let go of me. I've got to take the pan off the hob.'

She yelled upstairs, 'SINEAD!… SINEAD! Run your father a bath, sweetheart.'

Martin looked deflated and released Bridget.

'Are people trying to tell me something today or what? You're the third person today to suggest I take a bath.'

Sinead strolled into the kitchen and sunk her face into Martin's chest as she wrapped her arms around him. Her face pulled back within seconds, and she exclaimed, 'Da, you reek.' Pretending to be insulted, Martin chased her around the kitchen. She giggled and screamed as Martin pretended to stick her head in his armpit.

Out of breath, Martin said, 'Go and run your dad a bath now, darling.'

Sliding the bottle of prosecco into Sinead's palms, he continued, 'I'm gonna lie down for a minute before I jump in the bath. Pour this down the toilet, darling, and get shot of it.'

Bridget interrupted and shouted back, 'NO!... for God's sake, place it in the press with the others. I keep them and give them to Sinead's teachers at the end of the term; and Christmastime.' Turning her head while concentrating at the stove, she continued, 'They're a grand present with a card. Besides, teachers drink anything when they get home to unwind from all the noisy bleaters throughout their day.'

Sinead placed the bottle with the others and disappeared to her room after running the bath. Skipping his nap, Martin sneaked into the bathroom, locking the door behind him to hibernate, at least until dinner was served. Open shampoo bottles and shower gels lined the bath as Martin slipped beneath the water and drowned out the world around him. His nose was visible like a periscope as he submerged under the water, his feet playing skittles with the various bottles of shampoos guarding the taps, until they cascaded into the water.

Forty minutes later, Martin re-emerged. Steam and wet footprints followed him down the hallway. His skin was blotchy and red, the result of using Bridget's blunt razor and splashing cologne all over his shaven face. By the time he made it down to the kitchen, Bridget and Sinead had already eaten. Martin slumped down at the table as Bridget placed his dinner in front of him. Sizing it up and finding it lacking, he stuck it back into the oven for when he would come back home later.

'I can't eat this yet. I'll grab a sambo in the pub. I let that bath run too hot, and now I'm overcome with the heat. I feel like shite. I've left the bathwater for you, my love.'

'Did you shave in it?' Bridget asked.

'Yes!'

'Did you use the toilet?'

'Yes!'

'Did you flush it?'

'Erhh?'

'Did you take all the fresh towels in with you?'

'I forgot to bring them in, love.'

'So, what did you dry yourself off with then?'

'I used your bathrobe on the back of the door.'

'For crying out loud, Martin, I was looking forward to a long soak, and now you've ruined it. Did you put your clothes in the laundry basket?'

'I knew something had slipped my mind as I came out. Sorry love, in fact, just bin my pants; they're not fit for washing anymore. You'll see what I mean when you pick them up.'

'Chrissake, Martin, you've now given me an extra job or three before I run a fresh bath and curl up for the evening. I hope the toilet is flushed for your sake, Martin. Did you leave the door open while in there?'

'You know me, Bridge.'

'You're a bold piece, Martin Lynch. If I've told you once, I've told you a thousand times; there's enough damp in this house as it is. That means the toilet paper is now soaked. Wait a minute… did you hang a fresh roll up the way I showed you before and not just lay it on the holder? I give up... Don't I deserve to indulge myself at the end of a day, Martin Lynch?' she railed angrily.

'You come home, get your dinner on the table, your bath run for you and leave the place in a heap for me to clean up before you head out to the pub. What do YOU ever do for me? Why can't I take off to the pub for a night and forget everything going on around me? In fact, why can't I just take off on my own? That's right, Bridget making a life for herself; that would shock you all. Oh go on,' she said to his crestfallen face, 'just clear off out of here, Martin.' Bridget felt deflated. 'It's like looking after three children in this house.'

Martin didn't reply. He didn't know what to say. Stretching out, he left the earnings for the car delivery out for Bridget and grabbed the loose change on the sideboard and counted it. Bridget headed upstairs to clean up the bathroom. Reaching the front door, Martin shouted out, 'You'll need the mop in there, Bridge… LOVE YOU,' the front door slammed.

Martin's meagre earnings had always gone straight to Bridget to take care of all the household outgoings. He buried his head in the sand when it came to paying the bills. Instead, he let Bridget manage the lot. The ending of the day had been a relief for Bridget; she'd slogged through another tough shift in the care home. Martin's stressful day now over led to relief of sorts too. The future would hold a different scenario entirely if the Guards caught him driving a stolen vehicle. This was the predicament that Martin and Bridget (to a lesser degree as she was mostly kept in the dark) faced weekly and monthly.

No regular work for Martin concerned Bridget. He never told her about the illegal work he got. Bridget was no fool, though, and she knew that cash income was more than likely to be dodgy money, but it still went towards paying the bills. She turned a blind eye when it suited her. Martin was on top of the world, ready for the night's events ahead of him. His pockets were empty, but that hadn't stopped him planning a birthday drink for one of the lads, Gerry McGinty, in The Telegraph. Little did Gerry know, though, that it was probably going to be at his expense. Martin was happy.

Bridget padded upstairs, following the wet footprints in reverse. The hallway walls were dripping with condensation, reawakening a musty smell. As Bridget drained the bathwater, she dismissed the grime with a lazy wave, then headed into Shane's room. The door was open, and the hallway light gave her a glimpse as to what was ahead. His bedroom was a tip. Musty crumpled shirts sat dumped in the corner, layers of deodorant ingrained in the fabric to cover up the lack of washing. Dumped dirty football boots hid behind the door, only recognisable by the tatty laces dangling outside the clump of mud that encased each boot. His kit lay strewn across the bed, his shorts entwined with his boxers. Bridget picked up the material caked in mud, and as she turned them between her fingers, she dropped them, exclaiming, ‘Oh my God, that’s not mud.’

Sighing inwardly to herself, she felt defeated and left his room. After one more look in the bathroom, she listened to the gurgling as the bath drained. The tub had a lining of scum and grit around it, the ghost of Martin’s presence that trailed down to the plughole. A bar of wet soap had moulded itself to the bath. It took one more exerted effort of cleaning before she could refill it and soak away her troubles. She wanted to submerge herself in the water with her scents and oils to ease the tension from her shoulders.

Forty minutes later, after untangling the knots in her damp hair, she settled downstairs next to Sinead with a book and a glass of wine. Sinead nuzzled into Bridget’s neck and inhaled the scents in her hair while glued to the TV screen. It was the perfect ending to another stressful day.

CHAPTER 23

The Telegraph was quiet. There were just a few characters who sat in their regular daily spots. It was a way of life for them. They nursed their pints, determined to make them last a full hour before emptying their pockets of loose coins to balance up the cost of buying another. On cue, they then left to go home for their dinner. Dillon greeted them with the same pattern of mundane conversation every time. Every day seemed like Groundhog Day. Dillon grew tired of the monotonous discussions about the weather and tried to create a diversion by supplying newspapers at the bar. He'd hoped this would have stopped them talking to him. It didn't.

Some of the regulars had girlfriends. These lasses joined their partners every night. They never drank and acted as the nominated drivers, dropping off their partner's friends. Looking interested at first in their men's discussions, the novelty soon wore off, and they resigned themselves to a lifetime of boredom and regret. They usually had conversations with the staff instead of their partner's friends, and innuendo and comments from other male drinkers served as pick-me-ups to their tired egos. Trade picked up at the weekend, though, when drinkers filled the bar, and the pub had theme nights. It was bustling and entertaining, and the client base broadened somewhat.

Dillon had finished serving two customers when Martin arrived. Something caught Martin's eye perched up on the bar as he walked in. It was a printed A4 sign propped up against the optic bottles. The sign read 'Buy None! Get One Free!' Next to the sign was a stack of DVDs with one copy stood upright on display. Seeing Martin looking at the sign, Dillon glanced up and wiped his brow with the back of his hand, frowned, and said, 'Just don't fecking ask – I'm cursed I tell ye.'

Martin held his hands up defensively and replied, 'Jeez, you look like you've put your face on backwards there.'

Dillon reached up for a pint glass when Martin interrupted him and asked, 'Hold that for now… did you tape that programme I asked about last week?'

Dillon still had hold of the glass and replied, 'What? That lottery crap. Look, I pressed record from about 7 pm and switched it off around midnight. So, it's on there somewhere with my film...'

'Dillon, will ye be a good man and take us upstairs to have a gander at the recording.'

Dillon's eyes bulged as he shook his head in exaggerated shock, replying, 'You've got a hard neck on you, Martin. Are you off your rocker? If Declan caught you upstairs, he'd eat the head off me before skinning me alive in front of you.'

Martin had an edge to his voice and had to be careful not to come across as disrespectful. 'Calm the fuck down, Dillon. Look, we'll go upstairs, and if Declan finds out from anyone, you can just say I was helping you with the picture quality setup or something. Chill the fuck out, Dillon. Come on, man, it will take us no time up there.'

Dillon relented and, checking no one needed serving; they trailed off upstairs to the staff room. It was a basic room with a sofa bed, mini-fridge and a television. A satellite box rigged with cables connected to the big screen in the main bar. Fast forwarding through the recording, Martin came to the section with the lottery draw. He watched the numbers called out and then wrote them down.

As they retreated downstairs, Martin had a look of satisfaction on his face. He said to Dillon, 'Can ye pull that pint for us now?'

A smug look flashed across Dillon's face as he gently tapped his fingers on the bar top. Some years back, Martin had chalked up a hefty slate behind the bar. A slate which he could never pay off. Declan caught wind of the amount and came down heavy on Dillon. From then on, Martin had to clear the debt, and was only granted a twenty-euro tab. Once the limit expired, Martin had to pay for pints upfront.

Martin reluctantly said, 'Jaysis – Is there no let-up from you?' He dropped a fiver on the bar. Dillon poured the pint as Martin watched a burst of bubbles from inside the glass.

The door banged shut behind him, and he turned to see David saunter in, give the DVD display a sneer and remark, 'What's that all About?'

Standing straight with his knuckles pressed against the bar, Dillon looked defeated as he rubbed his nostrils. 'There's no two ways about it... I'm truly cursed. If I tell you what happened lads, will you keep it to yourselves?'

Looking bemused, Martin replied, 'I suppose so, yeah.'

Dillon remembered something and pulled out a book wrapped in a carrier bag. He handed it to Martin for his appraisal. After examining it, Martin dismissed it by saying, 'Right, Seamus Heaney. Nice tidy book. *Eleven Poems* could fetch you a handy stash, but only if it's the first edition. You'll get something for it, but don't go thinking you can buy a holiday from selling it. Again, sweet little number that.'

Pinching it back, Dillon took a deep breath and leant forward before he spoke softly,

'Irene's father passed away about six weeks ago. Being an only child, she's been left everything. What he had in the house was of no use to us. Well, when I say that, I mean it wasn't to our taste, so we decided to scrap the lot.' Dillon rolled his eyes.

David interrupted and firmly asked, 'Erhh! Before you carry on, can you pour us a pint there?'

Dillon poured the pint and carried on. 'There's an auction house in town, so we listed everything we thought was of value. Well, this grandfather clock was fecking huge. And as I loaded it, the bastard trailer started to tilt. Before I knew it, the clock and a wall cabinet with a statue of our holy lady on top of it came towards me. I could only save one of the pieces.'

Releasing a heavy sigh, Dillon wiped his brow. 'I grabbed hold of the clock, and the statue hit the deck and exploded into smithereens. This thing must have been 4ft tall. The missus says it came from Lourdes or some shite like that. Anyway, between the jigs and the reels, many lots had gotten underway, and the auction room was packed. We found a spot, and a lot had already started. I didn't have any catalogue, and I just heard 'Lot of 111 DVDs'.'

'Nobody had bid on it, the starting price was ten euros, so I thought, fuck it, and stuck my card number up to bid. Well, I thought there must be something decent in the box I could watch out of 111 films, and if not me, then something for the kids. As soon as I bid, yer man smacked the hammer down quickly. I rubbed my hands, thinking I'd scored a deal until I heard him say, 'Sold to the gentleman in the brown hat. Now, the proud owner of 111 copies of Cindy Crawford's workout DVD'.'

David choked on his pint as both the lads burst into hysterics. Once Dillon had their attention again, he carried on. They sensed a but coming. 'This doesn't end here, lads. Most of the stuff we had in our lot hadn't met the reserved asking price. I told Irene not to fecking set any reserve prices, as I would be the bastard loading it all back up again.We quickly paid up and loaded what didn't sell back onto the trailer, and I thought, sod it, I'll leave the fecking DVD box in the foyer and let someone else have it. We got back home that evening, and I was worn out from lugging all that shite around all day. Irene was worn out from all her nagging.

'Sunday morning, I got up bright and early but with a twinge in my back, so I thought I'd walk it off with a trip to get a newspaper. On my way back, I bumped into the Jehovah witnesses doing their rounds on our street. So, I thought when the doorbell goes; I'll sit tight until they piss off. Low and behold, I was sitting with my feet up, reading the paper when the bell rang. I could hear Irene had answered it, and she shouted back to me asking for a pen. I told her it was in my blazer hanging up. Irene walked into the front room with a box in her arms. It was the same fecking box of DVDs that we'd left back in the foyer of the auction house. They'd only checked our address to send them back to us by fucking cab. Being a Sunday, there was no courier service. They thought they were doing us a good gesture, but the driver at the door was waiting for payment. The silly mare only paid him from my wallet, and the bastard walked off with my pen after Irene had signed for it.'

'Jaysis, fucking Christ, I said to her. The bell rang again, and I thought it was yer man coming back with my pen. I told Irene I'd get it. I answered it, and it was only the fucking God Squad from earlier. I couldn't fecking shake them off for ages. Irene was there pissing herself in the background.'

The two lads were creased with laughter now. David complained between bursts that his stomach muscles were aching. Dillon, unamused, looked defeated behind the counter. They regained their composure as Dillon went on.

'It doesn't stop there, lads. I put the DVDs up on the bar counter to get shot of them, telling everyone there is no return policy. Mick McCormack took one home on Monday night, and his missus barged her way back in here the following day, slamming the DVD on the counter demanding a refund. A REFUND? I fucking said. How can you have a refund on something that's FREE? Mick told her he paid five euros for it, the cheeky bastard. I told her a shop wouldn't even take it back after you've viewed it for Chrissake! Then, to add insult to injury, she said, 'You can't view it, you daft bastard. The DVD is for Region One. The only way I can watch it is if I take a flight to America or Canada. Keep your DVD and shove it up your arse.' She then stormed out on her fecking broomstick.'

'Now you see, lads, as I've told you from the start. I'm fecking cursed. I can't even give them away for free, and people are still trying to give them back. They're haunting me, and it's all down to that fucking holy statue that got smashed. I swear to God that blasted thing.'

Dillon swiped the two empty glasses that the lads had finished and trudged over to fill up the dishwasher. It was a lonely walk for a desolate man.

CHAPTER 24

Martin and David continued to dwell on Dillon's latest tragedy.

Martin shouted out, 'Dillon will you pour us another two pints there, good man.'

David looked at Martin puzzled and asked, 'How are we going to get through tonight with fuck all to spend later?'

Squeezing David's cheek, a grin brimmed across Martin's face. 'I'm a man with a plan. Get these two in, and I'll be back in a couple of minutes.'

With a skip in his step, Martin headed off out to the grocery store next door. A local girl, Andrea, was serving. 'Do you have a birthday card that's cheeky and cheap? It's for one of the lads tonight,' Martin asked.

Andrea peered up from her magazine and pointed to the lower section of the card stand, 'Try over there, Martin.'

He picked the cheapest card and muttered to himself, 'That'll do nicely.' Placing it down on the counter, he winked at Andrea behind the till and said, 'How are you doing, my lovely? You're looking swell today.' A flood of red filled her cheeks. Martin knew that Andrea had a soft spot for him and often let extra things amount on the slate to take him over his limit. Her husband, Caimh, would never let this happen.

Andrea replied, 'I'm grand, Martin, thanks for asking. Is this for Gerry's drink up? Myself and Caimh are hoping to pop in there later.' 'That's right, should be a great craic tonight. Can you sort us out with these numbers for tonight's lottery draw?' As she handed him back the printed ticket, Martin pitifully asked, 'Can you stick this on the slate for us? Please? Pretty please?'

Andrea's face reddened again. 'I can let the card go on it, but the lottery ticket has to be paid for upfront, Martin.'

Martin realised his predicament and surrendered all the money from his pockets out onto the counter. It just about covered the cost. Kissing the ticket, he said to it, 'You'd better do me proud tonight.'

On Martin's return, David was in conversation with Dillon, and his pint was ready. After patting David on the shoulder, he downed half the pint. He sighed in contentment as the stresses of the day slowly released. Martin handed the card to David with the lottery ticket and said, 'Do the honours and sign and seal this.' he joked, 'my writing is shite.'

Scanning around him, two women caught his attention as they entered. Dressed up for a night out on the town, they looked around disapprovingly. Martin snatched the card back after David had signed it and downed the rest of his pint. Before they had a chance to order drinks, he sauntered over to them. One woman caught sight of him in her peripheral vision and turned her back to his approach, shielding her friend. That wasn't enough to deter him. David and Dillon looked at each other and rolled their eyes in unison. They watched Martin ready to fall flat on his face.

Dillon remarked, 'The dark-haired one is some flah. She's well put together with that rack on her, but her companion is a sniper's nightmare. She's nice from far but far from nice for me.'

David sniggered, 'You're right there! Blondie is so skinny with that waist of a wasp. When she turns sideways, she's like a golf club. No fun bags at all; you'd be banging just hair and heels.'

Sensing Martin's presence, the women ignored him while they queued to order drinks.

Martin summoned his easily accessibly bravado and spoke, 'Could you possibly help me, ladies?'

With their backs turned to him, the brunette shouted over her shoulder, cutting Martin short in his tracks. 'Look, fuck off! We're married. Just out for a drink before we go into town.' A firm hand marked out the women's territory. The brunette continued, 'Christ, we haven't even got a drink in our hands yet, and you're like some chancer leeching over us. So, no hard feelings, ok, but fuck off.'

Martin squinted and pulled a face as if injured as the lads giggled back at the bar. He apologised for his interjection and coolly said, 'Indeed, you are married. Because it would be a crying shame for any man not to wake up to your beauty each morning.'

Turning her head around, her blonde friend egged her companion to take a look. Meeting their gaze, Martin raked his hands through his hair. Reluctantly, the brunette engaged, pouting just enough to intimidate Martin. 'Ok, Mr Dimples, you have a look of the older Boyzone about you. You've caught our attention.' She wore a ruffled top with a plunging neckline showing off just enough cleavage. She was confident and countered with a tight smile, 'But quick and be on your way.'

With a glint in his eye, Martin raised a brow and replied, 'I think it would be fair to say Ronan Keating has the look of *me*. I have another five years over the young man; he's a bit of a short-arse, although he is still a handsome devil. So, I'll accept your comment as a compliment, thank you very much. Plus, there's a saying, 'A dimple on the chin, the devil within.' The brunette's neckline flushed pink as her eyes flittered.

'I have a very good friend whose birthday it is tonight,' Martin confided. Refusing to draw his eyes down to her chest, the brunette noticed, and it displeased her. 'I'd love you to plant a kiss on his birthday card, that's all.' Both women obliged and left two lipstick prints above the verses.

Martin chortled, 'Thank you, ladies, for your contribution. As you are married women, I will decline from offering you drinks as it may be construed as my trying to take advantage of you in some capacity. So, with that in mind, I will oblige you and graciously fuck off.' Martin smiled and walked backwards away from them, leaving them in fits of giggles. Then, taking them by surprise, he leaned back towards them and whispered, 'Great tits by the way.'

Both women fell about laughing, holding on to each other. Martin returned to David and Dillon and gleefully took his seat, flashing the lipstick printed card in front of the lads. Dillon laughed uproariously. David hesitated; however he knew from experience that trouble wasn't far away when Martin was full of himself and full of drink.

Dillon's phone beeped; he read the text, and said, 'The birthday boy is in a cab and around the corner now, lads.'

David started the conversation again. 'I saw Gerry last Saturday, taking one of his clients around on a test drive. I stepped off the kerb and waved to him, and the fucker ignored me. He was driving around like he was one of that Jaguar crowd with their noses stuck in the air. Sure he's only a fucking second-hand car salesman.'

Dillon chuckled to himself and replied, 'Arhh! To be fair now, he has done well for himself with a row of flash cars on his lot. I think you have to have a bit of pride driving your customers around. Where were you going?'

David belched before he answered, 'I had finished doing a spot of bricking that morning and was on my way home.'

Dillon flinched, 'Dressed like shite then when he saw you! No bloody wonder he avoided you.'

David relented, 'Fair play then.'

Old man Mick hobbled past, coughing and wheezing like a set of abandoned bagpipes releasing air. He was a die-hard regular who collected all the empty and leftover glasses as tables became vacant. He had been around forever, and no one ever questioned his presence around the bar. The reward for this meaningless task was to be given a couple of free pints during the evening.

Martin nodded his head towards David and, gesturing to Mick, snidely said, 'That mouth breather is still holding out. When will he just fuck off and die so I can take his position rounding up the glasses? Christ, he came in here with the footings.'

David tutted in response, 'Jesus Martin, is that the future for you? To sip on everyone else's dregs left in glasses as you collect them for a free pint. You set your sights high in life; I give you that.'

The front doors shuddered open and squeaked closed. Gerry blocked the glass panels with his larger than life figure. He tucked his shirt into his trousers after his uncomfortable cab journey.

David turned around. 'Would you look at the hack of the big man there?'

Gerry McGinty was a local man who had grown up with Dillon and Martin. He had come from nothing and built up a successful business. At first, second-hand cars graced his forecourt before Gerry progressed to high-end vehicles. He was once an attractive man with a good physique. Now those days were long gone. Bags under his eyes sloped into dark patches from the long hours at work, and he looked jowly around the face. As a successful man, he enjoyed the finer things in life,and it showed in a permanent paunch. Dandruff glistened on the shoulders of his expensive suits. A running joke among his friends was that Gerry developed a twitch in his right eye from the excitement whenever money was mentioned in venue or bet.

As an affluent man, he could pick wherever he wanted to wine and dine in the city. However, he stayed in the same area, drank with them in The Telegraph and looked after his closest friends. A rapturous drum roll of beer glasses banging against the bar greeted Gerry as he approached. He greeted the lads with a firm handshake. 'Evening ladies,' he chirped. 'Will you join me in a celebratory libation as this evening commences?'

Martin piped up, 'How's the form Jezzer, are you buying?'
Gerry frowned and replied, 'Aren't I fecking always?'

Dillon greeted him with a wink. 'Well, hello there. How's the battle, Gerry?'

'Can't complain, Dillon, unlike the state of the heads on these beers. Give us an empty pint glass there, will you.' An empty pint glass appeared instantly. Gerry took a second look at Dillon and said, 'Wish the full ones appeared as quick as that, Dillon.'

Gerry stuck a couple of euro notes into the glass as part of a whip around. Martin's eyes bulged at the sight of drink money for the next hour or so. He pulled the birthday card out and handed it to Gerry. 'It's a token from us all.' Gerry looked humbled and opened the card on the spot.

His eyes flickered over the verse and signatures but brightened up at the sight of a lottery ticket. 'You guys are legends. Could be my lucky night; you never know.' He then, bizarrely, wrote the lottery numbers on the back of his hand.

Martin looked quizzically at him and asked, 'What's that all about, Gerry?'

Gerry confessed, 'I buy the lottery tickets myself each week, and I always rub off the ink on the ticket with sweat waiting for the draw.' His hands were animated. 'So now, I just write the numbers on my hand instead and put the ticket away safely.'

Nodding in agreement, Martin looked Gerry up and down; he was restless. 'Looking rather smart, dressed to the nines tonight, Gerry, are you not stopping all night here?'

Gerry looked flushed and wiped the sweat from his brow. He pulled a handkerchief out of his jacket before speaking. 'I've been to a curry house with the missus and the kids. The sauce hasn't quite settled in my stomach yet.'

'I see the good life is treating you well these days, Gerry,' Martin commented.

Gerry clasped his stomach in admiration, 'Let me tell you something, it takes years to get to this size.'

'Is it a gland problem ye have?'

'No, it's a repetitive knife and fork problem I have.' Laughter erupted. Dillon interrupted, holding up three empty pint glasses, and said, 'Same again, lads?' They all nodded.

David, who knew Gerry the least, asked, 'Is it just the two children you have, Gerry? I lose track with everybody's families these days.'

The first pint appeared on the bar, and Gerry swiped it before Martin caught sight of it. He downed half of it to cool his stomach down before answering. 'I… we planned to have at least three children but have now only two... I met the missus eight months before our first son was born.'

The surrounding men squinted eyes at one another as Gerry continued. 'Then we had trouble conceiving the second one – well, the missus did. Let me tell you, we were like two ferrets in a bag in the fun days. When the first child was born, it was a delight all around. Little Robert was born 8lbs 1oz. Next, Ryan came along.' Gerry's mobile rang and broke the rhythm of the conversation. He held it up and mouthed 'It's the missus,' before he turned away and answered it.

David looked at Martin, shocked, and said, 'I fecking wish I never asked. I didn't know one of his kids died; you should have nudged me for fuck's sake.'

Martin raised his hands in defence. 'I didn't know either; I always thought he had the two kids.' Martin's train of thought was cut short when the other two pints clanged onto the bar. Before the foam had time to settle, the lads guzzled them.

Gerry appeared back, 'Sorry lads, it's herself indoors, checking if I reached here ok.'

Gerry could see the lads had a look of dismay on their faces and realised where the conversation had paused. He carried on from there, 'As I was saying… the first and second-born was a miracle... and that's where the family tree stopped. As soon as the boys were born, the baby hatch was sealed and healed up for good. No matter how hard I tried to convince the missus to try for another.' He took a swig of lager and wiped the foam from his lips. 'She insisted I had the snip.'

The conversation stalled, then continued, 'Did you lads hear about

Michael Shannon's boy?' Gerry changed the subject. 'What's his name? Thingy-ma-jig?'

'What, dumb arse Dougal? That boy is a bag of lady's genitals. Fuck's sake, what's he done now? His old man must be in despair with that lad.'

'He's in despair, alright, because dumb arse may be getting a numb arse if he stays inside the clinger for any longer.'

'How do you mean, Gerry?'

'By all accounts, Dougal, was part of a group of lads on a stag do, over the way there in Liverpool,' he gestured, pointing his finger outside. 'Anyway, he met a lass in town and pulled her. He then walked her home and one thing led to another, and he ended up shagging her on the bonnet of a security guard's car in a school car park. He was picked up on CCTV, and the Gardai were called, I mean the police over there.

'Anyway, the police caught him mid-action with this lass with his backside bobbing up and down and told him to – what's the best way to say it… *withdraw*. Anyway, Dougal took offence to the request and ended up thumping the officer on the chin for interrupting his strokes. Naturally, the police arrested him for striking an officer and had him locked up for court the next day.'

Wiping the sweat from his face, he continued. 'I tell you what; the police don't fuck about in England either. The long and short of it is that he was charged and convicted for displaying his mickey on school premises and GBH. Then he was added to the sex offenders register over there. His defence said, technically, his mickey was always inside the lass. It was only on display when the altercation with the officer took place, and the officer instigated the conflict.'

'God knows,' muttered Gerry, 'what goes through that boy's head. He's a brick shy of a load and now banged up across the waters there.'

'How's the wife taking it? She was always worrying herself over all the boys when they were at school. She always had a face on her,' Dillon asked.

Gerry continued, 'Those kids worried her so much, she abandoned them for the grave.'

'Oh shite – I'm sorry to hear Michael's on his own now.' Dillon replied with a shake of his head.

'For the love of God, I pray that my boys don't cause me that much anguish in my later years.' Gerry countered.

Martin added, 'Well, I suppose there is no real lesson to learn from this, except that like Michael Shannon loves his boy, we all love our kids.'

'We'll all drink to that.' The overzealous chinking of glasses took place.

Dillon dabbled with the jukebox behind the bar. He wasn't shy about putting on his favourite tracks and boogieing behind the bar in front of the revellers. The speakers around the pub came alive. It startled the drinkers as a trumpet arrangement sounded and the track 'There Was A Time' blasted through the pub. Tapping the bar with his wedding ring, Dillon said, 'Yeh can't beat a black man's record to get your feet moving. Come on now, lads; we're gonna have great craic tonight.'

Dillon threw some shapes behind the bar. For a heartily-shaped man, he did produce some thought-provoking moves. The track finished, and Dillon, worn out, slumped back against the bar. Martin commented on his fitness and his odds of surviving the rest of the night shift.

Dillon, rebuffing the mild insult, said, 'I'll have you all know, I won championship trophies for Irish dancing when I was a boy, and I still practice from time to time… after I've had a shower.'

Hilarity broke out as the lads fell against each other, spilling their pints and trying to stay on their stools. That offended Dillon even more. Noticing punters, like traders in the stock exchange, trying to gain his attention, Dillon picked up a euro and flicked it over to Martin. 'Tell ye what, find 'You Ain't Woman Enough' on the jukebox, and I'll show you I still have it in me.'

Martin's face scrunched up as he replied, 'I never had you down as a romantic.'

Dillon paused and countered, 'I haven't the feck what you're on about.' Flustered, as his extra staff hadn't turned up, Dillon started clearing off the bar and returned out back to change a barrel. Meanwhile, Martin located the song, and to his delight found one credit left on the jukebox which he used to play the song.

The vibe of the bar was warm and friendly. Conversations swirled as laughter occasionally overpowered the music. The tinkle of glass on glass blended into the background as the dishwasher was loaded, and empty bottles were discarded out the back. Overpowering perfumes and colognes lingered in the air as groups of youngsters rushed out to their cabs letting the stagnant odour of the carpet rise in a haze again. The front doors squealed shut each time there was a departure. The missing bar staff staggered through eventually, partially removing her coat and scarf as she hurried. A trail of cigarette smoke wafted in behind her from smokers outside. She apologised to Dillon, blaming the buses for making her late. Dillon wasn't interested. Typically, as soon as she handled the pumps, the trade slowed down. Dillon, now winding down a bit, mingled on the other side of the bar, patting himself down with paper towels.

An Irish ballad had just finished, and Dillon started psyching himself up, ready for his performance. A few of the other revellers had overheard Dillon's boasting and were intrigued to see his moves. Using his arms to form an open space for himself, Dillon confidently said, 'Now, focus lads... these are trophy-winning feet.'

The intro to 'You Ain't Woman Enough' started and picked up pace fast. Dillon clicked his ankles together before flicking his legs up in front of him. The move stopped dramatically as Dillon's legs didn't even reach above the waist. He made excuses about wearing the wrong trousers as the crowd broke their hearts in laughter. Dillon tried to redeem himself. 'Hold on now, folks… I'll gather my senses for the bit at the end... it'll all come together for that.'

The track ran into the start of another diddley riff. After absorbing all the focus around him, Dillon sprang into action with a sequence of jig moves followed by the high-rise ankle click again. Once more, the performance ended abruptly as Dillon's trousers constrained his legs. He grudgingly recognised his defeat and finished by saying, 'I can do this spot on at home when I'm in the bathroom, but that's when I have no clothes on.' The crowd roared with laughter.

'Spare us the picture of that for God's sake,' Martin howled,

Retreating behind the bar, Dillon looked like he'd just engaged in a ten-round boxing match. Sweat poured from every orifice, and he briefly disappeared out of sight behind the bar to towel himself down. He gave himself a few minutes before he re-emerged and, clapping his hands in front of the lads, shouted, 'Tonight's craic has only just begun lads! Who's ready for a refill?'

CHAPTER 25

As Dillon lined pints up on the bar, Martin checked his watch and leaned in to whisper, 'You need to switch the TV on and run the recorded show in the next five minutes to run in sync with last week's, so it all looks legit… away with you man, run upstairs and play it.'

After flooding the spill tray, Dillon shook his hands free of froth and fled upstairs. Pixels danced around the big screen before it came to life. Pausing for breath, Dillon emerged downstairs, not looking a well man; the effort had taken it out of him. The recorded show played in the background as conversations chattered on around. The voices competed with the music from the jukebox and were finally drowned out with the voice-over of the lottery introduction on the big screen. Dillon switched off the jukebox temporarily.

David had headed off to say hello to a couple of guys from his work. Creased up against the bar, Martin and Gerry were nursing pints in deep conversation; batting raised eyebrows and gentle shrugs back at one another. Gerry's curry still hadn't settled, and the fast-paced lager drinking had bloated him. This wasn't a good sign for the evening to draw out into the early hours. Dillon had a short break as his extra staff handled the pumps.

On the other side of the bar, Dillon joined in with Martin and Gerry keeping one eye on the stack of DVDs. So far, only one had vanished, but Dillon thought that would be the start of them disappearing. Within half an hour, it appeared back on the pile, to his dismay. With a shake of the head, he looked up to the heavens and muttered, 'For the love of God, I'm fecking cursed.'

David had rejoined the lads just in time to hear Gerry questioning Martin. 'Every time I see or hear of you, Martin, you're always in here,' Gerry gestured around the space with his hand. 'So and so is meeting

Martin in the Graft… I was talking to Martin in the pub last week; it's all I hear.'

Martin sarcastically answered, 'That's why they call me the *Everyday Man* in here. One... because I'm in here every day and, two... because… well because I'm also a man.'

Gerry chuckled and conceded, 'To be fair like, I can't argue with that. Jaysis… I don't know how you do it each week. Her indoors gives me a curfew, and she won't take any of that... "Oh, I couldn't get a cab back early enough," crap.'

David and Martin glanced at each other. Martin had to be careful about how he responded. David – being family – wouldn't take any wisecracks about Bridget being under the thumb. Martin hesitated, then spoke, 'Bridget and me have an understanding. If I'm upfront with her and I don't feed her any bullshit, then most of the time, she'll let me go out. There are no flies on her mind you, as she'll catch me out before I go out for the night.

'This morning, for instance, I said to her, "I'm popping out for a couple later." She said, "Now do you mean drinks or nights? You still haven't redeemed yourself since St. Patrick's day, when you said the same and came home two days later."'

Gerry chuckled, 'You're some quare wan, Martin, I tell you. You were locked out of a tree like a monkey who forgot his keys. We did have great craic that night. Every year it's getting harder to recover from it, though.'

Martin had now turned to focus on the big screen as the lottery draw took place. Nodding deliberately to Dillon, he muttered, 'Will you turn the sound up, Dillon? We can't hear a fecking thing over here.'

Nodding back, Dillon scuttled behind the bar to raise the volume. Cushioning his pint gently into his stomach, Gerry gazed at the big screen. Martin nudged David in the ribs and pulled a face to compose himself. He didn't want his laughter to ruin things now. After all, Martin's drinking money had been riding on this. Gerry gave a brief double take at the lads as the first winning number appeared, wondering what the commotion was all about but went back to examining his ticket. He recited the numbers off to himself. The second ball flashed up. Gerry peered at the numbers again and chuckled to himself. Dillon whispered into David's ear, 'He'll go fucking berserk when he finds out that ticket is worth the same as an old pound note…'

David, struggling to control his mirth, kept his hand over his mouth. Martin nudged David back and, with a nod of the head, motioned to pull himself together in the toilets before Gerry cottoned on to any stitch-up. The third number is displayed on the screen. Biting his nails, Gerry's eyes lit up in delight as he released the crease of his double chin; he turned to the lads and said, 'Would you look at that.'

Martin and Dillon pretended not to hear. Gerry turned back to the screen. The fourth number flashed up on the screen, and Gerry glanced again at his hand.

Martin shouted out, 'Did you say something, Gerry? I missed it.'

With his wide eyes fixed on the screen, Gerry had just worked out that he relied on just two more numbers. Breaking his concentration, he timidly said, 'Argh nothing, I was miles away.'

Martin guzzled his pint with a flourish, touching it down on the bar. Just as the fifth number blared out, Martin winked fiendishly at Dillon and said, 'Is he panicking yet? I daren't look over at him?'

Dillon bowed his head, squinted with one eye and replied, 'He's like a fecking statue; he hasn't even flinched.'

David arrived back from the men's room, more composed now. The sixth number had been announced, and attention had diverted away from the TV, back to the room. Gerry was in a trance; his jowls quivered as his eyes focused on the big screen. His heartbeat pounded and echoed inside his head. Each beat of time had slowed down. In the background, the second hand slowly crawled around on the clock, tic…tick… tic… tick. The final number flashed up on the screen again as his stomach rolled over with nerves.

It took a minute or two for Gerry to realise that he had the winning ticket. The men watched as, like a curtain being lifted, the realisation came over him. Standing motionless and still glued to the screen, the momentum of time resumed. The cacophony of conversations that echoed in the bar brought Gerry back to the land of the living. He muttered to himself, 'For the love of God.'

'Are you alright there, Gerry...' Dillon spoke, 'you look like you've seen a ghost, for Christ's sake.' Keeping his assumptions to himself, Gerry hadn't arisen any suspicion that he had the winning ticket. Clasping his pint, he released a discrete belch. The aromatic sauce from his earlier meal regurgitated in the back of his throat. Martin and David looked at each other puzzled. Was Martin's plan going to backfire? There was going to be no wild celebrations for anyone tonight by the looks of things.

Dillon could see the lads looking perplexed. He asked Gerry, 'So, what does the future hold for Gerry, now you're another year older and wiser?'

Gerry's eyes darted from side to side, thinking of an unassailable excuse to go home. His mobile rang, he flashed the screen to the lads with feigned seriousness, 'I gotta take this; it's the missus.'

As he disappeared outside, David surveyed the whip money. Holding it aloft, he reluctantly said, 'Shite! Still, at least we have enough for another round, as long as we don't have any crisps.' Martin, buoyant with alcohol, released disappointing belches.

David winced, sniffing the air, and said, 'Never mind, it was worth a try. Do you think he sussed us out, or is he a slippery bastard?'

Gerry slowly walked back in, white as a sheet. Looking disconcerted, he clutched his stomach. A false grin stretched across his face as he chirped, 'Oh… I'm sorry, lads, I'm gonna have to cut my evening short... that curry hasn't settled, and it's not mixing too well with the beer... I tell you what... have a drink on me for the rest of tonight.' Pulling out a handful of notes, he stuck them into the whip glass. Martin and David looked stunned, and before Martin could make any wisecracks, Gerry had backed away from the bar and said, 'I'll be off now so, and make sure Dillon gets a drink out of that whip money.'

Like a gust of wind, Gerry left in haste. Martin and David looked at each other; raising their eyebrows, they laughed in surprised amusement. 'Well,' said Martin, 'I told you we'd be on the tear, but this is not the way I planned it. All's well that ends well as they say.'

David replied, 'Well, to be fair; nobody can accuse Gerry of having dry balls; he's always pretty handy with the money.'

Martin waved Dillon over, who had just finished serving a customer. 'Dillon, will you count the money in the glass here and take out the twenty euros to clear my slate. Then we'll let the evening commence.' Martin slugged Gerry's leftover pint down.

'Slow down guzzle-guts,' David chided, 'Chrissake, I can't keep up with you.'

Rivulets of lager streamed down the corners of Martin's mouth as he replied, 'Rev up or fuck off.'

Dillon counted out the remaining cash and announced, 'Right lads... you have just over eighty euros, minus the twenty for Martin'stab, leaves sixty between you.'

Martin, delighted, addressed them all, 'You see lads, upstairs is for drinking and downstairs is for dancing. Dillon, take the money and start pouring pints and line them up on the counter here.'

Squinting his eyes at Martin, Dillon corrected him, 'NO! – Upstairs is for thinking and downstairs is for dancing, I'll think you'll find, Martin. But whatever,' Dillon said. 'You're gonna be in for it if he comes back.'

Martin knew exactly what he was doing. On another occasion, whip money left was reclaimed by a different punter after an argument halfway through an evening. So there would be nothing left to reclaim if the money was spent on the off chance of Gerry coming back. It didn't bother the lads having pints lined up and going flat. Beer was beer.

Forty minutes passed before Gerry stormed in and lunged at the bar, searching for the whip money. It was apparent it had disappeared. He could see the pints lined up at the bar. David nudged Martin, who shouted out, 'Well, HELLO there, Gerry!'

Gerry's face was puce. The drinkers around the lads moved their stools back as Gerry let loose with venom. YOU BASTARDS. The staff at the lottery HQ asked me if my real name was Marty McFly when I read my numbers out and told them I had won the lottery. They asked me was I travelling back to the future a week late as last week's numbers were already claimed.'

David jumped in and placatingly offered Gerry a pint. Gerry, tired now and starting to see the funny side, accepted defeat. He grabbed a pint and downed it. Gasping, he came back up for air and confessed, 'Jesus Christ, an hour ago, I thought I was made up for life with all the money beyond counting.'

Martin's fast-paced drinking had begun to show signs it had caught up with him as he swayed back and forth. He held back with any further wisecracks as Gerry still looked a bit pissed off. Gerry hadn't wanted to go back to the pub after being suckered in like that, but it was better than being at home and having it rubbed in his face by his wife.

Dillon appeared back from the men's breathing heavily and said,

'I think I'm coming down with something. I had to get out of the bath earlier for a piss and felt a bit woozy, and now I feel like shite.'

David nodded as if he knew exactly what the problem was. 'I think it's down to stress, Dillon,' he assured him, 'stress from your Irene nagging at you to shift all that furniture and shite.'

Gerry nodded in agreement, 'For God's sake, man, just do as the missus asks of you. Believe, you, me, I've learnt the hard way in life that 'A happy wife is a happy life.'

The conversation flowed past Martin as he caught words and endings of sentences but was now too drunk to engage completely. Something bothered him. Gathering himself together, he focussed on not swaying before he spoke, 'Fuck that, Dillon! Getting out of the bath to have a slash? I just piss in the bath sponge and squeeze it out in the basin next to me.' All three men guffawed as Martin stood, swaying slightly, unperturbed.

David replied, 'Are you serious? I've washed my teeth in that sink many a time.'

Martin waved his hands dismissively, 'Arhh! Don't fuss, man; I squirt a bottle of mouthwash around the rim.' Then, to Dillon, he said, 'You see, Dillon, you have done well for yourself. You have a few quid about you, but you still live in a council house with the split bathroom facilities just like me. Gerry, here, my good man… he lives in a new build house with how many bathrooms and extra pissers?'

David grabbed Martin's arm pulling it in. Shoulder to shoulder, he whispered in his ear, 'Pull your fucking neck in, will you. You're starting to draw attention to yourself saying stupid things, and you're saying them too loud. Do you get my drift? Cop yourself on, man.'

Martin's heavy eyes blinked as he held his hands up to Dillon in a sign of retreat. Dillon gave a slow nod back to him – a private way of telling him to behave himself.

Dillon tried to lighten the mood. 'Do you know how to tell if someone is doing well in life? Looking at Gerry here, he has the top of the range car and – as Martin puts it – extra pissers in the house, but the real test is in the jacks. If he or she has those Molton Brown handwash products in their bathrooms with those scented sticky things in pots, then you know that not only have they done well, but they've also moved up a class in life.'

Raising his nose in the air with a mock-aristocratic look, Gerry proudly stated, 'There's nothing wrong with a bit of snobbery to get you through your day.' Gerry's pinched face took the strain of holding his pretentiousness, and he burst out laughing.

Giddy laughter surrounded them. The bar staff kept the pints flowing as Gerry and Dillon animatedly compared notes on their wives with much-mocked tips on how to keep them happy and content. David had now switched into parent mode, keeping a steady eye on Martin. He knew this could be the start of a long evening ahead, and he had to be on his guard.

CHAPTER 26

That same evening, as Martin was enjoying himself in Declan's pub, Declan reflected on the information the detective had supplied him with earlier. His initial thought was to drive straight to Martin's front door and smash the living daylights out of him. Restraining himself from acting on impulse, he instead planned out his strategy.

Billy and Johnny joined him on the way to The Telegraph. Knowing Martin would be there caused his blood to boil. The likelihood would be that he would end up hitting him. He wanted to do it, and he wanted to do it in full view of everyone, including the clandestine watchman. The devil sat on his shoulder, agreeing with his thoughts. Believing this would send a message to everyone not to undermine or underestimate what he was capable of, Declan felt he had to show dominance. The situation surrounding O'Driscoll had been unclear. He could not be certain that O'Driscoll was involved in any of the insurgency with his business affairs. He needed word to get back to him, though, to prove that he still had the gumption to protect everything he had built up around him.

As Declan pulled up outside his pub, the waft of nicotine caught him as curls of smoke from the huddled crowd outside made their way into his open window. Parking the car, he took a moment to think through his choices. The devil sitting on his shoulder egged him on.

His stern face twisted around to Billy and Johnny in the back before he spoke with conviction. 'Do not dare intervene or question my SHITE in front of anyone in here tonight. Am I clear?'

Rubbing his sparse chin he thought some more. He wanted to get this done without dwelling on it much longer. Both men knew he was pissed off and that he needed to leave his mark. They were concerned, though, about how far he was prepared to go.

Sensing his anxiousness, they glanced simultaneously at each other before answering, 'Sure Boss, clear.'

All three stepped out in unison, gravity etched across their faces. Two bystanders finished their smokes and thought twice about lingering when they spied Declan. They hurried back inside like naughty schoolboys. Billy and Johnny stood behind Declan, and all three stopped for a few seconds. Declan nodded to both men in a sign of solidarity. Feeling wired and alert, he drew breath, stretched his arms out, and thrust the doors open.

The volume of sound inside was overwhelming as masses of conversations merged into one continuous noise. The body heat generated by the crowd had caused the stale smell of cigarettes to rise out of the old, matted carpet. Declan surveyed the bar and marked out David from the crowd, then spotted Martin's figure next to him in the reflection of the bar. His breathing intensified as his rage fermented. Declan marched dramatically over to Martin, barging past people as expletives echoed behind him. As he faced him, the conversation with the detective echoed over and over in his head... 'You my friend are being played.'

Martin hadn't realised Declan was there until he was just upon him. Red blood vessels lined the whites of Declan's eyes as his arm swung out, cutting through the air. Patrons barely had time to blink before his arm swung towards Martin's body. With fingers stretched out like claws, his fist embedded itself into the fabric of Martin's shirt at the neck, twisting the material until he had pulled him closer. Seams ripped, and buttons popped off as Declan's other hand grabbed Martin by his belt buckle. Martin yelped on impact from the force. Declan snarled as his muscles flexed and Martin's two feet left the floor.

As Martin cleared the ground, he caught bystanders in the chest with his flailing feet. The force of the lift made his arms swing out on either side of him, causing his fingers to smash against the hanging glasses above the bar. Full pints ricocheted across the surface and exploded in front of people. Dillon reacted instinctively, shielding his face as two full pints somersaulted in his direction. They soaked him from top to bottom. Stunned, Martin gasped with ragged breaths as the vessels in his neck protruded as his body sought air. Before he realised it, Declan's forceful arm had grappled him by the throat, and his body careered across the counter, clearing everybody and everything in his path.

Martin fell off the end on his back, landing on a square table in the middle of the bar. Disorientated, his head began to spin as Declan relinquished his vice grip around his throat. The suction of air into Martin's lungs brought tears to his eyes. Shards of glass tinkled on the bar surface, glistening, as alcohol ran down the bar and soaked into the carpet. Patrons remained frozen in shock, gawking faces tasting the spray of lager as it settled around them.

Declan drew his arm back again, stretching the seams of his leather coat, and he powered a punch into Martin's face. The force of the swing partially missed Martin's face but caught him on the side of his eye socket, causing it to split. Blood cascaded down his face. Martin gasped as alcohol spewed from his stomach, causing him to choke. Blood blinded his right eye and saturated the shoulder of his shirt and the carpet.

David attempted to step forward, but Johnny clutched David's arm and drew it up behind his back. David knew he couldn't take them both on, so he retreated. Patrons gasped in horror at the spectacle in front of them. Declan walked around the table, his feet squishing into the beer-soaked carpet. He stood and watched for a moment as Martin's body regurgitated bile as he drew in heavy breaths, coughing and spitting to clear his throat. Declan grabbed him by the throat again and pulled him up in view of everyone. His eyes fixed on Martin. His voice, loud and rasping, commanded the attention of everyone around him.

'Did you not think that I wouldn't find out about you working for the O'Driscoll's? You were caught on the Garda surveillance. You were caught in my fucking van. They traced the plate back to me. YOU COMPROMISED EVERYTHING I STAND FOR. And to top it all... YOU... OWE... ME... MONEY.'

Declan's fuelling anger caused spittle to bounce off his teeth onto Martin's blood-soaked face. 'You've taken advantage of my good nature and my generosity.' His laboured breathing caused perspiration to line his face. He carried on, 'Now, there will be new terms and conditions for our agreement. I'll be around your house every fortnight to collect the SAME monthly sum. Do I make myself clear?'

Declan fronted up in Martin's face as Martin groaned and nodded. Martin's alcohol intake had partly stemmed the pain inflicted on him. His face had turned a shade of purple; his eyes watered as he gurgled with each intake of breath. He still didn't have any comprehension of what had happened to him. Peering to his side, Declan caught sight of the so-called watchman visibly shocked, taking note of everything. Releasing his chokehold on Martin, he strutted around the table like a gladiator in victory.

Shouting out to the crowd, his voice became low and husky. 'Let this be a lesson to you all. I run things smoothly around here... you request it... I supply it... that goes for any merchandise and loans, but I'm running a tighter ship from now on. In simple terms... don't FUCK with me.'

Angling his neck, Declan purposely picked out David in the crowd. Avoiding eye contact, David bowed his head in guilt. Declan retreated away from Martin as he lay broken on the table. Frail whimpers echoed through the silence as Martin squirmed and gasped for air. Slowly coming to, he sat up with his elbows supporting his back. A wry smile faltered as he spat blood onto the carpet.

With a twinkle in his eye, he looked at his assailant and said, 'Will you say hello to Kathleen for me, Declan?'

Declan froze, as did David, Billy and Johnny. Beads of sweat crept across Declan's forehead as the set of his features shifted, and the muscles in his jaw tightened. Swivelling round, he stomped back over to Martin, his nostrils flaring, his eyes filled with fury. Martin looked like a condemned seal awaiting his fate. The inevitable happened.

Without a word, Declan hammered Martin with a straight punch to the face. A clean shot caught him on the chin as his head flew back, causing his shoulders to concertina. The momentum of the hit caused his body to jack-knife and leave the table, slumping in a heap behind it. Dwarfing him, Declan followed through with repeated pummels that held him down on the floor. Martin did not attempt to get up. Fellow drinkers scampered back from the blood bath. With knuckles soaked in blood, a vicious grin crept over Declan's face.

CHAPTER 27

Arriving home with Kieran, ready to chill out and watch TV for the rest of the night, Shane realised he had misplaced his front door key. Venting his frustration, he kicked the front door. Knowing his mother and Sinead wouldn't be back for hours, meant he would have to go find his father to get a key. There was only one place to find Martin Lynch on a Saturday evening.

Kicking back on the windowsill, Kieran examined the gum stuck between the grooves of his sole. He felt it every time his heel lifted off the pavement. Annoyed, he shouted out, 'Fucking shite. New fucking trainers and all this SHITE is stuck to them.'

Shane ignored the comment. 'Look, I need to get to the Graft to get the key off my old man, so let's get a move on, sunshine.' Hobbling down the street, each lad's dilemma seemed more important than the other's.

Back at The Telegraph, Declan had grabbed Martin by the scruff of his neck and dragged him towards another area with seated booths. Glancing up, he nodded to Billy, who reluctantly nodded back, knowing his instructions, and left the pub. Drinkers gasped and whispered to one another of Martin's fate. Billy returned, clutching a sports bag. The drinkers continued their whispers, speculating as to what purpose the bag might serve. Declan pinned Martin's shoulder down across the table with his forearm overhanging it. Slowly, Martin came to. Disorientated, his vision blurred around him as his hands scrambled for purchase on the table. His tongue was split and swollen, but no teeth were dislodged. Declan opened the bag to reveal an aluminium baseball bat. A ripple of trepidation filled the room as onlookers gasped. David stepped forward, but Johnny again stopped him dead in his tracks, defying him to advance.

Forcefully shunting Johnny's arm down, David shouted across, his head in disbelief; he couldn't believe what was going to unfold in front of him.

From a distance, Declan's car was visible outside the pub. Smokers huddled outside looking scared alerted Shane to something untoward. 'Something is going to kick off in here tonight; I can feel it.' The colour drained from Shane's face as it dawned on him that if his father was in there, and trouble was brewing tonight, then Martin usually had something to do with it.

As Shane cantered ahead, he turned while running backwards and shouted down the street, 'Meet you there, not too happy with both our old men in the pub. I've a bad feeling about this.'

Changing direction, Shane found a steady rhythm as he ran with purpose, pounding down the street. Reaching the pub, he bent forward, resting his hands against his knees to catch his breath. Glancing up at the doors, Shane heard the jukebox playing a 70s ballad. The pub sounded deserted, which he thought was strange. He walked on in.

Purposely staring at the watchman, a line of sweat formed on Declan's upper lip. His knowing sneer indicated he knew who the watchman was. His breathing was laboured as he reached for the bat, swivelling to find a comfortable position. Declan aimed to break Martin's arm with one full swing. Drawing a deep breath, he tightly gripped the bat, arching his back to make the strike.

At the same time, Shane pushed through the crowd to find his father cowering on the floor at the mercy of Declan. Lunging forward he tripped, before crawling over to his father. Reaching out, Shane laid his arm out across like Martin's.

Declan flinched at the sudden interruption and shouted, 'It'll make no difference, young man. I won't shed a tear breaking two arms.'

The jukebox had finished playing music. Shocked murmurs flittered amongst the crowd. The crowd parted as another figure walked in. Declan drew the bat back, summoning all his strength. Kieran emerged from the crowd, watching his closest friend facing the onslaught of his father. Without thinking, Kieran dived in the direction of the table and, falling beside his best friend, stretched his arm out across Martin in line with Shane's.

In a sudden change of direction, Declan swung the bat down

towards the floor and then up towards a line of drinks spread across the bar. The impact of the swing shattered the glasses into smithereens, hailing like confetti through the air. Alcohol showered the revellers, tiny pieces of glass covering their bodies. The sound of shattered glass continued to ricochet around the room. Declan stood back and dropped the bat onto the bar. The impact dented the counter and left red and bluepaint marks scored into the woodwork.

His legs felt shaky and his confidence shattered by the appearance and defiance of his son. In that one moment, his whole world had turned upside down as his flesh and blood upstaged him. He felt betrayed. Declan was shocked his son had the nerve to stand up for something he believed in. Standing back, hands by his side, Declan felt tired. The crowd around him started to disperse, afraid to be seen staring at him in this state. Declan pressed his body against the bar counter as he cursed himself. He needed time to reflect on what had happened. His legs felt heavy and leaden as the fight drained out of him.

Billy noticed this and shielded him as he whispered, 'You've made a holy show of yourself in here tonight.' Billy ushered Johnny to move the crowd around to the other side of the bar. Declan pushed Billy aside and looked at his son. Kieran looked downcast, watching Shane consoling his father.

Declan let out a wild cry that rang around the pub, 'BOOOOOY!' Flecks of saliva covered Kieran's face. Declan lurched back and headed for the exit. While moving, he pulled Johnny forward, leaning into his ear, and said, 'Get my boy out of here, NOW.'

After heading out to his car, Declan attempted to slide into the driver's seat, but his shoulder had locked. Wincing in pain, he tried to manoeuvre himself into a comfortable sitting position. Resting his arms against the steering wheel, he bowed his head, drifting off into a trance. Declan pictured himself standing up for what he believed in years ago and ignoring his mother's advice about not pushing too far. The evening's events hadn't gone to plan. He had lost face. This was the worst thing that could happen to a man like Declan. Once word got around that Declan Hennessey had gone soft in his son's presence, all bets were off. Kieran exited with Billy and Johnny on either side of him, looking scared. Declan dropped off Billy and Johnny and continued the remainder of the journey home in silence. Declan's thoughts were not about his boy but about how he could save face and repair his reputation.

On the floor of the pub, covered in blood and broken glass, Martin lay silent too. Despondency filled the air. Some of the elderly drinkers were too upset to get back into the mood of the night. They had intended to end their evening in the company of friends, but instead, they had just witnessed a barbaric event. Some of the younger men were impressed with what had happened, and they heckled each other, reenacting scenes like from a movie set.

Dillon had to step up and control the chaos. Checking his staff were ok, he gave them instructions on cleaning up. Revellers found glass fragments in their pints and queued up for replacements. Some cheeky patrons downed their pints, fragments and all, hoping for an additional pint in apology.

David and Shane got Martin up on the sofa area. As he regained consciousness, the seriousness of his injuries emerged. Dried blood had stuck his lips together, and judging how his pupils were, focused his vision seemed impaired. Purple and crimson bruising were starting to bloom amidst the gash on one side of his face. The volume of blood on his shirt highlighted the seriousness of his injuries. As his son and brother-in-law tended to him, Martin lay dazed; he didn't understand what had happened. As he touched his face to feel the swelling, blood mixed with snot came away on his hand.

Dillon approached the three of them and gently advised David to bring Martin upstairs to clean him up. Martin had a piercing ringing noise in his head but could speak enough to convey that he intended to carry on drinking. Dillon didn't refuse him that, but he wanted Martin out of sight.

An older couple looked visibly distraught as they passed Martin. They sympathetically patted him on the shoulder and left for the night. The evening had taken its toll on them, and they decided not to stay. Martin struggled upstairs; his aiding comrades hunched up behind him. After examining the extent of Martin's injuries, the decision was made to take him straight home as he refused to go to the hospital.

A handful of drinkers had joined in with the clean-up operation. Dillon gave them a nod in appreciation as a plastic dustbin skated across the floor. Dustpans and a shovel appeared from nowhere. It wasn't long before something approaching normal resumed. It would take a further clean-up operation the following day to completely rid the bar of glass fragments.

The queue at the bar was now two men deep, and all were braying for service. Dillon summoned the staff back off the floor to start pulling pints. Many of the revellers who had initially stayed after the fiasco to clean up began to put their coats on and leave. The queuing at the bar had put them off, as had the violence. Dillon had to think fast to calm the situation down. He focused on the drinkers, who were agitated at a slow pace. Reaching for an empty beer crate, Dillon turned it upside down and stood on it, raising his hands like a preacher.

Trying to engage everyone, he shouted to gain their attention, 'Settle down now... settle down... OI, LOOK AT ME YOU BASTARDS!' His voice moved down a notch as everyone stopped talking and focussed on him. 'This evening's spectacle has now finished, and to get you all in the mood for drinking; there's a FREE DVD for each of you who comes up and collects your replenished pint.' He pointed at the stack on the bar. 'Bear with us now. We are pouring as fast as gravity allows us.'

Disappearing momentarily behind the bar, Dillon appeared again with another cardboard box packed with Cindy Crawford workout DVDs. He slammed them on the bar, and drinkers grabbed at them, not knowing its title but cheered at a freebie. A few drinkers studied the title and choked, then used the DVD as a frisbee, tossing it mid-air across the bar. Other patrons found them on the other side and pocketed them as trophy finds, only to be disappointed once they took them home and tried to view them. Order was beginning to be restored.

CHAPTER 28

Loud voices and profanities stirred the neighbours on Holmewood Road as David held Martin up, helping him walk back home to his house. They floundered along the pavement and slammed into wing mirrors of parked cars as they passed. A streetlamp flickered, and their silhouettes cast shadows over neighbours' windows as they lurched by.

Martin had lost his keys during the attack. David breathlessly banged on the front door whilst trying to support Martin. Inside, Bridget stirred, then slowly and reluctantly slid out of bed. She blinked her eyes, willing them to adjust to the darkness. The room was cold, and goosebumps surfaced across her skin. She thought she could hear voices and scrambled to find her slippers. She skittered down the staircase, noticing the hallway light on and shielded her eyes with a hand. The door locks shunted across, and Bridget stepped back as the cold night air breezed into the hallway carrying David and Martin with it. The door closed. SLAM. Bridget focused on them, then yelped, forcing herself to fully awake before shock pinned her to the spot.

'For the love of God, didn't the driver stop? Why isn't he in the hospital? He's in no fit state to go to bed. David, what happened?'

David focused on Bridget's sleep-ruffled hair as he prepared himself to respond, 'Bridget, calm yourself down. There was no accident, only Martin opening his mouth.'

'How many of them did this? How come there isn't a mark on you? You'd better start talking, David,' her voice rose.

'Look, there's no easy way to tell you; I didn't want to burden you. Martin took out a loan with Declan during a card game and lost. Before you say anything, I did my best to stop him, but you know what he is like with drink inside him. DON'T look at me like that.'

'So, what's that got to do with him looking like this,' Bridget begged, 'he's half beaten to death. I don't understand.'

'To be honest with you, it came out of the blue. Martin owed money from another loan he took out for yer man, Aiden O'Driscoll across town there. Part of the repayment was to move cars around for him and take a small cut out of it.'

Bridget's mouth fell open.

'I swear to God, Bridget, I knew nothing about this one until he needed me to pick him up from his drop-off points. It looks like we got found out, and Declan went for Martin in the pub. To make things worse… Martin asked him to 'say hello to Kathleen for him' in front of everyone there. Then Declan completely lost it and threw Martin around the pub.'

Martin slurred and lisped, his words not forming. Wincing in agony; he coughed, licking the blood that coated his teeth. Bridget and David dragged Martin into the kitchen, heaving him onto a chair. Despite her fury, Bridget's face wore a mixture of shock and vulnerability. This was her husband, now broken in body and mind.What mess and danger had he brought upon himself and his family now?

Bridget got to work cleaning his face up and stripping him of his blood-sodden clothes. His body was marked in red lashes from the blows, marks that would turn black and yellow as days went by. One side of his face had swelled up, cuts and grazes covered his throat and collar bone. The antiseptic wash cleaned the worst of the blood away. The bowl of warm water turned crimson with blood. Martin didn't flinch or open his eyes. Instead, he snored as he breathed shallowly, swaying on the chair. David felt guilty. He couldn't look Bridget in the eye.

Bridget threw him a look, and composing herself, spoke in a calm and unhurried voice, 'What's done is done. I still think there is more to this. Nobody gives out a beating like this as a warning. It looks to me as if he tried to kill him. I can't do any more tonight. Lift him into the front room for me; I can't have that body in my bed. I'll speak to Kathleen tomorrow and see if she can shed some light on tonight's goings-on.'

Martin blinked his eyes open as he urged himself to come alert. 'Right,' he slurred, 'I'm off to hit the Four Springs nightclub.'

David and Bridget lugged him to the sofa, and after acknowledging his surroundings in a blur, he fell asleep as soon as he laid down. David declined a mug of tea and made his excuses to leave. He knew things would get worse here before they got better, and he needed to make himself scarce. Bridget knelt by her husband, checking his airways just like he did for Sinead when sleeping. Sadness created an ache in her stomach. Fatigue stretched across her laughter lines. She studied him. His head, body and pride would hurt in the morning.

As she returned to bed, she tried to put it out of her mind so she could sleep. Snuggling into the duvet, she curled up in the fresh linen, the smell of hair conditioner fragrancing her pillow. Her eyes closed. She tried to push the thoughts away. It was too late. The damage was done. Her brain became active with questions about her life. How much did Kathleen know? Could she sway Declan? Who else did Martin owe money to? Was this going to break the family and her friendship with Kathleen?

She didn't know what was going to happen, but she couldn't stop thinking about what might. She lay wide awake in the darkness under her warm duvet and struggled to work out what the future would hold. It would be time to get up soon. After hours of fitful worrying, eventually, her eyelids grew heavy, and she fell asleep.

CHAPTER 29

'Wake up… wake up now, Declan.' There was something sharp in Kathleen's tone as she wrenched the duvet back and stretched the curtains open, flooding the room with light from Kings Avenue. Declan flinched as he strained his eyes, glancing at the sideboard. It took a few seconds before the painful memories of last night come to the fore.

Kathleen said, 'You'll get your coffee when I get some answers.'

Pulling himself up with a pillow behind him in the spare room, Declan chided Kathleen with sarcasm. 'No good morning kiss either, my love?'

Kathleen's expression was solemn as she held her mobile aloft, 'I've had Shauna Higgins on the phone, texts from Niamh Murphy and Rachel Ryan. Not about the fiasco that happened in the public house that has my name above the door, but about my husband *creating* the fiasco and nailing somebody in front of everyone.

'I never hear from these women unless it concerns ICA business… no, no, let me rephrase that; the Association that I am the Chairperson of, that I represent as a role model. The very group I stood up and made a speech to recently! Do you realise that you have destroyed my reputation with last night's exploits? Now, don't aggravate me with any of your baloney. I want the truth and make it clear and simple for me.'

Declan rubbed his face, revealing the marks on his knuckles. Kathleen noticed them and scowled further, waiting for his response.

'Look, it got out of hand last night; I admit that –'

Kathleen interrupted, keeping her tone level, 'Who was it, anybody I know?' she demanded, holding eye contact with him. A five-second delay irritated her further.

'The Lynch fella,' he admitted sheepishly.

Kathleen's shock quickly turned to fury. 'Oh my God, Declan.

What's Martin Lynch ever done to you? Don't try and dress it up. I'm not the meek wife behind her husband. Surely, any altercation could've been handled by any man at your side. Why did you have to get involved?'

Rubbing his scalp back and forth, Declan searched for an excuse before he answered truthfully, 'You want the truth, well, Lynch owes me money. He defaulted and made a mockery of me. I had to take a stance. This is money we use to keep our home and life and family going, so don't start on me.' His reply came without remorse.

Kathleen went rigid as if she had been pushed too far and needed to control her response. 'Wait, wait… WAIT! Why did you lend Martin money of any sorts? You should have known not to after the slate he left behind the bar. I thought that you'd learnt your lesson not to lend him anymore. It was embarrassing for me to hold face with Bridget after that, but I did it for you. You agreed that Martin only had a short tab that wouldn't get out of hand. The Lynch's are always struggling, and I need to support my friend in any way I can, especially with Sinead. What did Martin do to justify the state of your knuckles? It can't just be that? One step at a time, Declan, and don't leave anything out.'

Kathleen flicked her hand in frustration as her voice rang clear, 'Never mind me answering to the women's group, even though you have put me in a compromising position. I have to face Bridget and Sinead now to somehow defend you in all of this. This is an impossible situation, Declan, do you realise?'

Declan breathed in, thinking of his words, but nothing could dress up the beating that he had inflicted. As he started to tell her about the events of last night, Kathleen absorbed all the details in increasing frustration as her hands raked through her hair. When he had done, Kathleen spoke without making eye contact.

'I can get my head around the situation with these intruder brothers fronting around town. You've made sure your name rings around in conversations with last night's showdown to put the frighteners on these fuckwits. I understand that… but Martin Lynch isn't a troublemaker, and judging by the state of your hands, he didn't deserve that.' She finished with a heavy sigh, 'I bet he didn't even fight back, did he?'

Raising his eyes to the ceiling, Declan muttered in mock seriousness, 'Don't go all sanctimonious on me, woman.'

Kathleen bit her lip before she answered, 'Do you realise that was child abuse – threatening to attack Shane? He's a minor.'

Declan looked shocked. He hadn't mentioned anything about the boys being there.

'Oh, and yes, my dear husband, I did get the whole rundown, including the part about the boys getting involved. You seemed to have left that detail out in your version of the events.'

'The boys are eighteen, for God's sake,' Declan replied stubbornly.

Kathleen cut him off with a hard edge to her tone, 'Don't try that with me, Declan. The boys are in the same year, they're still in school, and Shane isn't eighteen until June. They're children, and certainly, they're still boys in their mother's eyes.'

Declan tried to lighten the situation, 'What is with you women remembering everyone's birthdays?'

Kathleen's glare intensified the seriousness of her tone. 'What is happening to the Declan Hennessey, I know?' she pleaded, her anger fading. 'Not the husband but the man Declan Hennessey? The man I know would never make rash decisions, would never lash out like that and lose control in public. The man I know always takes a step back and thinks, planning methodically to get what he wants.

'You don't have to be proud to admit to me that you are afraid, Declan. Let's face it; you're getting older whether you like it or not. There is always someone fitter, faster and younger than you out there who wants the same things you did thirty years ago. Why not just hang your boots up? It's time for peace. It's not a case of admitting defeat, it's knowing when the time is right to stop. We have money, our health, our precious Kieran and a future ahead of us. Even after this, haven't you thought of the consequences that could come from this? Martin, pressing charges perhaps?'

'He wouldn't dare,' Declan's blood boiled.

'Bridget would! Martin couldn't stop her, and nor could I.'

Declan ignored the comment as Kathleen made a final plea to him, a warning in her voice. 'Let me make this clear to you, Declan. You find a way to dissolve the loan that stands between you and Martin. Make it disappear. I can put on a steely face and make my excuses with the ICA, but I have to be true to my friend.'

Kathleen fixed her eyes on Declan. Forcing him to look at her, she spoke with soft regret in her voice, 'Why Martin Lynch, Declan? He's no better than he ought to be. You could have settled your score with a handful of people in there last night. It wouldn't be anything to do with you digging up my past and concerning yourself with it?'

Declan ignored the question.

Kathleen continued, 'It's a sad state of affairs. I sincerely hope it's purely business Declan. I would think you a lesser man if that was the case. Love comes and goes, but jealousy is bred in the bone, dear husband. Do you have anything else to add? I want everything out in the open to end last night's saga.'

Declan shrugged warily, deferring any more conflict. The exchange was one-sided. Leaving the bedroom, Kathleen spoke in a subdued tone,

'I'll have your coffee ready for you downstairs. I've lost my appetite for breakfast, so please excuse me if that puts you out.'

Declan knocked his head against the headboard in rhythm with Kathleen's steps down the stairs. Searing pain shot across his shoulders as his back complained. He sat up straight. A pang of regret slithered down his spine as he contemplated his actions of last night. *Shite*, he thought.

CHAPTER 30

It was the date of the Robbie Williams concert, and Sinead could not have been more excited. Martin, on the other hand, was still carrying the bruises from the hands of Declan. The worldwide tour was a sell-out across the UK with rave reviews of the London dates. The generous hospitality package provided for Sinead included a night in the hotel next to the concert venue in Manchester. Martin was impressed to find that the room service tab offered by the concert promoter had no limit. He had to pinch himself to remind him that this was Sinead's special night away and not his own. Money worries always laid a heavier burden on Bridget, and she had felt forced to work, so Martin got the lucky job of escorting Sinead.

Hand luggage was packed, and Bridget had given Martin a comprehensive itinerary of dos and don'ts surrounding Sinead's welfare during their visit. The list was more like a mini brochure. Martin glanced through it but had no intention of reading it. The local newspaper had arranged for transport to take Martin and Sinead to the airport. The understanding was that they would take photos of them on their send-off for an article. The swelling on Martin's face had gone down considerably, but there was no getting away from the fact it showed signs of him taking a beating. Bridget had tried to persuade Martin to wear some of her makeup for the photo session to hide the bruising, but he was having none of it. The photographer arrived on time at 9 am, but after taking one look at Martin's face, they were reluctant to use him in any of the photos and just took pictures of Sinead alone.

After meeting the family, the newspaper had set up an appeal fund for Sinead, so inspired by their story. Since they'd run the first interview, the story had been receiving so much attention they had gone one step further and branded a minibus with her photo on it to raise awareness. The brief interview to take place before they left for the airport was longer than Martin expected.

The reporter went through a series of pre-scripted questions relating to Sinead's treatment and schooling and, of course, her love of Robbie Williams. Martin, tired and dishevelled waiting around for the team to finish, started to grow weary of all the attention on Sinead and began to make noises about it being a publicity stunt for the newspaper.

Bridget pulled him to one side and warned him, 'LOOK!... look at me, Martin. Whatever is going on in your head, STOP. Don't ruin this for our Sinead. You have sole parenting over the next 36 hours and by God, you'd better do good by her, Martin, or I will never forgive you. This is her time in the spotlight for a little over a day. Martin, let her have some happiness for this weekend and not make it about you.'

Martin, upbeat with his reply, didn't soften Bridget's mood, 'Of course, my love... I won't let Sinead or you down... honest. Cross my heart and hope to – well, hope to at least try.'

Bridget's lingering stare gave Martin the indication that she meant it. He knew he couldn't mess this up. Because of the unsettlement with Declan and Martin, Bridget was already anxious. She had wanted Kathleen to be there for Sinead's send-off, but Kathleen was too embarrassed to join in after what had happened. She couldn't look Sinead in the face knowing that her husband had inflicted such injuries on the girl's father. However, she was firm in understanding that business was business and accepting what was needed to secure Declan's position.

Finally, they headed off to start their journey to Manchester. The cold wind picked up and cut right through them as it hounded through the open entrance of the airport. The last of the photographs flashed by the check-in desks. Martin stood to one side and let Sinead absorb all the attention. He found himself a spot to sit down, from where he could keep an eye on Sinead. A shadow fell over him. Peering up, he saw two security guards glaring down at him. Straining his neck to look around, he saw no reason for them to be near him. Ignoring them, he carried on watching Sinead pose in front of the camera.

An authoritative voice spoke, 'Be on your way now, and we won't have to escort you off the premises. This is no place to be sleeping at any time of the day.'

Craning his neck around again, Martin frowned. 'You what? ... Do you think I'm fucking dossing here? You cheeky bastards.' Affronted,

Martin stood up, ready for an argument when a little voice inside his head restrained him. It was Bridget's voice. The words "Don't ruin this for Sinead" rang clear.

The guards stood firm and waited for Martin to make the next move. Martin could tell that they meant business. He glanced at Sinead. Catching his eye, she waved in his direction. Attempting to wave back, his emotions got the better of him as he choked on his words, 'You see that little wonder over there? She's mine.'

Realising their error, one of the guards spoke up, 'Is that the little girl from the appeal fund?' He gestured at the poster erected behind her, 'I read about her in the paper.'

Martin took in a long slow breath as tears brimmed in his eyes. It dawned on him suddenly how dishevelled he looked.

The Guard could see the upset and showed him a little compassion by saying, 'We have a teenage daughter. My wife said it must be a real strain for parents to cope with any serious illness. I'd be a broken man myself. She'd be carrying our daughter and myself.'

Ignoring the comment, Martin watched the joy in Sinead's face. Sheepishly, the guards attempted a parting gesture and said, 'God speed on your journey today. Hope she has a great time.'

Martin gathered his senses, swiping his face of teardrops, then returned to Sinead, who, now finished her photos, was itching to get going. With the flight itinerary in one hand and Sinead's hand luggage in the other, the entrance into the departure lounge overwhelmed him. The large glass windows absorbed light that cast beams across the lounge flooring. Plasma screens blinked with arrival and departure times suspended above them. Flight announcements repeated themselves, as a sea of people moved chaotically in pursuit of their departure gates.

A wave of panic set in as the flight and destination information overwhelmed Martin, who had never flown before. Suddenly, he felt the presence of two people over him again. Sinead tilted her head up to see an overbearing face meet her upside down. The security team had been watching Martin on CCTV. The pixelated screen had shown a man looking flustered and nervous. Either he was a drug mule with a considerable amount of drugs shoved up his arse, or he was a man who couldn't figure out where he should be going despite the considerable information at his disposal.

Laying his palm out, one of the security guards asked Martin for his ticket. After looking at it and looking at Martin's confused face, his demeanour softened. He took their boarding cards and passports, guided Martin and Sinead to their correct boarding gate and escorted them through the checks.

Boarding the plane, Sinead had butterflies in her stomach. As they arrived at their designated seats, Martin picked up on a whispered remark about the state of his face from the passengers in the seats behind him. Waiting while another passenger faffed around with the overhead storage, Martin stared the couple out until they diverted their attention to reading the passenger safety information about emergency landings at sea.

Once seated, the flight attendants were about to demonstrate the safety procedures when Martin stopped one of them and furtively asked her, 'Are you serving alcoholic drinks from the front of the plane first, or do I have to come up to collect them? Also, what size bottles of vodka do you serve?'

The flight attendant's eyes flashed concern before she quickly remarked, 'Sir – this is a short domestic flight; we don't serve alcohol. However, we do serve soft drinks or hot beverages.'

As she went to walk off, Martin said, under his breath, to her, 'Could you pour a miniature vodka bottle in my orange juice, Miss?'

Pretending she hadn't heard him, she briskly walked off. Sinead, dazzled by the newness of everything, was oblivious. The journey was swift and exciting. Sinead was elated with her new experience while Martin, feeling somewhat dejected, worried he had missed out on the freebie spirits.

CHAPTER 31

A week had passed since Martin's beating at the hands of Declan. With Martin and Sinead gone for the weekend, Bridget thought the time was right for her and Kathleen to meet appropriately and discuss it. Bridget had spoken to Kathleen briefly about it, but Kathleen had only heard second-hand accounts from a couple of her friends whose husbands were in The Telegraph that night. Declan had been in a terrible mood for the first couple of days after the incident. Kathleen had had to wait a week until the situation, and Declan's temper had calmed down before she could get to the bottom of what had gone on.

Martin and Sinead had only left a matter of hours ago. There was only so much tidying up Bridget could do to stop herself from worrying about them. She didn't know what to do with all this time on her hands and wanted to settle down for a few hours sleep in the afternoon before her night shift. Before leaving, Martin hadn't come clean about the outstanding money owed to the O'Driscoll's and Declan, so Bridget still felt somewhat in the dark. She hadn't slept properly throughout the week as Martin had passed the topic off whenever she picked at him for information. Planning the trip for Sinead had kept her mind active in a positive way, but every time she looked at Martin's face, she felt scared and angry.

Bridget snapped at Shane that morning as the grunting from his workout in the hallway got on her nerves. Unable to think straight with the relentless noise, she had barked at him to move the punch bag to his room. When Shane left the house without saying a word to her, she regretted the tongue lashing. Bridget needed closure on this whole mess and rang Kathleen as soon as Martin and Sinead left. Kathleen hadn't wanted to talk on the phone and said she'd call around at lunchtime.

As usual, Bridget had devoted her time to ensuring everyone else's needs were met and had neglected to look after her own. With tired eyes,

Bridget looked at the clock; it was 11.50 am. Her whole body felt tired. Bruised shadows sat wearily under her eyes. Her lank hair trailed across her face. She hadn't eaten properly in days. Her mind wouldn't allow her to sleep, and she needed answers to question after question. Her phone beeped, and Kathleen's name flashed up: *5 mins away, put the kettle on.*

Kathleen arrived with another box of cream cakes. It had slipped her mind when picking them up that Sinead had already left. Bridget opened the box while Kathleen hung up her coat and kicked her boots off. The waft of her Eternity perfume filled the air. Bridget made tea, and the two tentatively sat down to talk in the kitchen. Kathleen cupped her mug while Bridget devoured a cream cake.

'God, that tastes so good; I'll regret this when I jump on the scales,' said Bridget.

'B, when was the last time you ate a square meal?' asked Kathleen.

'Arhh, you know what it's like in this house,' answered Bridget, 'I'm always bogged down with too much to do in and not enough time to do it in.'

Kathleen studied her friend. The worry lines were now permanently grooved across her forehead. 'I'm serious, B; when was the last time you stopped for five minutes? You look wrecked.'

Bridget ignored the statement. 'Uhmm, Kathleen, these are too good! I'm sure Sinead won't mind if I polish off her one. Hmmm.'

'Bridget, listen to me.' Said Kathleen. 'I can't sit back and let you carry on like this. You're driving yourself into the ground. I'm going to arrange for you and myself to have a spa weekend when Martin and Sinead get back. I'll treat us to this, and I won't hear another word about it. We both need it,' she added softly.

Satisfied after her second cake, Bridget sloped back against the chair, finally winding down from the past couple of days. She briefly closed her eyes in the peace of the moment. Kathleen felt angry that her friend was suffering so much. Running her finger around her mug, she contemplated what to say next. She had news that wasn't good, but she knew she couldn't dress it up.

'Look, B, I've spoken with Declan,' said Kathleen reluctantly. Her wedding ring started to tap annoyingly against her mug. 'I deliberately waited for the heat to calm down so I could get my head around what happened. I heard Declan's side of the story, and it seems to tally up with all the tittle-tattle about that night.'

Stretching her eyes to keep them open, Bridget rubbed the backs of her hands over them as she straightened in her seat. Kathleen, looking at her, noticed how dry her skin was, with red blemishes around her nostrils and cheeks. The rubbing irritated it.

Bridget, catching her friend staring at her, said, 'Just spit it out, Kath, I need some closure on this to finally catch up on some sleep.'

The tapping stopped. 'Right, Bridget, well the thing is: apparently, Martin had a skinful last month and took out a loan to finish off his hand at the card game. Look B, nobody pressured him,' Kathleen aimed her finger pointedly. 'Anyway, he lost the hand and flumped paying the first instalment.'

Bridget pursed her lips to talk but couldn't find any words.

Kathleen continued. 'Declan paid him a visit.' She looked down, unable to meet Bridget's gaze. 'Martin understood the arrangement afterwards.'

Bridget inhaled and held it. She shook her head, tilting it forward before she replied. 'God almighty, David wouldn't have let that happen. There has to be more to it than that? Did you see the state of him?'

'B, you are not Martin's keeper and nor is David,' Kathleen reminded her.

Bridget recoiled back in her chair.

'There's more to it than that, yes,' Kathleen continued. 'David and Martin were caught on surveillance using Declan's van for something.' She waved her hand across her face dismissively. 'It's a long story. Anyway, it turned out Martin was doing some work for the O'Driscolls and was caught on camera and that, in turn, compromised Declan.'

Bridget's head dropped back against the chair. 'So, how much did he borrow? The truth, Kath. Martin can sweet talk himself out of situations with these O'Driscolls, but the money owed won't disappear.'

'Two thousand,' Kathleen's words trailed out in a whisper.

'Two thousand! David shouldn't have let that happen. I knew something was up. He was secretive about collecting money for something, I knew it had to be bad, so I didn't ask; I didn't want to know. I never thought it was that bad.' Bridget moaned as she pressed her face into her hands.

'Apparently, he had only needed a grand to cover his hand, but he thought he needed higher stakes to continue further into the night,' Kathleen elaborated. 'It all backfired on him when he put the lot on the one hand.'

'Dear God, how am I going to get us out of this?' Searching for answers, Bridget looked to the floor as she placed her hand to the base of her throat.

'B, I have an understanding with my husband that I won't interfere with his business activities as long as he is straight with me. It has served our marriage well. I can't intervene between Declan and Martin's issues. Martin is a grown man, and what he owes the O'Driscolls is of no concern for my husband.'

Bridget felt betrayed by her husband's lack of judgement, but she knew this situation was nobody's fault but Martin's. Her eyes flickered from side to side across the floor as she tried to piece together the situation Martin had placed her in. Questions raced through her mind. How were they going to pay off this debt? How long were these repayments for? How was Martin going to find work? How long would her body allow her to keep doing double shifts? It all overwhelmed her. Bridget couldn't make sense of it all.

'But his face Kathleen? Why did Declan beat him like that?'

Kathleen spoke hesitantly. 'Declan confronted Martin in the pub with no warning. I admit I wasn't happy when he told me that. By all accounts, Martin provoked him further in front of everyone, and that's when he lost his cool.'

Bridget sighed as she rubbed her face again. Feeling overwrought, she shared her deep concerns. 'I thought about what you said that night about leaving Martin. He's breaking me, Kath, and I can't take it anymore. As they say, "Fine words butter no parsnips," and with Martin, it's all words, no change. I blame him, you know, for everything, for the way our life has turned out.

'I think if Martin were straight about everything he had done from day one, then I wouldn't have this resentment towards him, this worry, this stress. That's what Sinead has picked up on. That's why she has this blasted disease; I'm convinced of it. It's all the negative energy in our home. My blood is boiling all the time trying to get ourselves out of this shite… this shit hole. Take a look around you, Kath. This is what my life has come to. Worry, stress, sickness, and shite.'

Bridget's blinks became slower; exhaustion was overcoming her. Kathleen studied her friend carefully and paused before speaking. 'You're dead beat B, and not thinking straight. You need plenty of rest, and your body needs to build up all your reserves before you can get your mind on the right track. This isn't a 24-hour fix; it could take weeks before you're ready to make any big decisions. As they say, time is a healer, so you'll have a different outlook in time to come.'

Kathleen got up and collected both mugs. Placing them in the sink, her eyes noticed a packet of medication by the side of the kettle. Kathleen read the label: *Mrs Maureen Finnigan - Tramadol – repeat prescription.* She quizzed her friend. 'This medication, B, please tell me you're not taking them?' There was a note of accusation in her voice.

Bridget's eyes were heavy now; she flinched, annoyed, at the question. 'Don't start, Kath. They belong to one of the residents at the hospice. She passed away, and the medication had to be binned, so I just took a few. They've taken the edge off for me; they've helped me get by these last few weeks.' Her eyelids began to droop again.

'Christ, B, this isn't the way forward,' Kathleen waved the medication leaflet in front of her. 'These are not helping you; they're making things worse. Look!' She read out the side effects. '*Anxiety, skin rash, hallucinations, drowsiness*' the list goes on. Please tell me you'll stop taking these, she pleaded. Her voice was shaky with concern.

Bridget remained docile in her chair. She mustered a slurred sentence, 'I just need them until everything is straight.'

Kathleen began to pull open the kitchen drawers and rifle through them, searching for more tablets. Second drawer down, she found more blister packets. There were enough pills to last her months. Scooping them into a carrier bag, Kathleen collected the medication and, leaving Bridget asleep, went outside and stashed them in her car. As she came back in, the wind caught the front door, and it slammed. Bridget came to and apologised for falling asleep, their previous conversation forgotten. She offered to make more tea.

Kathleen helped her out of her chair and took charge. 'Right, my girl, the best place for you is a bed, and that's just where you're going. 'Where is your mobile, by the way?'

'What for?' asked Bridget, puzzled. 'It's in my apron uniform for work.'

Struggling upstairs, Kathleen stripped Bridget's outer clothing off, made her comfortable and tucked her into the bed. She fumbled around the bedroom until she found her apron and the phone, then rang Bridget's staff nurse and called in sick for her.

Next, she rang Declan. 'Hi, love… yes, everything is ok… I won't be home till late so you and Kieran will have to get a takeaway or suit yourself. I'm spending the day with Bridget… DECLAN!... That's more like it!... Thanks for your understanding… love you.'

Unable to stay awake any longer, Bridget's eyes gave way to sleep. Sitting down on the edge of the bed, Kathleen examined her best friend's face as she slept. Her laughter lines had flattened out. Dry skin flaked from her hairline, her lips looked pale, and her eyes had dark shadows under them. All of this was the result of a body deprived of sleep and peace and twisted with worry. A good night's sleep was the first step. Kathleen smiled, tears glistening in her eyes, as she watched her best friend suffering, even while her body tried to rest. Stroking Bridget's hair, she was determined to help her as best she could. Getting up, she left the room, locking the front door behind her. Her first stop was to go back home.

She ignored Kieran when she arrived home and headed straight upstairs. There, she removed cash from a safe in her bedroom and, after counting it, split it into three amounts, separated into envelopes. Her next stop was a quick grocery run then to an organic bistro down the road. She left with a takeaway of homemade soup and fresh bread. Back at Bridget's, she filled her fridge with the groceries then hid each envelope in places only Bridget would find them. She stashed them underneath her uniform and in drawers that only Bridget would open. Finally, Kathleen cleaned as much as possible in the kitchen, then made herself comfortable reading a book whilst waiting for her best friend to wake up.

CHAPTER 32

A driver was waiting with a placard to greet Martin and Sinead in arrivals. Martin felt overwhelmed as he approached him; it was strange to see his name being held up by a chauffeur. He was intimidated until the driver opened his mouth to speak, and a broad Manchurian accent greeted them.

'Alright there. Does youse two wanna follow me... can I take that bag, young lady?'

The driver made light work of the luggage. Following him, Martin and Sinead exited the airport. Heavy dark clouds blanketed the sky as a gush of cold wind chased them into the car. The driver chatted away about being a chauffeur to Robbie Williams and his entourage during his UK tour. Martin felt at ease with his way of speaking. The language was brash but not offensive. Martin, however, knew from experience that Sinead picked up every detail of the conversation.

The vehicle pulled up outside The Stock Exchange hotel in the heart of Manchester. They were escorted into the lobby by the driver, where they checked in. The porter showed Martin to their room, an enormous suite, and instructed them on how to use the key card. Once their bags were dropped they were given a tour of the suites two bedrooms and living area. He asked if they had any further questions, then nodded as if waiting to be excused, clearly expecting a tip.

Typically, Martin had next to nothing in his pockets. He knew precisely what the attendant was hinting at, so he coyly played along and said, 'Before you go, my good man…' Reaching into his jacket pocket, he fumbled around. The attendant graciously nodded a second time in acknowledgement. Martin pulled out his phone and handed it to him. The porter looked puzzled. 'Could you take a couple of photos of us before you leave?' Martin asked politely, trying not to laugh. The porter obliged disgruntledly and left. Martin and Sinead burst into fits of laughter and when they had composed themselves, they unpacked and had a nap.

Sinead woke up first and switched the TV on. She took out her knitting and worked away at it. Martin soon woke up, too; all he could hear was the bass thumping from the music channel.

Feeling worse for oversleeping, he looked at Sinead and sarcastically said, 'Did you need to bring that frigging knitting with you, darling? It's the same with your Auntie Sheila. We all need a break from it.'

Sinead scrunched her face up in derision as she lost track of her stitch counting. She ignored him. They briefly discussed what they could eat, and both agreed on a selection of cakes and hot drinks. Room service was ordered and delivered, again without a tip. Afterwards, the concierge informed Martin his driver was waiting for them. The driver's instructions were clear: hit the renowned shopping precinct in the city.

Bridget had given spending money to Sinead, but Martin was dubious about how had she saved it up. He thought that Kathleen might have given Bridget the money as a treat for Sinead. Bridget would never admit that to him as she knew he would be self-righteous and refuse to accept Declan Hennessey's money. He decided not to ask about it and let Sinead buy whatever she wanted.

After an afternoon of shopping, they both had weary feet and hungry stomachs. Back at the hotel, they called the lift to head up to their room. Before they reached their floor, an elderly couple dressed in dinner attire entered the lift. The elderly gentleman eyed Martin up and down suspiciously, clearly speculating from his bruised and battered face that he had no right being in this fancy hotel. They looked flabbergasted when Sinead told them they were staying at the hotel. In their suite, Martin slumped down next to Sinead on the sofa.

He took one look at the hip-hop music video she'd put on and said, 'Is this what you'd be watching at home if we had the satellite up and running? Chrissake, this is a lot of shite.' Sinead dismissed his comment and raised the volume higher. Martin shook his head and shouted, 'I'm going to take a shower and shave in case one of the photographers are at the concert later. Do you wanna take a look at the menu while I'm getting ready so that we can order something?'

Sinead, looking downbeat, replied, 'Guess so, Dad.' Martin looked at her curiously, but she raised the volume up higher and waved at him to go.

Martin could have stayed in the shower until he collapsed from heat exhaustion it was so nice, the spray was hot and strong, a far cry from the facilities at home. Pulling fresh socks up over damp feet, Martin forced his foot into the air just as Sinead knocked on the door.

He called out, 'Yeh! Yeh!... come in, sweetheart.'

Looking pale and withdrawn, Sinead quietly said, 'Will you promise not to be mad with me, Dad?'

On edge, Martin hopped into the main suite with one sock partially on to see what had happened. He panicked and immediately thought that she might have broken the TV. On inspection, everything was intact.

'Jaysis – Yeh made me jump there, darling, what's the matter?' he said.

'I don't wanna go to the concert, Dad. This hotel is deadly. Our suite is smashing. We'll never be able to stay in one like this again. What I'd like to do is to order dinner and dessert, then snuggle up in this bathrobe and watch a movie... you can pick, Dad... I don't mind what.'

Flummoxed by the pure simplicity of her request, Martin couldn't speak for a moment. As far as he was concerned, it was music to his ears. The flight followed by the shopping extravaganza and the hot shower had drained his energy levels completely. If Sinead wanted to bow out of the concert, he had no problem with that at all.

Cupping Sinead's cheeks, Martin said, 'Darling, you jump in the shower, get your pj's on and get yourself comfortable. Tell me what you want for dinner, and I'll order it up for us. It's a great plan.'

Sinead had been worried that Martin was excited about going to the concert. The truth was, he'd have hated standing amongst screaming fans for up to two hours. Martin dialled for room service and placed their order.

'Oh, also, can you send up a bottle of Cointreau too, please? In an ice bucket?' he tagged on at the end of the order.

Within half an hour, the delicious smell of food from the service trolley filled the room. After dinner, Martin let Sinead pick the movie. It was a teen love story that had Sinead enthralled from beginning to end. Martin half watched it, drinking the Cointreau and enjoying the time with his little girl. Sinead let Martin stroke her patchy scalp. Next to the bottle of Cointreau, two cups of hot chocolate were made fast work of.

Eventually, towards the end of the movie, Sinead started to drift off. Martin didn't stir her. Instead, he listened to the rhythm of her breathing while he reminisced on the day Sinead was born.

2006

Martin rang for an ambulance as Bridget's wailing became incessant during each contraction. Reaching Rotunda hospital, they were rushed into the delivery wing, the midwives requests to push harder forced out more guttural grunts. As Bridget writhed in agony, pleading for pain relief, her face was ready to explode. After each push, the pain was like nothing she had imagined from her first pregnancy.

After each push, she collapsed back on the bed, with nothing left to give, and the drill sergeant psyched her back up to push with another heave. Martin had been at her bedside from admission and felt drained with exhaustion. Each contraction pulsed a surge of excruciating pain through him as Bridget clasped his hand in a vice. After several hours, Bridget felt the visceral tear of her flesh as Sinead's head pierced daylight before her body fully emerged.

Wrapped in swaddling, mother and daughter bonded under the strobe lighting. As the newborn flexed her muscles, her heavy eyelids broke tradition during her nursing and opened up, absorbing the new material world around her. It wasn't long before Bridget passed out through exhaustion; Martin then took on his fatherly duties. A short time later, Bridget awoke to a shrieking noise. As she came to, to the sound of her baby, a piercing throbbing pain drilled into her skull, which followed up with a thud that penetrated right between her eyes. Nausea overwhelmed her as she attempted to sit up.

Immediately, Bridget reached out to Martin for reassurance for the noise to stop. Her hand patted around the starchy bed sheets before she opened her eyes. Alone with a screaming baby next to her, she called out Martin's name in a weary tone. A beaming nurse appeared by her side instead of her husband.

Bridget felt groggy as she blinked around by her bedside and asked, 'Nurse, where's my husband?'

The over smiley nurse responded, 'I believe he's gone for a refreshment.'

Bridget blinked before her eyes opened wide.

'Hold on now nurse, that phrase can mean a whole different thing as far as my husband is concerned. Did he mention anything about thirsty work or celebrations being required? How long has he been gone?'

The nurse's fixed smile was still in place. It annoyed Bridget.

The nurse replied, 'Maybe half an hour. He was asking me where he could make phone calls.'

Bridget countered, 'So, he didn't say he was leaving the hospital and returning?' Dropping her head back against the pillow, Bridget lost the will to stay conscious.

The nurse noticed and tried to reassure her. 'I didn't get that impression. Please, you need to rest now, Mrs Lynch. My – your daughter has a powerful set of lungs on her.'

Bridget thought silently to herself, 'I want to punch that smile off her face' before she asked, 'Why is she screaming? My head feels like it wants to explode. Can you give me something to end it all?'

The nurse helped her sit up correctly and puffed her pillows out before adjusting the lift control of the bed. She spoke reassuringly, 'The baby crying is believed to help bring the mother around from the pain relief wearing off.'

Bridget responded prickly, 'This isn't my first rodeo, now take her away and give her to her father when he comes back up. I can't deal with this.'

The nurse persisted, 'Perhaps now might be a good time to bond with your daughter; she needs to feed.'

Bridget winced as she straightened her back, trying not to stretch any stitches. 'You've got to be kidding me. You're preaching to the wrong choir, sister. I've been drugged up to the eyeballs, and I can tell you this for free... that baby isn't swinging on these. I've got nipples the size of Rolos, and they feel like they've been sunburnt to the point that I can feel the heat on them from the fluorescent lighting through my gown. It's SMA all the way from here on in with this little one. I can assure you of that. Now, when is my husband back?'

A booming voice echoed from behind the curtain. Martin appeared with a spring in his step, and a broad grin stretched across his face. A bunch of flowers shielded his chest. He greeted his wife with a kiss on her forehead as petals bombarded her face.

'And how are my two beautiful ladies doing alongside each other?'

Bridget huffed, glancing at the attractive midwife, 'I do hope you do mean myself and your daughter, Martin. Where have you been?'

Martin beamed, 'I've just rung David with the news, and he's now spreading the word.'

'Martin, can you prepare a bottle for her feed so I can get myself together? I feel like shite.'

'Arhh, give over woman you look radiant, doesn't she nurse?' The nurse fixed a smile on him like a weather presenter and left.

Martin handed the baby over and watched in glee at mother and baby bonded. As exhaustion plagued her face, Bridget's eyes brightened on meeting her daughter's gaze.

Without thinking, Martin asked, 'Any idea what's for dinner tonight?'

As the words rolled off his tongue, Bridget flashed a mock grin rolling her eyes.

Bouncing on the balls of his feet, Martin asked again, 'Seriously, what's for dinner tonight?'

Bridget's tongue ran across her bottom lip before she spoke. 'Chrissakes, if I'd the energy to lift the flesh and blood in my arms, I'd swing for you. Now that this little guest has left my body; my hips feel like a wishbone has been split in two. I have stitches where you'll never be kissing again, and for your information – YES! The pain is worse than a bee sting. Mark my words, you'll be pulling your weight once we get back home, Martin Lynch. This is going to be payback for the past nine months.'

Martin had won at pissing off his exhausted wife, looking for an excuse to leave, so he added, 'Right – fish and chips it is then.'

Sinead was fast asleep when family members peeled the curtains back. Martin made his excuses to pick Shane up from school and bring some of the gifts back to the house. Scuttling down to the entrance, he searched for a porter he had spoken with earlier. He spotted him and made himself known again.

'Well, my good man, have you got a second piece of good news for me today?'

'I should've known better,' said the porter, 'Put a bet on the fast horses,' you said. You sold me the dream ticket, and I backed it as well. It fell at the first fence. In fact, I take that back; it's the first time I ever saw a horse trying to run through a jump.'

The betting slip balled up in Martin's hand. Leaving the hospital, he grabbed a cab on the way home. He should have been concerned about how he was going to pay for his journey but the joy that his daughter had been born into the world outweighed any of his concerns.

Snapping back out of his reverie and back into the luxury suite in their Manchester hotel, Martin saw that Sinead had fallen fast asleep. He gently woke and coaxed her to her room before tucking her into bed. He could tell by the shadows under her eyes that the day had taken its toll on her weary body.

As she laid down, she could tell he was studying her face and murmured, 'Da, I'm a big girl now. Don't fuss over me. I've enjoyed tonight. I'd still like to see the concert but will wait till it comes out on DVD. Da…?' she asked quietly. 'Could we come to a place like this again and do nothing but order room service and watch movies?'

Martin laughed and cuddled her before saying, 'Darling, that's a grand idea, but we'd have to win the lottery to be able to afford to stay here again.'

Sinead fidgeted with her pillow to make herself comfortable. She shifted up in the bed, tucking the pillow behind her back. Something was on her mind. Martin was seated on the chair beside her, his legs crossed, facing her.

Drawing her fingers lightly around the colouring of his marbled bruising, Sinead gently said, 'Da, it's not too late, you know?'

'Too late for what, princess?' Martin asked.

'You know, Dad?… For you to get a job, a real job, and help out Mam more.'

Martin flinched, then jokingly said, 'Do you want a bunch of fives in the mush?'

Sinead mimicked a closed fist and tapped his nose, 'Seriously, Da.'

'Well, aren't you the great recruitment agent,' he mocked. 'We've been through this before, my love. Let's not spoil a great evening.' He turned as if to go.

Sinead quickly responded, 'If you did it for yourself, Da, then Mam would see the benefits too, that's all.'

Exhaling slowly, Martin succumbed to her questioning. 'Look, I can't promise anything. I'll sit with your mam after all of this has flown by and discuss things. It's not as straightforward as you think, my little princess. This big wide world is often complicated.'

Sinead, unsatisfied, probed further. 'Da, why do you drink?'

'You, what?' Martin was shocked.

'I mean, why do you drink every day? Mam doesn't, Auntie Sheila and Kathleen don't.'

'Ah well, you see love,' he joked, 'I make up for what they miss out on.'

Sinead wasn't appeased. 'I think, Da, if you stopped – I don't mean – what I mean is… I think it's holding you back from what you could do in life. You don't have to stop. You could just drink at weekends after work has finished – what do you think?'

'I think you've been doing too much thinking, is what I think. what made you ask me that?'

'I researched it on Auntie Kathleen's iPad. Drinking all the time can cause a host of problems with people's personalities and their outlook on life. I think if you could make a change, we could see where it takes you – and us.'

'Now, what's with this "drinking all the time?" You don't see me at breakfast with a can of lager with my toast, do you?'

'I don't see you at breakfast at all, Da – you're always sleeping off the drink from the night before.'

Martin was ashamed but unwilling to concede. 'I think someone's been absorbing too much information for her own good around here.'

'I could put you in touch with groups in Dublin, Da; I wrote them down at home.'

'Groups, now, what kind of groups are we talking about here?' Martin said. 'Will I be able to go out for a drink with them?' he laughed, 'cause that's the only way I'd associate with them people.'

'Ah Dad,' Sinead looked forlorn. 'I just want to see a change in you. A chance of a change for all of us, that's all. I'm sorry. I didn't mention any of this to Mam if that's what you're worried about.'

'Look, Sinead,' said Martin, 'my life is like a damaged record.' He looked suddenly serious. 'It plays and gets to a certain point, and then the needle jumps to restart the chorus. I make mistakes and never learn from them, only to repeat the same mistakes again and again. The drinking takes the edge off the needle jumping back to the start.

'Thanks a million for looking out for your old, Da. I'm not mad at you. I'm annoyed for not thinking of this myself, and I'm proud of you for having the guts to speak to me about it. Can you show me what you were looking into when we get back home?'

Sinead beamed. 'Sure, Da, always look on the positive side. A change is going to come.' Happy now, she squashed her pillow back into form and snuggled back in the bed. Kissing her on the forehead, Martin rubbed the side of her cheeks before leaving. As he turned off the light, Sinead pulled the duvet up to her chin and spoke in a mischievous tone.

'Da... do you think they would miss my bathrobe when we leave tomorrow?'

Putting his finger against his lips, Martin whispered, 'Shhh, you know me too well, darling. It looks like they'll be missing two of them tomorrow.'

He closed the door gently behind him and went into his bedroom. Martin got himself ready for bed. It didn't take long for the day to catch up on him. He made himself comfortable amidst the fresh bedsheets and sagged into his pillow, letting the soft feathers form a mould of his face. Sinead's final question plagued his mind and, as he drifted into unconsciousness, tears settled against his pillow.

CHAPTER 33

The morning greeted Martin through the curtains. Stretching himself under the duvet, he revelled in the luxury of the soft bed. He spoke aloud, 'That's the best night's sleep I've had in ages. I feel like a new man.' After checking in on Sinead, he turned his attention to enjoying the en-suite shower and the comfort of the oversized fluffy towels. Whilst dressing, a booming sound rocked the room, startling Martin. Striding out of the bedroom, he witnessed Sinead standing on the glass coffee table performing dance moves to a hip-hop track with the music blaring. She was singing along shouting, 'Now Watch Me Whip, Watch Me Nae.'

Martin panicked and ordered her off the table and to turn the volume down. He wasn't concerned about waking up the guests next door but for the temperament of the glass table. He thought that if he was hoping to get away with permanently borrowing the bathrobes, then he didn't need any conflict with the hotel. They decided to skip breakfast, preferring to arrive a little early at the airport and eat there instead. Sinead wanted to hunt around the souvenir shop for trinkets for her mam and Kathleen.

As they exited the hotel, a rush of cold air accompanied them out the lobby. The morning weather had turned cruel. They fastened their coats up and mounted the collars, muffling their faces up to their nostrils. The bracing wind cut through them both as they sat in the car. Sinead asked if she could take out the *borrowed* bathrobe and snuggle up on the plane with it.

Wind funnelled across the entrance to the airport. Once inside the terminal, Martin was ordered to pitch down outside the shopping outlets to guard the luggage whilst Sinead shopped. Martin wasn't worried about losing her as it wasn't difficult to spot a young girl with a patchy bald head in the crowds.

Once aboard the plane, Martin couldn't be bothered annoying the stewardess with his requests. Instead, they both slept for the duration of the short flight. On arrival, Martin made Sinead rehearse answers for Bridget to prove they'd attended the concert. The newspaper bus was collecting them. The paper was going to have a reporter at the house to interview them again after their adventure.

The driver reminded Martin that the team would meet them at home on their return for another interview. Rolling his eyes, Martin just wanted to get home and relax after the journey. Martin and Sinead cuddled up in the cab and chatted briefly about their night away. When they got to the house, they saw the newspaper's car parked outside their home.

Bridget had already invited them in. Martin and Sinead had no further time to rehearse their story as they clambered in with all their bags. Thankfully, the questioning about the concert was brief. Sinead was very smart and said that the excitement had got the better of her and she couldn't recall much of the detail of the concert as the crowds and noise were overwhelming. The reporter accepted her response and asked to take photos with her holding her concert programme.

At that point, Sinead pretended to cry and confessed that she'd left her concert memorabilia in the hotel lobby. Martin, stone-faced, tried to communicate with Sinead to reel in the emotion, she was overdoing it a bit, but Bridget had noticed something was up. He knew once the crew had left, it would all come spilling out from Sinead, who couldn't keep a secret from her mother. Bridget made excuses that Sinead needed her rest, and the reporter duly left. The front door slammed shut.

Bridget marched back into the front room with her hands on her hips; she frowned and said, 'Okaaaaay! – who is going to start first?'

Sinead sang like a canary. Rummaging through her bag, she retrieved her souvenirs to show her mam in the hope of mitigating the damage.

Bridget's eyes lit up in annoyance as she shrieked, 'Are you telling me you both ended up dossing down for the evening while I was here on my own? You both missed the very event you went over to attend? I was worried about Sinead all night, wondering how she was getting on, was she safe in that huge arena, and you're telling me you pitched on the sofa all evening. Tell me, Martin, did you have a drink at all last night?'

Martin, in his defence, said, 'We were exhausted and needed to rest. I was dressed and ready to go out when Sinead said she preferred to stay in to watch a film instead.'

Bridget repeated herself, 'Did you have anything to drink,Martin?'

Sinead interrupted, 'Mam... I chose to stay in. I like Robbie's music, but after all the shopping yesterday I was too shot to go out to the concert. I chose the film and dinner, and Dad settled down next to me with his drink.'

Bridget glared at Martin and softly spoke to Sinead, 'Sweetheart, can you put your washing aside in the kitchen.' Knowing she was wanted away, she dumped her washing and headed upstairs to her room.

Although Sinead knew her mam treated her and her illness with kid gloves, by the same token, she knew that Bridget hadn't realised that she had matured over the last year. She was well aware of tension in the home with the pressures of money and Martin's drinking. She was still treated as a child that needed protection, and that annoyed her. If she could deal with cancer, she could deal with anything, she thought. Through plasterboard walls, Sinead could hear her mother's raised voice. Martin didn't retaliate or defend himself. The argument ended as usual with Martin walking out, slamming the front door behind him.

Over the past few weeks, Bridget had become an emotional wreck. Her body clock was all over the place from her gruelling night shifts and the tensions between her and Martin had gotten worse. The atmosphere went quiet, except for the clutter of crockery in the kitchen sink. Sinead appeared from her room and tried to reassure her mother.

Speaking quietly, she said, 'Mam... we had a great time last night, and Da was brilliant. He didn't shout or argue with me; it was my decision not to go out. If we'd had gone to the concert, I would have wanted to leave early. The day was too tiring.'

Bowing her head over the sink, Bridget replied, 'I'll see it all in a different light once I get some rest, sweetheart. Sorry, you had to hear the row.'

Watching the trauma on her mother's face, Sinead hugged her and responded,

'Sometimes, we are a happy family, and more times, we are at each other's throats! This family is going around in a loop with no pause to step out, Mam. I chatted with Da while we were away, and he's going to try to get a job, Mam. I know he lets you down, but you need to give him a break. I just want the shouting to stop, Mam. I want you both to be happy. Can't you tell that Shane doesn't want to be in this house? I can't say more than that. It's horrible here lately.'

Bridget turned to face her. 'Sinead Lynch, you and your brother have never let me down. I admit that recently your father and I haven't been getting along. I sometimes assume that you and Shane are still small children and that the tense atmosphere filters over you. You have enough on your plate dealing with your treatment. I am sorry both of you have witnessed the unpleasantness. I've been too concerned with my own point of view.'

Sinead brought out the souvenirs and left them on the worktop by the sink, then returned to the front room to watch TV. Bridget loaded the washing machine. Sinead had bought her a small white teddy bear with a badge that read 'I love Manchester'. She made herself a cup of tea, picked up the bear, then went in and kissed Sinead on the forehead before going upstairs to bed.

Sinead beckoned her back before she left the room and asked, 'Mam… what do you think of my new wardrobe?' Bridget gasped in frustration as Sinead held up the permanently borrowed dressing gown.

'For the LOVE OF GOD, Martin Lynch.'

CHAPTER 34

Martin hadn't gone far and, once Bridget went to sleep, he returned shortly after. He had timed it perfectly when he returned with some bacon, mushrooms, a French stick and a newspaper. Sinead heard the rustle of a carrier bag and knew that her favourite snack was on its way. Nobody made a bacon baguette like her Dad. Twenty minutes later, lunch was ready. The smell of fried bacon and mushrooms saturated the air. Sinead was folded up on the sofa in her oversized bathrobe.

Martin joked, 'Jaysis… it's a good thing your mam hadn't seen that before she went to bed. I suppose she'll do her nut when she sees it.' Sinead averted her eyes without responding. Unravelling herself from beneath the mass of material, she grabbed her plate.

Martin, satisfied after lunch, remarked, 'Arhh – now, that's a meal fit for a king and his princess.'

Sinead couldn't finish her portion, explaining the food hadn't settled comfortably; Martin grinned, 'Are your eyes too big for your belly, darling. Let your old dad help.'

Martin remembered that Shane had borrowed some device connected to the TV, allowing them to watch an array of films. It had to go back to his friend the following week. Once again, they settled down to watch Sinead's choice of film. It was an amicable agreement. The next couple of hours passed by quickly as Martin's heavy eyelids coaxed him to doze off. The movie finished, and both of them had fallen into a deep sleep. He woke up with a crick in his neck, giving him some discomfort. He didn't want to wake Sinead, so, grabbing the newspaper, he meticulously studied the days racing in the kitchen before gently disengaging himself to get stuck into some jobs.

Wet washing hung around the house as Martin completed his household chores for the day. The racing commentary on the radio kept him company as he deliberated backing a horse. After ringing David to put a bet on for him, Martin found that his credit had expired. He pondered over his dilemma, convincing himself it would be acceptable to leave Sinead asleep and pop out to put the bet on.

Martin reached the betting shop quickly. He chatted with two racing fanatics who quizzed him about the yellow bruising on his face and then placed his bet. Martin had to cut the conversation short to return home. By the time he got back, nearly two hours had passed by. Martin cursed himself. Hesitant, he went to sneak through the back door. The hum of the radio was still on in the background, and there was no sign of Bridget. Her handbag was gone, and he realised she had already left for work. He spotted a note from her on the back of the gas bill: *I have to pay this bill and fill the fridge up as there is nothing in there for the kids' dinner tonight. Where is the money for the instalment that is due tomorrow*?

'Oh, shite.' Martin slapped his forehead. He had borrowed €20 from the money put aside for the gas bill for his bet today. Even if his horse came in and won, Martin couldn't collect any winnings until tomorrow. Still, he knew he could count on David to lend him the money if he was stuck. Reaching for his mobile, he realised he had no credit to call him and cursed, throwing it across the worktop. The fact that he had been out and had the opportunity to top up his phone frustrated him even more. Bridget would go spare with the money short. He couldn't go back out again because Sinead was still asleep. She never slept that long during the day, even on medication. He presumed Bridget would have seen to her before leaving for work.

He peeked in at her through the door. The movie menu was still playing on a loop. Kicking off his shoes, he slumped down next to Sinead. Placing his arm over her shoulder, he stroked her head. As he pulled away, something caught his attention. Studying her, he realised her body shape and head position hadn't moved at all since he left. Surely, he thought, there should have been the slightest movements, even in the deepest of sleep. He tried to calm himself by considering how the last 24 hours had been hectic, and even a strong, healthy body would be fatigued after the whirlwind trip.

Martin placed his finger under her nose to feel for air. There was faint contact of air, not enough though to satisfy him. Unravelling the bathrobe from around her he expected to find her skin hot and clammy.

Her body was cold and still. Mild panic set in. Cupping his mouth with his hands, Martin tried to reason with himself. Suddenly, a glimmer of hope wiped all the sinister visions away from his mind as Sinead's eyelids fluttered. He needed to wake her by gently rocking her shoulders back and forth. Calling out her name, he commanded her to wake up.

Licking his finger, he placed it back under her nose. Sliding two fingers over her wrist, he waited to feel a faint beat. Previously, when Sinead was in a deep sleep for too long, he could wake her up easily. Even though it meant he had to sustain the wrath of her bad temper for doing so. This time he was in a situation that he had prayed he would never be in. As Martin tried to sit her up, her body fell into an awkward position. Laying her back down, he grasped the sides of her face, calling out her name in panic.

Sinead lay there motionless and pale. A rising feeling of nausea climbed from his stomach as the acid curdled in his throat. Martin took a few paces back to assess the room. Standing in the hallway, he forgot why he came out there for a second.

Craning his neck up the staircase, he shouted out, 'Mam!... Mammy!... Bridget!…' Realising there was nobody else at home, Martin ran for the front door and tried to open it – double locked. Bridget must have locked it on leaving for work. Racing into the kitchen, he tried to find his keys and again forgot why he was there. The radio interfered with his train of thought until he flicked it off. Pausing for a few seconds, he then remembered what he was looking for. 'Phone.' He swiped the mobile to dial 112. Nothing happened. He peered at the screen. SHIT. He hadn't realised he had smashed it when he had flung it across the kitchen.

His next thought was: keys. He found them underneath his newspaper. Hurtling back towards the front door, his hands shook as he struggled to do the simplest of tasks. With the lock undone, he flung the door wide open. The immediate moisture in the air hit his face. The rain had blitzed the street; it was soaking now, with drizzle hanging in the air. Darting into the middle of the road, Martin scanned around for anyone that could help him. His eyes focused on a car parked four doors up on the other side of the road. The vehicle was familiar, but he couldn't figure out why.

Turning back, he ran inside to Sinead, hoping there was some movement. There was none. Martin wrapped her body up in the bathrobe then attempted to lift her in his arms. The weight of her frame took his arms by surprise. Martin's head told him he could pick her up, but his legs protested as his muscles burned with the effort. Dropping forward on top of her, he lifted again. This time he was successful and slowly carried her limp body into the hall and out through the front door. Raising his left arm slightly, so her head made no contact with the door frame, he caught his other hand on a screw head and tore the skin away from his knuckles.

Wincing in pain, he laboured out across the road towards the car he had seen. He recalled why he recognised the vehicle – it belonged to a midwife that attended a neighbour who had recently had a baby. Martin's reserves of strength rapidly dwindled as the lactose built up, causing his muscles to scream with strain. His body failed him as he approached the car, and Martin slipped down onto his knees. The momentum of the fall caused Sinead to slip; the brace of Martin's arm softened the smack of her body on the tarmac. His elbows scored across the gritted surface as he broke the contact of Sinead's head, meeting it. The drizzle hadn't stopped. Blood was now seeping from Martin's elbow and knuckles. The rain mixed with his blood had caused drizzles of red to run over his hands, making his wounds look worse.

In desperation, he raised his eyes heavenwards and, in supplication, roared 'Please God, not like this, not like this.'

Sinead lay sprawled flat out on the road as Martin dashed to the neighbour's house. A blue banner pinned to the front door read 'Congratulations! It's A Boy.' Rapping his bleeding knuckles on the front door, giving no time for an answer, he repeatedly banged and banged. A male voice cursed as the door opened.

Gasping for breath, Martin shouted out, 'I need your nurse... get her now… PLEASE!'

The new father didn't utter a word and reeled back into the house, summoning the nurse out. She, too, was shocked by the state of Martin's condition and ushered him to come in so she could attend to his wounds.

Martin shouted out, 'It's not ME. It's my daughter; she's lying in the road.'

The nurse and house residents assumed there had been a road accident and immediately rang for an ambulance. Martin grabbed the nurse and pulled her out, trying to give her information about what had happened. His words came out all wrong, and his sentences made no sense. When the nurse saw Sinead's prone, frail and bald body in her dressing gown she soon ascertained there had been no road collision. Martin knelt and grasped Sinead's frail body to lift her. On attempting to hoist her, grit particles from the road surface embedded themselves into his knee.

A neighbour came out to let them know the ambulance was on its way. The nurse got both men to carry Sinead back to her own house to await the ambulance. Collecting her medical bag, she followed them. Sinead was laid back on the sofa for the nurse to examine her. Her bathrobe was saturated with rain and Martin's blood. She calmly instructed Martin to get a blanket and a towel to dry her off. Maintaining her body temperature was paramount. To Martin's relief, Sinead had a pulse, and her airways were clear. She was breathing, and her heartbeat wasn't erratic.

Just then, Shane arrived home. Quickly and calmly acquainting himself with the situation he could fill the nurse in on Sinead's medical history. Arriving promptly, the paramedics entered the house calmy, and the panic settled slightly as they set to work checking Sinead's vital signs and administering first aid. Shane rang Bridget's workplace to inform her of the emergency. There was no time for lengthy explanations. Guilt washed over him for the abruptness of the message being delivered. Bridget's employers reassured Shane she would be contacted straight away.

Still in shock, Martin couldn't comprehend what people were asking or telling him. He and Shane got into the ambulance to accompany Sinead to the hospital. The mood was sombre. No conversation took place. Martin was in a world of his own, fixated on Sinead. Shane was trying to get a signal on his mobile.

Martin fell to his knees and, clasping Sinead's cold hand, spoke softly to himself.

'Dear Lord, I can't find the right words. PLEASE, PLEASE, PLEASE, can you listen to my heart. I promise I will stop at whatever it is that has pissed you off. Breathe life back into our Sinead. You see, all these millions of people look up to you as their rock. Well, my Sinead is MY rock. I will get a job; I won't take the piss out of Sheila, and I will do whatever it takes to get you back on track. Amen.'

The journey was rocky as the ambulance accelerated, swerved and weaved in and out of traffic. An occasional siren was sounded as the ambulance briefly stalled in traffic . The siren's flare illuminated shop windows as they raced past, bringing mannequins to life for only a brief second. On arrival, there was a rush of activity as the ambulance doors burst open and more medical staff swarmed around to transition Sinead's unconscious body into the hospital. The urgency was more profound for the medical staff. They had followed Sinead's profile in the media and took her plight to their hearts.

CHAPTER 35

The corridors of the hospital were colour coded to direct people to specific departments. A prominent green line trailed along the walls, broken up with arrows for directions and fire exit signs. Fluorescent lighting reflected off the linoleum flooring, and a cushioned rail ran along the middle of the wall, absorbing the damage of bed traffic. Framed prints of sunsets and cities aligned the walls; their purpose nobody knew. Pounding down the corridor, Martin's heartbeat drummed in his ears. Shane held him back as the doctors whisked Sinead off into the treatment area. Somebody would be by soon to update them, they were told.

The room was unpleasantly sterile. Plastic chairs lined the walls, an indication that nobody was supposed to remain comfortable in there. A poster showing the importance of handwashing fluttered on the wall. The strip lighting emitted an annoying high-pitched sound that could only be drowned out by conversation. There was none. Talking to Martin to establish Sinead's history of seizures during the past couple of days proved pointless. Martin couldn't recall any relevant information, no matter how much Shane probed. Twenty minutes passed. Nervous energy was filling the room.

Voices suddenly rose outside. The door handle twisted soundlessly, and Bridget walked in. Shane immediately stood up and clasped Bridget in a tight hug while she glared with resentful eyes at Martin over his shoulder. Feeling her accusation penetrating through him, Martin bowed his head in defeat. Releasing his mother, Shane sat back down. Standing motionless, Bridget waited for acknowledgement or a plea for forgiveness from Martin. Anything. He remained silent.

A droplet of rain ran down from her forehead. Wiping her hand across her face, Bridget pulled an escaped thread of loose hair from her fringe and coiled it behind her ear. She sat down opposite her husband. Her eyes were bloodshot from crying. With tiredness and fatigue catching up on her, the raw emotion poured out of her and her face crumpled into tears.

Husband and wife sat on the hard plastic chairs silently, disconnected. Bridget could see Martin was a broken man, and no questioning or blaming him was going to help now, but she couldn't muster up the effort to comfort him either. The smell of institutional cleanliness was familiar to Bridget. It was the same smell in the hospice where she worked. She was hardened by these signs and portents of death and decay. Rubber soles trooped along the corridors, the murmuration of voices faded in and then out as staff shouted out along the corridor. The movement of a cleaning trolley rattled along.

Nearly two hours passed, it felt like time had stopped. The silence sharpened, spiking the air in the room. A haunting echo of the wind penetrated the room from the air vent over their heads. Wailing ambulances could be heard through the walls as they delivered more pain and suffering to the A&E. Shane sat quietly. A quiet atmosphere was a far better vicinity to be in than a war of words between his mother and father.

Footsteps approached along the corridor. As they got nearer, all three of them turned to the door expectantly. A nurse entered, followed by a doctor clutching a clipboard. Bridget noticed the way he held it. It looked like it was a barrier between them. The doctor introduced himself with an unsmiling gaze while the nurse remained silent.

'Good evening. My name is Doctor Mackey, and I'm a senior consultant in the Department tonight. I've reviewed your daughter's notes, and whilst progress on her radiotherapy treatment has remained stable after her treatment, I understand you were made aware of potential side effects as well as changes to wave patterns of her seizures.'

He paused. Bridget noticed his white knuckles squeezing the chart. 'I'm afraid Sinead's has suffered an intracranial haemorrhage. Your daughter collapsed because of a bleed on the brain. However, since she reached us here, her condition has continued to deteriorate over the past hours.'

The doctor broke eye contact and looked for reassurance to continue from the nurse. 'I am very sorry to tell you that when a haemorrhage interrupts blood flow around or inside the brain, depriving it of oxygen for more than three or four minutes, the brain cells die. The affected nerve cells and the related functions they control are damaged as well. Sinead can no longer breathe unaided and has required life supportive treatment. We have carried out the relevant tests to determine brain activity and, unfortunately have to tell you that brain activity has been irreversibly lost. This means that she is going to die. Sinead cannot wake up or breathe unaided. I am so sorry to tell you this.'

Taking a deep breath, the doctor slowly released it before continuing. 'Unfortunately, it wasn't a case of what you or the hospital medical staff could have done. It was simply that her brain developed a fatal haemorrhage, leading to her losing consciousness. Once again, I reiterate my sincere sympathy for these tragic circumstances. The specialist nurse here, Denise, will assist you in answering questions and let you see your daughter.'

The doctor bowed his head and left the room. The room was still and motionless as all three family members tried to grasp that their daughter and sister was now lifeless. The hairs on Bridget's arms stood to attention. She stood paralysed in the room, unable to breathe. There would be no more laughter or tantrums or witty wisecracks coming from their daughter again. It wasn't possible. They had educated themselves at the start of Sinead's treatment of possible worst-case scenarios, but this was never one of them. The nurse escorted them to another private room where Sinead lay peacefully on the bed, the whirring of the ventilator filling the air. The sight of her made them catch their breath.

Nobody spoke. A torturous silence descended again. The room seemed colder; the air made their skin feel dry. Tubes and monitors connected to her arm and finger played a rhythm of beeps. The gentle rise and fall of her ribcage pulsed life through her heart as a machine beeped in sequence. The room had an unearthly feel.

How could this child be dead? Thought Martin. Her skin was warm, blood pulsed around her body; surely the doctor must have been mistaken? Bridget sat at one side while Martin and Shane sat opposite. A deep wail resonated from the pit of Bridget's stomach. Not a cry, but a guttural wrench of grief that instantly dried her throat up and threatened to engulf her. She swallowed a gulp, but it remained in her throat.

Stroking and kissing Sinead's face; Bridget apologised to her for not saying goodbye or paying her enough attention that day. Tears streamed down her face and onto Sinead's cheeks. Martin held Sinead's hand and kissed each one of her fingers while Shane laid across her body, unable to cry or grieve. The gut-wrenching pain hit them hard and instantaneously. The actual fate of how fragile life could be was now their worst nightmare. Bridget was consumed with the thought, "How could a child be full of life in the morning and yet be so lifeless now?"

Leaving the room, the nurse waited outside. The glass window gave her full view of their grief unfolding inside the room. A short time later, the doctor returned with the nurse. This time he looked strained and ruffled. His tie was askew; his shirt button undone. Bridget noticed the confidence had drained from him. He now looked like an ordinary man, maybe a father himself. Waiting to be seen, he caught Bridget's eye before speaking. Bridget sat up and looked uncomfortable at being singled out.

The doctor spoke, less efficient this time as hope crept in around the edges. 'Sinead may appear alive; she has a heartbeat; she looks like she is breathing and ready to wake up at a sudden pinch or shout. She is warm to touch and everything else you associate with living. But she is not.' There was a pause.

'There is no life when brain activity ceases. Her organs are all functioning, so, at this point, I would like to talk to you about something you might not be expecting, and that is organ donation. It can save and transform many people's lives, starting tonight. As Sinead's brain tumour was classed as primary it hasn't spread beyond the brain stem and she is eligible to donate tissues. As parents or guardians, I need to ask you first was Sinead on a donor register list. If you are unsure, I can get the nurse to check.'

Bridget gently shook her head as the corners of her mouth quivered. Her strained red eyes couldn't cope with the questioning. Martin stood up in protest. He shouted in defiance, 'You're not touching her, you hear me. You tell them, Bridget. Chrissake, man, have you no dignity for us? Our daughter is still breathing. When I kiss her, I can still smell life inside her.'

The doctor tried to backtrack. 'I'm really sorry. I can see that you are finding this difficult to come to terms with. It is to be expected. I am sure you need some time on your own to talk about what I have told you. I will come back later; please think about the wider picture here. There is no recovery possible from here on for your daughter.'

Bowing his head, the doctor maintained eye contact for a couple of moments, looking for a sign of hope from either parent. None was offered. The doctor left, leaving the nurse outside the room again. A while later, the nurse came in and asked if any refreshments were required. She sensed the atmosphere was suitable for the doctor to return. The door briskly opened; the doctor walked in again with his nurse chaperoning him. Both parties knew how the conversation was going to start. The doctor looked ragged and uncomfortable. He took a deep breath, and looked down at the floor before, embarrassedly meeting Martin's and Bridget's eyes. Only when he met Shane's eyes did he feel intimidated by the family's grief.

'You are going to have to make a lot of decisions in the forthcoming weeks. I know you have been through a great deal already, but can you briefly tell me what you understand of the situation Sinead is in now. We must be clear on this. Right now, you need to make a decision about organ donation.'

Bridget wasn't clear-minded. She couldn't speak, frozen from the now where Sinead had parted from them. Martin looked at Bridget for reassurance. Trying to hold in his emotion, he said calmly and rationally, 'You can't have her.'

The doctor tried to convince him. 'How do you think Sinead would feel about giving the gift of sight to someone else, extending someone else's quality of life?' he asked. The doctor looked back at Bridget for a response, any motion to counter Martin's objection.

Shane grasped her hand tightly.

The doctor continued, 'We can confirm that Sinead was not on the donor register, so each of you must give the decision, united.'

'FUCK OFF! You hear me, is that clear enough for you?' Martin roared. The exertion left him weak; a hard knot stuck in his throat as he scrambled to make himself understood.

'Look at her; she is just a child, only just starting in life, making her own choices and decisions. This disease has robbed her of all of that. My wife and I raised her; we watched her grow, develop, she argued with us about what she wanted. She had fight and spirit. My daughter came into this world intact, and she will be buried intact. This is no religious view. It is a mother and father's wish; you have to understand that?'

Bridget, gaining confidence with Shane's support and her husband's stoicism, finally spoke up. Her tone was sombre but deliberate.

'I'm in full support of my husband's decision.'

The doctor let out a sigh; he looked deflated but relieved. He sucked his lips in, sealing them with his teeth, and nodded, admitting defeat. A final apology was offered for their loss, and he tried to maintain a professional air.

On leaving, Martin caught the doctor's attention and spoke apologetically, 'Doctor –'

The doctor interrupted him by placing his hand on his shoulder, 'No offence taken, Mr Lynch.' The door closed behind him. The nurse stayed inside to advise the family of the next steps. They agreed on turning off the ventilation machine, allowing their daughter to die peacefully surrounded by her family. After her chest deflated with a final sigh, Sinead's body died that night.

CHAPTER 36

A taxi brought the family home. Bridget switched the lights on as she went into the kitchen. The room was eerily silent. The dim, low-energy light bulbs cast shadows before brightening the room. Buzzing into life, the fridge compressor hummed, pulling her gaze to the fridge, which was covered in family photos. On the cooker top, solidified fat sat redundant in a frying pan. At the flick of a switch, the kettle grumbled. Martin walked out and straight in to the front room with a sick sinking feeling in the pit of his soul. Sinead's bathrobe lay strewn across the floor. Loss pierced his heart. Dropping to his knees, Martin embedded his face in the soft material absorbing the scent of his daughter's life.

From the kitchen, Bridget heard Martin sobbing. She listened to him plead to God to relinquish Sinead from his grasp. It was a plea he could carry on for an eternity. Shane joined his mother in the kitchen. Everywhere he looked, there was a reminder of Sinead. A hospital appointment card hung next to a calendar on the wall, photos of her on the fridge, her handwriting on a piece of paper on the table. Bubbles erupted in the kettle. Bridget made them tea and joined Martin in the front room. Shane came in with candles from Sinead's room. He placed them around the room and lit them before sitting down with Martin and Bridget. Silence wrapped around them. Their whole world was now distorted as if they had stepped on a landmine. The thoughts of what to do next exhausted them. They needed rest but relatives and friends needed to be contacted and told of the news. It all seemed so impossible.

Before they had left the hospital, a bereavement team was assigned to the family. A hospital liaison officer would begin to make the first steps of funeral arrangements. They simply couldn't go there yet. Bridget and Shane went to bed while Martin sat on the sofa where Sinead had lain, as he knew now, dying all day. He cursed himself for leaving her for that short period. Martin went through every possible scenario he could have done to prevent what happened. He tortured himself. He needed to be around someone or something that would not judge him as harshly as he now judged himself. He craved consolation.

From upstairs, Bridget heard the creak of drawers opening and closing, then the hinge noise of the drinks cabinet clinking shut. Martin had crept into the back room and found his solace. It was a bottle of scotch whiskey won at a church or school fundraising event that still had the winning raffle ticket stuck to it. Its brand was unknown, but it had the correct consistency; 40% alcohol. It was going to give him all the consolation he needed.

Martin searched for old photo albums of the children when they were younger. He took them on his lap and sat on the sofa where Sinead had lay hours earlier. He gathered up the bathrobe and pulled it around his shoulders. The screw cap twisted quickly off the scotch and bounced off the wall. There was no need for it; he had no intention of the bottle's contents lasting until the morning.

As the hours passed through the night, insidious thoughts crept into his mind and refused banishment. Martin had drunk most of the whiskey by the early hours of the morning. As each gulp went down, it didn't touch his taste buds. Instead, it bypassed them and came alive as it hit his tonsils, making his gullet heat up like a funnel of fire. Slumping back on the sofa, his last recollection of the night was the sounds of Bridget sobbing upstairs through the floorboards beneath her.

The following morning it felt like an electric pulse had woken Martin up as he gathered his senses. Confused for a second, he had a brief moment of normality before he realised where he was. His head pounded. With the curtains drawn, a fallen side lamp shone a dimmed circle of light across a corner of the room. The central heating awakened the damp smell of the robe. As his mind processed the graphic images in his head, he tried to ascertain if they were real or merely scenes from a terrible nightmare. It only took a few moments for the terrible dream to become a reality.

Catching sight of old photos scattered across the sofa, he eyed the almost empty bottle on the floor. Slouching back into the couch, Martin felt the emptiness of the seat next to him. Avoiding reality, he finished off the rest of the whiskey. His throat felt acidic and sore. Multiple triggers set off flash memories sparking like fireworks in his head before he drifted off into a trance, and sleep dragged him back into oblivion. Martin had been out for the count for under an hour when there was a knock at the door. It startled him, but he ignored it. The knocking became louder. Lifting his head to acknowledge it, he shouted out, 'FUCK OFF!'

Whoever was outside heard his voice but couldn't make out what the slurred words were. There was silence for 30 seconds. The knocking, then banging, intensified as the bottom of the front door reverberated. It wasn't long before it rattled Martin. Mustering enough strength to rise from the sofa, he stomped over to the door clutching his head. The door hadn't been bolted from the evening before. Martin released the catch and wrenched it opened while cursing. Trying to focus his eyes in the sharp sunlight, he covered them with his forearm as the figure of a man took shape. Declan Hennessey stood in front of him.

Today was collection day on the new two-week rota. With Martin's senses distorted, his eyes felt dry and gritty. The images of Sinead lying motionless in the road flashed before him. Raw emotion kicked in as he stumbled back. Then, out of character and out of his tree, he lunged forward with fists clenched and swung wildly at the air. The first punch caught Declan clean on the chin; the second one caused him to lose balance. The speed of the lunge caught Declan by surprise. The contact sent him spiralling backwards, landing on a car bonnet. Multiple images of Martin danced in front of his eyes before he knew what had hit him. Beads of blood dripped onto his shirt as throbbing pain stung his lips. He never thought Martin ever had the nerve to try anything like that.

Regaining his composure, Declan lunged forward and grabbed Martin by the throat. Declan's nails raked his skin as he dragged him outside onto the pavement. Goosebumps covered Martin's shirtless body as the fresh morning air filled his lungs. Tremors took control of his body. Not attempting to shield himself, Martin closed his eyes tight and spread his arms open wide; he wanted to be rid of his guilt and pain. Declan obliged, and when Martin fell after the first punch, Declan pinned him down and repeatedly smashed him in the face. Bile spewed out of Martin across Declan's arm, soaking his groin. Declan scrambled off him, wanting rid of the sticky, stale alcohol puree that stuck to him. Standing back up, he turned and skimmed the worst of the puke off himself. An empty whiskey bottle hit Declan flush on the back of his head. He grimaced, clutching the back of his skull and groaned in shock and pain.

Bridget appeared at the doorway. Her face was slack; her eyes deadened as she took in the scene. She stepped in front of her husband, shielding him. The whiskey bottle, meant for Declan, bounced off a car and spun around on the pavement before stopping, revealing the raffle ticket, number 159.

Bridget snarled at Declan. 'We lost our Sinead last night… she's dead... DEAD!... Go on, finish him off. It's what he wants you to do... go on and do it.' Bridget pointed down at Martin; there was a husky tone to her voice. 'He was the last one to see her alive, and now he has nothing to live for... GO ON!... HELP HIM!... FINISH HIM OFF!'

Declan stumbled back in disbelief. He knew instantly it was true. He knew it couldn't be a delaying tactic to avoid paying. This news would devastate Kathleen. He stared down at the state of Martin. His face was in a mess. He had vomited up the last portion of the whiskey, and it was smeared across his face with blood and tears. Declan thought briefly about how he could tell Kathleen what he had just done to Martin and share the news of Sinead's death. With his hands behind the back of his head, he backed away unsteadily from the house. Staring at Bridget, he mournfully said, 'How could I have known?'

In haste, Declan fumbled back into his car. He rang Kathleen, then cancelled the call when he realised he needed to tell her the sad news to her face. Examining his split lip, he rolled his tongue around it, viewing it in the mirror. It had felt like licking the end of a battery tip. Conscious and sitting up, Martin was now staring at him from the driveway. Fresh blood ran down Martin's swollen face, soaking into the waistband of his jeans. Declan watched Bridget tending to Martin on the pavement in his rear-view mirror before their images blurred out of sight. He headed home, all the while planning the best way to tell his wife the grim news.

Kathleen's silhouette danced in the ripples of the net curtains as Declan braced himself before going inside. As he entered the hallway, the distinct fragrance of Febreze hit him at the same time as a thump of fear kicked his gut. Loud music blared from the next room, overpowering the roar of the hoover as the front door clunked shut. Declan turned the hoover and the music off. Cursing to herself, Kathleen thought the cable had become snagged on some furniture. Barefoot, she went back out into the hallway and was startled by Declan.

She screamed. 'Bejaysis, you frightened the shite out of me.'

Out of his comfort zone, Declan blurted out, 'I had no way of knowing – I would have left him otherwise.' The swelling on Declan's split lip caused his speech to slur.

Kathleen frowned and said, 'You're worrying me, Declan, what's going on?'

Declan gently questioned her, 'When did you last speak to Bridget?'

Kathleen gathered her thoughts instantaneously and said, 'Erhh – two days ago – why?' She looked scared now.

As guilt wrapped around Declan's throat, he couldn't release the words to break Kathleen. Knowing something wasn't right, she tried to question him about work, about Martin, about another argument. A tone of panic crept into her voice as she shouted out, 'Damn it – shout it out, MAN.'

Kathleen's bottom lip quivered as Declan held his hands out towards her. 'I was collecting the money from the Lynches. Martin smacked me one as soon as the door opened. I took him to the ground when Bridget stopped me –'

Kathleen interrupted. Her nose wrinkled as she shook her head. Utterly confounded, her voice rose, 'Martin couldn't pose a threat with an opened razor, and you're saying he did that to your face? There's something you're not telling me, Declan. Wait… WAIT! … We've had this conversation before about Martin. Why were you at the front door of my best friend's home?'

Husband and wife narrowed glances at each other.

'I explicitly asked you to undo the arrangement with Martin as it personally put me in a difficult place with Bridget. You *agreed*!' Kathleen flashed him a scathing look. Searching his expression, she looked for the truth.

'So, tell me, did it make you feel good about yourself hitting Martin, Declan? I think the money has nothing to do with this; I believe you went there to torment him. I still can't understand for the life of me why my relationship with Martin still – in fact, I'll take that back WHY it ever bothered you. You weren't around. You never existed in my life until years later. It had absolutely nothing to do with you, just like some of the business arrangements you've had that have nothing to do with me.

'I deliberately don't question what you do. I'm not stupid; it's a sad state of affairs. I've heard of some of the stunts you've pulled in the past. I've heard whispers in company when people won't make eye contact with me, but I keep schtum out of respect for my husband. I should be upset, but I'm embarrassed for you, Declan. You've made yourself look like a small-minded man. I never thought that you could ever make me feel this way about you.' Unexpected tears gathered in her eyes before she blinked them away.

Looking away, Declan focused on a stain on the wall. Hesitantly, he replied, 'They've lost their little girl.'

Kathleen's lips parted in surprise before pulling a face of incomprehension. She shook her head, raised her hands in a flurry and said, 'You're not making any sense... lost what?'

Declan chose his words carefully to avoid using the D-word, it was so harsh, but he had no choice. The reply came out as a whisper. 'She's dead. Sinead's dead. I don't know how, when or why.'

Kathleen's gaze flickered back and forth across his face. Disbelief and a wave of nausea coursed through her as she tried to deny it. Her body went cold, and her face bloodless as warm tears glided down her cheeks, 'NO! – NO! NOOOOOOO.' As her hand covered her mouth, her chin took over the emotion by quivering. 'And what of Martin? You beat upon a man who lost his daughter?'

Declan held the back of his head with one hand. Kathleen tried to breathe slowly and deliberately. Without a word, she turned and went into the kitchen, searching for her mobile. Declan followed her, listening as the dial tone chirped. There was no answer. Pressing her palms against her eyes, she rubbed disbelief away in despair. Clenching her fists tightly, she willed the bad news to go away. Declan attempted to lean in and comfort her but, sensing his movement, she flinched away. Kathleen spoke with prickly politeness as tears bubbled along her lower eyelids before she quelled them, announcing practically, 'Right! I need to get over to Bridget's and do something… help her... talk to her... I don't know what to do... but I need to be over there.'

Declan nodded in agreement and again tried putting his arms around her, but she ushered him away. After waking Kieran and breaking the news to him, Kathleen collected her bag and left. The front door slammed with no goodbyes.

Kathleen arrived at Bridget's with an ache in her throat. Already, a small bunch of flowers had been left on the windowsill with a card. Soon the whole street would know. After a gentle knock, the door opened. As the pair embraced, Kathleen broke down in tears. A cyclone of questions whirled through her mind. Bridget consoled her, stroking the back of her shoulders. She was unable to grieve herself yet.

Over endless cups of tea, Kathleen listened to the circumstances leading up to Sinead's death. The two of them remained together for hours, aware of Martin out of sight in the back room, drowning his sorrows but unable to comfort him. Kathleen listened. She gently rubbed her thumb along the back of Bridget's hand as Bridget began to describe her pain.

'During Sinead's diagnosis, it hit me hard, you know. Learning and reading about the different strains of it. Your deepest fear of losing a child makes you shudder with denial. You dismiss it immediately, and you build yourself up to each stage of the treatment and just getting through each part of it, trying not to look ahead.' She rubbed her dry eyes.

'The consequences of the treatment plagued my mind when she had a bad day. You try to be strong and continue with your day-to-day life. You look at other families, and you think: What did I do to deserve this? Why me? Why us? Why her?' But you feel her pain as well. Right in here, it's piercing you daily.' Bridget's fist tapped against her chest.

'Then there are all the unknowns. How long? How much more pain? Will she survive? Will it come back? Will she be able to have her own family? I'd look to talk to Martin about it, but he didn't take any of this seriously. I often looked at him and thought: Are you actually concerned for your daughter? Because why do I feel like I'm carrying all the worry alone?'

Kathleen interjected, 'It's because you are a mother, B.' She reassured her, patting her hand.

Bridget snatched it away before she continued. 'This is going to sound wicked of me, but I believed that Martin was kind of glad that Sinead got this illness.' Bridget looked relieved by the unburdening. 'Yeah! I did, it's a terrible thing to admit, but I did.'

Kathleen interrupted, 'B! Martin loved Sinead every bit as you did. Martin cloaks everything with humour. He is hurting really bad at the moment. He is a fella. They have their methods of dealing with things. Unfortunately, Martin's is drinking.'

But Bridget needed to finish the character assassination of her husband. 'You know, I believed he was glad she had the illness because it gave him the excuse for me to stay. I can't take it anymore, Kath, carrying him. If Sinead hadn't developed this illness, I would have walked away with the kids in tow. I can't take not having anything anymore. I have no life. I'm living to work, not working to live. What kind of life is that for anybody. Look at this house. It's a disgrace. Nothing has improved in our marriage. Martin's drinking has become worse. Look at him now. I don't know where to turn to, Kath.'

'It wasn't so long ago you told me you still loved him, B,' Kathleen tried to diffuse the situation.

'Is still loving someone enough to let them bring you down with them?' Bridget asked plaintively.

Kathleen bowed her head before answering, 'The only advice I can give you is that you both need each other to get through this together. You need to open up. Both of you… to each other… with nobody else around, no interferences and definitely no drink.'

Bridget agreed with a hurried nod and continued, 'I'm anxious about Shane. I've tried to talk to him, but he refuses to acknowledge he's hurting. He can't stand to be in this house for a minute. Jesus, I can't blame him. Has Kieran mentioned anything? I know he adored Sinead just as much.'

Kathleen listened but didn't want to come across as disingenuous in her comment.

'Don't take this the wrong way, B. Kieran has said Shane is distant at times and takes himself off to the park with bottles of booze. This has been going on for months' Bridget started to cry harder.

'B, he will be ok. Let the boy find his space. Don't tell him Kieran has spoken of this because it will just push him further away. Don't be getting any ideas in your head about Shane following in his father's footsteps with the drink. The boy needs to deal with this his way, and he will. And when he is ready, his mother will be there with open arms for him.'

CHAPTER 37

The last couple of days had been tearful with the trauma of sorrow. Kathleen had been a true friend to Bridget and helped her navigate all the administration surrounding the death of a loved one. She greeted the family members and close friends at the home. She ensured everyone was fed and rested as much as possible. The neighbours rallied round, and Mrs Mercer had made lunches and dinners for whoever required them at the Lynches house. Well-wishers had ordered flowers or simply left them outside on the pavement. Mrs Mercer tended to them and lit a display of candles on the windowsill.

David tried to coax Martin out of the house, but Martin was in a pitiful state. He was a husk of himself, held up in the back room. He hadn't changed clothes or washed in days; the clothes he wore stank to high heaven of sweat and lager. David had brought Martin a steady supply of strong lager that was finished and tossed aside in the room. Bridget insisted David stop, as Martin became withdrawn from everyone around him. Martin was consumed with bleakness, suffocating in morbidity. Alcohol numbed his senses briefly before the guilt came back with a vengeance.

The black dog firmly nestled itself in Martin's mind, cloaking him. He was zoned out, drifting along with childhood memories of Sinead rotating in his subconscious. Only to have them sullied by the image of her lying dead in the blood-soaked bathrobe. He was unable to relate to anything said to him. A nod or a grunt was his only response. The rare food he ate, he couldn't taste. His stomach was hard with acid like a volcano pit from the alcohol. He felt no grief, only guilt and pity. Guilty that he never got to say he loved Sinead one more time. Guilty that he couldn't remember the last words he spoke with her – pity for himself.

Bridget asked Kathleen if she would try to talk to Martin. To at least get a response from him . Bridget was engrossed with Mrs

Mercer, organising the constant flow of flowers left outside when Kathleen knocked on the back room door. There was no response. She entered the room and muttered, 'For the love of God.'

The smell in the airless confines of the room took her aback. She pinched her nose. The room was dark except for a shaded lamp that shone dim light. Flicking the lights on, Kathleen pulled a footstool out and sat in front of Martin. Lifting his hand, she linked fingers with him. A pained expression lined her face as she took a hard look at him.

She spoke in a passive tone. 'Martin, I can only partially imagine what you and Bridget are going through.' Choking back tears, she willed herself not to cry. She focused and took a deep breath, maintaining eye contact with Martin. Controlling her breathing, Kathleen continued. 'I could tell you about the tears I cried for our baby all those years ago. The anger I felt. The bitterness I felt looking at other mothers with their babies. Losing a child is the loneliest, most desolate journey a parent has to take. It's a wound that never heals, but I promise you the pain does decrease.'

She paused, convincing herself she was the strong one, adding a smile in her voice. 'You have thirteen years' worth of memories of Sinead to cherish and share. Don't push Bridget away. She needs you now, Martin. She may usually be the strong one holding this family together, but she isn't strong enough now without you. Get out of this… this hole. It stinks like you. Clean yourself up, sit with Bridget and Shane, pull out every family photo and rekindle all those moments together. It's the first step together. Focus on small tasks and think about the future in small steps. Forgive yourself for being imperfect.

'There will be triggers along the way that will set you back, like when someone asks you how many children you have. Then there are the first anniversaries. The next birthday. The first Christmas without her. It will hurt, I can't dress it up any better than that, but you have to go through it. Hope will help you along the way. You have to believe that. Remember, Martin, your wife and son are also suffering, and they need you. All this Martin? You must take a real hard look at yourself and see what it's turning you into... LISTEN to me, Martin!... ALCOHOL isn't your answer. Bridget and Shane, God bless them, they need you to be strong... Once alcohol comes and takes everything you have, it's relentless… it will then come and take YOU.'

Staring ahead, Martin didn't respond. The emptiness consumed him. Kathleen stood up. Rubbing her fingers through his hair, she attempted to leave.

Martin's timid voice spoke, 'Please don't go, yet... please.'

Easing herself back down, Kathleen made more room for her feet by nudging beer cans away. She collected Martin's hand again, studying his eyes.

He looked forlorn as he spoke. 'It's only in death that I now know the meaning of that phrase… "Your son is your son today, but your daughter is your daughter forever." I'm sorry I wasn't there for you, Kathleen all those years ago... First, the baby didn't seem real to me. Then, I buried my head in the sand – I didn't want the responsibility. I carried on partying, drinking and getting charged up. It was inevitable we would never make it.' Martin swallowed a hard lump in his throat.

'This is Sheila's God settling a score with me for all that cursing of him I've done. It has come back to haunt me. I feel detached from my body. People are talking to me; I know they mean well, but I can't get to their level to respond. It has only been a couple of days, and it already feels like a lifetime of suffering.'

His voice turned hoarse as anger caught up with him. 'Sinead once said to me, "Dad, you must at least have one person in your life who you can tell anything to and have them listen and understand you. I'm lucky," she used to say, "I have two people, and you are one of them." What she didn't know was that I only had one person, and that was her. I can't even talk to Bridget about her, and we have the same loss,' he turned his head in shame.

Kathleen tried to reassure him, 'Martin, it's a true saying that you never get over grief; you learn to live with it. You need to talk to Bridget, not just about Sinead's death. You need to let each other into your thoughts and your lives. For two people who live together, you are so far apart from one another.'

Kathleen squeezed his hand tenderly. She looked at Martin's face. It was a picture of remorse, of shame. Martin felt his throat closing up. Kathleen passed him a bottle of water. Slugging it back in haste, Martin felt his throat easing as he carried on.

'Sinead had this hamster years ago, do you remember? The bastard thing was up all-night chomping away at its cage. I often used to sit and watch it. Night after night, it chewed at the same spot. I knew its fate was never to break free, but it persisted. It died. Sinead, bless her though, thought it had a great life. My life is like that. I know my place in it. I've tried to better myself, and it just kicks me back into my place. I have accepted it. Sinead was the reason for me to keep trying. What do I have to live for now?' His face shrivelled up. No tears.

'You can't talk like this; it's unhealthy,' Kathleen protested.

Martin spoke restlessly, 'Look at my face, what do you see?'

'It looks like shite, Martin,' the reply came out before Kathleen realised what she had said.

'No, not the marks or the bruises. Really look,' Martin summoned, as Kathleen assessed his face carefully.

'I don't know, Martin; it looks even shittier,' Kathleen remarked.

Martin answered, 'I'm not embarrassed to say, I've cried in my life. I am ashamed to say I can't cry for my daughter. I can't grieve, Kathleen,' His voice sounded pained as the last few words trailed off.

Kathleen chose her words hesitantly, 'All of that will come in time, Martin. There is no rush; you don't owe it to anybody. Nobody will judge you for it. It will come in its own time.' Kathleen kissed his hand. The softness of her words cleansed something inside him.

Martin looked up at her, 'Thanks for listening, Kathleen.'

'Don't worry, I'm not going to be too far away. Good night, Martin, and God bless.'

Slipping her hand out of his, Kathleen switched the light back off. The door quietly closed behind her as she watched the light disappear and vanish from Martin's figure. She bid Bridget good night as she cuddled her, reassuring her that she'd be around tomorrow to help again. Bridget and Martin slept for the first time in days.

CHAPTER 38

The next day the local newspaper that had supported Sinead's recovery was told of her sudden passing. A representative visited the family home to offer any support they could. A cheque changed hands with Bridget for Sinead's appeal fund. With goodwill, they suggested that the money goes to Sinead's funeral costs. The news team decided to issue a memorial poster of Sinead in the next edition as a tribute to her, whilst also continuing to support the awareness appeal for her illness.

Shane got up each morning and met up with Kieran, away from the constant reminder of death. Ten days had passed when summoned back home; he dragged Kieran along to help prepare for the forthcoming wake by shifting furniture.The central heating system has a leak resulting in the radiators not performing, so two old paraffin heaters were brought down from the loft that needed cleaning up. It was a skill to decant paraffin into each tank because if fuel spilt out onto the flooring, the fumes hung around for days. The lads had to go down to the hardware store and buy enough fuel to fill both tanks. Shane collected the plastic containers and bothered Bridget for cash, who was being looked after by Kathleen and having a hair treatment. Kieran followed, and the pair trudged off down the street.

This allowed Kieran the opportunity to speak his mind to his friend. 'Look, Shane, stop, listen to me… You're like a brother to me; that means Sinead was my sister too. You can lie to everyone around you but don't mug me off. When you're ready, I'm here to listen. Fuck my dad and fuck yours. I want to hear from you – are we tight?'

Shane nodded his appreciation and, staring ahead, drew in a long breath. As he exhaled, the air misted in his face. They touched their clenched fists to each other's, and knuckles clashed, sealing a bond of brotherhood.

Approaching the hardware store; an uncomfortable feeling caused

Kieran's nerves to tense. The same car that Shane had had his face smashed up against stood parked outside the store. Shane only noticed it as they reached it, but he wasn't uncomfortable with the situation alone. It was the commotion they heard as three figures became visible inside the window that unnerved him. Raised voices interrupted the sound of smashing bottles.

Kieran grabbed Shane's shoulder, tugging him back out of view. The men inside spotted them, and the entrance door opened. A colossal figure came out and grappled with both the lads. Kieran freed himself, scuffling backwards onto the pavement. Shane wasn't quick enough or strong enough, and they effortlessly dragged him inside. His resistance was futile as he tried to prevent himself from entering through the doorway like a wild animal. The two containers they'd brought with them spiralled across the pavement before the door slammed, leaving silence behind. Out of sight now, Kieran sat up with his hands pressed firmly into the cold stone pavement. His backside and fingertips numbed quickly. Trying to focus with eyes wide and full of fear, he gently tapped the back of his head against the wall as he tried to figure out what to do.

Inside, forced face down on the floor, Shane had hurt his shoulder during the struggle. He scanned the floor around him for his missing trainer but couldn't spot it anywhere. Dermot, the store manager, who had worked for Declan for years, sat behind the counter. Bloodied tissues were held up against his nose. The till was open and empty. Shane looked around. He felt the shadow of a tall figure behind him. He rolled himself over until he caught sight of the character and recognised it was Liam O'Driscoll, the son of Aiden O'Driscoll, Declan's rival gang boss. Both the lads knew Liam and referred to him as Liam the Lummox. He was Aiden's youngest son who hadn't been working for his father for very long. What Liam lacked in intelligence, he made up for in size.

A voice emerged from nowhere. 'Well... look who we have here.'

Footsteps sounded along the aged floorboards; Patrick Finnerty, the elder and wiser brother, emerged with a grin stretched across his face. Shane looked around for the other brother. Beneath the floorboards, the persistent smashing of glass bottles echoed in the cellar.

Patrick stood over Shane, sneering, 'What is it with you two? This is the second time you're under our feet.'

Shane peered over at where Dermot sat, shocked and bloody and asked quietly, 'What's been going on, Dermot?'

Dermot removed blood-drenched tissues to reveal his nose and upper lip broken and swollen. It appeared that at least one of his front teeth was missing. 'I couldn't stop them,' he muttered.

Patrick gave Liam a gentle nod and signalled to Shane to get up off the floor. Liam grabbed him by the ankle, spinning his body around before he picked him up by the scruff of his neck.

Patrick shouted in Shane's face, 'Where's your fucking sidekick? I want him to see this.'

Footsteps stomped up from the cellar. Thomas, the dimmer brother with not a lot going on behind his eyes, appeared. Shane tensed his stomach awaiting a sudden blow from either of them.

Patrick spoke, 'This is fucking precious,' he snarled at Shane,'what brings you in here?'

Unable to put weight on one foot, Shane replied, 'Just for some fuel.'

Patrick smirked at his brother, 'Well, don't let us stop you.' Shane hobbled over to the counter whilst shielding himself from a potential blow.

Patrick spoke to Dermot, still prone and bleeding behind the counter, and sarcastically said, 'My good man. This customer requires your attention.'

Shane gestured to the door, 'My container is still outside.'

Thomas intervened, unknowingly licking his lips. 'Do you think we're stupid or something?'

Patrick interrupted his brother, 'Our good friend wouldn't wish any more harm to our favourite shopkeeper now, would he?'

Shane had got the message. Thomas nodded at Liam to allow Shane to go outside. The door opened, Shane reached for the paraffin container and spotted his trainer lying on the path. In his eye line, he saw Kieran propped up against the shop. He pulled the plastic fuel container into the shop, looked at the brothers and begrudgingly said, 'I need my trainer. It's out by the car.'

Neither brother replied. Patrick pretended to strike out at Dermot. Dermot flinched as Patrick grinned and shouted back, 'Let him get it; I'm sure he won't do anything stupid.'

Liam shunted the door open. Shane walked towards the shoe and kicked it further away in the direction of Kieran.

As he moved towards it, knowing he was far enough out of sight, he spoke swiftly. 'Ring your dad and get him down here. I'll have to go back in. Dermot has taken a hiding. The bastards have smashed up all your dad's stock. I'll delay them here for as long as I can. Run, NOW.' Looking stricken, Kieran moaned, 'I left my phone at your gaff with yours when we were lifting stuff.'

'Shite, you'll have to run back to mine then and get your mam to ring him.' Shane hastened back to the store. As he returned, the look of relief on Dermot's face told a story as Thomas trotted back downstairs.

Kieran bolted away on the run to Shane's house without stopping, his lungs burning with the effort of it. With his tracksuit top saturated in sweat, steam rose from his shoulders as his adrenalin ebbed. His legs felt heavy and laden as he reached the house. He knocked on the window. Bridget felt a rush of cold air as she opened the door. Flooded in sweat, Kieran panted hard as his heart rate tried to find its natural rhythm.

With panicked politeness, Kieran asked, 'Can you call Mam out here please?'

'Don't be silly lad,' she replied, 'get yourself inside to take the chill off you. Is Shane far behind?'

Ignoring her question, he hurried in. Trotting into the front room, he tried to grab his mother's attention.

Bridget asked, 'I thought you would have brought one of the containers home with you?'

Kathleen could tell by the look in his eye that something was wrong. She quizzed him, 'Right, spit it out... let me guess... you've bought the fuel and smashed the container on the way home... am I right?'

A vacant look covered his face. 'Mam... can you come outside for a minute?' His words were broken and panicky. Kathleen could sense the situation wasn't as straightforward as she thought.

Bridget felt the tension in the air and firmly asked, 'Where's Shane, Kieran?'

Kathleen deliberately lowered her voice so as not to freak Kieran out as he shifted on the spot. Her soothing tone calmed him. 'Kieran... just tell it how it is... in your own time, love,' she watched his every expression as he spoke.

'The fellas from outside of town are after smashing up Dad's basement,' he stammered, his tone full of despair. 'Shane got out but had to go back in there to help Dermot, who is in a bad way.'

After inhaling a quick gasp, Bridget interrupted, 'You mean to say, the SAME two who gave you both a hiding before?'

Kieran nodded, and a wave of trembling overcame Bridget.

She cried out, 'NO!... NO!... PLEASE… God, not today.' A jolt of panic passed through her as she started sobbing. Her head filled with anxiety as the blood drained from her face. She grabbed hold of Kathleen's arm and pleaded with her, 'We have to get my Shane out of there. Why is Kieran here instead of Shane?'

Kathleen pulled Bridget around to face her with more force than was necessary. She tried to calm her down. 'Bridget, listen to me now. I need you to focus and not fall apart on me. Both our sons are in danger.' Bridget stopped sobbing. Kathleen marched Kieran outside and, stroking his cheek, slowly spoke to him, 'Listen to me, my love.' Her fingers moved to stroke his eyebrows as she continued, 'I want you to go back to the store and do whatever YOU need to do to protect Shane and yourself. Talk the talk in there to at least distract them until your father can get down there.'

Kieran understood her every word. He mustered up a smile to mask his fear. She flashed a nervous smile back at him and, gripping both his hands, looked into his eyes and said, 'I love you, son.' He ran.

She released an unsteady breath. As anxiety crept along her spine, she gathered herself and rang Declan. After two rings, he answered the call. He was in The Telegraph. As he heard her chilling words, he stared directly at the watchman on duty. The watchman didn't miss a thing but had no idea of the saga that was unfolding. The call was brief. Kathleen ended it. Declan's last words were 'Ring Billy and Johnny.' Sliding his phone into his pocket, he glared at the watchman. A red mist clouded Declan's judgement as he stalked over to him and grabbed him by the throat. Dragged up against the wall and pinned there, the barstool disappeared beneath him. With bulging eyes, the watchman's face grew redder as Declan growled at him.

'Ring O'Driscoll, NOW. Tell him he has overstepped the mark with his lackeys on my territory, raiding my fucking store.' The watchman's body dropped like a sack of shit. He coughed for air.

'He knows what consequences to expect – ring him – NOW.' The watchman made the call. Patrick's phone rang; he ignored it. A text message pinged to Aiden. Declan left the pub and sped off as his own

phone rang. He told Billy and Johnny to meet him at the store.
Back at the Lynches, Kathleen was trying to calm Bridget down.

'Bridget, I need you to get a grip. It's both our sons in there. Do you understand?' Bridget's eyes focused as she tried to compose her panic-stricken self.

'I can't lose another child, Kathleen. Dear God.'

'I know, love, you won't.' Their eyes met as they embraced.

'Listen to me, B. Both our boys have each other in there. Declan is on his way down to the store. Kieran won't let Shane down. They're going to be ok.'

Bridget nodded, grasping Kathleen's hands. She looked terrified.

'Now, I need to leave you, B, and head back to the pub if Billy or Johnny head there instead of the store. Are you going to be ok on your own? I can knock for a neighbour before I go?'

Bridget shook her head, 'I'll be fine, be sure to ring with any news.'

'Of course. It won't surprise me if the lads waltz on in here soon as if nothing has happened.'

Bridget nodded, holding back her emotion.

They embraced one last time before Kathleen left. This was the first time Declan had embroiled his family in any of his operations, and it would be the last. Kathleen reached The Telegraph; Dillon had opened up but left part-time staff on duty. They informed her of the altercation involving Declan and the watchman. Kathleen tried to stop her mind going into overdrive. Permutations clouded her judgement as to how the scenario could end. She felt vulnerable waiting for any news as time ticked on.

CHAPTER 39

The tension had reached fever pitch inside the hardware store. Fumes filled the air around the counter area from where the paraffin tank had been damaged in the fray. The rich smell of scotch whiskey saturated the air as Patrick and Thomas wreaked havoc, demolishing Declan's contraband stock with a sledgehammer. Dermot tried to move the paraffin container closer to the door but it was filled to the brim and he struggled with its weight. Shane got up and helped him haul it across the shop floor to the front door, where Liam stood guard. Shane was trying to figure out ways to get out, but when he saw how Dermot struggled to move, he dismissed the idea. Trying a different approach, he tried to reason with Liam to plant a seed in his head.

'I can't believe your father has ordered this. I don't know much about the guy but from what I've heard this is way out of order.'

Liam reacted, 'My father's a good businessman; shut your face.'

Shane sneaked a look at him and realised something. 'He doesn't know anything about this, does he?' Liam ignored the comment but looked awkward. Shane knew Liam was as thick as shite, and this could be their ticket to getting out of there.

'Tell me, Liam – what do you think the boss man is going to do once he finds out you've wrecked his store?' he challenged. 'From what I've heard, he has a shocking temper. He's going to come gunning for your dad who knows fuck all about this.'

Shane walked away and left Liam to dwell on his predicament. A pair of eyes peered up from the basement steps. Thomas walked up into the shop. He held a sledgehammer in one hand. Shane didn't know if he had heard any of the conversations. Without saying a word, Thomas stood nose to nose glaring at him. In one motion, Thomas dropped the hammer onto Shane's toes. As it landed on his shoeless foot, the pain instantly shot through his nervous system, and he crumpled to the floor. Thomas calmly picked the hammer back up and walked around Shane before switching his gaze to Liam with a disapproving look. Without warning, the hammer swung through the air and smashed into the fuel container. The force of the impact caused the vessel to explode, sending fuel over the shop floor and drenching Shane.

Kieran made a trembling run back to the hardware store, his heart rate hammering. He was standing next to the store, hidden, he reciting all the things he would say if he got inside. His attention was caught by one of the appeal posters of Sinead stuck on the inside of a window. With all the best intentions, his courage failed him. Anxiety welled inside, and he forgot everything he planned to do. Pacing back and forth, he tried to psych himself up again. Kieran's world paused as a thousand images and fond memories of Sinead, flashed before his eyes. Raw sadness erupted from within before he broke down uncontrollably.

Sliding down the wall outside, holding his face, he slumped to his knees and cried. After a minute or two, he pulled himself together. A different mindset developed inside as his fear solidified into a rage. Wiping his tears away, he gritted his teeth and took a deep breath through his nose. A surge of adrenalin made his head buzz as he approached the store window to peer in. Leaning sideways, he glimpsed Shane squirming on the floor. He readied his muscles for action. Anger and hatred welled up from inside, and he began to tremble with rage.

A roar ripped out of him as he charged through the doors. Liam was the first person in sight. Kieran steamed across the floor and shunted his elbow out in front of him. He made contact with Liam's jaw, and the force of the impact rendered an almighty crack. The side of Liam's head ricocheted off the adjacent shelving, knocking him clean out. The loose stock tumbled down as his body slumped in a heap.

Thomas appeared on the periphery of his vision, having swapped over from Patrick smashing stock. Hauling himself to his feet, Kieran propelled himself forward before the pair met, immediately locking arms. Adrenalin coursed through Kieran's body. He took a swing at Thomas and missed; he then feigned a right hook to dupe Thomas, who went to shield himself, leaving himself open on the left side.

Thomas yelled out to his brother while Kieran took a lungful of air, reigniting his muscles. 'PATRICK!... Get your arse up from that basement.'

Kieran lunged again at Thomas; a miss-timed run that left him grasped in a headlock. His struggle was frantic as he tried to overwhelm the larger man. With speed, Kieran smashed his fists into Thomas's rib cage. Each blow was intense and winded Thomas as he gasped for air. As Thomas doubled over, Kieran instinctively smacked blow after blow into Thomas's face. Bile and spit covered his shirt as he continued his war cry with every punch.

Shane continued to lie helpless on the floor and was blinded by the fumes hindering his ability to escape. Footsteps clambered up from the basement. Shane squinted and could make out Patrick's frame encroaching onto the shop floor; all he could do was scream out to Kieran, 'Mind your back – behind.'

Amid his fury, Kieran dropped Thomas to the floor and, gaining momentum in his footing, took the force of Patrick running into him. The pair slammed into shelving behind them, sweeping up loose stock under their feet as they too became soaked in fuel. Both were locked in a tight clinch. Rapid gasps filled the air. They slammed each other across the aisles, neither relinquishing their hold on each other.

Kieran wormed himself free and skated backwards. This gave Thomas breathing space to regain his composure. He looked around for something to use as a weapon and found boxes of screws as missiles. The screws splintered off everywhere, confusing Kieran and, mixing with the paraffin, laying a dangerous path underfoot. Shane could only see through one eye now, and he needed to do something fast. Anything to prevent the brothers from getting on top.

Thomas rose to his feet, looking dazed. Shane sat himself up and searched around for a weapon. The only thing within reach was an iron weight used to hold the shop doors open. Once in his grasp, he had only one shot at throwing it. He mustered every ounce of power he had and swung. The weight skittered across the wet floor and slammed into Thomas's ankle. He let out a scream and recoiled in agony.

Kieran and Patrick were now on top of each other, grappling on the floor. Just when it seemed the fight was never-ending; a large metal tool case came crashing down from a shelf above onto Patrick's face. He was knocked unconscious. Kieran rolled off him and laid on his back, gasping for breath. Glaring at the fluorescent light above him, he saw Dermot's face looming over him, 'Got the fucker.'

Dermot looked around slowly, taking in the state of the store and said to Kieran, 'I'm sorry I couldn't do much to protect any of this.' Hobbling back to the counter, he looked dejected.

Kieran got up and tried to reassure Dermot. 'There was little value here; this just kept the other businesses ticking over. It was out of your control, Dermot.'

There was a silence in the store now except for the hum of the radio. Shoppers stood outside, attracted to the drama inside and gathering information from each other. One of them had their face scrunched up against the window and acted as a correspondent relaying commentary back to the baying crowd. The cold temperature outside frosted up the window as the informer's warm breath coated the glass with condensation. Kieran helped Shane to his feet; they hugged one another.

Shane complemented Kieran, 'You're the fucking man you are. Let's all get out of here before this lot come back around.'

A car ground to a halt outside. The lads had seen a glimpse of it but didn't recognise it. The driver got out and escorted an overweight figure from his seat. A smaller saloon-type car pulled up directly behind it, and two more men jumped out. The people outside the store screamed and scattered as they saw firearms on show in broad daylight. The group were not a welcoming committee. They blocked off one end of the street. The Finnerty brothers were making motions of coming to on the floor.

Dermot spoke up, 'Look, boys! I'm not one to be firm. I admit that I'm planking it, but I'd rather take my chances with what I don't know outside than wait for these two to find their feet. Let's get out of here.'

Kieran agreed. 'Well, lads, it has to get worse before it can get better. I haven't been this nervous since my mam went through my browser history on her laptop and then told my dad in front of me. We'll have to whistle in the dark here.'

They fell about laughing while holding onto each other. Reality hit them then, and they quieted down and stood inside the door, mustering up their courage to face what was coming for them.

Shane spoke softly to Kieran, 'So, what did your dad say to you then when he found the porn?'

'Not much... after Mam was out of the he gave me a clip

around the back of the head and said, "Next time, sharp-like Son... DELETE!... DELETE!... DELETE!"'

Both lads chuckled under their breath, but their laughter died as a figure approached them. The men outside had formed a protective barrier in front of the store. Armed assailants flanked either side of the portly figure in the middle. Through the door they heard him speak to them.

'Are the Guards on their way? I need a quick answer, NOW.'

Dermot called back, 'Not unless you made a call.'

The figure spoke again. 'We don't have time either way. My name's Aiden O'Driscoll: I've now gathered that my son is part of this shit-show today. Is he still in there? The big lad.'

Shane answered first, 'Yeah. And those two fuckwits are in there with him.'

O'Driscoll abruptly interrupted and shouted, 'I don't give a shite about those two pricks. Just tell me, is my boy in there. I give you my word; all that is done is done and had nothing to do with me. I didn't arrange any of this.'

Without warning, the doors released and opened. Kieran spoke up, 'Sir… I did what I had to do in there to protect us.'

O'Driscoll looked at him in agreement; he lifted his head and said, 'You're Declan's boy, are you not?... I have no argument with you or especially your father. We have remained distant for years but yet always kept an eye on each other. That's as far as we ever needed to concern ourselves with each other. NOW – where's my boy?'

Kieran stood tall but tense. He replied, 'He's taken a hit and is out cold.'

O'Driscoll nodded and waved two grunts in to recover Liam. Once inside, raised voices between the Finnerty brothers and O'Driscoll's men echoed loudly. Shouts and further punches were dished out, and then Liam was carried out; conscious but disorientated. Aiden stepped inside to view the extent of what had happened, shaking his head on the way out.

From a distance, they heard the sound of a revving engine from the other end of the street. The car slammed its brakes on hard when it arrived outside the store. Another vehicle ground to a halt beside it. Declan jumped out with Billy and Johnny behind. They could see Kieran standing in front of Aiden. A wave of torment washed over Declan's face. He looked at lads and said, 'Billy and Johnny, I'm going in. If I get shot, DO

NOT run in behind after me. Do I make myself clear?'

Declan marched over from his car with no concern for his safety. One of O'Driscoll's men pointed his handgun at him, waiting for instructions. Declan knew that the closer he got, the safer he would be. Holding his arms out in a show of surrender, he was adamant that he wasn't going to slow down. O'Driscoll held his stance, his legs wide apart, both hands deep in his pockets. Both assailants raised their guns and aimed with precision in Declan's direction.

O'Driscoll made the first move, signalling to his men to lower their guns as Declan approached.

Gesturing for Declan to keep it together, O'Driscoll cautiously said, 'This is an outrageous attack in your terrain and all elements of its planning look like it came from my ordering. Hand on heart, I can honestly tell you I didn't know or sanction any of this. God's honest truth. Before this goes any further, I need to know that you believe me, Declan.'

Looking to the ground, Declan gritted his teeth and said, 'You know that's my boy over there.'

O'Driscoll relented, 'I'm aware of that... I need an answer from you, Declan?'

Nodding his head in response, Declan looked up and abruptly said, 'Alright… I believe what you say. But this isn't finished, not by any stretch of the imagination.'

O'Driscoll held his hands up, nodding in agreement, and ordered his men to put their weapons away. A wave of an arm commanded Aiden to come back into the store. Declan nodded, permitting him to go inside.

Grasping Kieran's face, Declan asked, 'Are you good, my boy? Take all three of you back to the car.'

Kieran clutched his father's wrists and calmly said, 'Dad, we are all fine. You'll have to keep it together, Dad.'

Declan knew he had to keep calm. Once Aiden walked back out, all hell would break loose if he didn't. The penny had dropped for Aiden, and things weren't going to be pretty. Aiden realised the Finnerty brothers had audacious plans of their own. Instead of carrying out his orders, they were attempting a coup. Declan apologised to Shane and Dermot for their being caught up in turmoil before ushering them in haste back to Declan's car with Kieran. A yelp came from inside before one of O'Driscoll's men dragged Thomas. Thomas glared at Declan, then Aiden. Aiden stopped the procession and stood in front of Thomas. His eyes burned into Thomas' as he questioned him.

'You thought you were so smart and that one day this was all going to be yours. Well, I've got news for you; I'm finished with you two shits.'

Thomas looked up at him with disdain, still held between the two men, and replied, 'For Chrissake!... you're still stuck in your little world... both of you,' he looked at Declan. 'This city has got so much more to reap, and you just can't see it.' Thomas mustered a glob of phlegm from the back of his throat, which he spat at O'Driscoll's chest.

O'Driscoll lashed out at him, slapping him hard across the face with the back of his hand. Grabbing out with one hand, O'Driscoll locked his grip around his jaw and slammed his head against the shop window. The glass panel shuddered as the vibrations ricocheted throughThomas's head.

O'Driscoll roared at him, 'The problem with you two is that you've got no respect for the people who have put a little bit of trust in you. You think it's your God-given right to take what's put in front of you. You're nothing but parasites. You'll *never* achieve anything like myself and the man whose store you've destroyed. You'll *never* achieve anything because you'll *never* have any loyalty from anyone.'

Without relinquishing his grip, he could tell that none of what he had said had registered with Thomas. Dropping him to the ground, he issued instructions for his men to drag him back to one of the cars. He wanted to give them one last private send-off that would ensure they would never set foot in Dublin again.

O'Driscoll turned his attention back to Declan. Offering to cover his losses, he asked him if they could venture in together to assess the damage. As they entered the store, the heavy tang of paraffin spiked the air and burnt the back of their throats. O'Driscoll summoned one of his men over to hold the doors open to let air in. The pair stumbled across stock strewn across the floor. Declan was more concerned with how much capital was now destroyed in the basement than anything in the store. Declan had accepted O'Driscoll's vague offer of recompense but wanted a face-to-face with the Finnerty brothers to give them a parting gift of his own.

Outside at the cars, a commotion had broken out. Patrick had caused a diversion by grappling with one of Aiden's men after he waited for the weapons to be packed away. When the other man came to his aid, Patrick sprayed a can of WD40 in their eyes that he had sneaked out of the store. Coming to his brother's aid, Thomas punched the third man repeatedly in the balls and, grabbing the cigarette from his mouth, he ran back into the store.

Over in Declan's car, Kieran was poised to jump out and run back in to warn his father, but both Shane and Dermot persuaded him to sit tight. The three of them watched as Thomas disappeared inside the store. Once inside, the doors slammed shut.

Caught off guard by the sudden arrival of Thomas, Declan and O'Driscoll watched in slow motion as Thomas took a long drag on the cigarette, holding it aloft. 'I thought it was only fair and proper to leave you with a parting gift before I go,' he said. He slowly exhaled and flicked his cigarette into the air. Declan and O'Driscoll watched it fly through the air and start to come down towards the floor as if in slow motion. O'Driscoll, panicked, headed for the basement.

Stretching out his arm to block his way, Declan grasped him and shouted, 'You'll burn alive down there... this way, *quick.*'

The cigarette hit the deck and ignited in the blink of an eye. The path of flames followed the trail of alcohol and paraffin towards the staircase and down into the basement. A loud WHOOSH bellowed up the stairs as the fire engulfed the store. Black plumes of smoke ballooned across the ceiling into every crevice. Exploding canisters giving off intoxicating fumes further fuelled the fire. As the flames grew, intense heat channelled down towards the back of the store, engulfing everything in its path.

Declan dragged O'Driscoll towards the back door, one arm shielding his eyes from the smoke. Declan knew that the back door was always locked. So, without stopping, he shouldered through it, smashing it on impact. His shoulder ruptured on contact before he hit the tarmac dragging O'Driscoll on top of him. They collapsed, coughing for air, knowing how lucky they were to escape with their lives. Declan got to his feet, surveying the destruction.

From the ground, O'Driscoll called, 'Will you give us an arm up, man?'

Deflated, Declan looked down on him and said, 'I thought your guys were trained. I had a salvageable store before you arrived. YOU OWE ME.'

Kieran watched the orange glow from the store as Thomas exited the front doors, hurtling back towards the cars. Shane and Dermot wrestled with him as he tried to set himself free to go after his dad. They held him back, and the three watched as the store burnt to the ground. Dropping to his knees, Kieran gazed at the intense flames and listened as glass panels exploded.

After watching them being packed away, Patrick, managed to get out of the car and retrieve one of the guns in the midst of the chaos. Distracted by the explosion, Thomas had seized the opportunity to take control of the smaller car. Faced in the direction of Declan's car, it partially blocked the road. The brothers looked ahead. They planned to drive straight forward to clear their path. They got in the car and started the engine. With a high-pitched revving noise, the wheels screeched, and the vehicle lurched forward towards Kieran, who had broken away from the others. The speed picked up as the car found its rhythm and hurtled down the road. Shane and Dermot shouted at Kieran to warn him. As the car came closer, Shane dragged Kieran clear. The smell of burning rubber lingered as the car clipped the rear end of Declan's. The brothers' vehicle then side-swiped and smashed off another parked car. The driver slammed the brakes on, and tyres screeched as the vehicle swerved from side to side and zoomed out of sight. Dermot held his neck as he stumbled across the road to check on the boys. It was starting to sink in that no one could survive such a devastating fire.

As the fire continued to rage, cans of aerosols and tins of flammables exploded on heat impact and streams of them fired out through the vacant windows. Shane and Dermot quickly helped Kieran to his feet and out of the way. The group stood in awe of the spectacle, watching the store as it burnt to the ground.

Just when all hope was lost, two figures emerged side-by-side from the rear laneway. Kieran was the first to work out that one of the figures was his father. The way his shoulders dropped and his left knee swung out at an angle confirmed his father was alive. Kieran ran past the waves of heat and clutched onto him. Aiden stumbled to his car and wiped his face clean of soot. Sirens rang out as Gardai and emergency services arrived at the scene. Routes into the nearby roads were blocked off, and neighbours emerged from their houses to watch the spectacle. Word had spread that the store was ablaze, and opportunists had appeared on site trying to steal anything that may have been salvageable. The damage was too severe; everything inside the building had turned to ashes. Looking back at the foundations, Declan watched as thousands of euros worth of damaged disappeared in the blink of an eye. He could come to terms with the loss and rebuild again, but the damage to his pride came at a greater loss.

CHAPTER 40

Thomas held a firm arm on the steering wheel as the car's back end fishtailed in haste to leave the scene. The suspension protested as the wheels bounced off kerbs before, some distance achieved, the motor slowed down. He broke the silence.

'Patrick, do you fancy taking a wee peek at our future pub? I wanna get a feel for the place before we etch our names above the door.'

Patrick smirked, 'Go on then, you know the way.'

The car stopped outside The Telegraph. Anxiously watching out the window, Kathleen first thought it was Declan. Her heart fluttered as she rose from her stool in relief. Thomas and Patrick walked in. Nobody took notice of them except for Kathleen. As her eyes widened, her heart pounded. She gave them a cursory glance, somehow knowing who they were. Turning away to the bar in a controlled panic, she tried to figure out what their presence could mean for her husband and son. She placed her hands firmly against the bar, her arms shaking uncontrollably, and she willed herself to calm down.

The brothers entered as if they owned the pub. Kathleen's blood boiled. The fear from not knowing the fate of her family had hardened into anger. Against character, she stood up and approached the brothers. She tried to keep a smile fixed on her face but was aware that she was sweating. Unaware of who she was, they noticed her but dismissed her until she caught Patrick's eye.

Patrick, confident and triumphant, sized her up and found her acceptable. 'Well, hello there, little lady, can you give me a grand tour of this pub... forgive me, let me introduce ourselves as the future owners of this establishment. My name is...'

Kathleen stalled his pitch, much to his brother's amusement. Her face tightened as she hissed, 'I know who you are,' her tone was clipped, 'and I know *what* you are.'

Patrick looked bemused, while Thomas remained straight-faced, having just realised who she was. Patrick offered his hand to Kathleen. Thomas intervened, 'Let me deal with this one brother; I specialise in whores.'

Kathleen hurled her arm across Thomas's face. He didn't expect it. Her nails caught the side of his cheek and the tip of his nose, which stung with the contact. 'I see manners don't come naturally to you,' Kathleen snarled.

In an almost impulsive reaction, Thomas lashed out with the back of his hand and caught her flush on the chin, sending her sprawling backwards onto the carpet. Patrick leapt to her defence, still not recognising who Kathleen was.

'Fuck's sake, Thomas, do you have to become jealous of every piece of skirt I chase?'

Thomas chuckled to himself, entertained at, for once having the upper hand over his brother. He smirked, 'Patrick, let me introduce you to the wife of the present occupier of this establishment.'

Patrick, wrong-footed, gaped at her on the floor.

An elderly drinker, appalled by the attack, tried to intervene, but Kathleen politely but firmly steered him away. Patrick attempted to help Kathleen up, 'Here, take my arm. I'm the gentleman of us two brothers.'

Kathleen ignored him and clambered up on her own accord, praying her legs wouldn't betray her. She gazed back and forth between the brothers, defiant, ignoring the red hot pain in her chin. With a steely resolve, she spoke. 'My father has a saying: "Treat every man as a gentleman until he proves himself otherwise." You two are no gentlemen.'

Patrick, embarrassed, tried to make light of the situation, 'You see, brother, now we are both tarnished with the same brush.'

Thomas ignored him and continued to stare right through Kathleen. Kathleen noticed it, and yet refused to look away, she would not be cowed in her own pub.

'What are you gawping at, woman?'

Kathleen gave a wry smile, not giving away anything.

Patrick slapped his brother across the chest, indicating it was time to leave. Looking her up and down, he slowly walked around Kathleen and said, 'Your husband is a lucky man getting to come home to a woman like you. It will be a shame when you are all he'll have left soon.'

Kathleen stood still, hiding her trembling.

Thomas couldn't help himself and, passing by, whispered in Kathleen's ear,

'Mark my words, the next time we meet, you'll never see me coming, bitch.'

She held her breath and felt her heart pound hard against her chest. Sensing the growing sensation of a loud vibration in her ears, she leaned forward and, with an air of finality, said, 'Get the FUCK out of my pub.'

The road out front was a mass of Gardai, emergency crews and onlookers at the hardware store. Declan, still dazed and receiving treatment for smoke inhalation, was being questioned. Somehow Aiden and his posse had managed to vacate the vicinity before their involvement was noted.

The investigation continued down at the station, and, unsurprisingly, the finger remained pointed suspiciously at Declan. The Guards didn't believe it was an accident that started the fire. He didn't care at this stage. Nothing mattered to him now, only the prospect of meeting the Finnerty brothers once again.

Word had got around the neighbourhood about the fire, and by the time Declan got home, his mother had joined Kathleen and a newly heroic Kieran to welcome him home. Wrapping her arms around her son, Geraldine praised him for securing everyone's safety. In the same sentence, she managed to tell him off too, but her heart wasn't in it. He filled them in on the story with the Finnerty brothers then went upstairs for a shower.

When he emerged cleaner and calmer, Geraldine sat down with him and, cupping his hands in hers, voiced her concerns for his safety. For the first time in his life, she opened up and expressed her terror at how his lifestyle might result in his demise; It pained him to hear it from her. In front of his mother, he was, like always, a small boy, trying to keep her happy. Declan looked relieved when Kieran joined them and lightened the mood. All three sat in the lounge as Kathleen poured Declan a whiskey on ice. She handed him his drink and began to pace up and down in front of him. Sitting back, Declan waited patiently to receive the riot act from her.

'Kieran has filled me in somewhat on today's events. You do know that these brothers will be back to terrorise you again if you do nothing.

You need to find a way to defeat these parasites. They have no morals, no honour, or code of conduct.' Kathleen continued, 'Your mother and I have always remained out of your business by choice. You promised us you would never become involved in anything to do with drugs from the very start of all of this. Is this what this turf war is all about? Don't bullshit me, Declan.'

Declan flinched at the accusation. 'I promised you I would never become involved with drugs, and I've kept my word.'

'Ok, Declan. I believe you. Now, what are you going to do about this?' she asked. 'These bastards will come back and take everything you have worked for. You and O'Driscoll need to put your pride aside and work together on this. Christ, you two had the perfect understanding for years before these culchie bastards turned up.'

Kathleen dropped to her knees in between Declan's legs. He took a slug of his whiskey. As the spirit slid down his throat, it relaxed him enough to slow his senses down. Kathleen cocooned his head in her arms, leaving the warmth of her lips on his cheek. She could see that her husband was now a man slowing down in age and body. He looked like a broken man in body, but Kathleen knew the fight was still in him. She needed to make him believe in himself to get on top of his biggest battle yet.

Lifting his head, she cupped his ears. She wiped the tiredness away from under his eyes and spoke softly, 'Declan... love, listen to me.Your mam and I have always been your biggest supporters. Now you need to believe in yourself. You've always set yourself a goal and achieved it by thinking methodically. As we all sit here now, darling, we believe you can get through this. Once this goes away, then you can think about relinquishing some control so that we can all take a step back and enjoy our lives.'

Declan didn't respond but smiled softly in agreement. He leant back and closed his eyes. Kathleen moved across on her knees and was cradled by Geraldine. Geraldine stroked her hair and said, 'You told him exactly what he needed to hear. Let him rest now, and God willing, he'll find a way to settle this.'

CHAPTER 41

The morning after the fire, Declan woke up on the sofa covered with a blanket. Kathleen had heard movements in the room and greeted him with a mug of tea. The overpowering fug of stale whiskey lingered in the room before Kathleen pushed the bay window open. The aroma of a cooked breakfast wafted into the room. Kathleen had sent Geraldine home in a cab last night, and Kieran was still asleep. It was just the two of them.

They ate together and didn't speak. Declan was alert but in deep thought, and Kathleen watched him warily. She had an appointment to keep, so she made her excuses and kissed her husband goodbye. The minute she left the house, Declan scrolled through the contacts on his phone until he came to Aiden O'Driscoll. Ringing him, he hung up immediately. Pressing the phone against his chin, he toyed with it and cursed aloud, 'Arhh, fuck it.'

Declan ordered a cab to take him to the other side of town to O'Driscoll's pub, The Running Horses. He made another call to Detective Muldoon and arranged to meet him mid-afternoon. Arriving at the pub, Declan was surprised to see how upmarket it looked from the outside. Dark green, glazed tiles surrounded the lower brickwork. Large panelled windows gleamed, having been cleaned that morning before opening. Blossom-filled hanging baskets gave a warm, inviting feel to the place. Pausing for thought as he wiped his feet on the bristled floor mat, he wondered if O'Driscoll had ever been to The Telegraph and made the same comparison.

The bar bustled with a suited gentleman wearing tweed overcoats. Huddled together in small groups, they voiced their opinions, tearing at their racing pages as they squawked about dead cert winners. The pub was about half a mile away from the national racetrack; a big race meeting was took place that day. Lively punters scrambled at the bar as they ordered pitchers of beer, spilling them in haste on the retreat back to their tables. One busy customer passed Declan with a heaping tray of pints, soaking his shoe as he squeezed by. A youthful Declan would have had the man lying on his back with the pitcher poured over him. This older and wiser Declan decided not to cause a scene. He reached the bar and waited to be served.

'I'll have a whiskey American, young man. More of the whiskey and less of the American.'

The bartender placed the drink along with the bottle in front of him. Examining the bar, Declan admired the arrangement of optics. Some of them he'd never heard of, and others he knew he didn't want to try. A phone rang from behind the bar, and the bartender answered it, staring up at the security camera. He looked back at Declan and the ten euro note on the bar and said, 'On this occasion, Sir, it's on the house.' Declan nodded in appreciation. Within a minute, he felt a presence beside him. Turning, he saw O'Driscoll seated next to him, his glass soaked into a coaster. He looked away. Both sat staring ahead without making eye contact.

O'Driscoll spoke, 'I'll give you this… you've some balls coming down here after what's happened. Tell me, when was the last time you ventured into my pub?'

With fleeting glances at each other in the mirrored bar, Declan replied, 'I'm just resting my balls after saving yours. I thought I'd come down to see how the other half live. I must say I'm impressed.'

Chuckling to himself, O'Driscoll waved his finger, summoning another round of drinks. Both men continued to talk comfortably, acknowledging each other through their reflections in the mirrored bar. An hour later, they had come to an agreement on an allyship. They would reconvene when Declan had more information about the Finnertys.

Before parting ways, Declan asked, 'Look, I've someone inside the force who is supplying me with reliable intel on you-know-who. I trust my man, and I've got a meeting with him after leaving here. Problem is, I've left it late to cover him for his services. He has taken care of something that could have incriminated me in a wider investigation.'

O'Driscoll stopped him with a raised hand. 'How much do you need?'

Declan winced and said, 'Two thousand.'

O'Driscoll choked in astonishment, 'For fuck's sake... for that kind of money, I'd be expecting him to bring the pair of bastards *to me*!'

Declan winced again, 'That's the price in the climate we live in today.'

Knocking his drink back, O'Driscoll went out of the bar, telling Declan to wait. Before he was out of eyesight, Declan had one more request, 'Could you put it in an envelope for us?'

A frown sloped across O'Driscoll's face. 'Do you want me to lick the seal for you as well?' He turned and went behind the bar.

O'Driscoll returned with a sealed brown envelope. As he handed it to Declan, he whispered in his ear, 'Is this what it costs me to save my balls?'

Declan didn't reply but nodded in gratitude. Gazing around, he asked, 'Thinking about it, could you ever risk losing this magnificent pub?'

O'Driscoll answered, 'There is only one man here at risk of losing something, and that's you. I'm here to stop you from losing any more.'

They bid each other goodbye. O'Driscoll disappeared upstairs, and Declan left the pub to hail a cab to meet Muldoon. During the ride, his mind searched for a weak link in the Finnerty brothers set-up.

The meeting with Detective Muldoon was in the same coffee shop in town as previously. The lunchtime whiskey left a warm glow on Declan's chest and watered his eyes. On arrival, Muldoon was already there and keen to start.

'I took the liberty of ordering you a cappuccino; you can't go wrong with that.'

Declan thanked him and made himself comfortable. The whiskey fumes caught the attention of Muldoon. He commented, 'Jaysis – late night or an early start today?'

Declan shrugged, 'Early business meeting.'

Studying the lines on Declan's face, Muldoon leaned forward and spoke in a knowing tone. 'I hear there was a ruckus at your place with you in the heat of it – so to speak – the other week. The duty sergeant had to hold the reigns on a couple of hotheads wanting to visit you that night. I hear that it got – or you got – out of hand. Then there is the fire. I wonder if the two are linked – a reprisal for kicking off in the pub. The truth be told, I don't give a shit. You know, if the public is put at risk, I can't call in any favours for you. The uniforms will be all over your vicinity. Keep your shite in-house, do you hear me?' he advised.

Declan slouched lower in his chair in response. He let one arm hang over the back of the chair as if he was in charge of the conversation.

Muldoon cut to the chase, 'Look, these pair is bad news. My team has a scope on them, and if you're planning anything, I can't interfere or bail you out if you are caught in the mix of things. Do I make myself clear? I will deny all avenues of contact with you. My burner phone will never be traced. These fish are getting bigger, and there are many a detective that wants to be the ones to reel them in.'

Taking a deep breath, Muldoon looked around. 'My acquaintances back in Limerick tell me… Let me tell you, these fellas are bad players. In their hometown, whatever goes down is entirely run and orchestrated by them only. The main guy who runs the outfit is called Dooley. He is one bad apple that you wouldn't want in your cider. He will always leave a bad taste in your mouth. By all accounts, if you do something to upset him – you'll always be watching over your shoulder.'

Muldoon rubbed his tired face. 'This Dooley character started by running a skip firm in Limerick. Gradually, he owned all of them along with recycling companies. It was strictly cash-based revenue. He earned his fortune that way. Later he bought a pub, that's his castle. It has been reported that two guys have been murdered over the years since leaving the business. Nothing was ever pinned on this Dooley.'

Declan stroked his chin before tipping his fingers together, hiding his nose.

The detective continued. 'He now operates an enterprise selling and transporting drugs throughout Limerick. It was something that these Finnerty brothers were keen to expand on after proving their worth to Dooley on some low-key scams. It's been rumoured that Dooley has contacts with criminals in South America, and he was proposing to ship excess quantities of class A drugs through Ireland and into the UK via his recycling companies.

'He had allegedly tied up contracts with UK-based firms to ship recycling containers on route to China. It is believed he was using this decoy as a diversion to ship drugs across Europe and Asia. My advice is to stay clear from them altogether. Sort your shite out your way and away from any surveillance. After today, destroy your burner and, in due course, we'll arrange contact in the future.'

Muldoon looked at Declan, seeking reassurance from him. Declan nodded. A folder was slid in front of Declan, and the detective abruptly rose and said, 'We are done now.'

Leaving his coffee untouched, the detective waited for his envelope and left. Declan finished his coffee and peeled open the folder. Inside were photos of Dooley and his pub. It was called The Manor Arms. He looked closer at the prints. What the fuck? He thought the place looks closed down.

With the meeting completed, Declan knew he needed to get back home and plan his next move. He thought about finding a secluded pub to gather his thoughts in, but the cold weather put him off. He took the folder, left the coffee shop and took a cab home. Comforted by the chatter of the cabbie's voice, Declan asked him to stop off at an off-licence. He bought his favourite whiskey and some snacks to bring home. On arrival at his house, Declan generously tipped the driver and wished him good evening.

Kathleen had left him dinner in the oven with a note explaining she was at Bridget's. After dinner, he settled in and watched TV with the sound muted. Downing another whiskey, he shuddered as the liquor burnt his chest. Declan picked up the folder and, in despair, flung it across the floor. After half the whiskey bottle had settled in his stomach, he began to delve back through fond memories. Fatherhood had always taken second place behind running the business; Declan tortured himself over that. It was only in recent weeks that he had come to realise that instead of his son respecting him, he only feared him. At that moment, it hurt him. He was tempted to finish the bottle but needed to be clear-headed for Sinead's funeral tomorrow. Strange days he thought. Who would have thought they'd all end up where they did?

CHAPTER 42

The funeral took place at the church connected to Sinead's school. Bridget knew the parish priest, but it had been some years since she last attended any church services. However, the priest had visited Sinead at home after she was being diagnosed. There was a strong relationship between the Lynches and the previous priests of the parish, as Bridget's parents had known them for many years.

The day was planned to be a celebration of Sinead's life. The Publicity generated through the local newspaper had stirred up a lot of interest, and many were expected. The community felt great sympathy for the family, and the entirety of Sinead's school were expected to attend. The school music teacher had liaised with the head of the church choir to accommodate the pupils in Sinead's class to sing during the service. After the ceremony, a private gathering was planned for family and close friends.

Initially, it had been planned for the Lynches home, but The Telegraph pub was deemed a more suitable location to accommodate Bridget's large family. Kathleen had persuaded Bridget to use the function room upstairs, and she would staff and supply food for the buffet. Bridget tried to hand Kathleen money to cover the costs, but Kathleen refused and wouldn't hear another word about it. Declan was fuming at the gesture, not because he wasn't generous but because he considered it disloyal for Kathleen to suggest it. He wanted to distance himself from the family, but he owed Kathleen, so no more was mentioned about it. After the reception in the pub, Bridget wanted to have some of her family back to her home later to reflect more privately.

Restlessness had kept Martin awake all night. The parish office entrusted himself and David to set up the seating arrangements organise the flowers. On arrival at the church, they were overwhelmed by the influx of flowers and ended up moving half of them outside on the church grounds. Meanwhile, Shane's duties included tidying the house to accommodate the family members arriving. Sheila had taken it upon herself to prepare hot food for hungry guests to enjoy when the family returned later.

The morning was cold and crisp. The funeral cortege pulled up outside Number 22. Neighbours stood outside the house, dressed in black, and a respectful silence stretched down the road. Bridget hadn't needed to be told that the procession had arrived. It was her biggest fear, seeing the coffin, experiencing the sharp impact of her loss so physically. Neighbours bowed their heads in respect as the procession slowly departed from the street. The Lynches sat stunned in silence as they followed the hearse.

A couple of local photographers had arrived to document the funeral. The scale was such that the local Guards arrived to escort the procession along due to the volume of traffic that flowed through the area. On arrival, the church was overwhelmed, and crowds of people spilled along the streets outside. Bridget recognised familiar faces of mothers with their children by their sides but couldn't make sense of anything, so dazed, was she. Martin looked haggard and old as himself. David handed out candles to people who entered and kept a close eye on Martin throughout. As the procession entered the church, the organist played 'All Things Bright and Beautiful' in the background.

Martin showed no emotion as he lifted and shunted the coffin with the other five men. Each pairing of men stretched out and linked arms over shoulders as they began the slow march down the aisle. A selection of Sinead's favourite songs played, the most appropriate was 'Long as I Can See the Light' which brought tears to even the hardest of men when sung by the choir.

As the opening verses echoed out through the main entrance, Martin became floundered; an almost imperceptible dropping of his stature was followed by a complete collapse under the weight of his daughter. The other pallbearers braced themselves, managing to spread the weight difference. A strong arm reached out and caught Martin before he hit the floor. Declan stood above him, reaching out with his other arm to hold Martin's weak body in the circle of his arms. Martin hadn't eaten properly in days and was almost faint through exhaustion. He tried to thank the figure in front of him, tears dripping down his face blurring his vision.

Martin hadn't realised it, but it was the first time Declan had laid a hand on him without inflicting violence. Feeling embarrassed in front of the congregation, Declan wished it had been someone else who had helped Martin.

The old burnished wooden benches gave off a distinct smell. Martin and Bridget held hands tightly throughout the service. Sheila read a moving poem that she had written in honour of her niece. Reading it slowly but clearly, she choked on the final line as her eyes drifted to the coffin. In reflection, silence wrapped around the church. The distant muttering of prayer and the rattling of rosary beads prevented the silence from taking over completely. The motion of the congregation kneeling reverberated around the church like an old wooden Tudor ship changing direction in high seas.

The eerie quiet was rent by the muffled shriek of interference from the microphone. All eyes focused on the source of the sound as Mrs Callaghan took to the lectern. Taking in a deep breath, she exhaled and then she spoke.

'For those of you who don't know or recognise me, I am – I was Sinead's teacher. For all of you who knew Sinead, she warmed our hearts with her dry, witty humour. For me, her understanding of humanity and life in general was abundant. I tutored Sinead throughout her illness and personally grew attached to this lovely young girl with a passion for learning everything there was to know. She was a wise young lady who had all of life's potential to fulfil. If it were not blighted by the disease that finally took her life, I am sure she would have stood out in adult life and secured a positive future for herself.' Mrs Callaghan stopped herself as she choked on her final words and stood down.

A mother struggled at the back of the church, comforting her baby, who continuedly cried. The priest spoke to the congregation, 'Can I just say to you all, all children are welcomed in this church, with or without a parent, with silence or without. The bible says, "Let the little children come to me, and do not hinder them, for the kingdom of God belongs to such as these. Truly, I tell you, anyone, who will not receive the kingdom of God like a little child will never enter it. And he took the children in his arms, placed his hands on them and blessed them."' When the service ended, there was silence once more.

CHAPTER 43

Family members filled the funeral cars as they followed the coffin in convoy. Kathleen and Mr and Mrs Mercer were the only non-family members invited to the burial. The procession was slow and took a detour past Sinead's home address on route to her final resting place. Cars crept along into the graveyard car park, an open area with no tarmac to welcome the procession. Wheels crunched over gravel, avoiding disconcerting puddles that showed no depth.

The priest was waiting by the graveside. His white and purple cassock stood out like a beacon amongst the mass of grey stonework that commemorated lost lives. Dates crumbled away on slanted gravestones, weathered and blighted by moss and decay over decades. Generations of ancestors, forgotten, as time and scheduling left no space to remember those gone. Here was one place in the city that was so full of people with nobody visiting them.

The sky was a grey haze. Swathes of broken clouds threatened to burst into rain but thankfully withheld their deluge. A thin continuous mist dampened everyone instead. Soft footing greeted the followers off a path onto soft grass. The morning dew dampened everyone's shoes. The priest's hair whipped up in the light winds as he issued instructions to the dishevelled-looking groundsmen. Their fictitious faces showed the respect that wasn't believable; their only concern was for the service to hurry up, so they could get away from the unforgiving wind.

Family members lined up in black, side-by-side, around a deep black hole awaiting the body of Sinead. Failing members were held up by their elbows as the service started. Bridget's family escorted her like a state President to the front of the grave. Her hair was pinned up and fastened up with a headscarf only to be whipped off by the wind. Martin and Shane clasped each other's hands. The priest's words were kept brief, the pain now almost too much to bear.

Bridget sobbed, held by Sheila and Kathleen as he blessed the place where this young child was to lay. Together their voices merged into a keening sound, like a low pitch of a cello that repeated itself. All three women united for once. The magnitude of despair in Martin's and Shane's faces was held back somewhat as they tried to hold themselves together. The mourners were separated by this invisible dividing line. On one side stoicism, the other; untamed grief.

The white coffin was lowered into its final resting place. Bridget said goodbye to her only daughter. Martin acknowledged her words; his own words held prisoner in his chest. Shane dropped a folded message in on top of the coffin, and then, one-by-one, the mourners tossed in single flowers as they said their final goodbyes.

The Telegraph was packed. Bridget had put some money behind the bar to cover everyone's first drink; what she didn't realise was that Kathleen had given instructions that not a till drawer should be opened that day. They hadn't anticipated the extent of mourners who had come to pay their respects, though.

A pint appeared in front of Martin, but unusually for him, he didn't touch it. The pub was now no longer a sanctuary for him. He sat in a daze, looking around at all the people. A sea of heads flitted around each other as conversations flowed with the drinks. Most of the people he'd never met before. If he had, it was when he was drunk or when they had witnessed him taking a beating from Declan. He didn't feel people in the pub were there for him or Bridget. Instead, he felt aggrieved by them, people who wanted to partake in the drama surrounding Sinead's death. A numbing ache occupied his chest. He felt utterly alienated; nobody truly knew what the loss of his daughter meant to him. People approached him with sentimental tokens of condolences. Martin stretched his lips into a smile, nodding at murmurs of consolation without hearing a word. For once in his life, he wanted to get away from the pub.

He watched as folk drank and chatted, even laughed and told stories. Pints of lager were held aloft to avoid spillage as patrons moved through the crowd. Sympathy was dished out with air kisses. Martin was in a lonely place of his own and couldn't relate his grief to anyone.

Martin and Bridget were unable to reach each other in their grief.

The last few days, they were like shift workers changing over rotas. Her family surrounded her all day; he remained in the background carrying out chores, neither of them looked at each other. Both of them needed to spend time together to grieve unitedly, but Martin felt her family had put up a wall, and he was left on the other side of it.

The sight of pints being drunk and the sound of jokes being told became unbearable. He couldn't stomach any more of it. Threading his way through the jovial crowd, he slipped out of the pub. Cigarette smoke hit his face as he emerged outside and began the walk home.

The long-awaited forecast of snow had finally come to pass, and the wet mist transformed into light flurries of snowflakes that settled on his shoulders before disappearing. When he reached Number 22, he realised he had no key. He rested his forehead on the front door in despair. The thought of having to go back to the pub to get a key from either Bridget or Shane was unthinkable. He chanced the door and to his bewilderment, it opened.

Walking into the kitchen, he sat down amongst the warmth of the catering dishes set on low heat. Fond memories of Sinead filled his tormented mind. The exhaustion made holding in his emotion difficult, and he burst into a frenzied state of crying, releasing all his built-up tension. After a few minutes, he composed himself, hiccupping back the remaining sobs.

The front door opened, and Sheila unexpectedly entered. She was surprised to see Martin there as nobody had noticed that he had vanished from the pub. Martin tried to mask his bloodshot eyes by pretending to read some of the cards on the table. Sheila, feeling like she had intruded on him, fumbled with an apology.

'Sorry, Martin, I hadn't realised you had come back to be on your own. I needed to check on the cooking before it burnt dry –'

Martin interrupted her, 'Can I make you a cup of tea?'

Hesitating, Sheila didn't know quite how to take this unexpected kindness. 'Martin, it's a lovely gesture, but I've tasted your tea. You kick back there, and I'll make us both a cup,' she smiled at him.

Sheila insisted he sat in the front room while she tended to the food. As he sat, he heard the rest of the family come clattering back. Loud female voices bellowed through the hallway. Hushed melodramatic voices cancelled them out before Bridget poked her head in the door carrying two cups of tea. They spoke briefly about the church service, and then Sheila knocked and announced that the food was ready to be served. An influx of family members came in, claiming seats as they tucked into the infamous Irish stew that Sheila had prepared. Martin and Bridget shared a brief moment of solace before the room was full of hungry, chattering family.

As the evening drew in, alcohol loosened up some of the moods. The conversation carried over to loved ones and friends who had died over recent years. Exclamations were made over how much time had passed. At each name of a person departed, hands made signs of the cross.

'It's a true saying; you're only ever praised in life when you are dead.'

'That's true, even if they were a bastard,' laughter followed.

Even though it was early evening, the warmth of the house caused weariness to set in. The day's event had caught up with a lot of people. Bridget braved the backlash and thanked everybody for their attendance, and invited them to head home. This allowed herself and Martin to settle down for the evening and reflect on the day.

Shane had found an excuse not to be at home. At the back of Bridget's mind, it concerned her how he was dealing with the loss of his sister, but she knew he had to grieve his own way. He had his distractions, plus Kieran was at hand to confide in. Sitting amidst the mass of cards and condolences letters, Bridget and Martin snuggled side-by-side and went through them together. Scanning over the verses, Bridget read the handwritten messages.

After a while, Martin left the room and returned with one of Mrs Mercer's bottles of prosecco; it fizzed everywhere as he uncorked it. The contours of her face changed as quickly as her mood. Feeling aggrieved that he could think of alcohol now, she erupted into a frenzy of rage, dismissing the flute glass.

'Do you think this is a moment to drink, Martin? I know this is the norm for you... bury your head when things get tough and blur it all out... but Christ, Martin! We have to live on now with no Sinead... how can we do this? Everywhere we look, she still has a presence with us in this house... I can't see past tomorrow without her, and you want to get obliterated tonight?'

Taken aback by her sudden personality change, Martin bit back. 'Do you think this is how I wanted our lives to be? To live out our time in this shit-hole life. I wanted the dream, too, Bridget. I wanted it all too. But it's never going to happen for us, so I deal with things the best way I know how... I didn't want this life either. Both of us to be scrimping away from week to week, surviving to make ends meet, no joy no…'

Bridget interrupted with a scream, 'I WORK, MARTIN!... I work for this shitty life you're talking about, not you. I DO!'

Martin retaliated, 'That's not fair, Bridge. I put my neck on the line to bring money into this house. I'm always looking over my shoulder.'

Bridget interrupted, 'And, whose fault is that? I don't tell you to go straight into the betting shop and piss our money away. I don't tell you to get in trouble with your dodgy dealings. We won't be in half of this trouble if you put your money straight on the table each time you got it and settled on a proper job.'

Martin felt betrayed. 'I can't get a nine to five job Bridget; you know I can't. I can't do it! Rules and regulations – Yes, Sir! No, Sir! Fuck you, Sir!'

Bridget cut him short, 'But I HAVE TO, Martin. I have to clean up people's shite and pick up the extra shifts. I can't say well, "FUCK YIS ALL, I'M OFF" cause then we wouldn't have this shite hole that we have to live in and call home.'

Feeling drawn into a corner, Martin defended himself the best way he knew how. 'JAYSIS woman, I can't do nothing right by you. All I was offering you was a drink.'

He slammed the bottle down, knocking over the glass in the process. Out of character, he stepped right up, his face up into Bridget's face, and let loose.

'I can't do anything right by you… I don't NEED you to remind me of that… I feel it every single day, and at the end of each day, I can see in your eyes the way you detest me. You're not the only one hurting over our Sinead... I LOST HER AS WELL... I see the way your family looked at me today... "POOR BRIDGET... putting up with that fucker, MARTIN…" as if the loss of a child isn't terrible enough to deal with... she has to carry that bastard husband of hers as well... I can SEE it, Bridget...

'Listen to me, Bridge... I lost a daughter and saw her for the last time today... that wee girl was my best friend... she understood me... she accepted me and didn't judge me... It pains me to say it... I've learnt it's better to keep silent around you than to tell you how I feel because I know it will hurt when you DON'T listen, you don't UNDERSTAND me. She was the only person in this God-forsaken world who did... AND NOW... I have no one,' his voice trailed off, 'What am I going to do now to get me through each day?'

Searching her face for acknowledgement, he saw only blankness. Martin got up and left.

Bridget shouted after him, 'Oh, so, it's *my* fault now that I don't understand you. Maybe it's because I'm always too damn tired to sit and listen to you, Martin. THAT'S RIGHT… OFF TO THE PUB YOU GO.'

Leaving the front door ajar, Martin left with no jacket. Taking a few steps forward, he felt a crunching sound under his feet. Looking down, Martin saw the ground was white and glistening. Leaning his head back, he felt snowflakes tingling as they fell on his face and melted against his eyelids.

He looked up at the dark sky and whispered to himself, 'My darling, you longed for this snow... I hope you're looking down and watching it settle.'

He dropped to his knees, admiring the breathtaking sight of the snow gently falling. Bridget had settled back down amidst the mountain of cards when she heard footsteps come through the door. Martin appeared as a man possessed. Bridget, riddled with guilt after the argument, decided to make the first move.

'I haven't got the energy to carry on like this all night. Give my head some peace. Have your final say and go back to the pub –'

Covering her mouth with his hand, Martin cradled her at the same time and said, 'For once, woman, be quiet. Don't say a word and let me show you something that is going to take your breath away. Trust me'

She nodded silently. Releasing her, Martin asked her to slip her shoes back on. She did, and he guided her out into the hallway. He picked his coat up, covered her shoulders and said, 'Right, close your eyes as you step out.'

Bridget waved away his gesture and replied, 'Away with you.' She looked out the door and stopped in her tracks. The entire street was illuminated. Every house had candles lit, lined up on the top and bottom window ledges; lights flickered the whole length of the street. The scene was breathtaking. The shadows and flickering flames bounced off the bricks from each side of the street. Bridget took a few paces forward and let Martin's coat slip to the ground.

Bridget stepped out into the snow. A streetlamp was faulty, causing the lamp to surge and flicker randomly. Holding hands, they watched as fellow onlookers passed from the top of the street and stood in awe of the spectacle, taking photos before they disappeared from view. Footsteps approached them in the crunching snow. Mrs Mercer had come out of her house. Looking embarrassed, she admitted she had knocked on all the neighbour's doors to hand out the candles and ask them to help. She had declined the invite to the pub after the burial; she hadn't felt comfortable rejoicing in a drink on a funeral occasion. This was her gesture to say farewell to Sinead. As she trailed back home, the glint of the moonlight shimmered across the rooftops.

Bridget gazed at Martin, 'I don't want us to go back in yet. Will you sit with me?' Snatching at his coat, he rested it over her shoulders, and said, 'Give me a minute,' and returned to the house.

Mist covered Martin's face as he returned from the house slowly, carrying two rolled-up sleeping bags to sit on.

Bridget broke half a smile and said, 'What I said back there, I…'

Martin shushed her and put his arm around her. They sat in the snow for some time, silent and reflective and said a final farewell to their daughter.

CHAPTER 44

For over a week, Declan had thought hard about the best course of action to take in tackling the Finnerty brothers. Shielding Kathleen had proved to be an impossible task; she was resolute that she wanted to be kept in the loop.

Sitting up in bed one night, Declan and Kathleen waited for Kieran to come home before they could settle. Declan took the opportunity to talk through his plan to get rid of the Finnerty brothers by introducing himself to their previous employer and forming an alliance with them. Once he had spelt out the alternatives, she realised he had no option but to follow through. Her only concern was who he involved in his plan. She found out that Billy and Johnny were the only men going with him to try and find this Dooley character in Limerick. He was the key to the Finnertys' weakness as they were now wanted men by him. Declan was sure of it. Knowing that there was no way of talking him down once he had made his up, Kathleen at least respected that he told her the truth.

The front door opened with a jangle of keys and then closed. After a patter of footsteps, Kieran knocked at their bedroom door. They shrugged. Bridget asked him to come in.

Kieran partially opened the door and asked, 'Are you two both decent?'

Declan replied in haste, 'Behave, son. We knew you were coming back home.'

Kathleen gave a three-second stare emphasising the remark was way out of line. Kieran rubbed his nose before speaking, 'I've been thinking stuff over this past week, and I want to say something. I want you to back me up on my decision. If I go to bed now, I'll talk myself out of it by the morning.' Both parents looked quizzically at each other.

Declan spoke before thinking, 'Have you got a lass in trouble, Son.'

Kathleen, offended, said, Declan, how dare you. No, he hasn't.'

'Has he spoken to you about this then?'

'A mother would know these things; he'd have confided in me.'

'You mean you wouldn't have told me? Declan asked him.

Kieran intervened, 'You guys, I'm standing in front of you, I *am* here.'

Sorry, my love, ignore your father, carry on.'

'I want to be involved with Dad's business. I want to be included in going after these brothers. I want you to stop treating me like a teenager. I want you to respect my decisions.'

Declan sat up straight in the bed. 'Not a CHANCE. You're too weak, Son, up here,' he tapped the side of his head. 'I've spent my life shielding you from this kind of stuff, protecting you from men like these. Joining the business is one thing; this is a different matter altogether.'

Kathleen rolled her eyes, 'DECLAN... I think what your father is trying to say is that we have provided a life for you where you can educate yourself and have choices. A life where you are not looking over your shoulder, a life where you are safe.' Declan darted his eyes at Kathleen.

'Guys, please, think about it. Meet me halfway on things, at least then, instead of a straight NO. Mam, I'll go to the referral at the hospital, and I'll keep you in the loop Dad. I want you to teach me to defend myself your way. From now on, I don't want both of you to keep mugging me off. That's all I want.'

Both parents again looked at each other in surprise at the maturity of their son.

Declan frowned at Kathleen, 'What hospital referral?'

'Declan, that's another conversation between you and me. Don't push it.'

'Mam, Dad, do we have an understanding now?' Kieran asked.

'Yes, love, we do, don't we, Declan.'

'Yes, Son, we'll think about it.'

'Thank God.' Kieran nodded goodnight and slowly closed the door behind him.

Declan and Kathleen looked stunned at Kieran's request. Kathleen shouted out as the door closed, 'That was sweet of you to confide in us, Son.'

Declan followed up with, 'Thanks, Son.'

As their door closed, they heard movements in the bathroom before Kieran trudged off to his bedroom. After settling their differences on Kieran's choices, they continued to talk it through in bed. Kathleen reiterated Kieran's sentiments about wanting to spend quality time with his father. Declan didn't respond; instead, he shrugged his shoulders as an answer. He was still unhappy about being kept out of the loop about the hospital referral. Secretly, though, he was proud of Kieran and how he had spoken up for himself.

The couple caressed briefly before settling down to sleep. Declan snuggled up behind his wife and spooned her. Tentatively, he stroked her hair, panning his fingers through her strands before he caressed her earlobe. As if a tut and the strain of a deep sigh wasn't enough to repel him, Kathleen had her suspicions of what Declan's notions were and had it confirmed when she felt a soft, warm prod at the base of her spine. The prod developed into a pulse that gently pressed against her backbone. From past endeavours with her husband, she knew what the next move would be and cut him dead in his tracks.

Kathleen swivelled over and grabbed his crotch in the palm of her hand and squeezed it. She flicked it, causing him discomfort, and said, 'You can pack that back in your pants for tonight... and if you make it back from your suicide mission to Limerick with *these* still intact... then *maybe* you can put them to some good use with me. CRYING OUT LOUD, did you really think I'd be in the mood for bedroom gymnastics after burying our friend's child?'

Rolling back over, she released her grip on him. With her eyes fixed in front in the darkness, she remarked, 'I can assure you; tonight isn't going to be *Magic Night.*' Kathleen punched her pillow, shaping it for comfort as she blinked in the darkness.

Declan's face squirmed as he spoke out in duress, 'Damn you, woman, I've waited three weeks.'

A voice in the dark answered back with an air of finality, 'And you'll be waiting another three weeks more, Declan Hennessey; I can tell you that now.'

Her defeated husband mumbled back, 'Is there no let-up from you, woman?' Feeling stung, Declan's romantic notions lay dead in the water. Chuckling to himself, he rolled over and punched his pillow before burying his head in it as he tried to clear his mind for the troublesome day ahead of him.

White rays penetrated the net curtains the next morning and woke Kathleen up. Tentatively turning over, she reached out for the mould of Declan. Feeling his space empty, she looked around the room for him. She could make him out standing in front of the window casting a shadow across the floor. She got out of bed and slipped on her dressing gown. Joining Declan by the window, she wrapped her arms around him as the sun embraced them. He didn't speak. He seemed disturbed by something.

'What's wrong, love?' she asked. 'Look, if you're still pissed with me over last night; well, I'm sorry this whole week has been exhausting, and a midnight poke was the last thing on my mind.'

Grasping her wrist gently, he turned her around and spoke softly. 'I'm scared, my love. This is the first time in my life that I'm fearful. I'm old, and I struggle to be top dog. I'm travelling into another county and waltzing into another man's territory, making myself known. If this happened to me ten years ago, I would have torn him apart before he spoke a word. I have no choice but to do this, and for the first time in my life, I'm not confident of how this could turn out. These boys down there don't fuck about.'

Grateful for his honesty, Kathleen tried to bolster his confidence. 'Where's the bravest and boldest young man I fell in love with all those years ago? Admittedly, you are getting older, and your body is showing signs of age and slowness; but your mind is sharper and wiser than anyone else that I know. You don't let anything slip past you or let anyone else get the better of you, Declan Hennessey. If this situation worsens, then at least you will have Billy and Johnny to back you up. Please, God, tell me you are taking them with you?' Worry looped around her mind about the possibility of Declan travelling to Limerick with no backup.

Sensing her tension, he reassured her. 'Of course, those two are travelling down with me. Who'd you think is driving there?'

Breathing a sigh of relief, Kathleen placed her palms on Declan's chest and patted a rhythm as she said, 'A fresh cup of tea is in order.'

She sauntered out, tightening the belt of her dressing gown as she went, as she passed, Declan leaned in and whispered to her,

'As the boy is sound asleep, is there any chance of a sha–?'

Kathleen finished off his sentence for him, 'NO – and put some pants back on.'

As Kathleen disappeared, Declan stared at the ceiling. 'PLEASE, GOD! If I make it back home after the next couple of days, please give me the stamina to make it up to my good wife... Amen.'

Kathleen prepared breakfast, and the grill sizzled, releasing smells that saturated the room. Declan repeatedly turned his phone between his fingers and thought about ringing Billy and Johnny. Instead of deciding to send them a message, he tapped out a brief instruction to cancel plans over the next couple of days and meet him in the pub at midday.

Kieran emerged from upstairs and collapsed on a stool. Stretching, while rubbing the sleep from his puffy eyes, he spoke, 'I could smell the bacon in my sleep, and then my stomach woke me up; I didn't eat anything last night; I'm starving.'

'The last time I recall you getting up this early on your own – you must have been eight or nine years old and had wet the bed.' Kathleen teased. 'Do I need to go up and check your sheets?'

'Funny, Mam. While you're up there can you get my jeans and wash them, they're...'

'Let me guess… they're on the floordrobe.'

'Even better, open his window in there, Kathleen; every time I walk past his room, all I can smell is his arse.'

Kieran threw a look at Declan and slumped onto the work surface. He raised his head before he pleaded, 'Can you make us one of your lovely cups of teas, Mam*, please?*'

Possessed by his phone, Kieran relayed text messages to friends with a speed and accuracy that reminded Declan of his mother knitting. Declan knew there wasn't going to be any dialogue with him until he had finished. With breakfast ready, a gentle swipe across the back of Kieran's head advised him to put the phone away. The conversation was light and jovial about Kieran's tales of pranks he played with his mates.

The morning's breakfast had been an eye-opener for Declan of how he wanted his family life to be in the future. His son was growing out of his chrysalis and showing signs of becoming a buoyant young man. Declan knew that Aiden and himself had been tired of how demanding their roles had become. The criminal world they operated in now stretched outside of Ireland and across the whole of Europe. Both men were way behind on how territories performed. Cash was no longer a binding bond as all transactions were now done online within seconds. An old-fashioned handshake meant nothing. Things had changed beyond recognition. Transactions left a digital trail, making them accountable for their activities.

CHAPTER 45

Declan stepped into the shower, and the cold surge of water spiked his skin before the heat built up. Declan finalised many a decision under the spray of hot water that stung and soothed his muscles. Kathleen had spread out his clothes for him on their bed. Declan examined them and chuckled; she had laid out an outfit as if he was going to a job interview.

Gently folding them back into the wardrobe, he wore a fresh pair of his signature black jeans and a crisp, clean shirt. He had to go back downstairs to put on his beloved boots. Kathleen insisted he left them inside the porch. An awkward farewell left a hard lump in Kathleen's throat as she deliberately kept it brief, treating it like any other morning of him going off to The Telegraph. By choice, Declan left Kieran in the dark about the seriousness of the trip along with its consequences.

The morning flew by as Declan had a meeting with his insurance agent at the hardware store regarding his claim. There had been no diversion big enough to convince Declan to abandon his road trip. He arrived at the pub before noon, trailing slush from his boots, startling staff who hadn't expected him. The usual regulars pinned themselves to their designated seats. Declan sat at a round table and ordered coffee. Checking the weather forecast for the journey ahead, he was relieved that no snow had fallen across his route.

Leaning back, feeling subdued, he closed his eyes for a moment only to be rudely awoken by the sound of Billy.

'Wakey! – Wakey! – Boss.'

Declan shuddered, rubbing his dilated eyes before he snapped,

'Fuck sake, man, don't sneak up on me like that. I was a million miles away.' Billy dropped a travel bag by his side and sat down. Johnny appeared from behind him, balancing two coffees.

Declan's eyes dropped to the travel bag, and he asked, 'What the fuck's that's for?'

Billy looked puzzled, 'It's for the flight and overnight.'

Declan looked bemused, 'First of all, what gave you the impression we were flying somewhere, and secondly, how do you know what I've called you both here for?'

Johnny dumped the coffees down and interrupted, 'Kathleen phoned us to make sure you had contacted us about fucking off down to Limerick.' Declan felt riled up and wanted to slam the table. He resisted and tapped the surface firmly instead.

Clapping eyes on Billy's travel bag, Johnny looked agitated and said, 'Nobody told me we're having a stay-over.'

Declan intervened, 'Well, that's because we're not. We're driving down to Limerick, and Billy has very kindly offered to drive.'

Billy slumped back in his seat and muttered to himself, 'For fuck's sake, man. I was looking forward to a meal and watching a movie on the plane.'

Declan broke his heart laughing and said, 'For the love of God! We're going to Limerick, not Limassol, man!'

Billy tried to defend himself, 'Well, I'm not driving my piece of shite down there. It'll have to be yours, Boss.'

Declan burst into laughter again and consoled Billy by saying, 'We couldn't get a direct flight there anyway. We'd have to fly somewhere in the UK, then transfer to Shannon to make our way to Limerick. I can assure you we will be driving in luxury down there, and I'll even supply you with a complimentary drink. Now, I can't say fairer than that.'

Being slightly appeased but still stung from their laughter, Billy said,'Well, I'll still be taking my travel bag with me.'

More coffee quietened down the trio before Declan brought up the seriousness of what was involved and outlined the repercussions of what could happen. He explained he had information about the pub that Dooley's family ran, and that was their first port of call. The faithful pair always backed Declan's decision despite knowing it could all kick off in the county nicknamed Stab City.

Setting off, Johnny had a back seat with Billy's travel bag for company. Billy admired himself in the driver's seat. Declan slouched next to him, finding it difficult to adjust not being in control of his car. As Billy adjusted to the width of the road, he reluctantly pushed weight onto the accelerator. Declan didn't mind the slow pace, so he never forced the issue, unlike Kathleen's driving.

The shortest journey down to Limerick was around 125 miles, roughly taking under two and a half hours. The roads were clear as many people had refrained from driving in the slushy snow. Every scenario played on Declan's mind before he settled on a plan of action. However, this was the first time he did not know who he was meeting or where he was going. He felt out of control.

Billy and Johnny were good servants to his needs and loyal, more important to him than anything. He felt a slight sense of guilt, bringing them along. Billy had a wife and family to come back to after this journey. Johnny was a rolling stone crashing ahead into everything through life. Declan decided that he would go into Dooley's pub on his own and only give them a sign if he needed their support. Keeping this to himself proved difficult, as he had always been upfront with them.

The conversation fizzled out as they took in the breathtaking scenery. Acres of combed fields and farms passed by them, bordered with hedges and colonised stoned walls. The cultivated fields had remained much the same over generations with very little change to the landscape.

Johnny buzzed his window down and shouted out, 'Take a gander at the scenery over there, boys.' Inhaling the fresh smell of cow dung, he wallowed in its scent and said, 'I tell you what, lads, this takes me back to a former life. I must have been working with cows once before.'

The unsettling smell stung their senses, infuriating Billy and Declan who shouted to close his window.

'Close the fucking window,' Billy remonstrated, 'I bet you *were* a cow in a past life; you seem to love the smell of your own shit so much. Getting pinned down by a beast of a bull, giving you one, with your nose shoved in shite.' Declan and Billy became giddy with laughter.

Johnny tried to defend himself, 'I meant, I must have been a farmer, you pair of gobdaws.' Zapping the window down, the wind lashed Johnny's hair back and pinned his skin to his cheeks. He shouted, 'Breathe in that country smell, lads. Take a deep breath through your nose and exhale. It's so grand out here in the open countryside. I could see myself being a helmet with a couple of chickens and a drop of milk for my tea, fending for me-self.'

'You mean, hermit?'

'No, I think he was right the first time around.'

'I could be quite happy being self-sufficient. No one around to bother you, just the sounds of nature. I'd cut a reek of turf off the bog of the land; for the fireplace, to warm the evenings. I'd also harvest my own tatties and store them away for the winter so I could hibernate.'

'And how would you produce the milk?'

'Oh, I'd have that delivered; I couldn't be arsed milking anything; it would taste like shite.' Cackling erupted. Billy closed all the windows while Declan flushed the air-con through.

Gazing across at Billy, Declan asked, 'Did you pack any sweets with you in your travel bag? I've got a bad taste of that shite lingering in the back of my throat.'

Billy squashed his face up and replied, 'All I've got is a packet of Rennies.'

Reluctantly, Declan answered back, 'They'll do… Johnny, throw his bag over here and keep talking; it will shorten the road.'

The bag zipped over the headrest, catching the top of Declan's head; Johnny reeled in hysterics and said, 'You said, to throw the bag – so, I threw the bag.'

Declan flinched and yelped out, 'You, bastard.' The bag had so many compartments that Declan had to rummage through them all. He muttered, 'Fuck sake, where am I supposed to be looking?'

With eyes concentrating on the road ahead, Billy instructed, 'Try the toiletry bag that the missus has packed.'

Declan continued his search and eventually found it. 'Fuck sake, this has had a more thorough search than a customs officer at the –' Declan cut his remark short when he opened the bag. 'What the fuck are these doing in here?' Mustering half a smile, he dangled a packet of condoms for Johnny to see. Raising an eyebrow, he said, 'Me and you have to talk when we get back home. Did you think we were all going on a boys' piss-up for a couple of days?'

Billy straining his eyes ahead of him at the road, said, 'Hold on now, fellas – the wife packs my bag, and they are always in there for when me and my good lady go away for a night's stay at a hotel. She keeps insisting that I go in for the snip at my age. I tell her, I'm too old to worry about more kids, and I'd rather wear the willy socks.'

The laughter mellowed. Declan hurled the travel bag behind him at

Johnny and said, 'Right back at you.' The bag stunned Johnny in the chest. He shifted it to the floor then settled down to find comfort, closing his eyes. The scenic views soon became monotonous. Declan craned his neck around, listening to the grunts from Johnny. Tempted to join Johnny in some shuteye, he didn't feel comfortable leaving Billy solely in charge of the road.

As the conversation tapered off, the hills softened and flattened, and greenery was slowly replaced by brick and fences by traffic lights. Residential homes and local buses flashed past them as random people darted across the road, banging on the bonnet and greeting them with a cutthroat sign welcoming them to Limerick city. Nevertheless, it was still lovely to be welcomed.

CHAPTER 46

It took another half hour to drive past the grassy wasteland circling the city before they reached the backstreets where Dooley's pub was. On approach, it looked like an area of deprivation. Billy crawled through the narrow streets as Declan eyed the houses. He had built up a profile of the type of characters that drank in the pub. As he scanned the rooftops, he noticed hardly any homeowners had satellite dishes. Black bin liners lay dumped outside homes, substituted for dustbins. Many of them had been pulled apart by stray animals, and flies danced around them. Gas meters were missing their fibreglass surrounds, evidence of tampering. It seemed appropriate for residents to dump furniture and tyres at the end of roads with disposable nappies used as makeshift footballs.

The picture all this conjured up in Declan's mind was that of a feral environment. People worked hard and had nothing to show for it except the comfort of drinking in their local bar. Declan knew that in areas like these, the bond between people would be strong. They wouldn't accept someone messing with their own.

Billy reacted, 'Christ, man, we're stepping beyond the pale setting foot down here. Well, I never! – the land of muck savages.'

Declan waved the car on and instructed, 'Don't stop, keep going… left here… that's it, now next right… follow it around and check the next turning. Right, I'm happy now, spin back around to the pub; I'll explain later.'

Nervousness set in as they arrived. The pub stood on the corner of a desolate street. Curved bay windows adorned the front of the building. Many of the surrounding windows had metal grilles shielding the glass. Billy cautiously parked up. Sleeping Beauty woke up, stretched out and farted. Billy and Declan had no choice but to unwind their windows. A red flicker in Billy's wing mirror caught Declan's attention, the vehicle's presence was noted on the surveillance cameras. Declan bounced out of the car and scouted around the premises, locating exit points he memorised for a fast getaway.

Settling back in his seat, he gave his instructions to the lads. 'In a minute, Billy, I want you to swing the car around and park it outside, just in front of the main doors. The cameras have already clocked us outside here, so there's no point in playing silly beggars with them. They know we're here, but they don't know who we are. I doubt many cars pull up like this outside here, so alarm bells are ringing. I've decided to go in low-key and suss the joint out. If I get the impression that I'm not welcome in there, I'll give you guys a sign to come on in. I'll ring and hang up or ping a blank text to you. If the shite hits the fan inside, then look out for a reaction by the front doors –'

Uncomfortable with Declan's plan, Billy stopped him mid-conversation, 'Hold on now, Boss? We've all travelled down here on this fucking journey to reason or tackle these people on their turf. We haven't had as much as an invite, and you wanna waltz on into this shebeen like a fecking regular?'

Declan intervened, 'I have thought this thing through, lads, and I'm going in low key.'

Johnny spoke up, 'I'm with the big man on this. For fuck's sake, how can you go in low-key in a deprived shit hole like this? Christ, man, the pair of us wouldn't even go in there together. By the time the bar had taken money for our drinks, we'd be lynched.'

Declan paused, raising his index finger to his lips; seconds later, he said to Billy, 'Pop the boot.' Declan nipped out and around to the back of the car.

Johnny looked to the roof and muttered to himself, 'Please God, he's not pulling out a shooter to go in there with?'

Billy shrugged his shoulders. 'I have a horrible feeling about this.'

Declan reappeared from the boot, donning a dark grey tweed flat cap. That was his decoy for entering the pub. Billy and Johnny both shook their heads in despair.

'Well, fellas, how do I look?' Declan muttered.

Billy rolled his eyes and said sarcastically, 'Well, feck-er-de- feck, that's a helluva disguise; I would never have guessed it was you; what a transformation.' Looking at Declan seriously, he said, 'You're going to get us all killed in there, and I won't be able to use my overnight bag down here for tonight.'

Declan unzipped a sports bag and sniffed the air as he pulled out architectural drawings and road maps with red pen markings across them. 'Right, fellas, gather your senses; you need to take heed of this info. I've planned our route around the side roads if we need a quick getaway.

'On the other sheets, here are the architectural layouts of the pub so you can see the exits. Luckily, Dooley had an extension fitted on the back for an additional saloon area, so I was able to access the drawings showing all the fire exits via Limerick Council's planning office.'

Declan tapped on the bag before he carried on. 'I don't know what kind of arms Dooley's men are packing in there. Do you realise, this Dooley character can make us all disappear for good in here tonight? Dumped and burnt in some desolated cillín. Nobody would know where we went or if we would be found.'

Billy, nervous now, cut him short, 'Alright, I think we get the picture.'

Smiling broadly, Declan continued. 'For strictly precautionary measures, I have these devices in here,' he motioned to two small metal boxes in the sports bag. 'One for you guys to strap onto these two doors… here…' he tapped the page, 'and one for here, in case we need a quick escape. These explosives will blow locks, so they need to be positioned correctly. Don't worry; they aren't volatile. I have a key fob to detonate them, providing they don't find it on me. Are we clear on this, lads?'

Johnny raised a finger.

Billy snapped, 'Fuck off with your finger, man, you're not at school asking for permission to speak.' Turning to Declan, Billy carried on, 'Jaysis, are you out of your warped mind, man? We've started out with fecking illusions of flights and fancy foods to come down and have a word with yer man. *Now,* we're ending the night with the possibility of wearing concrete boots and everything we own going to the missus. We're way in over our heads here, and I'm shitting myself about what might happen over the next hour.'

Johnny intervened, 'Well, technically, it could be all over if *Deco* here takes a stray bullet between the eyes as soon as he walks on in there. That's game over in under two minutes. Yer man here keeps saying he wants your watch; then can I have this car?'

Declan looked shell shocked. An eerie silence drained their faces of confidence before sniggering broke out amongst them. The men nodded in approval before they embraced hands together in one last solidarity clench.

'In the worst-case scenario, if shots get fired at me as I enter the pub, at least they'll miss the car outside and save on paintwork repairs,' Declan said.

'Boss, I'm messing – are those two bastard brothers worth us walking into this? As I live and breathe, we've got your back in there, but this is way out of our league. We should have come down here prepared.'

Declan sighed; his tone was firm. 'You two are both good men. I have learnt over time that some people aren't loyal to you, others are loyal to their need of you, and once their need changes, so does their loyalty. You two are different. You've been at my side from the start of all of this.' Both men felt humbled.

Billy sighed with apprehension and replied, 'You're the boss.' Declan fixed his cap and flashed his set of teeth.

Johnny said, 'I bet you don't come back out with all those teeth intact.'

Declan looked searchingly at him and replied, 'Have a little faith in me, lads. You can't go swimming without getting wet. Turn the engine off. You lads take one of these explosives each. They have a rubber backing and stick to anything solid. Make sure they are positioned correctly on this door by the lock and not the hinges. I'll step in front of the cameras to divert attention away from you. When you get back to the car, remember to watch out for a sign from me to steam in at the right time. Oh, and one last thing... don't forget to engage the alarm on the car... I don't trust none of these fuckers around here.'

Declan left. Johnny clipped Billy gently around the side of his head before he jumped into Declan's seat. Folk songs played in the background as the men watched shadows of people walk back and forth passing the pub's front doors. Suddenly, the doors opened, and the light from inside shone out across the pavement. A heavyset woman trundled out, looking worse for wear. She looked Declan up and down, stumbling as she passed the car.

'There's a fine woman to keep you warm at night,' Billy said.

Johnny gazed at her before turning to get Billy's attention. The woman disappeared out of sight. 'She looks like shit beaten up in a bucket with a face like a blind cobbler's thumb. Not even the tide would take her out. Man, I'm telling you, you'd get a look in.'

Puckering his lips, Billy leaned in for a kiss.

Johnny flinched. 'Away and wash the back of yer bollix.' They exited the car and hurried around to their designated points to attach the devices as instructed and were back in a flash.

Given the nod, Declan grasped the door handle hard and paused. After a deep breath, he stepped inside. Johnny whipped down the sun visor catching sight of his crucifix's reflection in the vanity mirror. Squeezing his eyes shut, he recited a short prayer.

Little fella on the cross,
Whose had my back when I've been at a loss,
I need your hope and your insight,
To take us all home safe tonight.

Johnny blew a kiss at the reflected crucifix and said, 'Hang in there, little fella.' Meanwhile, an unpleasant smell of wet dog greeted Declan as he entered Dooley's bar; from his early vantage point, he took in the pub's layout, noting the exits. Each exit was guarded with men who looked like they could handle themselves. Nobody batted an eyelid at the presence of a stranger. It made him feel like there was a trap set for him.

Declan skimmed against a pool table as he passed towards the bar. A game had been paused. The remaining black and white balls was in a stand-off. Declan winced at the probability of the black being potted. As the player concentrated on his shot, he caught sight of Declan looking at him.

'This is a local pub – that's locals only. We don't welcome strangers in here, do yourself a favour and take a hike, my friend.'

An unhealthy silence wrapped around the table as spectators shuffled, looking agitated. Declan ignored the comment. Staring at the green baize cloth, he told the player to resume his shot. At speed, the balls made contact; Declan lunged forward catching the white ball. Swinging his arm back, he threw it directly at the player. The ball bounced off the cloth, striking the player directly in the forehead. It sent him spiralling backwards as he collapsed in front of his audience. Scooping up the black ball, Declan then threw it through the glass entrance doors.

CHAPTER 47

'I'm fecking bored already,' Johnny muttered.

'I'm not exactly enjoying this either,' Billy countered. 'I can't sit here and do nothing. That's not how we've rolled over the years together.' There was silence.

'The thing is... at times, don't you think to yourself about life? How mankind has evolved and the nature of man himself,' Johnny mused.

'You're in a deep and meaningful mood – hold on a minute now, I fecking well told you not to roll up any of that skunk hash. You told me you were going to cut it up and bag it up with the milder weed to get shot of it all. That shite was too pure; it would smoke your brain out. Christ, the last thing I need to be explaining is why you're climbing the walls. And if Declan finds out –'

Johnny held his hands up in protest. 'I didn't touch any of that gear. I sold it on to the tinkers. No! – I'm serious... look, things like? Errr... who on earth first thought about making cocaine and thought to themselves, "I know I'll shove it up my nose and see what happens." The same with beer and wine? "I know; I'll walk around squashing these grapes, then ferment them, then drink it."

'Do you know that everybody on this earth affects one another? Our choices, even the smallest of decisions, affect the way we lead our lives. Also, things like... do deaf people communicate with each other in the same sign language worldwide? Do deaf people talk to themselves and what does it sound like... Other things like, say for instance: if yer man is up in court, and he's an atheist, and he's asked to swear on the Bible. He's an atheist. He doesn't give a fuck.'

Billy interrupted, waving a finger, and replied, 'No, you're wrong there. He has the choice of an affirmation or an oath. It's about yer man's moral judgement, not his faith that he is swearing on, so to speak. Mind you, if he's trying to get away with murder, the bastard will say anything.'

'Fuck away off.' Johnny pushed the question again, 'Ok, take Muslims in court… Are they asked to swear on the Bible?'

'Don't be daft, man. They'd be offered the Koran to swear on instead,' Billy answered.

Johnny looked flummoxed as he replied, 'The fucking Koran?'

'Yeah, it's their big red book. It's their equivalent to the Bible,' Billy answered.

Johnny's eyes glinted as he clarified,

'You mean like the one Eamon Andrews used to hand over on 'This Is Your Life'? The one they use for praying to yer man Abba?'

Billy cottoned on, shaking his head. 'It's fucking, Allah, man. I can just see yer man swearing on the Koran and then singing to a rendition of 'Take A Chance on Me' whilst on the stand. I swear to God, you're having me on with this shite, and I fall for it every time.' Johnny winked and both men chuckled together. Billy tried to regain his composure as he watched for Declan's movements.

A loud shunt sounded as a circular object hurtled across the road, ricocheting off a nearby parked car. As the object passed them, its shape became apparent; it was a black eight ball. It bounced off a vehicle and trickled down the street before it finally settled in the gutter.

Johnny had a hand on the door handle; he was ready to bolt.

Billy restrained him. 'Let's not overreact here. Just take a deep breath. Do you think that was the sign? Surely, it was too quick?'

'We should go straight in there, man,' Johnny said.

'But, if we steam on in there now, and it's not the sign, then the boss man will go ape.'

Johnny paused for thought as Billy released his grip. In agreement, he said, 'You're probably right. But how will we know the sign then?'

Billy responded positively, 'Well! The boss will let us know. WON'T he? I tell you, you're a daft bastard at times. I'd say that this is a regular occurrence around here, hence the metal grilles.'

Shaking his head in contempt, Billy signalled at the gutter, 'Well don't sit there, go and get the bloody ball.'

Declan's stance was that of an athlete ready to start a race. All eyes were trained on him as beads of sweat ran down his face. Surrounding him at all angles were men just about to run at him.

He called out wildly, 'WAIT FOR IT.' He looked around frantically. Nobody came to help him. The men launched at Declan, pummelling him to the ground. There was a brief moment of resistance before flailing arms rained down on him, and stray boots kicked him from all directions. Profanities filled the air amidst the frenzy of blows. Many shots missed Declan but struck others. Drunken heckling played a soundtrack to the chaos.

Declan laid in a foetal position amidst the scrum, gasping for air. The weight on him decreased as bodies were lifted off him, causing blood to rush to his head as bubbles fizzled through his temple. Declan muttered to himself, 'Shite… what do those fellas need to signify as a sign? A fucking shotgun going off?'

A shrill whistle silenced the baying crowd. Scanning around, Declan looked for the exits. Two burly men lifted him to his feet and placed him in front of the elusive Mr Dooley. Dooley wasn't an attractive man. Acne had plagued his face and left scarring. Cruel lines ran down the side of his cheeks, dividing his nose from his face. Scars riddled his skin, breaking up the lines that aged his face. Hearing the flick of a knife, Declan braced himself as a sharp blade was deftly placed against his throat. He gulped.

Dooley scowled, eyeing Declan up and down. 'I'm going to ask you a series of questions. How you answer them is up to you. I may not like the answer, but I expect it to be the truth. Work with me, and you might make it out of here alive. Do I make myself clear.' Declan nodded in response.

Dooley spoke again, 'That's not an answer.'

'Knife,' Declan said. Dooley dropped his chin for the heavy to release pressure. 'Thank you,' said Declan.

'You still haven't answered; I need one.' The silence solidified.

Declan's coat squeaked as he breathed in slowly before answering, 'Yes.'

Dooley paused, glancing at Declan. 'GOOD. Then I'll begin... Question one... ARE YOU WIRED?'

'No.'

Dooley waved at his men to scan Declan's body. Once Dooley was satisfied, he said, 'Congratulations. You have survived question one.

Question two: have you brought Gardai with you?'

'No.'

Dooley's eyes skittered across the bar at another henchman with a walkie talkie. His response acknowledged that it was all clear.

With piercing eyes, he fixed his gaze on Declan, pressing on with his next question. 'Third question... how many men are with you outside?'

Sweat glistened on Declan's forehead. Agony rippled through his body as he replied, 'Two.'

Dooley raised his eyebrows, offended by the answer. Tilting his head to one side, he unnervingly said, 'You taking the PISS? You're telling me you've waltzed into my playground only two handed?' His jaw muscles locked in disgust. Studying Declan's face, he searched for tell-tale signs of lying or weakness. Dooley gestured for the pressure to be relinquished. Cocking his head towards the men at the front exit, he waited for his reply. Interference scrambled over the walkie talkie; two fingers raised up.

'Question four... are your two tooled up?'

As the pain shortened his breath Declan started to laugh. 'Jaysis!... Tooled up? They're a pair of fucking spanners. They were supposed to back me up when the ball passed through the glass.'

Dooley motioned for the grip on Declan to be relaxed. He whispered to his men to make themselves known to Declan's accomplices. Within no time, gritting their teeth, Billy and Johnny were escorted in and paraded in front of Declan. They quickly scanned the room for options; it looked bleak.

Declan grimaced at Billy. He spoke sarcastically, 'Wait for my fucking sign, I said, I threw a fucking ball out the fucking WINDOW.'

'We thought it was something that happens here on a regular occurrence,' Johnny answered.

A blank expression glazed Declan's face as he turned his attention to Dooley, 'Have I passed this initiation trial or what?' Dooley folded his arms, owning his space. Glaring at the men in pity, he offered a sympathetic smile before snatching it back.

His adam's apple bobbed back and forth as he spoke. 'Lord almighty! I'll give it to you, coming down here with just the three of you. You've got some balls.' A smug smile of satisfaction covered his face. 'Now I've established you haven't come all the way down here to cause me any harm; that leaves me with the assumption that you're wanting something from me... and that will cost you.'

Easing the pain from his battered body, Declan stretched his back and replied, 'No, I have something to give you. What I have to offer is priceless. I've come here as a professional courtesy.'

Dooley looked intrigued and chuckled. 'Is that so?... Well, now that this welcoming ceremony is over, you can tell me what your priceless suggestion is over some drinks.'

An adjacent set of doors opened onto a private bar. A gleaming American pool table stood prominently in the room.

Lowering his voice to a grumble, Dooley spoke to Billy and Johnny. 'Fellas, if I were you, I'd shift the motor and make sure it's belled up or wait in it while I listen to what the main man has to say. This neighbourhood isn't a safe place at night. Believe it or not, there are some unruly characters around here.' Both men looked annoyed.

'If it's all the same to you, I'm still not comfortable splitting back up just yet. The car can stay where it is while your crew keep an eye on it,' Billy said.

Dooley smirked, 'CREW… Listen, lad-o, I'm not running a God damn cruise ship down here. Your boss man will be safe talking to me… RELAX… Believe me; if I wanted your legs broken by now, it would have already happened.' Dooley walked off, turned back and said, 'Now be a good girl and lock daddy's car up.'

Johnny's eyes bulged at the cheap jibe. Forcing his way past Billy, he lunged at Dooley only to be restrained by Declan.

Dooley turned around with a sly grin across his face and said, 'I like men with a bit of fight in them.'

CHAPTER 48

Dooley's men guided Declan to a large circular table draped in a green felt cloth used for poker games. Staff removed the covering and placed a bottle of whiskey and vodka out. A set of glasses and an ice bucket were added. The adjoining doors closed, and a sentry with a thick neck guarded them as feedback through his ear piece frustrated him.

Dooley spoke as he poured, 'You probably already know of me. I know of you of course, Declan Hennessey,' he pointed at Declan. 'I know you have a little outfit in Dublin. You have a reputation that holds you in high regard, as I understand. I like that; people respect you because they fear you. It can carry you a long way in life.' He hailed his glass in the air, 'Remember that! For you guys to travel on down to Limerick, I'd take an educated guess that you either want info or merchandise.' Dooley poured another whiskey then slid the bottle Declan's way.

Declan topped his glass up with ice, raised it and toasted. Their glasses clinked. Dooley's forceful nudge took Declan by surprise. 'This is some set-up you have here. Your men have a good size on them. Are they ex-military?'

Dooley paused a beat as a sly smile curved across his face; everyone waited for his response. 'Let's keep it to business questions only. Personal questions make me think you're trying to get on my good side. I don't have one, by the way.'

'I don't have anything to sell to you. I do have something to trade with you, and it won't cost you a single euro,' said Declan.

Dooley slurped his whiskey back, ice cubes clattering against his teeth. Maintaining eye contact with Declan, he forcefully said, 'Nobody trades anything worthwhile for fuck all.' Savouring the warm glow in his chest, Declan replied, 'The Finnerty brothers… like I say, it's professional courtesy.'

Intrigued, a flutter of recognition sparked in Dooley's eyes as he rose from his chair. Taking in a slow deep breath, his fingers formed a prism against the table. 'I've waited for nearly a year for that name to resurface,' he spoke, seething. 'Are you telling me those two bastards are working with you? You better not be pissing me about now.' Declan knew he had stirred a hornet's nest.

Declan answered, 'They've tried to ruin everything I have built up. They've burned my store to the fucking ground and are planning to try and take over. I've formed an alliance with the O'Driscoll family, who run the majority of Dublin City. These brothers aren't playing from the rule book, and we need them permanently removed from Dublin.'

Dooley nodded as he leant back on his chair, balancing himself as it teetered on the back legs. He considered Declan with real focus before suggestively saying, 'You're scared of them, aren't you? They've frightened you.'

There was something about his intonation that made it sound like an insult. Billy and Johnny felt slighted by the question. Dooley noticed it as he saw a flicker in their eyes.

Unable to hold Dooley's eye, Declan knocked back his whiskey and said, 'You're right... I'm scared for my wife and my family's safety. I'm scared for my two best men to the side of me who also have families... is that what you want to hear?'

Dooley remained silent. He poured himself and Declan another whiskey before he continued, 'It takes a sincere man to admit his frailties. I like that about you... it shows dignity in a man.' He nodded in admiration of Declan's honesty. 'I've owned this pub for twenty-odd years. Over that time, many rogues have tried their luck and failed until those two crossed my path.' He began his story.

'Something like five years ago... every Monday morning, I would tidy up the backyard, binning all the food from the Sunday trade.This bastard boxer dog appeared from nowhere, and he would ransack the bins and leave me all the clearing up to do. This dog came back every other day to feast on the leftovers. No matter what I did to secure the bins down, this bastard animal would still get into them.

'This one particular Monday morning, I caught him feeding off the leftovers again. Anyway, to cut a long story short, I'd had a skinful the night before and was short-tempered that morning. As I heard him throwing the dustbin around my yard, I caught him by surprise and kicked him clean in the ribs. He dropped like a sack of shite, then got back up. He still hovered around for the food scraps and wouldn't be done. He had a strong spirit, and for some strange reason, I admired him for that.

'I asked around; nobody seemed to know the dog's owner. Low and behold, the next Monday morning, he was back for his banquet, so when I appeared to shoo him away, he braced himself to be booted. I assumed his previous owner had beaten him as he took it as normal behaviour. Something inside me let him help himself to the bin. From that day on, I decided to keep him, and he stuck to me like glue. I later felt ashamed for kicking him, and it's the only thing in life I've regretted. I named him Tanner.'

Declan, unsure where the story was leading, tried to show interest by asking, 'Was that down to his colour?'

'Yes! You're right, that was his colour, but the wife found something on the computer, Urban Dictionary or something like that, about how the name Tanner referred to a man of great magnitude, so the name stuck. From that day onwards, I never hit the dog again. However, I can't say that for anyone else who has got in my way since.'

'Look, this is all very poignant,' Declan said, 'but what relevance does this have to my dilemma?' A flicker of anger shrouded Dooley's face. That was the calm before the storm. His whole demeanour changed as he reared up out of his chair. He prodded his finger for emphasis in Declan's face.

'You come down HERE, wanting my help? Then you sit and shut the fuck up in my pub.' Dooley burst out with rage, grasping the underside of the table. Declan and Billy were both taken aback and stood up, bracing themselves, holding their hands up in surrender. Dooley sat back down, indicating the others should do so too.

He continued vehemently. 'That dog was more loyal to me than any man working for me in here tonight.' He began to calm down. 'One afternoon, I was out on some business, and I got a call from the missus.I had the phone switched to silent, so it rang out. It was another forty minutes before I went home. By then, when I checked my phone, I had eight missed calls and five text messages waiting for me. My heart sank when I read through the last one: *Tanner attacked at home, come now*.

'I tell you now, not a Guard in sight would've pulled me over the way I drove home. I shot through every red light and didn't stop; the wheels were smoking. I ran through the pub, and the missus greeted me in tears. She pointed out to the yard, and I could see him there lying there looking back at me. I dropped to my knees to cradle him. I tried to make him comfortable, but his mangled body wouldn't let me ease his suffering. He died in minutes in my arms. My boy held on to his last breath for me to come home, and I ignored all the calls pissing around at some fucking meeting letting him die. I promised my boy I would kill whoever did this to him and make them suffer for it. I had CCTV covering the whole area, luckily. As I watched it back, I saw a man in a balaclava scale the yard and beat the living daylights out of my best friend with a baseball bat.'

Dooley clenched his fists, pressing them into the table. He looked across at all three men and asked, 'Have any of you experienced the fear and weakness that comes from the loss of someone close to you? Let me tell you; it's not good for the soul.' Declan felt a modicum of sensitivity.

Dooley held his head up with pride and said, 'I'm not ashamed to admit it, but it was the first time in my life I cried. My father died many years ago; he was a proud and violent man. I saw him off at his funeral and didn't shed a tear. It was the same for my mother's funeral, as well. My first wife left me for another man, and even then, I still never shed a tear... however, I nearly did when she wanted to come back sometime later, but that's another story.'

Laughter eased the tension. Declan apologised for interrupting him earlier. Dooley duly accepted it before asking, 'Do you have a dog?' Declan looked at him blankly. Dooley continued, 'Didn't think so... let me tell you something... until you have one, you won't realise it's a bond that can't be broken. Not like people. No matter how bad your day has gone, when you come home, your dog won't judge you by the decisions you've made that day. He just wants to greet you because he's missed you.'

'To have an operation like you and I run, you must have people around you like dogs. I mean that with the utmost respect. You must have a bond with people who trust your every decision and back you up all the way. Without that unity, your goals and achievements will amount to fuck all. That's why I had to cut those bastard brothers the fuck loose. It soon became clear they had their own agenda. So, at first,they were on a short leash, and it soon became evident they were no longer suited to my operations. I gave them severance pay and a one-way ticket out of my fucking city, but they took it badly.

'They thought they had done enough to run their own show. I put them straight; I was the main man running and controlling everything that operated within the city. So, they thought of leaving me with one last send-off gesture. They knew what would devastate me... and they succeeded.'

The table went quiet. Declan and Dooley had enough hatred for the Finnerty brothers to conclude that they needed to work together on this one.

A bald wiry man came into the bar. He was carrying a wager book that required Dooley's signature. The hushed conversation went back and forth between them behind cupped hands. Taking advantage of the interruption, Declan stretched his legs around the pool table, admiring it. Billy pulled faces at Johnny and ridiculed the man who wore glasses that made his ears stick out prominently. Johnny had to leave the meeting table to avoid the embarrassment of sniggering.

'Apologies, gentleman,' Dooley returned his attention to them, searching Billy's face for signs of disrespect, 'but business calls.' He rubbed his calloused hands together. 'I'll lay my cards on the table with you. Do you have any idea what I'm going to do once I get my hands on those brothers? You've to ask yourselves can you live with that outcome. For the first six months after Tanner was killed, I sent men out to find and bring them back to me so I could just kill them myself outright. It's been the best part of a year now, and since they disappeared off the face of the earth, I've had time to reflect on it.

'When I get hold of them, I'm going to break both of their legs and make sure they'll never walk again. I'll personally torture them and make sure they will have to be spoon-fed for the rest of their lives. I'm only interested in the one who murdered my Tanner; the other one can watch.'

'We're with you on whatever you choose to do with them,' Declan replied. 'You have to be sure it was them before going further, though?'

Sinking his whiskey, Dooley sat up. 'When I watched the re-run of Tanner's slaughter – because that's what it was… a slaughter – I caught sight of a Celtic tattoo on the forearm of yer man when he left. It was definitely Thomas Finnerty. Don't worry yourselves about catching the right bastard. It'll be me that has the sleepless nights before I catch them.

'I have enough on my plate at present with the state of the world's economy affecting my businesses. It's all gone tits up. They have Humpty

Trumpty over there in the states, building his wall or fecking stairway to heaven. Then across the water there, they haven't got a clue how to fix this Brexit malarkey. They can't keep a leader to fix it, let alone agree on a deal or no deal – it's all bollix. And our fella running the country here can't keep the peace between the divide because of the clauses of this Brexit shite. I think they should get rid of the lot and put Mrs Brown in charge of it all. She may not be clued up on her politics, but she has a bigger set of balls for making decisions. I have freight coming into the country and out across Europe. I incur shipping costs, permits, fuel, tolls, emissions testing, and fecking politics.'

Dooley ended the meeting by saying, 'I'll give you a contact number for our next meet. When I come up to collect those two, you deny any knowledge of me. I don't want to be followed up by any dick squad. Do I make myself clear, gentlemen?'

Declan offered his hand across the table. Dooley accepted and, with an intimidating tone, said, 'The enemy of my enemy is my friend.'

Thanks to Johnny's prayer, all three men travelled safely home to Dublin.

CHAPTER 49

Declan slept in until 10 am the next following day. Whenever this happened, he cursed himself. He thought that a couple of hours wasted meant opportunities had passed him by. However, this morning was an exception. He listened to the soft patter of Kathleen's feet as she walked out of the bedroom. The aroma of coffee stirred him as he turned over. Kathleen had left it next to his mobile.

Switching off airplane mode, a rake of text messages came through, as well as missed calls from Aiden O'Driscoll: The Finnerty brothers had been found, and Declan was to contact O'Driscoll as soon as possible. Declan rang him. O'Driscoll answered after one ring. 'Good morning, are you part-time running about town now, or have you got a young lass on the side?'

Declan took offence to the insinuation but offered mock laughter instead of a response. 'I'm a lucky man – let me tell you now – I have the best looker in town married to me.'

O'Driscoll laughed. 'Well, I have some news that will excite you more than your good lady. Those pesky brothers have been playing foul again. I have a crane operator at the port who tells me what I want to know. He's been keeping an eye on a cargo shipment the brothers were dealing with before we went our separate ways. It turns out our boys have kept themselves busy looking after the arrival of the shipment. They have taken receivership of it and agreed on a timeslot to collect the consignment.

'The fuckers must think of me as fucking stupid. I deliberately let the operator feed them the information they wanted to hear. So, it turns out, your good self and I are granted one last opportunity to bid these bastards a final goodbye – If you get my drift.' There was silence from Declan.

'Did you hear all of that, Declan?' O'Driscoll questioned him.

Declan sighed and replied, 'I'm afraid I had no choice but to secure services from an outside candidacy, who will tie up this situation for good.'

O'Driscoll was confused. 'The fuck you on about, man?'

'We need to meet.' Declan was short.

O'Driscoll, feeling out of the loop, angrily said, 'Have you organised something without me? DON'T SPEAK. I'll be down to your shite hole in an hour, and your bar better serve fresh coffee.' Declan listened to the dial tone and realised his relaxing morning had ended.

Breakfast with Kathleen was of the silent variety. Kathleen stood in front of him, arms folded, with a frown across her face as she listened to Declan's explanation of the day before. 'Fuck you, Declan, if you expect me to believe your tale of events. You're telling me, all three of you walked into the bar and introduced yourselves and this character that you feared simply invited you to sit down for drinks. You all then patted each other on the back and left with some agreement between you all. Tell me Declan, did you swap addresses so you can write each other letters?' she mocked.

'Alright, woman, it didn't quite go to plan, ok, are you satisfied now?'

'No, shite! And I suppose you walked into a lamp post to give you that fat lip when you were blowing kisses back to this Dalton… Dooley, or whatever this character's name is.'

Declan gave in and chuckled to himself, knowing there was no pulling the wool over Kathleen's eyes. Sitting her down, he started from the beginning, this time with the truth. Kathleen sighed, digesting the retold story. A short time later, Kathleen had an appointment to attend to and kissed Declan goodbye. As her perfume lingered on his cheek, he asked her a surprise question. 'When you were growing up, did you ever have a dog around the house?' The question caught Kathleen off-guard.

'My mother did all the barking in our house, and my father pissed up the wall when he was boozed up and couldn't open the back door. So, having a dog would have been too much competition between them both.' Kathleen winked and closed the front door.

Declan was in a good mood as he made his way inside the pub. Ignoring text messages coming through, Declan secluded himself away from the rest of the bar. Splintered light came through the windows illuminating the pub. Declan thought it would make an excellent photograph to remind him of his days here. Bar staff appeared with coffee and hurried off.

Out of sight, a loud voice bellowed, 'I believe someone is expecting me, young man?'

The bartender replied, 'Who would that be then?'

'Your employer, you fuckwit,' O'Driscoll aggressively yelled.

O'Driscoll looked around the bar. 'Jaysis, half of them in here look like they've slept in their clothes.'

Declan thought it was best to make himself known and raised his hand to signal him; O'Driscoll swaggered over in his long overcoat. The two men chatted about the pub trade until more coffee appeared, and they were left alone. Declan folded his arms, 'My contact's information paid off for me on this occasion... or shall I say for us –'

Aiden interrupted, 'What the fuck have you been cooking up?'

'I've got the name of the Finnerty brothers' previous employer. He's more upset than us with their moral compass, to say the least.'

O'Driscoll was trying to make sense of where the conversation was going to lead. 'Please, God, tell me you haven't made contact with them yet? Those fuckers aren't a patch on us. Christ, they've killed people in their path, and you wanna go and dance with the devil? Those boys control everything in and out of that county. That slum city is a bigger shit hole than what I've walked into here today.'

Declan grimaced, but he didn't challenge the remark, 'I'm afraid it's a little late for a pep talk.' A stone-cold look washed across O'Driscoll's face.

He paused before speaking. 'Please God, you haven't contacted them yet? The family that runs that city are the –'

Declan cut him dead, 'The DOOLEY family.'

O'Driscoll fell back in his seat, shaking his head, 'You have no idea what you've unleashed here. CHRIST… at first, we had a few grass snakes snapping at our ankles. Now you have spoken to a heavy outsider who has the clout to peg us off one by one.'

Declan looked away before answering, 'I've been down there to introduce myself and explain the predicament we are in.'

O'Driscoll felt undermined, 'Yeah, and I can tell by the state of your face what his answer was. God damn you, man. I'm trying to move into retirement slowly and set my sons up within the business. If this family try to establish themselves in our city? I don't want to be worrying about this mob making a hit on us. I'm too fucking old for this shite.'

Declan leant forward, standing his ground, 'I went down there and nearly got lynched walking into their pub. They have no interest in our dealings up here. Believe me, Aiden. Dooley wants these bastards for his own gratification, and we're going to deliver them straight to him. He has given me his word that is all he is interested in.'

O'Driscoll crossed his arms and calmly said, 'Do you know he'll kill them. If this guy wants them that badly, he'll kill them.'

Declan locked eyes with O'Driscoll and replied, 'It was only a short time ago that I dragged your sorry near-dead arse out of my store. Have you forgotten they tried to kill us both? I, too, have family futures I want to protect. Dooley is the connection we both need to secure this.'

Declan gave O'Driscoll the grace to contemplate the news. O'Driscoll knew in his heart of hearts that Declan's plan made sense for all parties concerned. Nodding reluctantly in approval, he committed. He pushed his coffee aside and said, 'Do you have something with a kick to it?'

Declan obliged. 'It's a little early for me, but I'll join you in a toast. Tell me, Aiden? What do you and your good lady plan to do when you hand the reins over to your boys?'

O'Driscoll took a sip and twisted the glass around in his palm before answering, 'The missus wants to travel a little. Of all the places in the world I can offer her, she wants to travel the whole of fecking Ireland!... can you believe that?'

Declan chuckled, 'Now, what would your missus do if a message came back that one of your lads was severely attacked or God Forbid…?' Declan waited for a reaction.

O'Driscoll pushed his empty glass forward for a refill and gently replied, 'I know what game you're playing, you sly bastard. But you're right, my missus would fall apart. I can't live with that… *so...* I'm in… whatever it takes to ensure these bastards never set foot on our soil again, I'll support.'

O'Driscoll still looked uncomfortable. Declan studied his facial expressions; something was wrong. He politely asked, 'Are you having second thoughts there? Take a day to think it through if needed.'

Aiden smirked and replied, 'On the contrary. It must happen tonight. I've already planned and set a honey trap for the bastards for thinking they can take receipt of my shipment and ride off into the sunset without me noticing anything. They must think I'm an old bastard for missing the set of keys they stole from one of the cars before they set your store on fire. The keys are for a lock-up. I've stored expensive commodities, bootleg liquor and fags. Also, merchandise of a particular custom that seeks high revenue.'

O'Driscoll's words didn't fool Declan, 'I never had you down for a man dealing in drugs, Aiden. Especially you being a family man, seeing the youth of today around the city growing up into young men. How does it make you feel knowing that your shite is probably in their bloodstream, distorting their focus on life?'

Taking offence, O'Driscoll bit back in a fury,

'DON'T YOU fucking sit there preaching and judging me at the same time. CHRIST'S SAKE MAN, why did you think I needed safe passage through your territories when we first met? What did you think I was bringing through, food for starving babies? You and your fucking righteousness, it's held you back for decades. But from what I hear, it's your good lady who holds the reins in your home anyway, so really, she's the boss of your business.'

Declan remained silent, staring across at him. O'Driscoll finished his whiskey and said, 'I'll text you the address of my lock up with a time to meet up before the brothers show up. This is my burner number; I'll need yours. They are a pair of thick eejits if they think they can get away with my merchandise. If your new friends from out of town want these two, then tonight is their opportunity. Let me make it clear. I want nothing to do with this mob when they claim their prized possessions. I want the dirty deed to be done outside of our city. I don't want any bodies dumped on our borders. It will draw attention to my activities from the Gardai... are we clear?... can you vouch for your man? You sure he's only after two trophies to take back home?' Declan nodded.

O'Driscoll stood up, nodded goodbye, and whispered, 'All of this ends tonight. If the shit hits the fan, then so be it. Are we good?' Both men locked hands in a tight grip. O'Driscoll walked off, then paused and looked back. 'Perhaps we can finish that bottle together after all of this has died down.'

Declan nodded, 'I'll be sure to hold you to that.' O'Driscoll nodded again and disappeared.

Declan waved the bartender over and ordered another coffee. The coffee arrived as he phoned Dooley. There was a silence. Declan spoke first, 'I have some pressing news.'

Declan got no response except for heavy breathing. Muffled conversations hissed in the background. Next, he heard the phone passed from person to person before Dooley spoke, 'It will be good to hear your news, but I need to hear it face to face from you, are we clear?' Declan understood.

'I'll fill you in later then. The celebrations are happening tonight. I'll text you the location to meet me and take you straight to the event. It will be good to see the look on their faces when they see the effort you've made to come up to see them. I look forward to it.' Declan hung up and left Dooley to stew.

A text message appeared from Dooley seconds later with a new number to text the location details to. Declan sent them off with a meeting time of 10 pm. That would give Dooley ample time to drive up to meet Declan and be introduced to O'Driscoll. Declan convinced himself that within the next 24-hour period, all would resume in his city. The evening looked like a perfectly orchestrated planned event that couldn't go wrong, but he still had a gut feeling that something wasn't going to plan. He usually relied on his gut feeling, but he had to try and override it on this occasion. Things were happening.

Dooley had summoned a handful of men for a briefing on dealing with the Finnerty Brothers. One had been given the task of preparing cars for the journey up to Dublin. Three vehicles needed to have full tanks for their return trip. Until the brothers were collected, the final destination had been withheld. One of the transport vehicles was an ex-postal security truck that had caged racking in the rear. Dooley was confident that the van was going to be carrying extra cargo on the return journey. It was the perfect layout to allow passengers to feel every bump, twist and turn while in transit. Two men accompanied this vehicle, dressed in security uniforms.

Dooley had waited a long time for this moment. Even though it had come at short notice, he wasn't going to leave any detail out. Just in case the brothers squealed like pigs in the back, a sedative was on hand to be administered. All his men were briefed not to harm either of the brothers upon capture grievously. Dooley wanted the pleasure of inflicting every blow himself.

Back in Limerick, a valeting company was on standby to receive the security vehicle upon its return. This was no ordinary valeting procedure. Blood and skin needed to be sanitised from every crevice so that if screened, no trace of DNA evidence could be found.

During the briefing Dooley spoke clearly and defined each role so that no misunderstandings or mistakes could ruin his plan. These were experienced men, and they knew how meticulous Dooley was. Each driver was given the postcode and advised to hold back ten minutes before setting off after the car in front. This was to avoid any suspicion. In the unlikely event of Dooley being pulled over, the team had been instructed of a plan B. He wanted the plan to run without a hitch. He knew that he would probably never get another chance if the brothers caught wind he was after them.

The plan had been for O'Driscoll to liaise with the port operator to allow the Finnerty brothers to receive the cargo container, which he then knew they would try to double-cross him on. It was then to be transported to O'Driscoll's lock-up around midnight, where Dooley and Declan would meet. What the brothers hadn't realised was that a tracker had been pinned to the vehicle, one of O'Driscoll's vehicles, that would show him their every move.

CHAPTER 50

Adrenalin flushed through Declan's bloodstream giving him heart palpitations. His forehead broke into a clammy sweat as he revved the engine. Holding the steering wheel in a vice grip, he depressed the accelerator, causing plumes of smoke to surround the car. Pins and needles numbed his fingertips, and his feet lost sensitivity in the footwell. As far as he was concerned, he had just suffered a mild panic attack. Either way, he hadn't planned to breathe a word to Kathleen. The pressure of keeping on top of his game and looking over his shoulder constantly drained him. It was time to change his lifestyle. He opened a packet of cigarettes and took a deep draw on his first inhale.

He had intended to go home and rest before the evening's showdown. He also wanted to stay out of contact with Billy and Johnny. They were surplus to requirements, and he didn't want them knowing about the plan. If they got wind of what was going on, they would back Declan up to the hilt. He didn't want them involved. Driving off with no destination in mind, he wanted to be on his own. Knowing the possible repercussions of the night's events, he convinced himself he could live with them. After all, it was for the good of his future and his family. Driving past the church which had held Sinead's funeral, he recalled how many people had turned up. He decided to turn around and park up outside. He got out and stared up at the spire of the church, taking in all of its glory. The stone structure was visible for miles across the city.

Studying the engraved stone blocks, he sniggered to himself and said, 'For the love of God, what the *fuck* am I doing here?'

'How do,' a voice shouted. Declan ignored it. The voice spoke again. 'If you regret something you've done, then you may regret it even more if you turn away now... after all, you've come this far, why walk away now?' Declan peered around to find a sunken-looking, older man wearing a heavy coat and a woollen hat struggling to turn the key in the lock of the church doors. He waved Declan over to help him. When the doors were secured, he greeted Declan, 'Good day to you, Son... I know who you are... I also know your mother well... and I also know what you are thinking right now.'

Declan, bemused, tried to find an excuse to be on his way quickly. 'Well... I was just passing.'

The wiry old man looked at him knowingly, 'Son... no one passes a church, then turns around to stand outside it with nothing on their mind.'

Feeling embarrassed, Declan said, 'I'll be on my way now, Father.'

The older man acted as if he hadn't spoken, 'I won't be having it, Son... I'm not going to unbolt everything again, so you'll have to follow me home, and then we can sit and talk. It's not every day I have one of your kind turning up at God's front door to ask questions or to find answers.'

Declan glowered, 'My kind, Father?'

The man had already turned around and walked off towards the priest's house when he stopped and abruptly said, '*Yes*... your kind... shady people... people who operate outside the boundaries of the law and avoid paying taxes. Don't insult my intellect, young man. I may be an old man, but I also keep my ear to the ground. Don't worry – you don't scare me, and I don't scare you, so follow me.'

Declan felt like a schoolboy caught in the act of mischief. Digging his hands into his pockets, he rocked back and forth, trying to figure out an escape. This old-timer took no prisoners. The man sharply motioned Declan to follow him. Relinquishing his inhibitions, Declan followed, curiosity getting the better of him. Inside the parish house, the man laid his overcoat across one side of the sofa then settled down in an old, rugged armchair.

He glanced up at Declan and asked, 'Would you like tea? I don't drink coffee.' Declan declined. The old man looked perplexed, then said, 'You're supposed to follow my line and say, "*Yes*, I would love a cup of tea, but you stay there, and I'll make us both one." Do you follow me, Son?'

Declan smiled and knew the wiry old goat had played him. He got up and flicked the kettle on. The man gave instructions from the comfort of his armchair. 'The sugar is in the silver pot by the stove, and the milk is inside the fridge. Make sure the water is boiling, Son, when you pour it into the tea. There is nothing worse than a poorly made cup of tea.'

Declan smirked; it reminded him of his mother shouting at him when he was a teenager. He made the tea and brought it in. The old man had fallen asleep. Declan studied him. His thin legs in his oversize trousers looked like they couldn't carry his tiny frame. Purple veins highlighted his weak wrists, and his skin was wrinkled and decayed looking. Declan muttered, 'For fuck's sake.'

The man woke up startled. 'That's one euro in the collection box for blasphemy in God's house.'

In defence, Declan replied, 'Jaysis, this isn't the church.'

Folding his arms, the man forced himself to sit up. 'That's two euros, and now make it five for denial. This is God's lean-to of a house, and that counts as well,' he said. Shaking his head, Declan reached into his pocket. The man stopped him and said, 'You can deposit it the next time you come to church.'

'Next time?' Declan replied, 'Here's a ten; I'm sure the blasphemy will keep adding up.'

The older man nodded, 'Yes, Son. I believe you wanted to come into the church. Will this be your first time of many to come?' Declan ignored the question. 'Never mind. Please, make yourself at home, if you want to tell me what's on your mind – I'm a good listener. Unlike some of the congregation within the church, I promise what you say here won't go any further.'

Declan sank back into the frame of the old sofa. The old man sipped his tea and stared at Declan. 'Your mam has taught you well, young man. This is a lovely cup of tea.'

The whites of his eyes were yellow and watery as he focused on Declan, 'Go ahead, start talking, it's only you and me.' The old man's knee unknowingly swung like a pendulum as he settled in to listen. The movement was almost hypnotic. Declan felt relaxed and decided to unburden himself.

'I don't know what I'm doing here. I don't go to church. The only times I attend are for weddings, funerals and christenings. I couldn't even tell you what the difference is between Catholics and the Church of England. I know one of you lets all your priests marry but doesn't celebrate the whole gay thing, and the other clan won't allow it full stop.'

Raising his arm slowly, the old man intervened. 'Right you are. That will be us then, the Church of England. We decided some time ago to move forward and embrace the ever-changing culture of modern-day society. To change the stigma of homosexuality, to register civil partnerships within the priesthood and congregation… to keep the church's population thriving. The difference between the Catholics and us is simply one word: *Indoctrination.*

'They haven't evolved from the original translation of the scriptures. They have accepted beliefs based on what they were told that could not be disproven. This has purposely forced their clergy to stay locked away from humanity for all these past centuries. Sadly, it has created a place where the disgusting behaviour of fiddling with all the young altar boys could flourish too. Those Catholics are still getting found out in today's age after continuously denying that anything so damaging ever took place within its church walls.

'Initially, they paid compensation to keep it all hush, hush, to cover it up. The magnitude was so systemic that they had no choice but to come clean and admit that countless young boy's childhoods were scarred and ruined. I'm not saying it never happened within our religion, but at least we have evolved over recent decades to accept that all of God's children have different sexual orientations. As long there is love and respect for each other, everyone is welcome under God's umbrella.

'In Genesis 2, the Lord says, "It's not good for man to be alone. I will make him a companion." St Paul writes, "It is better for a man to marry than to burn." So, it's good to share our lives with another. Neither of these says, "But not if he is gay." It's all open to interpretation. Let love thrive, I say.'

Declan was enthralled by how candid the older man was about life in general. Finally, he said, 'The thing is… I'm engaged in a tricky situation to protect my family. To protect everything that I've achieved and worked for... and to do that, someone has to suffer the consequences.' Bowing his head, he paused.

The old man sat up and said, 'You mean, what you have worked and achieved for, yet paid little taxes for?'

Affronted, Declan rose to his feet and, raising his voice, said, 'Look... I don't need this shite from you lot.'

'Arhh, save your breath to cool your porridge, young man, and that's another euro in the collection box by the way. Sit yourself down now and sip your tea. It would be a shame to let it go cold.'

Declan sighed and sank back into the sofa, holding his hands behind his head. Worry lines crossed his forehead. The man could tell that Declan was looking for justification, enough to protect his family. He spoke again with maddening calm.

'Young man, hindsight is the perfect gift that none of us can offer each other. I'm not going to pretend I know how or why you live your life the way you do. But if I can give you one piece of advice, it would be this,' he pointed the finger at Declan showing signs of tremors. 'I have learnt the hard way in life that I cannot count on others to play ball or respect my wishes, even if I respect theirs. Being a good person doesn't guarantee that other people will be good too.' Sitting forward, he clasped his hands together, steadying his shakes.

'What I'm trying to say is that you only have control over yourself and how moral you choose to be. As for other people, you can either choose to accept them or fight them to live your life the way you feel is right. You already know the answer to your dilemma because you are seeking righteousness in God's house. It's not going to change the outcome of how you feel. If you are looking for an escape in here? My answer to you is to follow what your soul tells you to do, whether the outcome is lawfully correct or not.

'God forbid if something happened to your family, I could see it would devastate you. Then, all that would live inside your soul would be vengeance. Before you embark on a journey of retribution, dig two graves, Son, because no one wins. A wise man, who then became a famous writer, once wrote, "Anger is an acid that can do more harm to the vessel in which it is stored than anything on which it is poured".
That's no way for a man to live each day.'

Declan's found solace in the older man's words.

'The life you lead, Son… protect your family at all costs. I can see you are a wealthy man. You have a nice car outside, probably a grand house as well. One day you will realise that material things mean nothing. And all that matters is the well-being of the people in your life. Don't let that time come too late for you. You and me, young man, are worlds apart.

'No matter how much wealth you have in your bank account, how nice your car is or how luxurious your home is; our graves will still be the same. There is no such thing as rich earth. No large fee will escort you through the gates of heaven like them blasted speedy boarders at the fecking airport. In the meantime, what God has in store for you won't pass you. Stay humble, Son. Once again, your mother has taught you well. Oh, have you a euro for me, for the box? I let one slip out.'

Declan, amused and stirred by the words, thanked the man. 'Father, you've truly given me some insight into how I'm feeling. I thank you for that. I tell you what, here is twenty euro for your collection box.'

The old man chuckled to himself, waving the money away, '*Father?*' he laughed, 'I'm NO priest, young man. Were you expecting me to assign you a penance of twelve Hail Marys or something?' Giddy with hilarity, he fell back into his armchair in amusement. 'Sure, I'm just the churchwarden around here. Whatever gave you the impression I was a priest?'

Declan had a look on his face akin to that when his winning horse had been disqualified. 'What do you mean you're not a priest? You said you knew my mother and you invited me into your home. This is the priest's house!'

'Ahh,' the old man replied, 'That is correct, Son. I can see why you're confused. I'm on the parish committee here, and that's how I know your mother. I've helped out here for years now and knew your father before he sadly passed away. It's only in recent years that thieving bastards have been helping themselves to the contents of the Lord's house, so I was offered the post of churchwarden; to lock up and secure the church after daytime activities. One of the benefits of the job is that I have access to the lower floor of the priest house to have lunch or take a nap if I wish.'

The older man coughed then started to choke. His whole body felt the impact of him trying to breathe. Pulling out an inhaler, he sucked in three squirts. He held his breath as his eyes widened, then he slowly released it.

'Young man, you haven't revealed anything to me, so don't feel cheated by me. Your mam thinks the world of you and worries as much as you do about your own family. My final piece of advice to you, Son, is… to not pass over the burden of worry to your offspring. Try to enjoy the little things in life because one day you will look back and realise they were the big things.'

The old man sighed and went to get up. He could barely lift himself out of the chair. He was weary and fatigued. Unfolding himself from the sofa, he went into the kitchen. 'Right, can I offer you another pot of tea, young man?'

Declan had carried the tea tray with him and replied, 'No, thank you, I best be on my way.' Placing the tray down, he asked the old man, 'Forgive me; I won't pretend to say that I haven't noticed you here before because I rarely come here. The last time was after my father's funeral when I was a boy. So, what's your name?'

Waiting for the kettle to whistle, the man answered, 'Brendan Kilkenny.'

Nodding his head respectfully, Declan replied, 'Mam has mentioned your name many times in conversations over the years.' Declan held his arm out, and Brendan obliged in a handshake. His aged limp hand held together with skin offered the briefest of clinches.

'After your problem has been sorted, I'll look forward to seeing you back in church, young man.'

'Stranger things have happened. It would be good to talk to you again.'

'I mean it, young man. Oh, and I want to see you place that twenty euro note and the one you settled for myself in the collection box before you go.' Brendan winked while escorting him to the front door. 'God has a reason for allowing things to happen. We may not understand his wisdom; we simply have to trust his will.'

CHAPTER 51

Declan felt rejuvenated after his short sleep and the conversation the night before. All was well on the home front, too, which helped his mood.He had told Kathleen he would be heading out to a private poker game, and she accepted his account of where he was going. He didn't want her to worry, and he was glad she didn't suspect anything.

Kathleen was focused on preparing for a girls' night, so it suited her that Declan was going out. Kathleen had pestered Bridget to come along and wouldn't accept no for an answer. Martin had agreed to stay sober for the evening and pick her up, so she had no excuses about the cost of cabs. Both Martin and Bridget realised even a few hours apart would be a break; their mutual grief was beginning to stifle each other as neither had gone back to work since Sinead's death.

Declan enjoyed what he subconsciously called 'His Last Supper'. He checked his phone and was thankful that Billy and Johnny hadn't contacted him; they seemed to accept his story that no further action would be taking place. He let the kiss linger, kissing Kathleen goodbye, then got into his car after one final goodbye. Declan relaxed to music as he drove to O'Driscoll's meeting point.

When his phone rang, it was O'Driscoll. The conversation was short and direct. O'Driscoll spoke first and in vague terms, 'Is everything in place at your end for tonight's proceedings? Will those guests be able to attend tonight?'

'Yes, they are looking forward to it,' Declan replied.

A message flashed in from an unrecognisable number. He knew it was Dooley. The Limerick gang were en route and expected to arrive on time. Everything was falling into place nicely. Still, Declan had an uneasy feeling that something was going to scupper their plans. A ripple of fear ran down his spine and trepidation coursed through his veins. *Was tonight going to be his final on this earth?*

O'Driscoll's lock-up was on the borders of farmland about forty minutes away. A secluded dirt track was a good destination point to meet. Declan tried to avoid the hedgerows from scoring the paintwork of his car as he navigated the narrow lanes. The mud had hardened, making driving less troublesome until potholes appeared that gave way to robust terrain. The steering wheel took a course of its own as the car rumbled over the rutted track from side to side. The tyres followed the grooves worn into the trail until it eventually evened out before he stopped. It was pitch black as he levered himself out of the car.

Flapping birds hustled in branches above him. He lit a cigarette and paced back and forth. Headlamps beamed from a distance as they crested over the hill, bouncing up and down as they headed towards him. Declan held his hand across his forehead, trying to shield the glare as it cut through the darkness. The car's speed didn't slow on its downhill descent. Its handbrake ratcheted, and it clipped the side of Declan's car before screeching to a halt and blowing up a frenzied dust cloud.

Next, it reversed fiercely towards Declan, knocking him off his feet. Clasping his ears, he rolled around in the dirt as fragments of fibreglass ballooned into the air. A lone figure stepped out and moved towards Declan. Dust motes came to life in the headlights as the looming figure glared over him. With his face smudged in dirt, a familiar voice called out, 'Well, Well, Well. I thought you burnt to a crisp in that store, and yet somehow you survived.' A hand reached out to Declan, offering him a lift up from the ground. Taking it, he got to his feet.

A second figure held out a bottle of water and spoke, 'Hold your hands together and clean your face with this.' Thomas Finnerty came into Declan's view and poured water into his outstretched hands. Soaking his face, Declan looked as the Finnerty brothers came to life. Declan tried to recall which ankle of Thomas's was the weak one.

Thomas spoke first. 'Did you think we were going to walk into this blind? We've worked hard to come this far. This shipment is going to be our pot of gold from working with O'Driscoll. The old bastard can't see the benefits of selling imported coke. Chrissake, London is crying out for tons of this shite, and they'll pay through the nose to get the pure stuff.'

Patrick continued. 'It didn't take much persuasion for yer man at the port to cough up what he knew. He was only too willing to spill the beans to save his other seven fingers. What disappointed us is that you two bastards thought you could take us out alone. Poor O'Driscoll will be spitting feathers when he sees our driver, and we'll be saving that shocker for the main event.'

Thomas took over. 'We got yer man's mobile and can see the conversation he had with O'Driscoll. The eejit didn't delete anything; how professional was that? You bastards have been planning this together? When we start selling this gear, everyone will recognise our name. We have contacts in the UK and across Europe to sell to, and you boys will be made obsolete.'

Patrick held his hand out, 'Give me your phone and don't mess about.'

Declan nodded and glanced at the messages that had come through on the home screen. Thankfully only two from O'Driscoll had been sent and came through as Brewery Rep. Dooley's name had been saved in the contacts as Consolidator, so it wouldn't flag up. Snatching the phone, Patrick let his guard down, and Declan punched him in the groin. He fell to the ground immediately. Thomas was younger, sharper and quicker. He kept Declan low to the ground, stomping on his upper body and head. The assault was too feral for Declan to offer resistance.

After a couple of minutes, Thomas released him. Declan sprawled out motionless as he tried to find a fresh breath of air in the moving dust. Every rib ached, and the slightest of movements caused him immense pain. Thomas stood over him like he was prized kill, smirking to himself. He snatched the phone from his brother and rang O'Driscoll. It answered after one ring. The voice that answered spoke immediately, 'Don't be hurrying me up now... I'll be there in minutes.'

Thomas breathed down the phone silently and waited, 'Declan… don't be playing silly beggars with me. We'll have this wrapped up tonight once and for all.'

'And how do you intend to do that, O'Driscoll, with Declan, laid flat out in front of me?' Thomas finally spoke, then ended the call. As Patrick limped back to the car, Thomas dropped the mobile onto Declan's chest and said, 'For the second time, I see you at death's door. Take this survival as a goodwill gesture and end your days running your territory in Dublin. If we meet again, I swear you will meet your maker.'

Declan wiped away bloodied phlegm from his mouth, 'Every dog has its day.'

Thomas nodded. 'It's the top dog that survives in this world, and the old dog gets put down.' He turned and walked away. Declan lay sprawled flat out and listened for the slow recession of the brother's footsteps. For God's sake, Dooley, don't let me down, he thought to himself.

The brothers drove off, leaving a gritty storm cloud behind. Declan felt helpless. His body told him he had had enough. He rang Aiden, who answered without saying a word this time. Declan spoke first. 'Your man at the port lost a finger until he broke his silence about your set-up. They took his phone and traced your messages.'

O'Driscoll cursed, 'For fuck's sake. I told that man to delete every communication each day.'

Declan replied, 'I can't believe the pair of you didn't have burner phones. This shite is REAL! The fuckers were looking out for us en route to the lock-up. They must have thought luck was on their side when I was in open view before they slammed my car and jumped me.'

'They still only think it's the two of us. We still have the element of surprise when Dooley shows up. How far away is he now?' said O'Driscoll. Bright beams flashed in front of Declan. Brakes screeched as the dust settled, bringing a car to a halt.

Declan looked at it, 'We can't take any risks missing these chancers. Right, Dooley has just pulled in, so we'll see you there,' he hung up.

CHAPTER 52

Two further cars pulled in behind as Dooley jumped out. He spoke with some of his men then looked at Declan. It was apparent Declan had been in a scrap; an anxious look flashed across Dooley's face. No pleasantries were exchanged as Dooley grasped Declan by his lapels, shunting him up against the car. His face was seething as he yelled in Declan's face. 'DON'T tell me you've tackled them on your own. DON'T tell me I've wasted my time getting up here. DON'T tell me they have escaped.'

Declan broke Dooley's hold of him, shoving him back to regain his own space. Two of Dooley's grunts tried to run at Declan as another yanked out a handgun aiming it at him. Dooley raised his arm to hold them back.

Declan stood his ground and said, 'Our location was found out. They cut off Aiden's man's finger before he squealed.'

Dooley interrupted, trying to regain some composure, 'Are we still on for catching them?' Declan nodded. 'They're at the compound loading up their transporter. O'Driscoll has a hoard of liquor and contraband tobacco. They're unaware that you are involved but still brazen enough to take the two of us on.'

An obnoxious look stretched across Dooley's face as he stood toe-to-toe eyeballing Declan, 'That's because you two are a pair of fucking pussies.' Losing his cool, Declan swung at Dooley, catching him on the side of his jaw. Dooley hit the ground but not before two of his men steamed into Declan and pinned him to the dirt track.

Dooley yelled out, 'ENOUGH is ENOUGH.' Standing back up face-to-face with him, he said, 'For the love of God, the only reason I'm keeping you conscious is that you're needed for me to get those brothers. Any other God-forsaken day, and you would have been slain by now. Keep your gob shut and take us to them directly. Don't take any chances. DO

I MAKE MY SELF CLEAR?' Declan could only nod, his swollen mouth hurt badly.

Dooley, now extremely aggravated, said, 'Drive directly to the holding area. Once you see those fuckers, flash your hazard lights once. That will indicate to us to hold our ground and find a position to pin them in. After that, you're on your fucking own. Now, jump in and drive there. Just in case you try any funny business, my good friend will be laying in your back seat with his handgun pointing at the back of your head.'

Declan clambered into the driver's seat. The shooter took up position behind him and laid down in the footwell. Declan's phone rang again; the voice behind shouted to him to throw it behind him. He did. The shooter answered the phone and listened, then asked who O'Driscoll was. Declan answered, 'He's the other fecking pussy.'

Laughter rumbled from the back seat as Declan drove. Just before the entrance to the compound, a fast-approaching vehicle joined the mini convoy, and again, Declan's phone rang. The shooter answered the call and asked Declan, 'Brewery rep?'

'That's my man; he's arrived late to join us.' Declan said. All the cars crept in for the ambush, ready to ensnare the Finnerty brothers. O'Driscoll pulled up alongside Declan, and both car windows buzzed down. Declan put his index finger up to his lips, instructing O'Driscoll to be quiet, then gestured to his back seat. O'Driscoll rolled his eyes and said, 'You follow my lead; do you hear me?'

Both cars pushed forward to the lock-up, where the Finnerty brothers spotted them on their arrival. Ignoring the glare of headlights, they continued loading the merchandise onto a tail lift van with a handgun on show in the back of their jeans. O'Driscoll flipped his boot and pulled out a shotgun before he walked up to them. Declan attempted to get out of his car when the shooter shouted out, 'You sit tight there now, Hennessey... we only need one hero here tonight.'

O'Driscoll, seething now at the lack of respect the Finnerty brothers had shown him shouted out, 'I have let you pair of amateurs run your little sideshow for far too long. You've now reached the end of the line.'

The brothers split and darted in separate directions, both keeping their guns on O'Driscoll. Holding his ground without flinching, O'Driscoll said, 'Well, this is where we separate the professionals from the amateurs tonight… are you ready?' A gunshot rang out, and Patrick's leg exploded with blood as he fell to the ground. The noise was unbearable as Patrick squealed like a captured animal. Shocked, watching his older brother screaming, Thomas panicked. Coming out into the open, he aimed his handgun at O'Driscoll.

Declan's rear door opened; the shooter in the back fired two shots in Thomas's direction but the bullets rifled past him with no precision. Thinking about the broader picture, Thomas thought better of retaliating, then ran to find some cover out of sight. A bullet pierced the air from a distance, blinkering out the security light and shrouding the area in darkness. Declan's rear door remained open; the shooter shouted out to Declan, 'Those two shots just saved your pal's life out there.'

With adrenalin rushing through his system, Declan's hearing and sight were amplified as he jumped out and watched from behind his driver's door. O'Driscoll hurried back to find cover behind his car as more shots rang out. The shrilling screams of Patrick whistled through the air. The concrete loading bay was soaked in a sea of blood. The van's engine fired up and continued to rev, but one of the cars had blocked its path. Both brothers now had no means of escape. A lone hooded figure jumped out of the van cab and ran to assist Patrick under the illumination of the headlights. O'Driscoll watched the scene unfold, and his heart sank. It was O'Driscoll's son, Liam. Distraught, he walked out to the open ground, dropping his shotgun and leaving himself unprotected.

His strained voice shouted out, 'Liam... SON.' Struggling to believe Liam had been turned, O'Driscoll stood, stunned, unable to countenance what he saw. Liam paused but didn't look back at his father; instead, he clambered back into the cab of the van. Thomas seized the opportunity to take a clean shot at O'Driscoll. For once, the consequences of Thomas's actions played on his mind. He couldn't risk the chance of Liam returning to save his father if he shot O'Driscoll. Thomas came out from the darkness, aiming the gun point-blank at O'Driscoll. Declan stood up and shouted out to O'Driscoll, 'To your right side.'

O'Driscoll spoke faintly to Thomas, the gun level at his face. 'You knew my boy was weak, so you took advantage of him to get to me. You've turned him into a traitor. So, you promised him the world, did you? What were your plans for him once you got everything you wanted from me? You're nothing but a cold, heartless bastard.'

Thomas didn't answer and just glared at him knowing he had the upper hand. Releasing the safety catch of the gun, he said, 'This is for my brother.' He fired a bullet at O'Driscoll's leg, sending him collapsing to the ground. The older man didn't flinch or let out a cry; instead, he sat back, taking deep breaths, fighting through the pain. Pulling himself forward, he grabbed onto Thomas's leg and used it to pull himself up.

O'Driscoll's face trembled as shock took over his nervous system. 'That makes us evens for now. Tell my boy it's all over, and he's on his own. Then you can take off.'

Thomas berated him, 'You're in no position to ask for anything. Who are *you* to dictate to *me* about anything?' Frustration ballooned inside Thomas. O'Driscoll had no respect for him. In anger, Thomas lashed out at him across the face with the barrel of his gun, sending him crashing to the ground again. Declan couldn't take it anymore and went to leave the safety of his car, intending to distract Thomas.

The shooter in the car footwell grabbed him and said, 'You go out there, and you're on your own like that old fool.'

'I was on my own when I walked into your bosses shit hole and made it out in one piece. I'll take my chance with this brazen fucker,' Declan replied.

Thomas saw Declan step forward and shouted, 'Hennessey, I've put you down like a dog tonight already. You keep coming, and this time it will be permanently, hotshot.'

Declan riled Thomas, casually taking his coat off before replying, 'Do you want a chance at having a shot for the title, champ? I mean *boy*?'

Thomas fired into the night sky, clearing the barrel, then unclipped the magazine, throwing both parts in opposite directions as he rested his foot on O'Driscoll's body. 'One down... one to go,' he goaded Declan as fury spiked him. 'I've heard so much about you as if you're some kind of fucking folklore hero since I've been up here. But let me tell you, your time is up. Myself and my brother have the vision to operate this city. Your problem is you don't know when to give up.'

Declan continued to listen in a bid to waste time and draw Dooley and his men into position to make the final strike. Thomas's anger grew before he hit out at Declan, landing a punch square on the jaw. Declan let Thomas have a few shots to let him feel he had the upper hand, but after four strikes, he let loose, attacking Thomas with a barrage of solid punches to the chest and ribs. His rhythm was slick and took Thomas by surprise, who retaliated with a string of missed shots. The pair pivoted back and forth as they grappled. Declan had soon worked out Thomas's pattern of punches and deliberately left his guard down for him to come forward. With the carrot dangled, Thomas snatched at it, falling into Declan's trap. He suffered a series of brutal body shots with a few to the head. A deep gash chiselled through his eyebrow as blood spurted, trickling down his face.

One last well-timed punch from Declan and Thomas hit the deck. He lay prone, breathing heavily, not even making an effort to get to his feet. Declan let his guard down and turned his back on him. Thomas, seizing the opportunity, pulled himself to his feet, scrambling over to him. Declan sensed it, but it was too late; he lifted his arms in defence as Thomas pummelled him. Declan protected his face, but then, feeling a sharp pain under his armpit, he suddenly lost all strength.

Thomas pulled back to reveal a screwdriver covered in blood. Crouching down on one knee next to Aiden, Declan tried to stem the blood flowing from under his arm. He looked at Aiden and back at Thomas and said, 'Do you remember when I told you that every dog has its day?' Chuckling to himself, he repeated, 'EVERY dog has its day.'

Thomas looked blankly at Declan, not understanding him until figures came out of the shadows and circled him. Taking in short, panicked breaths, he watched as the silhouettes came to life, their faces showing in the glow of the headlamps. Making a decisive run, Thomas hurtled away from the cars. The shooter in Declan's car now made his presence known as he aimed his gun at Thomas. Thomas froze in confusion. Turning around, he searched for another escape route. Hearing footsteps behind him, he realised he was trapped. There was a blind panic in his eyes as the inevitability etched across his face. There was no way out. The sound of a metal object dragging along came from behind him. Dooley jumped off the platform. 'You've made me wait a long time for this moment. Before you left me, you left something behind, and I thought it is only fitting that I return it to you.'

Forcing himself to look down at the metal object, Thomas recognised it as the same silver metallic baseball bat he had slain Tanner. Fear gripped him. Standing face to face, Dooley walked around while talking to him. 'I've waited a long time for this moment. The wait has given me a lot of time to reflect on how to deal with you. For the first six months, I was adamant that I was going to make it quick clean. Problem was taken care of... but *now*... I'm going to take my time over you.'

The whistle of the bat cut through the air with such force as it aimed at Thomas's leg. A visceral sound of metal against bone echoed across the wasteland, causing his leg to fold the opposite way as Thomas collapsed to the ground, screaming in agony. Dooley felt no remorse. He signalled at the security van, and there was a commotion as Dooley's men surrounded the cab, motioning Liam to get out. Unable to deal with the sight of his father in distress, he turned away and attempted to run but stopped to take a second look at his father lying prone in a pool of blood. Dooley signalled for him to be brought back and gave the nod for him to be taken care of.

As three of Dooley's men pounced on him, beating him repeatedly, from where he lay, O'Driscoll screamed out,

'Leave him be.' Grappling with the dirt, O'Driscoll dragged himself along towards his son. Dooley flung his arm out as two men held Liam firmly while a third one continued landing punches into his face. 'Who is he to you?... I want quick-fire-answers.'

'HE'S MY SON... he's my boy...'

Looking dumbfounded, Dooley whistled loudly. The men backed off, leaving Liam to get to his feet. Dooley winced and asked, 'What kind of fucking set-up is going on here for Chrissake?' He paced back and forth, considering his options. 'That giant bastard,' he said pointing at Liam, 'is an accessory to everything here tonight, and he's your fucking lad? Before I leave here, you better give me your word that he will never speak a word of what has gone on here tonight. I'd sleep better finishing him off knowing a dead man can never tell tales. That goes for all three of you.'

Declan stood up, clutching his arm, and answered,

'I can vouch for the lad and his father too. Our ties can be broken now. You have what you came for. We'll do what you want. We can look out for ourselves from here on.' Not looking convinced, Dooley whispered to his men. Weapons were disarmed and boxed back in the car boots.

Dooley looked back, 'The only way three people can keep a secret is if the other two are dead. You two better not come back to haunt me. I… I have what I came for...' he pointed at Thomas Finnerty, lying mangled on the ground. 'Don't ever contact me or come back down to Limerick again. WE ARE DONE.'

Declan nodded, replying, 'On one condition? Promise me those two chancers will never bother either of us again.'

Dooley looked offended, 'I can promise you; they'll never be able to walk again or even tick off boxes for a lottery ticket. Those bastards will pay for the rest of what little life they have left after what they did to me... is that good enough for you?'

Declan and Aiden sat back-to-back in the dirt, reserving what little energy they had left as Dooley concentrated on his clean-up. Screams shrilled out as his men herded Thomas into the security van. Dooley signalled for the van's shutter to open. Patrick had become delirious. It was evident he'd lost a lot of blood. Dooley's men dumped his body into the same vehicle as his brother. Dooley's mind was finally clear. He had one final thing left to do. Looking to his right-hand man, he ordered, 'Torch it... torch the whole FUCKING lot... don't leave a trace of anything that can be recovered from this site.' Dooley's men started to douse the inside of the container and cab with petrol.

Declan tried to stop them. He said, 'For Chrissake, you have your man. We can sort out the clean-up operation at our end.'

'I couldn't give two FUCKS what you think. That means all the evidence of loot and blood is left out in the open. Once the Guards are notified of this, they'll be all over it, examining it for forensics. I can't take that risk. Can you two? I've let the old boy keep his son. He needs medical attention right now to save his life. You both need patching up. Now fuck off and let me get on with this,' Dooley clicked his fingers. One of his men darted over to him with the explosive devices that Declan had tried to use at Dooley's pub. Unravelling the bundle, Dooley taunted Declan, 'Do these look familiar to you? They weren't even armed to detonate… fucking amateurs?'

Declan watched as the device was activated and thrown into the van. The dark velvet sky lit up as flames engulfed everything it came into contact with. In no time, the vehicle was beyond recognition; it had turned into a giant orange fireball, luminescent as it gathered momentum. The fuel tank exploded, and molten fragments of metal illuminated the night sky. The loud explosion was sure to attract attention, along with the dense smell of diesel fermenting in the atmosphere. Everyone in sight shielded their faces from the shrapnel fragments spiralling in all directions.

Dooley turned to Declan, 'What's done is done. We'll be on our way, and I suggest you all leave right now as well.' Dooley headed away into the darkness. One by one, each vehicle left after the next. The intense heat had now set fire to the loading bay roof, and the lock-up, and the wind's direction had channelled the heat towards Declan and Aiden.

Declan shouted out to Liam, 'Drag your father back to the cars, away from this heat. This whole warehouse could go up at any time. Lift him into the back seat. Get away from here and leave him at the nearest hospital en route to the city.' Liam lifted his father, crumpled, into the driver's seat of O'Driscoll's car. The door barely closed, and it needed Declan to slam it. The car pulled away, leaving a cloud of dust as Declan watched the red taillamps disappear into the distance.

CHAPTER 53

Declan needed to get away as quickly as possible. The warehouse's hot metal roof and side panelling had peeled off in the extreme heat. Poisonous vapours bellowed out from the wreckage. Covering his mouth, Declan clambered into his car gingerly, unable to move his right arm. His blood loss hadn't stemmed, and blood had soaked into his clothing. He had started to blow hot and cold and feel queasy and knew he needed medical attention.

He blasted the air conditioning in the car to keep himself alert. He took a moment to glance at a photo of Kathleen clipped behind the sun visor. It was a snapshot of her caught off guard that he had always loved. Declan kissed it, standing it up on the dashboard so he could see it as he drove.

The traffic was generally light, but this evening an event at the national football stadium had caused gridlock at the exits out of the city. Declan hit a wall of traffic and crawled along, the radio on for company. He decided to exit at the next junction; he'd dart through the backstreets to keep himself alert. He was losing strength, and his mind felt fuzzy. He reached a turn-off slammed on the accelerator and came off the motorway. Oncoming wind through the open window numbed his shoulder, while with his left arm, he changed gears and steered. He pulled over; afraid he was losing consciousness. The photo of Kathleen kept him somewhat alert long enough to call for help.

He called the ambulance services. Explaining his wound and blood loss, he directed them to his home address. His next call was to Kathleen. It switched to voice mail. He hung up, cursing. She immediately rang back. Her voice was low and tender.

'Are you far from home, love.'

'I don't want you to panic, but I've got myself into a bit of a scrap.

An ambulance is coming to our house.'

Kathleen paused, 'AMBULANCE? You stupid fool. You should've gone straight to A and E. Hang on now... Declan, what has happened to you?' Declan pressed his mobile to his head. Angry with himself that he had to lie to his wife about how severe his injury was. His words were starting to slur.

'I've a puncture wound that I can't stop bleeding, Kath. I'll be home in minutes, so sit tight for me.'

Kathleen needed answers. 'Please God!... Don't tell me you've been shot?'

Declan knew she would freak out, so she tried to keep the conversation short. 'Have the girls gone home?'

Kathleen could be heard whispering to someone in the room. She placed the phone back to her ear and answered, 'Bridget is the only one left. Martin has arrived to collect her. I'm not letting them go until you arrive home.'

'Right… right… right… I have no reception out here. I'm coasting on one bar, love you always,' Declan hung up.

Having drunk a fair share of wine, Kathleen sank on the sofa to think, her legs feeling weak. Mindfulness of Martin's presence, Bridget asked, 'Is Declan coming home tonight, Kathleen?' Kathleen burst into tears. A hundred different scenarios raced through her mind. Bridget consoled her, ushering Martin away into the kitchen.

Martin cursed to himself with his back turned. 'Jaysis – I only came around to pick her up, and now she's picking up the pieces... for fuck's sake, we'll be here all night.'

'Did you say something there, Martin?' Bridget snapped.

'Only a quick 'Hail Mary' for the good Lord to shepherd Declan on his safe journey home, my sweet,' he quickly improvised. Unable to make out the gist of the conversation, Martin busied himself instead of making coffee for the women. He brought the two coffees out. Kathleen hadn't noticed him as she was desperately trying to ring Declan back. Bridget thanked him as he scuttled back to the safety of the kitchen.

Kathleen's photo on the dashboard was Declan's lifeline in the car, helping him to focus enough to make it home. He had no strength left once the car pulled in, and he slumped forward against the steering wheel. Needing one last surge of effort to walk up to the front door, he mustered every ounce of energy remaining to get out of the car. Kathleen had rung Billy and was surprised that he knew nothing of any meeting or activity that night. That worried her further. Billy and Johnny should have been at Declan's side. None of this was adding up in her head.

'Why would he take a risk like that and not have any backup?' she voiced her thoughts to Bridget, 'It doesn't make sense. He deliberately went on his own from what I can make out. What could he have expected to achieve?'

Bridget held Kathleen's shoulders, trying to calm her down. 'Kath, you're not making any sense. Is Declan in some kind of trouble? Was it to do with those two outsiders who have caused havoc around town?'

Kathleen looked straight through Bridget, unable to formulate an answer. There was a knock at the door that startled them both. Kathleen ran to the door and fumbled with the lock before it opened. She nearly fell backwards. Declan clung onto the door frame, covered in blood. Kathleen grabbed hold of him and hugged him tightly while shouting at him, 'You stupid fool, what were you thinking of?'

As Declan tried to embrace her, Kathleen bore the full weight of him falling forward. Bridget helped catch Declan's body weight, guiding him to the floor. Kathleen saw more blood seeping out from under his arm and panicked. She tried to ask him questions to keep him awake as he slipped in and out of consciousness. Declan's eyes became heavy, he looked at the curve of Kathleen's mouth, and a small smile creased the contours of his cheeks before the whites of his eyes rolled back, and he passed out.

Bridget took control of the situation and stretched Declan flat out. Undoing the button holding his coat together, she attempted to peel it off him. They could both see the extent of blood loss. Kathleen froze in panic, 'You fool, you stupid old fool.'

Bridget raised her voice to Kathleen, 'WE NEED TO CALL AN AMBULANCE.'

Kathleen, in shock now, couldn't acknowledge any questions put to her. Bridget shouted out, 'Martin, come here NOW.' A second later, Bridget shouted again, 'Chrissake, Martin, what the hell were you doing in there? Didn't you hear all the commotion in here?'

Martin walked calmly into the room and said, 'I didn't want to take the risk of him being pissed off seeing me in his home. I'm hardly his favourite person. Jaysis though, for once he has been on the right end of a beating. He looks like shite.'

'We need to do something,' Bridget replied, she looked at Kathleen and whispered back to Martin, 'I think he's dead. What do you think?'

Martin swapped positions with Bridget and felt around over Declan's body to ascertain where the stab wound was located. 'Shite, it's a deep one; we need to stem the blood flow.' He looked at Kathleen; she had slipped into a trance. Bridget took hold of her and shook her. Kathleen came to, staring at Declan's lifeless body.

Inconsolably, a note of hysteria in her voice, she wailed, 'I'VE LOST HIM... HE'S DEAD... HE'S NEVER COMING BACK TO ME.'

Martin spoke firmly, 'KATHLEEN... listen to me, carefully... He's not dead, but I need to stem Declan's blood flow... do you understand?'

Kathleen nodded; Martin continued, 'That's grand... Right, now this is no time to go shy on me, Kathleen... I need you to fetch me your sanitary towels, and I don't mean those little swiss roll thingy-me-bob things either. I need the thick padded type… and a bottle of vodka.'

Bridget helped Kathleen to her feet and whispered in Martin's ear, 'That's great, Martin; you're doing ever so well!' Kissing his forehead, she continued upstairs with Kathleen to get Martin's requirements. Martin stared at Declan's lifeless body and contemplated if it would be such a bad thing for him to slip away and die? It would make his life run a lot more smoothly. Kathleen and Bridget raced back downstairs; he saw how distraught Kathleen was and was determined to make Declan more comfortable.

Kathleen handed over a pile of sanitary towels; Bridget held the vodka bottle left from earlier. Martin had ripped off one side of Declan's shirt to make his wound accessible. The padded towels soaked up the blood. He removed the sodden blood towels and cleaned the puncture with the vodka. He then compressed the wound with more vodka-soaked pads, keeping Declan's arm locked to his body for extra pressure. Declan didn't flinch as the vodka bleached out his flesh.

Kathleen rocked back and forwards beside him, repeating, 'He's never coming back; I've lost him.'

Martin tried to find a pulse. Both of Declan's arms were cold and still. He was winging it; he had no knowledge of first aid training. Even though he had managed to clean and compress Declan's wound, he thought saving his life was way out of his hands. Martin had to think quickly. He asked Bridget for a makeup mirror. She shrugged her shoulders, turning to Kathleen. As Kathleen searched for one upstairs, Martin reached for one of the wine glasses and poured a neat vodka into it.

'Christ, it didn't take you long to sniff one out,' Bridget remarked.

'It's for medicinal purposes… it helps to calm my nerves,' Martin replied bluntly. Kathleen reappeared and handed Martin the mirror. He waved it under Declan's nose to see if any condensation appeared.

'Jesus Martin? What are you doing?' Bridget naively asked.'I'm checking to see if he has a reflection… to see if he's a vampire. What the feck do you think I'm doing, woman? I'm checking to see if he's breathing.'

Bridget slapped Martin's shoulder hard, then scolded him, 'Why does everything in life have to be a joke to you, Martin. This shite is real.'

Martin sat back, rubbing his face and replied, 'In case you hadn't realised, I don't know what the fuck I'm supposed to be doing here. In fact, I'm not even supposed to be here.' Kathleen released a loud sob. Bridget glared scornfully at his lack of tact.

Trying to redeem himself, Martin attempted to resuscitate Declan. Positioning Declan's neck and head, he prepared Declan for mouth to mouth... Martin hovered over Declan's mouth, staring at his tonsils. As he pinched his nose, he attempted to bond his lips against Declan's. Their lips joined, and Martin breathed hard into Declan. After one breath he reeled back with a look of disgust on his face. 'I CAN'T do that again. I tried to pretend he was a lass, but his stubble ruined the thought.'

Bridget smacked Martin on his shoulder and angrily said, 'Chrissake, Martin, you're giving him the kiss of life not prepping for a sex scene. Get back down and do it.'

Martin puffed hard during six more renditions of mouth to mouth. On the seventh breath, Declan choked and regurgitated phlegm. Martin flew back up with mucus fragments stuck to his face. In disgust, he reached out for the first thing to hand and picking up a sanitary towel he wiped his face clean. Declan let out a murmur as his muscles briefly flinched, then he remained still. Kathleen exhaled in delight. Martin, having mopped his face, aimed straight for the vodka bottle again and gurgled a mouthful. He cleared his throat before spitting it back out into an empty wine glass. The next swig, he swallowed.

Blue and white lights flashed into the front room, and Kathleen rushed to her feet to escort the ambulance crew inside. Bridget and Martin looked at each other, trying to figure out which one of them had called the emergency services. The paramedics took over and worked to stabilise Declan's condition. They made him comfortable before prepping him for transfer in the ambulance. After explaining how he had resuscitated Declan, Martin felt deflated as the paramedic explained, 'That was good thinking, but there was probably no need for it. With the blood loss sustained, his body would have shut down and developed a slow rhythm to protect his organs; it might have looked like he wasn't breathing, but he was.'

Martin, panicking, held the ladies in the kitchen and said, 'Listen to me now! There's no need for Declan to find out that I did what I did to bring him around. For safety's sake, we'll say it was you, Kathleen, who resuscitated him. If he found out it was me –' Martin paused, shaking his head.

CHAPTER 54

Kathleen accompanied Declan in the ambulance, gently talking to him while stroking his hand. Once in the hospital, she felt calmer as the medical staff took over. Declan was placed on an intravenous drip and dosed up with a sedative. Even though he was still unconscious, the crew encouraged her to talk to him. His life wasn't in any danger as he was breathing unaided. It seemed to Kathleen like he had dodged a bullet, and this was a wake-up call.

Meanwhile, Bridget and Martin locked up the house and headed over to Geraldine's to inform her of her son's *accident*. They thought best that it wasn't a conversation over the phone with a worried elderly mother. After reassuring her of her son's condition, they would bring her to the hospital. Geraldine had prepared herself many times over the years for terrible news about her son. With too much time on her hands, she tended to dwell on her negative thoughts. She realised how lonely one person could be after the death of her husband. Her empty house held so many happy memories with Donal, her late husband. She detested having to rattle around all day preparing dinners for just herself.

Martin and Bridget pulled up outside Geraldine's home. It was a quiet secluded cul-de-sac. Her house was the furthest one away on the bend. When a visitor came right down, she knew they were coming to see her. Geraldine was a light sleeper and was roused from her bed by a brilliant light through the curtains searing along the ceiling as the car headlights approached. An engine idled before a car door slammed, and a hushed voice beckoned to keep the noise down. Immediately she thought: it's bad news. Her mind was full of dread. Her hands started to tremble. She panicked. The Guards only came to your home in the middle of the night with bad news.

She slipped her dressing gown and slippers on and made her way downstairs. She fully expected the Gardai to knock on her door and deliver bad news for many years, especially when Declan was a young man. The older he got, the less she expected it. Cinching her dressing gown tight, Geraldine opened her front door. Light filled the path as the security light flicked on. She expected to see uniformed officers and drilled herself to be calm, but it wasn't the Guards. She recognised Bridget and vaguely knew Martin.

'Is it Declan?' she asked, terrified as the two of them reached her front door, 'is my son dead?'

Bridget held her hands up in protest and replied, 'He's alive. He's at the hospital but has lost a lot of blood.'

Taking a deep breath in, Geraldine slowly exhaled, creating a mist in the cold night air. 'You'd better both come on in.' Standing aside, she gestured for them to enter as the cold air swept into the hallway. Taking them into the kitchen, she filled the kettle and ignited all four gas rings before joining them at the table. Awash of embarrassment filtered through her as she realised her false teeth were sitting in a glass of solution on display. Quickly inserting them, she rubbed her hands together to warm up.

'I won't be offended if you keep your coats on in here,' she shivered. 'Well, thank you for coming out at this hour of the night. I appreciate you coming instead of ringing me. As you arrived, I thought I would be mourning my son tonight. I need to know what happened to him, and *please* don't shy away from the truth. I know the kind of life my son leads, as well as the consequences it entails.'

The kettle whistled. Geraldine was grateful that Martin offered to make tea. Bridget started from the beginning, telling Geraldine what she knew, explaining Martin's technique of giving Declan CPR in lavish detail. Martin looked at Bridget in disbelief. So much for keeping that information between us, he thought. Swirls of steam wafted under Geraldine's nose as she wrapped her hands around the mug.

The journey to the hospital made Martin feel uncomfortable as Geraldine shared memories of Declan becoming a young man. Geraldine had no idea of the history between the men and freely aired how successful he had become, supported by his beautiful wife. Martin cringed as he had to endure the tales of Declan's glory days. The sight of the illuminated hospital entrance relieved him. He looked around for somewhere to park and abruptly said, 'Christ... how can a hospital car park be full in the middle of the night?' Geraldine walked on ahead into the foyer while Bridget spoke with Martin.

'Go on home, Martin. I'm proud of what you've done tonight.'

Martin insisted he would find somewhere to park and wait for her to return. He would ring Shane to contact Kieran and let him know where his father was. Bridget understood that it wouldn't be a good idea for him to come in with her. Bridget and Geraldine were directed to the ward where Declan was resting, and the doctor came to give them an update.

'The patient is still unconscious, which is to be expected. *Please* do not try and rouse him. He has had surgery to investigate and close the stab wound. His body is weak, and he must remain stable in bed with no sudden movements. He can see visitors, but once again, please keep the noise level down and to be careful of the line going into his arm.'

Geraldine broke down at the sight of her son. She still pictured him as her small boy. Kathleen embraced her and said, 'Just let it all out. It's all going to end well from here and now on. Things are going to change after this.'

CHAPTER 55

Martin, unable to get in touch with Shane, decided to head back to the Hennessey's home to wait for him there. He saw there were lights on downstairs, but the place was quiet. Perhaps, Kieran had gone inside and saw the signs of the disturbance and the blood-stained carpet and left in a panic, he thought. Going into the house, Martin saw Kieran staring at the mess, frozen like a statue in the middle of the sitting room. He called out his name, but Kieran didn't respond.

Martin knelt in front of him and softly spoke, 'Kieran... listen to me, Son... your father has been injured in a fight and is in hospital. I know this looks bad in here, but I can assure you he is in good hands and has your mother by his side.' Kieran started to quiver; Martin noticed the trembling and thought to himself, please God, don't have a fit on me.

Kieran looked confused and finally spoke, 'Did he get attacked in here?... Did Mam get hurt?'

Shaking his head with conviction, Martin replied, 'NO... NO... he arrived home with a stab wound, and it looks like he phoned the ambulance to meet him here – honestly, Son... this mess looks far worse than the injury your father has sustained.'

Kieran gathered himself together and tried to put on a brave face. Martin spoke positively, 'I can take you straight to the hospital, Son. I've already dropped your nanna down there, and she is in good spirits.' Martin pretended he hadn't noticed Kieran's trembling and waited for him to compose himself.

Kieran darted upstairs; Martin helped himself to a tumbler of vodka. He raised it in a salute while looking at a framed photo of Declan with Kathleen and said, 'Here's to you, big man.' He knocked the glass back and poured himself another. Winking at Declan, he pretended to talk to him, raising his glass again, 'I don't mind if I do… that's mighty generous of you... and here's one for the road... SLÁINTE.'

Footsteps trailed down the staircase. Martin pretended he was standing around waiting. 'Are we good to go, Son?'

They didn't hang around on the return journey as Martin negotiated the traffic with speed. He chuckled and said, 'Thankfully, Bridget isn't a passenger in the car as she would be questioning my every manoeuvre. "Martin... you're going too fast... Martin, you still need to slow down." God, that woman drives me crazy.'

As they arrived at the hospital, Martin directed Kieran in. 'Can you tell Bridget that I'll be waiting in the car park and to ring me when she is ready to leave?'

The three women were gathered around Declan's bedside when a nurse popped her head around and said, 'Can we squeeze one more visitor in here?' Kathleen jumped at the sight of her son, embracing him.That was Bridget's cue to leave. Kieran thanked her and explained about Martin looking after him and bringing him back to the hospital. It wasn't often Martin's name was praised like that; Bridget soaked it all up.

Voices drifted in and out of Declan's consciousness. As he started to come around, he could hear clusters of words, then whole sentences. He laid there happy, absorbing the conversation. He listened to Geraldine recalling stories of himself as a teenager and comparing him to Kieran at his age. Declan's lips were dry and tight as if glued together. He spoke softly, 'Mam, you're going to make me blush, revealing all my past secrets.' His eyes remained shut, and he could hear the gasps within the room and then felt touches to his hands and face. The bright fluorescent lights stung his pupils as he strained to open his eyes.

Gradually, Kathleen filled Declan in. Geraldine left the room to find a nurse, seeking more pain relief for him. She arrived back with a nurse wheeling a trolley of medication. Kieran took the opportunity to ask if anybody wanted anything from the cafeteria. Kathleen requested nothing. Geraldine offered to tag along with Kieran. Kathleen sat down and held Declan's hand while the nurse administered pain relief to him. As she tended him, she casually mentioned that he'd received CPR prior to the ambulance arriving. Declan responded, 'I'm a fortunate man to have quick thinking people around me to perform CPR on me; it probably saved my life.

Kathleen, needing to shut the topic down as quickly as possible, replied, ‘It was nothing sweetheart, I acted on impulse.’

The nurse recorded his vitals and left the clipboard at the end of his bed before saying, ‘It won’t be long before you’re back in tip-top condition. The only thing you need now is rest and plenty of it.’

She exited the room leaving Declan dwelling on his near-fatal experience. He shivered at the possibility of dying; he had never thought that he was seriously close to losing his life. The lack of sleep and worry had taken their toll on Kathleen. Thinking it was a good time to leave Declan to rest, she said, ‘My love… tonight has put a strain on all of us. We all need to get some sleep. I’ll drop your mam back home and collect her again to come back up tomorrow. I need you to rest now. I need you to be fighting fit again.’ Kathleen winked at him then kissed him on the lips. Noticing that Declan had something on his mind, she told him to spit it out.

He spoke tentatively. ‘I was thinking of a slower pace of life; a distraction from work… how would you feel about us getting a dog?’ Kathleen waited for the punchline. There wasn’t any.

‘Dogs don’t clear up their own shite, and I have enough to do picking up after you two at home. Now, don’t be getting any funny ideas. I’d be lumbered with looking after any mutt, and it wouldn’t be fair on it as it would never be setting foot inside my house. It’s a lovely thought, Declan, and that is all it’s going to be.’ Declan nodded. As Kathleen got up, he attempted to pat her on the backside,

‘Can’t wait to have me some of that,’ he smiled.

‘You’ve already had one near-miss; I wouldn’t want to be the cause of a heart attack,’ She smiled at him.

Geraldine and Kieran came back into the room, and Kathleen explained they were all leaving. Kieran hugged his father and told him to take it easy. Kathleen then asked Kieran to run downstairs and order a taxi at reception. She waited outside the room, leaving Geraldine to have a heart-to-heart with her son. It dawned on her that nobody had told Geraldine, not to mention that Martin had performed the resuscitation on him.

Geraldine had already read Declan the riot act about how stupid it was for a man of his age and experience to let himself get caught out like that. She ended the conversation by telling him he must promise her that he would be burying her instead of the reverse. Declan assured her that his lifestyle was going to change after this wake-up call. Holding his mother's tiny hand, he kissed her fingers and said, 'Mam, I met Brendan at the church, Brendan Kilkenny. You've mentioned his name over the years, but I didn't know you knew him well. What's his story?'

Geraldine sighed, shaking her head. Regret panned her features as she unravelled his story. 'As a young man, Brendan took to the drink after his wife's death and paid the price for it, wasting away in prison. He hadn't been married long when a hit and run driver killed his wife, Theresa. Yer man was caught after fleeing the scene and served time, but they couldn't prove he was drunk at the crash. Brendan took to the drink, and we lost the man we all cherished... God, it was awful. Your father and I were close with Brendan and Theresa and felt it was our duty to help him, but we lost him completely despite all our efforts.

'Anyway, the man who killed Theresa later went on to mow a young girl down; the Guards found him drunk at the wheel. Thank God the young girl made a full recovery, but this is where it gets worse... Brendan caught wind of this and found the pub where the man drank. He visited it one night, worse for wear and bludgeoned him to death in front of everyone. Brendan then went on the run for years before turning himself in. He served life before being released 20 years ago and found solace in the church. Brendan was a good man who wasted the prime years of his life; not in the name of love but hate. Your father and I should've pushed harder to help him. Anyways, what were you doing up at the church?'

Declan, astonished at the revelations, asked, 'How come nobody has ever mentioned that story? This town sings at the misfortunes of others.'

'Ah, these things are often let lie,' his mother said, 'no one wanted him to suffer more than he already did.'

'Mam,' Declan gripped her hand tightly, 'things are going to be different now. I have realised it's the two strong women in my life who have suffered the most, and I'm sorry for that.' He gestured to Kathleen outside the room, 'That woman looking in on us is the most courageous person I know. She brought me back to life. I don't think I could have done that if it was the other way around.'

Geraldine held her other hand over Declan's, 'You're right, my love; you've picked a fine woman there who puts up with a lot. But you're mistaken? It couldn't have been pleasant for her seeing you in that state, but it wasn't her that brought you back to life… it was Martin who gave you CPR.'

Declan let a roar out of him, 'MARTIN... MARTIN, FUCKING LYNCH... Gave ME mouth to mouth?'

Kathleen was glued to the window, trying to lipread the conversation between them when the penny dropped. 'OOOOOOOOOOOOOOOOO SHITE, she's told him.'

Declan looked over his mother's shoulder and out at Kathleen. With wild eyes, he let another roar out of him, his voice reverberated along the ward, 'KATHLEEN… KATHLEEN HENNESSEY.'

CHAPTER 56

A week had passed of Declan's recovery. The special treatment at home soon wore off after a couple of days. Boredom set in on day four, and he was itching to get back to the pub. Kathleen had given him strict orders not to set foot outside the house. The daytime television bored him. Billy and Johnny visited him once he was out of bed.

Kathleen greeted them on the path outside the house, 'Didn't you bring him any flowers? Arhh, jaysis, that will annoy him.' Johnny looked quizzically at Billy as Kathleen managed to keep a straight face.

'You daft bastard, you believed her, didn't you?' Billy teased Johnny. Ringing the doorbell, Johnny didn't even dignify the question with an answer. Declan hobbled out like an old man.

'You can cut out the limping, Boss. It's your shoulder that took a blow. Nice play for sympathy, though.' Billy said.

'It's bloody pins and needles, lads,' Declan replied, 'I'm bored shitless sitting in this house; I need to get outta here. The doctor said no manual labour or strenuous movements for at least a month, but I reckon I'm ok to go to the pub.'

Johnny spoke up, 'Never mind what the doctor says. You should take heed of what Kathleen says.'

'That woman would have me retired tomorrow from all of this if she had her way.'

Johnny made tea while Declan questioned Billy for all the gossip on the streets. Billy reeled off different people's names and proposals they had for buying and selling. The chat lasted an hour when Declan abruptly declared, 'I've got a meeting with O'Driscoll this afternoon. We're hoping to draw up some guidelines to work on future dealings together, bygones be bygones and all of that. He's renowned for being a slippery bastard, but I think after everything that has gone on recently, he'll have a different outlook on life now.'

'I'll still have one eye open when dealing with him though,' Johnny added, 'that boy of his is as thick as shite! We could use him as an introduction to pain when clients don't pay on time; that's all he's good for, I'm telling you.'

Billy nodded in agreement. 'That's not a bad call at all.' Both lads finished their second cups of tea and were leaving before Declan stopped them.

'Before you go, lads, I need to apologise for not letting you both in on the raid.' Billy dismissed the apology with a wave. 'No, lads,' Declan replied, 'I'm serious; this needs to be said. It was nothing to do with you guys; it was me.'

'You sound like you're breaking up with us, Boss.'

Declan smiled then continued, 'What I saw happen; I never want to be involved with again. Those two got their just desserts and are out of all of our lives for good. I won't even bat an eyelid over what happened. I can live with that, so you two don't have to.'

Appreciating the words, the lads nodded in acceptance. As they left, Declan pulled them towards him for a hug. Deep down, Billy and Johnny had been worried about Declan. Not for their position or the income he provided for them. He was more than a friend; he was a brother.

Declan was surprised O'Driscoll had offered to come to his pub. He phoned ahead and had his staff section off a private table. The doctors warned him not to drive, lift or operate any heavy machinery, so he took a cab to the pub. He was in a reflective mood and left the driver a decent tip. Inside, the same recognisable daytime drinkers resided in their usual seats. Declan greeted them, this time seeing them in a different light. He wondered what their stories were. What had brought them to find solace in his pub? He asked staff for his preferred whiskey and carried the bottle and ice bucket over to the tablewhere O'Driscoll was seated.

O'Driscoll greeted him, 'I'm resting my balls in your pub now.' The pair locked hands and embraced. Both muffled gasps of pain as their respective wounds caused discomfort.

'You're lucky to be alive. I thought I was going to have this whole city to myself,' Declan said.

'I thought you were a goner with all that blood you were losing from what my boy told me. There is one sure thing in life, and that is: The older you get, the quicker you used to be,' O'Driscoll replied.

Declan grimaced and tried to find a more comfortable position.'So tell me, how is it working out with your boy now?' O'Driscoll looked embarrassed. Declan noticed it and tried to backtrack.

O'Driscoll stopped him. 'He's my boy, and God knows I love him, but he's got shit for brains. I know it's wrong for a father to speak ill of his child, but the lad is a big-footed galoot with nothing going on behind the eyes. He needs to be told what to do instead of working things out for himself. I can't have him in the business anymore. I want to do what's right by the boy, and I've probably frightened him all his life without realising it. Can I tell you something in confidence… from one father to another?'

Declan put his arm across O'Driscoll's shoulder and tapped him to continue. 'I've decided to see one of these therapists, to talk about my relationship with Liam. Ermm… I'm ashamed to admit I've let the boy down all his life. Expecting him to follow the life that I led... the same life you and I lead. It's going to be a new road for Liam and me to take.'

Declan felt compassion for O'Driscoll. It brought back dark memories for him that Kieran might have witnessed his violence growing up. The pair continued to talk business, and finally, mutual agreement in place about how to proceed, they sealed it with a toast.

Declan had stood his ground that he would not distribute any form of drugs. O'Driscoll hadn't even mentioned the topic and agreed in principle. He hadn't ruled out letting a third party distribute in town and take a cut, but the unwritten rules had changed in the city. The risk was far too high for a man of his years to risk getting caught up in. It wasn't his morals that put him off; it was the severity of the prison sentence that weighed heavy on his mind. The bottle of whiskey had mellowed the two men. They let their guard down and relaxed in each other's company, making a new set of rules for themselves.

CHAPTER 57

Martin was woken by Shane scuttling around the house, searching for his sports gear. Bridget had been scheduled for day shifts this week and was ready for work. A neighbour had brought over a delivery addressed to Martin. Overhearing the conversation downstairs with Bridget at the front door, he was intrigued. When it was quiet, Martin decided to get up. He greeted Shane in the hallway, who was late for a match. Martin wished him luck as the front door slammed shut. A list of chores had been left on the table for him. Martin read them out loud. One, in particular, caught his eye: *Hoover the rugs in Shane's and Sinead's rooms.* Bridget had written it from the force of habit.

Sinead's room remained a shrine. Martin breathed the scent of her in. Nobody had attempted to move or change anything inside. It was perfect the state it remained in. He sighed and left and went back downstairs to start his chores. The radio was on low. Martin looked at the parcel that had been delivered for him. His heart sank as he opened it; knowing where it was from told him what it was, and he was scared to touch what was inside.

Rubbing the sides of his nose, he forced himself to look. Holding his breath, he pulled out Sinead's shawl. A note from the Hotel in Manchester fell out with it. Martin cradled the shawl like a newborn baby, gently and delicately. It released a scent that reminded him intimately of Sinead. He got up and left her room, taking the soft material into the front room with him. It felt like an emotional, gut-wrenching pain. The black dog had awoken inside him, and Martin needed to numb it. He located a bottle of whiskey, still sealed, and poured himself a glass.

Weeks had passed by, and it was collection day for many of Declan's clients, including Martin. Declan's team were out in full force, knocking on client's doors and rounding up all outstanding payments. Throughout the month, there were only two scheduled collection dates set up. They were on the 1st and the 15th of the month. These specific dates were to accommodate folk who were self-employed and those who were paid mid-month. The fixed dates discouraged them not to spend before their collection was due. The number of excuses also dropped.

Declan liaised with his collection team, informing them that he would personally collect payment from the Lynches until further notice. Nobody questioned him. Declan had prepared two brown envelopes with loan agreements for two clients. The first client was James Duffy; the second was Martin Lynch. Both clients were serial offenders. Declan planned on making sure they toed the line for future dates.

Kieran had been woken early by Kathleen. He wanted a lift out to join Shane for the match. Declan quickly sealed both envelopes in the car and, waiting for Kieran to get in, idly slotted one envelope in between his fingers, repeatedly turning it over. Kieran hopped into the car, breaking his concentration, and asked, 'A penny for them, Dad.'

'Hrrh?'

'A penny for your thoughts. Actually, can you make it ten euros instead? I wanna get a burger and chips after the match later.'

'Sorry, I was just thinking. Don't worry about it. Here's a tenner, Son.'

Kieran raised his brows in surprise and said, 'That's class, just like that. Dad, you're going soft in your old age.'

Billy and Johnny arrived, and Declan gave the lads instructions. They then followed behind. Declan placed the envelopes on the dashboard. Kieran had been on his phone; he ended the call and sighed, 'Change of plan, Dad, can you drop me off at The Telegraph? Shane has to go back home as he's left his football boots there. He was in a rush yesterday as he stayed at Siobhan's place last night.'

Declan showed rapt interest, 'Siobhan, she's a new one on the scene. You're telling me her parents let that boy sleep with their daughter under their roof?'

Rolling his eyes, Kieran countered, 'Dad, he's going to be eighteen in June; she's twenty. She's at Uni and has a house share with other students.'

'Don't you be getting any funny ideas about bringing lasses home,

Son,' Declan warned.

Kieran objected, 'Don't be like that, Dad.'

'It's not me that you've to get around; it's your mother,' Declan protested.

'Can't you have a word with her for me, Dad?' Kieran probed.

'Hang on now? So, are you courting some lass as well then?' Declan questioned.

Kieran spoke candidly, 'Well, I'm thinking about asking –.'

Declan interrupted, 'You spend too much time thinking, Son. I tell you what, do you want me to ask her for you?'

'Fuck off, Dad,' Kieran protested.

Declan burst into laughter. 'I hope you carry that pack of three lifesavers that I gave you, for when you decide to stop thinking and start doing… I'll leave a batch of them in your room. Don't fret, Son. I was a horny young man once, and your mother still stirs my loins, boy.'

'Fuck sake, Dad, pack it in, will you? I think I'm going to bring up my breakfast,' Kieran made a vomiting sound.

'I'm just saying, Son. Don't ever come home and tell your mother you got some lass up the duff. It will break your mam's heart, and of course, it will be all my fault.'

Kieran shook his head, 'Dad, some chance of that. The last girl I brought home; Mam knew more about her than I did. I've learnt my lesson well there. I won't be telling Mam her surname, so she can't search Facebook for info on her. It was bloody embarrassing listening to Mam grill her about photos of her at parties.'

'Your mam worries for you, Son. She doesn't want you being misled by some harlot.'

'Chance would be a fine thing,' Kieran echoed before Declan probed again, 'so, have you actually…?'

'Fuck off, Dad! I'm not having this conversation with you. Change the subject,' Kieran stared out the window.

'Alright, son. No need to get touchy. If you ever want to ask me any questions…' Declan offered a reassuring smile as he studied Kieran's face.

Kieran babbled, 'Right, Dad, got it.'

There was an uncomfortable silence in the car. Looking for a distraction, Kieran plugged in Declan's playlist. Curtis Harding played in the background, high enough that conversation wasn't required. Declan keptglancing in his rear mirror, making sure Billy and Johnny hadn't strayed behind. They reached their first stop, James Duffy's address, and parked mid-way down the street.

Reaching for the envelopes, Declan said to Kieran, 'Watch and learn, Son, this is how you command respect.'

Billy stepped out and leaned against the car, keeping an eye out. Declan walked up to the door and knocked. An apologetic Duffy greeted him with excuses. Raised voices echoed along the street. Declan handed Duffy the envelope with the contract. Kieran tried to look away from the rear-view mirror but found himself glued to it. Declan gave a quick side glance to Billy and walked back to the car. Billy met Duffy with a punch to the jaw sending him spiralling. Kieran flinched and turned away. Declan swaggered back to the car and sat next to his son. Together, they watched on with fleeting glances in the mirror as Billy continued to beat Duffy.

Kieran turned the music up loud. Billy continued to punch Duffy hard in the ribs until he could no longer get up. Billy then grabbed him by the jaw, yanked open his mouth and shoved the envelope in. Billy and Johnny stood over Duffy now, Johnny's boot on his chest. In the rear-view mirror Kieran saw a toddler come out to the doorway. The young child was crying and screaming at the sight of his father covered in blood. A hysterical woman came out and ushered the toddler back inside. Billy knelt and snarled at Duffy, who cowered at the prospect of being hit again.

'Remember! An agreement is binding. Next month's collection falls on the first. Don't make me have to come back again to remind you.' Billy and Johnny casually walked away and back to their car. Both men chuckled as the car engine purred. Declan turned the volume down and looked intently at Kieran.

'I can guarantee yer man won't default again. You let one slip, and others will think they can follow suit and take advantage of you. The way our positioning is at this moment in time, I've got to stand my ground. Do you think I enjoy this kind of work anymore, Son?'

Kieran turned his head to face the opposite direction and stared out of the window. 'Just get me away from here, Dad,' he said.

Declan shook his head and sighed, 'One down, one more to go.'

He signalled to the lads, and both cars left. Concerned onlookers pretended not to notice them. Kieran, all too familiar with the journey they were taking, knew something was not right.

'Who's the next victim, Dad?'

'You'll see,' said Declan. 'I don't treat all my customers the same, Son. Some just need talking to; others need reminding that I set the rules.'

Kieran became more uncomfortable as they pulled into Holmewood Road. Declan signalled to Billy in the car behind and motioned for Kieran to hand him the other envelope from the dashboard. 'This shouldn't take long, Son.' Declan walked up to Number 22. The street was quiet. He knocked and waited patiently; nobody answered. Putting his ear to the door, he could hear sounds from upstairs. He rapped his knuckles hard on the door again then shouted, 'Martin, can you come to the door? I need to speak with you.'

Martin came clattering down the stairs, singing. He was drunk and singing loud.

'*And through it all... she offers me protection... a lotta love and affection... whether I'm right or wrong... DU, DU, DU, DU, DU... I'm loving angels instead.*'

Declan shouted again, flicking the envelope between his fingers, 'MARTIN... will you open this door. I need to be on my way.' Declan looked through the window. Nobody else was visible. Martin continued his slurred singing in the hallway as he fumbled about, ignoring the shouting outside. Declan became irritated and hollered again, 'Martin, you know I'm out here, don't make this any worse for yourself. Open this bloody door.'

There was silence inside. Declan looked back at Billy then back at the door, concentrating on the movement he could see through the glass panel. His temper was frayed. Booting the front door, he roared, 'I call the shots around here, Martin. You hear me. Open this fucking door.'

Declan's heart raced. His temper boiled over. His nostrils flared as he slammed his shoulder into the door. Wincing in pain, his efforts made a hairline crack in one of the panels. He repeatedly kicked and slammed into the door at the weak point. Peeking in through the splintered wood, he could see Martin's figure in the hallway.

Billy leaned into the car and whispered to Johnny, 'He's fucking well pissed off now.' Johnny nodded and looked on at Kieran, who looked frozen in Declan's car. Declan turned and headed back to the cars, shouting, with his arms failing in the direction of Billy. Slipping, he regained his composure as he ran back to them. Billy shouted back in frustration,

'Can't understand a word, Boss?... the boot... what?'

Declan, frantically catching his breath, yelled, 'Pop the boot...pop the boot, NOW.' Billy and Johnny could see the madness in Declan's face. Jumping out, they popped Declan's boot. Inside the boot, Declan removed the compartment base to reveal a selection of firearms. He picked out a shotgun and blatantly checked it was loaded before placing a hunting knife in the back of his jeans.

Billy tried to calm Declan, 'Boss! For God's sake, get a hold of yourself. There is no need for this. Myself and Johnny can take it from here. We'll make sure he gets the message.'

With sweat pouring from his face, Declan shrugged him off.

Johnny whispered to Billy, 'What the fuck does he think he's doing?'

Billy ignored him and followed after Declan trying to reason with him. Standing directly in front of him, he refused to let him go any further, 'I'm telling you now, Boss; this will be the biggest mistake of your life. We'll all go down for this, and we'll be finished.'

Declan looked Billy in the eyes, 'It wasn't so long ago; you said to me you'd back me up wherever I went. I need to do this. Now, have you got my back? I need you to trust me on this.'

Billy let go of him, shaking his head, 'Not this time, Boss. This is one step too far.'

Declan grabbed his shoulder, 'I'm asking you to put all your trust in me here, after everything we've been through. One last time, for me.' Billy swallowed hard and, against his better judgement, nodded in agreement. Declan sighed and said, 'I'm going to aim for that lock. As soon as we break in, I want you to grab Lynch and hold him in front of me. Do I make myself clear?'

Both men looked back at the cars. Johnny stood by Kieran's door. Declan braced himself locking his elbows before coaxing his finger around the trigger. He took aim at the lock, held his breath and fired. A deep pain ricocheted down his shoulder. The door exploded; wood splintered everywhere. However, the lock was still intact.

Billy coughed, shielding his face, and shouted out, 'Fuck sake, Declan, have you ever fired that shotgun before. Jesus man, I live nearer than where the shot landed.'

Declan blinked and moved nearer. 'I have to get in there.' He refocused his aim through the haze of dust that settled in the air. The shotgun fired again, and the kickback from it opened the wound under his armpit. The gun fell to the road. Billy shouldered the door; it still resisted. Declan then slammed it with his boot, forcing the remaining pieces apart. The door flew open.

Billy caught sight of Martin's figure in the hallway and lunged towards him, grabbing him from behind. Declan fumbled backwards out onto the pavement gasping for air. Then, having found his footing, he reached for the knife and stumbled through the door frame, lunging at Martin. Martin collapsed in Billy's arms, spluttering. Outside, watching from the car, Kieran held his breath as he witnessed his father murder his best friend's Dad.

Declan's shadow loomed at the front door as he stood back from Martin's body. Billy collapsed under the weight of Martin, freed his legs from under him and got to his feet, staring down at him in shock. Martin gurgled, trying to take in air, then slowly his muscles relaxed, and his eyes closed. In the silence, a shadow emerged from the kitchen. Shane had returned for his football boots and expected to find his father in bed. Instead, his father was now prone on the floor, bullet holes in the door, it was like a scene from a movie. Curtains twitched up and down the street. Nobody had been brave enough to step outside and intervene, but everyone was watching.

'DAAAAAD,' Shane screamed and ran to him. Cradling his father in his arms, he called out his name again and again. Billy left the house and took care of the gun. Declan, hit by the reality of what had just happened, stood still, stunned, the knife hanging down by his side. He started to shake uncontrollably and watched with tears in his eyes as a young man, the same age as his son, broke down and consoled his dying father.

Declan picked the envelope up from where it fell on the pavement. Looking at Shane, he said, 'This was not my intention. I never expected this to end this way.' He dropped the envelope onto Martin's chest and walked out. Johnny was already back in the driver's seat of Declan's car next to Kieran. He glared at Declan and said nothing as he approached. Billy hurried Declan back, who seemed to be in a trance as they raced to the cars.

Taking control of the situation, Billy said, 'Johnny, take the boy home to his mother. Don't ask questions. I'll explain everything later.' Johnny took heed fumbling Kieran out of Declan's car and into the other vehicle before he sped away. Declan sat, trembling in his car, unable to make sense of things. Billy dialled 999 and started the engine.

CHAPTER 58

Kieran asked questions that Johnny couldn't answer. He needed to drop Kieran off and think. Johnny parked outside Declan's house. He could see Kathleen on her phone in the front room. Had she heard the news already? He was about to inform her that her husband had murdered an innocent man in cold blood. Johnny felt sick as he rang the doorbell. Kieran stood dazed beside him. Kathleen noticed something was up as she looked at Kieran.

'Alright, spit it out before I start getting phone calls,' she said.

'Mam, I don't know… I don't know Dad anymore.'

'Hold on there, what's going on? What's your father done this time? Is it the match? I told him not to go annoying the referee, Christ! I knew this would happen. Your father can't help himself.'

'Kathleen, this is something more serious than football,' said Johnny.

'Dad has killed Shane's dad,' Kieran burst into sobs.

'I know he would like to from time to time, but I'm sure your father knows that Martin is worth more alive to him than dead,' Kathleen choked on a chuckle.

'Kathleen, the boy is right,' Johnny confirmed.

'Oh, I see now… you're good, Kieran. You'll get one over on me one day but not for a few more years yet.' Kathleen chuckled, but neither Johnny nor Kieran moved. Noticing that Kieran's arm was shaking, she said, 'Johnny, what's happened?'

'It's like the boy said. We went to Lynch's house to give him new contract terms for his repayments. It should have been straightforward. Declan snapped and pulled out a shooter. He shot the door in. Billy tried to get him away. We thought he was going to scare him and make a scene. You know, so word would spread that Declan wasn't tolerating any nonsense. It got out of hand so quickly. Kathleen, it happened right in front of us.'

'Mam, Shane was there; he saw it all. We just left them.'

The colour drained from Kathleen's face. Her mouth dropped open.

'We saw it, Kathleen; there are no two ways about it,' Johnny backed up Kieran.

'I didn't see this coming; I knew Declan had issues with… it still doesn't make sense.'

Johnny held his hands up, 'The Gardai will be swarming around there. The street is probably shut off.'

'Where's your father now?' Kathleen demanded.

'He was in a state Mam; Billy took him away from there as soon as we left,' Kieran answered.

Johnny cut in, 'Kathleen; I have to ask you, was Declan on any strong medication that could have affected him in this way?'

Kathleen looked puzzled at the questioning and answered hesitantly, 'No, he was given pain killers, but he refused to take them because they made him sleepy. Does Bridget know? I can't sit around here waiting for Declan; I need to go and see her and try to explain. I need to get out and find Declan first to hear the words from his mouth…to believe him. Was it a terrible accident, Johnny? You must tell me, Johnny; it couldn't have been like you say it was. Was there a fight first? Declan wouldn't do this.'

'None of us knew a thing; it's all too late to try and change his story. Shane was there and will already have told them how it happened.'

Kathleen hadn't listened and asked, 'Was Martin definitely dead? Was he still breathing?'

Johnny couldn't defend Declan, 'Declan shot at the door, feet away with Martin behind it. Who could survive that?'

Kathleen tried to make sense of the scenario, 'I can't get my head around all of this. When was all this? Tell me exactly what happened.'

'We came straight here. It was maybe 30 minutes ago by now,' Johnny said.

'Right! I need to ring Bridget, now… hold on… shite her phone is off. That could be because she's on her shift… right, I'm going to go up to the house,' Kathleen paced herself.

'Mam, I'm coming with you,' Kieran announced.

'I need to look Bridget in the eye on my own,' Kathleen said. 'No, Mam, I'm coming. Shane needs me as well. I need to ask him what he heard away from Bridget,' Kieran countered.

'You're right, my love… Johnny, is the weapon still in the car?' Kathleen asked.

'For God's sake, it was never in mine; it's in Declan's,' Johnny protested.

'You're telling me my husband has had weapons in the family car?' Kathleen protested.

'Kathleen, this is not the time to start a row. I'll drive the two of you up to the top of the road. Then I'm to meet Billy and clean up the cars. Don't argue with me,' Johnny said tersely.

'Let's be on our way then, thanks, Johnny; I didn't mean to…' Kathleen backed down.

'Hush now, no harm intended,' Johnny made light of her comment.

Kathleen tried Bridget's phone a couple more times. She refused to leave a voice message. Johnny, in turn, rang Declan's phone. Kathleen locked up the house as they made the journey back to Holmewood Road.

CHAPTER 59

The Gardai had blocked off both ends of Holmewood Road. Kathleen reassured Johnny he could leave them and head off to Declan. He disappeared without another word. Kathleen and Kieran held hands as they approached the crime scene tape. An officer questioned their relevance at the location. Kathleen explained that she needed to be with her best friend without telling them her name.

They waited whilst the Guard went off to check if they could go through the cordon. A crowd had gathered and were busy narrating their versions of events. An ambulance was visible outside the house, its rear doors open. Guards littered the scene, walking in and out of the property. Camera lenses flashed where reporters, already tipped off by neighbours, had arrived to get an exclusive. An investigation team were on the scene.

A figure emerged with a female officer; it was Bridget covered in a foil blanket. Her face was bleak. Kathleen tried to hide. It was the wrong time to approach Bridget. It was all too raw. Bridget caught sight of Kieran first, then Kathleen. The foil blanket drifted off her shoulders. The female officer had stopped to speak to a medic. Bridget headed towards Kathleen. Her eyes were brimming with tears, her arms outstretched, seeking comfort. Kathleen started to shake. Kieran held her hand tighter. Kathleen couldn't control her emotions and wept as she tried to give a rambling explanation.

'I'm so sorry, Bridget. I don't know what happened; I don't know where Declan is. He can't have meant to do this. I'm so sorry, B.'

Bridget reached out with open arms; Kieran flinched. She grasped both of them in a hug.

'This is all too much. I don't know what to say. I didn't think he was capable of anything like this. It was all too much to live with. If it weren't for Declan breaking in to save Martin, he would be dead now. You must be so proud of Declan. We owe you.'

Kathleen's face froze. Her eyebrows knitted as she shook her head in disbelief. 'You're not making sense, B! Declan murdered Martin. He killed him... didn't he? There were witnesses. I don't understand.'

'No! No!, Kath, you've got it all wrong; Shane explained it to me. Martin received Sinead's shawl in the post this morning. She left it at the hotel when they went away to the concert. It was all too much for Martin; he couldn't deal with it. It was just the final straw. He fixed a strap up onto the punch bag joist and tried to hang himself in the hallway. Declan somehow realised what he was trying to do. He shot his way through the front door and cut the noose to save him. Martin is alive. He survived. They are taking him to the hospital now. It's all going to work out ok for us.'

Kathleen locked eyes with Kieran; they both released mutual guilt and then tension. Kathleen was speechless. She dropped to her knees, clutching her forehead. Bridget knelt with her, clasping her hands.' It's ok, Kathleen. It's all going to be ok. Declan came here to make peace. He was going to give us a new start in life. Come with me.'

Bridget took Kathleen's hand, and they ventured inside the house and into the back room. The Guards ignored them, talking into their radios and taking orders. Bridget opened the microwave and removed a letter. It was addressed to Martin. She handed it to Kathleen to read.

LYNCH, MARTIN – agreement – 1321

The decision has been made to terminate your loan agreement permanently. Do not question my decision. Do not speak of this to anybody else. My wife has had no input in this affair. Do not question her. This is a matter between yourself and I. Your slate in the store and The Telegraph remains unaffected. Do not question this. You will never be granted another loan from any of my businesses again. Do not question this. I am giving you a chance to turn your life around. You have lost enough in this lifetime. You still have a family; cherish it. We will never be friends or associates. This is a private and confidential agreement. Please sign below agreeing to these terms and conditions.

DECLAN HENNESSEY.

I agree to the terms and conditions of this agreement.

Print name : ....

Signed : ....

As the story unfolded to Kathleen, it pieced together to form a new jigsaw puzzle that showed a softer side to the man she married. Kathleen was stunned at Declan's change. He had never conceded on a loan agreement before. Kieran looked concerned at Kathleen's facial expression as she passed the letter to him to read.

'I deliberately hid this away from the Guards for now,' Bridget said. 'If Declan hadn't broken in, Martin would be dead. This changes everything. This house, our life, this poxy front door, the money, all of it is meaningless. We're going to start over again. The memories we can keep from here, there's nothing else we need.

'I knew Martin was in trouble for borrowing money. I thought he owed one lender that I was aware of. I forced the rest of it out of David. It took a lot for Declan to do this for us. I know that you have a good man there, Kath. The Guards want to question him, but Shane spoke to them, so it's just a formality.'

Kathleen looked at her son. They both felt guilty for misjudging Declan. They were interrupted by an officer who informed Bridget that Martin was on the move to the hospital. Shane appeared, looking distraught but oddly in control. He held his fist out to Kieran. A lifeline. The two boys touched fists. Bridget and Shane left to rejoin Martin in the ambulance. A detective fixed his eyes on Kathleen. He knew her but failed to introduce himself to her. Kathleen felt uneasy as they disappeared back into the crowd. The crowds dispersed as the blue sirens left the street.

A patrol car was parked outside the house when Kathleen and Kieran arrived home. A number of witnesses on Holmewood Road had confirmed Declan as the assailant who fired the shots. He had handed himself in with his solicitor at a local station. His account of the events showed him checking up on a friend of the family. Kathleen and Bridget backed up his story. He was a hero. It was plausible, but he didn't escape charges of using a firearm. His explanation was vague.

Further witness statements and Garda interviews would occur, but nobody on the street was prepared to go to court. An officer had been left on duty outside the Hennessey's home. Once Declan was released and arrived home, the officer left the address. It was dark; the lights were still off as Declan walked into the kitchen and was startled by the sight of Kathleen. Kieran came out of the front room and joined them. Unsure how to approach his father, he shrugged and then, guided by his father, all three embraced. The room was silent, uniting the family. After a bite to eat, Kathleen ran a bath for her husband. His big frame struggled to find comfort in it, but the heat soothed him. Kathleen returned downstairs to where Kieran was watching a film.

She walked into the room, caught sight of the TV and Kieran on the couch and yelled, 'Jesus Christ.'

'What, Mam?' Kieran jumped.

'Stop that right there… and take your hand out of your trackie bottoms, Jesus, lad; you could at least wait till we've gone out.'

'Mam, you scared the crap outta me; what's gone wrong with you?' Said Kieran.

'What type of film is this you're watching?' she asked.

'What?... It's Spiderman. I always sit like this. This isn't a film with nookie in it. For God's sake, Mam.'

'Jesus, thank God,' Kathleen breathed a sigh of relief. 'Hang on there a second. Rewind it to that lass speaking, do it now.'

'Jaysis, Mam, alright.' The picture went backwards to the beginning of the movie. 'Press STOP! Now, play from there on.'

The picture froze then played… a young girl was stood on a podium, dressed in a blue mortarboard hat and silk cape. It was her graduation speech. Kathleen stood with her mouth open, mesmerised.The girl's words hit her like a clap of thunder:

'What makes life valuable is that it doesn't last forever; what makes it precious is that it ends. I know that more than ever. Time is life, so don't waste it living someone else's life; make yours count for something. Fight for what matters to you, no matter what. Because even if we fall short – what better way is there to live.'

Kathleen chuckled to herself, breaking into private laughter. Kieran didn't get it. He didn't want to ask either.

Kathleen left the room tilting her head back, 'Keep your hand out of your trackies.

CHAPTER 60

Martin awoke, his eyes strained as he sucked in a breath. Gathering his senses, he realised he wasn't in his bed. Starchy sheets provided no comfort. The ceiling was white, a false ceiling with LED lighting. A distinctive smell lingered in the room. Martin knew it was a hospital. He carried out a quick body scan. As he swallowed, the pain was unbearable. Breathing sent shooting pain through his neck and shoulders. He moved on the bed, checking to see what movement he had. He could feel his chest, his arms, his hands, but wait… Panic rippled through him. His hand strolled down to his groin; he flicked it. The sensation was a relief.

Images came flooding back – the shawl, Sinead, whiskey – then nothing. Feeling someone's gaze on him, he twisted his neck; the pain was instantaneous. The fluorescent lighting caused his eyes to blink rapidly. Bridget's face greeted him. As memories and feelings came back to him, he was overwhelmed with images of dust, gunshots, the noose. What a mess, he thought. How unforgiving to desert his wife and son. He couldn't even finish himself off properly, and now his wife sat there dutifully. Swallowing guilt, it remained lodged in his throat. The pain he could deal with, the shame he couldn't. Bridget adjusted the covers on his bed. She held a glass to his lips, and in a low voice, she said, 'Martin.'

Bridget forced a smile, a genuine smile at her husband, and made eye contact. She didn't pity her husband; she felt ashamed that she had let him down. How low he must have been to give up on everyone still living around him. She caressed his hand. No words were needed. There was a twist of the door handle, and Shane entered. The crinkle of a carrier bag disturbed the silence. He had an eager look across his face.

'I'm sorry,' said Martin, 'I had nothing left to offer you both. Only debt, no prospects and no future. I couldn't see a way out.' Martin's voice rasped painfully in his throat, he continued, 'then Sinead's shawl arrived yesterday… it brought it all back… to see her die... How long have I been in here?'

'Ssshhh! Rest, Martin, the worst is over. You were brought in unconscious this morning. You were sedated and have slept for most of the day.'

'Dad, it was touch and go at first. I got it all wrong, though. Declan broke in to save you, Dad; I thought he killed you.'

'Save me! I don't remember. I don't understand. Today was collection day.'

'My love, things are going to change for us all, for the better. We're going to have a fresh start. A chance to live properly.'

'Ha, don't make me laugh; we're never going to dig our way out of this.'

'Right, listen to me, Martin. This is going to come as a bit of a shock. Declan has terminated the loan agreement… I know, I know, I know,' Bridget held her hands up. 'I know everything, Martin… The O'Driscolls… Declan… the lot. Don't say a word. We owe nothing to nobody anymore.'

'What?... Fuck off.'

'Dad, it's true. Kieran's dad came with this letter to talk to you, to give us a new start. When you didn't answer, he looked through the panel in the door, knew something was up and smashed the door in. Mam, show him the letter.' Martin looked for confirmation from Bridget; she pulled the letter out and showed it to him.

'I don't understand. How can that be? I owed money to both of them. There's no way O'Driscoll will let it go. They're going to come after me.'

Bridget told him the news he needed to hear: 'I didn't ask too many questions with Declan, but Kathleen filled me in on the missing links. You borrowed two grand from Declan, God knows what the percentage repayments were, but all of it has been voided. O'Driscoll has come to an agreement with Declan, which has suited both of them. You owe him nothing from now on either. No more rookie car jobs either.

'Just promise yourself you'll stay away from O'Driscoll's clowns. David will do no more favours for Declan so that you won't get caught up in any of Declan's businesses. You have your slate still in The Telegraph, but you are not permitted to step foot upstairs. There will be no more invitations either.'

Martin nodded repeatedly. An overwhelming relief came over him. A fresh lifeline was on the horizon. 'Bridget, this is a chance for me to live a life not looking over my shoulder. You have no idea how I've longed for that.'

Shane had agreed to meet up with Kieran at their usual spot under the willow tree. Bottles of alcohol clanged together in the plastic bags hanging from their handlebars as they cruised along. The park was quiet. The school rush to the park had elapsed, children had gone back home for their tea. The lads hadn't had a chance to catch up over the last couple of days. Their father's actions had stunned everyone; they had a lot to take in.

Their bottle caps formed a fortress line around the tree base. Nervous, they guzzled the bottles too quickly. As usual, Kieran sat on a carrier bag to ensure his backside wasn't damp. He tried to address the topic, 'How's the old man doing?'

'Ok, no thanks to yours,' Shane couldn't keep up the pretence. His face buckled under pressure, and he chuckled, relaxing Kieran.

'Fuck's sake, man, I'm serious. When is your old man coming home from the hospital?'

'In the next day or so, they say. He's got to have a chat about his wellbeing to decide whether they think he will try and top himself again. How's yours?'

'Surprisingly, kind of chilled out.'

The atmosphere felt peaceful. The lads drank their beers, enjoying each other's company.

'Thick fucks, aren't they anyway?' Shane said.

'Who?' said Kieran.

'Dads,' said Shane and they both laughed. 'My dad taught me three rules,' continued Shane, 'that he says will get me through life without getting into fights. 'Rule one: never ask a man about money or how much he earns. Rule two: never glance down at another man's mickey when you're having a slash. Rule three: never rob a working man of his tools.'

Both lads chuckled together. Kieran sighed, 'My dad's only rule in life is, *Happy wife... happy life.* He has to make sure nothing or nobody else gets in the way of the two of them. He truly loves my Mam to bits.' Shane smiled with his bottle in his mouth.

Kieran looked straight ahead as the sky faded and said, 'I guess, in a funny sort of way, our dads are similar. They both want the simplest form of happiness in life. It's just how they go about it that separates them.'

Shane opened another bottle and held it aloft, 'Here's a toast to our dads. God love them.'

CHAPTER 61

Declan had been up bright and early that morning and had trouble rousing Kieran. Kathleen told him to go back downstairs and wake him herself but he refused, insisting he needed Kieran for something. She was suspicious as to why Declan was up and why he needed Kieran with him so early. Typically, Kathleen had her ways of getting answers out of Kieran. She decided to leave it until later to get to the bottom of what he was up to. She was in a rush to go out herself to do some shopping with Bridget. Eventually, Kieran surfaced and joined Declan downstairs for breakfast. It would be another half an hour before Kieran's senses would be alert to gain his attention.

After breakfast, Kathleen was ready to leave and placed a chaste kiss on her husband's cheek. 'I don't know what you two are up to. But you do know that I'll get to the bottom of this.' Declan shrugged his shoulders.

Kathleen clutched her car keys and a travel cup; she took a second glance back at Declan and said,' Now, don't be creating a mess in here, you may be stiff and sore, but that's no excuse for being lazy. I want this house spick and span when I get back home at lunchtime. Do you hear me?'

Declan ushered her away with his good arm and called out,' Away with you, woman, stop fretting.' Kathleen left. Declan sighed with relief. He chewed his toast and spoke to Kieran, 'It's a good thing you're like a zombie first thing in the morning because when your mother gets her teeth into something, she won't let it go.'

Kieran was too busy pawing at his phone to answer. His fingers moved sporadically, responding to messages and checking his social media accounts. Declan shook his head at him,' Why don't you just talk to people, Son, instead of all this…' Declan mimicked him pressing the buttons and carried on, 'in my day, Son, we never had all these mobile phones. If I needed to speak to someone, I had to –'

'Yeah, I know, Dad. You had to go out to a phone box and put money in it to make a phone call.'

Declan chided, 'These mobiles consume you all; you never use it to speak to people. Yet, all the time pressing buttons with it. God forbid if you lose your fecking signal, then you get yourselves into a panic.' Kieran, continuing his keying, tried to silence his father.

'You sound like my old English teacher, Dad. He was always saying that these social media sites were strangling the future generations.' Declan nodded and sat up straight; he took a deep breath. Kieran knew what this meant. 'Christ, Dad, don't start with one of your sermons.' Declan ignored him.

'In my day, people communicated with each other. They spoke, they argued, they cursed, they fought. Arguments were settled, and things moved on. Nowadays, these Bookface sites create a divide. They pit people against each other instead of bringing them closer together. In my day, if a man were depressed, you'd take him down to the pub, buy him a drink, talk to him and get him pissed. Then, problem solved.'

Kieran challenged him, 'See, Dad, everything in your day revolved around drink. The trend is dying out, Dad. Pubs are closing down, and people haven't got the money to spend each night in the pub.When I've got a bit of money in my pocket, I go into town and meet up with some friends in one of the coffee shops. The pubs don't interest us unless it's the weekend. Even then, we use them to meet up in.

'You're talking about how the internet is ruining this generation; you forget how the pub culture ruined families over the past generations. A man would finish work, maybe go home for his tea, then straight back out to the pub, seven days a week. Dad, I've seen first-hand the damage done by alcohol. Children not seeing their fathers all week. Mothers with no money to provide for their families. I see that in our pub. I see that on our road. I see that in Shane's home.'

Declan was dumbfounded. He appreciated Kieran being honest about his feelings. Kieran rarely opened up much growing up, so this expression was welcome. 'I never thought much about how folk's lives functioned outside of the pub. Christ, son, you're a thinker, aren't you?

'I've waited in the car in town for your mother and watched the youth of today consumed with their phones and music. It keeps them withdrawn. There was this group of lasses; something caught my eye about them, and I couldn't work it out. Then it hit me. They all looked the same. I mean there were short, tall, fat and slim ones, but they all had the same shaped, shaved eyebrows, the same clothes, the same hair. Your generation has created a new species of elves among young women.'

Kieran burst into laughter and accidentally farted. Declan stood up, stretched his back out and said, 'Come on, Son. We need to be making a move… Christ, Son, that stinks… make sure you have a clear-out before you get into my car. I don't want you stinking it out.'

Kieran responded with glee, fanning the air away from him. 'That's Bisto, Dad – let the flavour flow.'

Declan made sure the kitchen was spotless before they left the house. They returned within an hour and suspiciously unloaded the car and hurried back out again.

'Now, don't start fecking interfering with my radio stations. I have it set up just the way I like it.'

'Son, the older you get, the more you realise that it isn't about material things in life; the pub neither pride nor ego that matters, it's about this. It's about you and me.' Declan thumped his chest, 'It's about this, and who it beats for.'

Making the most of his father's softer side, Kieran asked, 'Dad, speaking of material things can you lend us a hundred euros?'

Declan chuckled, 'Do you think I'm getting these euros handy, Son? I'm creating a moment with you, and already you're trying to mug me off.'

Declan slowly drove off. The conversation and bickering between them continued. It was evident in the past that Kathleen had ways to persuade Declan to change his mind over something, but she hadn't intervened at all on this occasion. This change of heart was solely Declan's, and he did for his sake and not his son's. No amount of money would compensate for building a bond between father and son. Declan's change in lifestyle and his family were the only focus now; today was a new dawn.

CHAPTER 62

Kathleen's shopping spree was a success. She loved shopping and could quite happily spend all day with friends in and out of shops breaking for lunch and making the day of it. She arrived home just after lunchtime. Declan and Kieran had left no more than an hour ago. She gathered her shopping bags and nudged the car door closed with her hip. Opening the front door she dropped the bags to the floor.

Trudging into the kitchen, She noticed a strange smell. Bloody Kieran again, she thought. She opened a window. After a quick inspection, she sighed, slipped her shoes off and headed upstairs to the bathroom. Something caught her attention – a noise. Pausing on the steps, she quietly listened for it to repeat itself. Dismissing it, she headed into the bathroom and then returned to the kitchen for a coffee. While the coffee was brewing, she went through her shopping. The strange noise occurred again. This time it was louder. It sounded like it came from the conservatory. A single door led there from the kitchen. She knew it was unlocked because the key was inside the lock. Generally, if it were locked, it would be hanging up on a hook. Her hand started to shake.

Quietly, she slid down on the floor tiles and crawled back around to the worktop area. On instinct, she grabbed hold of a sharp knife and slid towards the conservatory. Her mind went into overdrive as to who could be behind the door. The worst possible scenarios flooded her head. Maybe it was somebody seeking revenge for the Finnerty brothers? Perhaps it *was* one of the Finnerty brothers? Perhaps the intruder was a drug-fuelled maniac who was going to kill her so that she couldn't identify him. Kathleen had a spasm of nausea in her stomach. She recalled the last words Thomas whispered to her after she scratched his face.

A shrill scream escaped as she panicked on hearing a thud at the bottom of the door. She girded herself to open the door and surprise the intruder. Her confidence wavered as fear ambushed her. She recalled fear like this from her childhood when she slept over at her grandmother's house.

Kathleen remembered going to use the outside toilet at night. Trying to wee as fast as possible to escape the feral noises outside. Kathleen counted to ten to calm her breathing. Blood pumped through her veins. She reached across for the door handle, feeling her pulse banging in her index finger. The door opened. Her breath caught in her throat.

She looked at the glass patio doors to the garden. They remained locked and undamaged. A shadow moved to the side of her, and she screamed and dropped the knife. Her heartbeat lost a steady rhythm as it fluttered in fear. Trapping her from getting back out of the room, the shadow moved behind her. She was terrified but forced herself to turn around.

At the door was a white and tan boxer puppy skidding around in a puddle of urine. The puppy yelped once and stared wide-eyed at Kathleen. It was unnervingly bold, with its hind legs stretched far apart. It darted off and jumped up onto the cushioned seating, then started biting at the draped curtains.

Kathleen's eyes grew wild. Her hands cupped her mouth. 'For the love of God... NO… NO… NO… NO... my beautiful home.'

She watched as the puppy's footprints smeared urine all over her furnishings, and it tried to clamber up her curtains. Seconds later, another noise came from the corner, and another boxer puppy came skidding across the floor, tugging at a box of Christmas decorations it had found tucked away. This one was brindle in colour and slightly bandier than the first one. Kathleen clutched her chest and moaned, 'How could he do this to me... My lovely home... And *two* of them.'

Dropping her arms down at her side, she realised she'd stepped into the puddle of urine, soaking one shoeless foot. Kicking the tiled floor with the ball of her foot, she looked up to the heavens and shouted at the top of her voice, 'DECLAN!... DECLAN HENNESSEY!'

THE END

ACKNOWLEDGEMENTS

From the outset, the most crucial process in bringing this story together has been down to working with Emma Walsh of *The Literary Professionals*. After writing the first draft of my manuscript, I knew I needed help to pursue my goal. With the themes and dialogue in this story, I knew I wanted to work with an Irish consultant. After research, The Literary Professionals' website stood out a mile for me. It was well laid out, informative and inviting. I think when my first manuscript dropped on Emma's desktop, she felt she was being punked. I can joke about it now because I have an end product that makes me feel proud.

This project has been a work of dedication and self-discipline for me over five years involving Emma's input. From the beginning, it was apparent I was not well-read. Emma's initial constructive report broke down the elements of my writing that needed improving; her suggested reading material and blogs to research were beneficial for me to improve the basics of my book. Emma managed to be informative, perceptive and apt but with humility to help me build my confidence in writing. I continued to read and rewrite each year before coming back to Emma for further improvement in my manuscript, including edits and additions to my storyline. I now have a finished product today that has been the single most important thing I have ever done for myself.

Emma has been aware of the relevance of this story to me. Although she filled the criteria for each assessment report, she has always surpassed herself with additional information, breakdown edits and, as always, tactfulness. I am sure she does this for each of her clients. Emma Walsh, if there were not so many rules and regulations in the workplace nowadays about conducting yourself, I would come over to your office and kiss you on the forehead for everything you have made me believe in with my writing. I have so much respect and admiration for someone I have never met.

After analysing my assessment report, part of my criteria was to take up a writing course to develop confidence in writing. I joined an evening class for creative writing headed by Declan O'Keeffe. During this course, Declan glowed with enthusiasm as he brought creative writing concepts alive with his fusion of, and his admiration for, screenplays and books. This seed that sparked me to research and write a screenplay for this story as a five-part drama series. I hope, Declan, you continue to wake up students' imaginations and broaden their horizons with the medium of books and film.

Part of a self-publishing author's remit is to source a designer who can listen and design a format for a book cover. Whether it is the first or fifteenth cover design, each is important to showcase the story that an author wants their audience to see. I contacted Peter and Caroline at *Bespoke Book Covers* with an idea of how I wanted the cover design to look. In addition, I sent them the first couple of chapters to give them an insight into how the story develops. I read the endorsements left by previous clients worldwide, saw their showcased work, and I was positive they could do a good job for me.

Knowing the landscape of the city he grew up in, Peter convinced me that he could deliver a scene evoking the story's background. He did not fail and captured a moment of one of the main characters collecting his thoughts in the city he owned. It is indeed a skill to get inside an author's head to envisage what they want to bring to life, and Peter has achieved that spectacularly.

Throughout my writing, I need to thank Michelle and Melanie Conroy for their help and patience in putting up with my tantrums, all because I don't know my way around the keyboard and Word format.

Last but not least, I would like to thank a well-known author who unknowingly was the spark that inspired me to start writing my initial story. This writer is Lynda La Plante. Some years ago, I broke into her home; I took all my clothes off and walked around aimlessly, searching for ideas on starting my story… Okaaaay… that's not quite the truth…right!… some years ago, I attended Lynda La Plante's address as a service engineer dealing with her secretary as a point of reference.

On entering her home, I was drawn by the elegance of the main hallway. The wooden panels evoked a smell that brought back flashbacks from a dream I had involving an old pub. I thought nothing more of this until I went through my monthly payment statement and saw Lynda's name as a reference. I have a spiritual side to me and took that as a sign for me tell my story. I wrote to her explaining my story, and she replied with an encouraging letter wishing me luck in my pursuit, and here we are today.

Dear reader

Firstly I would like to thank **YOU**, the reader, for purchasing this book amidst the array of select titles available to you. As self-published independent writers, we as writers solely rely on feedback from customers who have taken a punt on a newbie and purchased a book from Amazon. I would love to read your thoughts on this story as it creates a profile for writers to generate sales and helps other readers to buy this book. I would greatly appreciate your review on Amazon and Goodreads.

J F Conroy

Book Club Questions

1) How does the book's title work in relation to the book's contents? If you could give the book a new title what would it be?

2) How did the book make you feel? What emotions did it evoke?

3) How do the characters see themselves differ from the way others see them.

4) Were there times you disagreed with a character's action? What would you have done differently?

5) What are your thoughts on the book's structure? Did it serve the story well.

6) Which character did you relate to or empathize with the most?

7) How did the characters change throughout the story? How did your opinion of them change?

8) Are there any characters you'd like to deliver a lecture to? If so, who? What would you say?

9) Was the story what you expected it to be, based on the summary?

10) What scene resonated with you most on a personal level (Why? How did it make you feel?)

11) Did the characters seem believable to you? Did they remind you of anyone?

12) If you could ask the author anything, what would it be?

Printed in Dunstable, United Kingdom

66250589R00211